W9-DGF-279

Chinese Industrial
Society after Mao

Chinese Industrial Society after Mao

Rosalie L. Tung
The Wharton School
University of Pennsylvania

LexingtonBooks
D.C. Heath and Company
Lexington, Massachusetts
Toronto

HARVARD-YENCHING LIBRARY
HARVARD UNIVERSITY
2 DIVINITY AVENUE
HJAS
Feb 24, 1982

W 4355.55/88

HC 427.92 .T86

Tung, Rosalie L. 1948-

Chinese industrial society
after Mao

Library of Congress Cataloging in Publication Data

Tung, Rosalie L. (Rosalie Lam), 1948–
    Chinese industrial society after Mao.

    Bibliography: p.
    Includes index.
    1. China—Industries. 2. China—Social conditions—1976–
3. China—Economic conditions—1976–   . 4. China—Economic policy—
1976–   . 5. China—Politics and government—1976–   . I. Title.
HC427.92.T86   338.0951   81–47183
ISBN 0–669–04565–9   AACR2

Copyright © 1982 by D.C. Heath and Company

All rights reserved. No part of this publication may be reproduced or
transmitted in any form or by any means, electronic or mechanical, including photocopy, recording, or any information storage or retrieval
system, without permission in writing from the publisher.

Published simultaneously in Canada

Printed in the United States of America

International Standard Book Number: 0–669–04565–9

Library of Congress Catalog Card Number: 81–47183

Dedicated to my Mother

Contents

List of Figures
and Tables

Preface

The year 1976 marked a milestone in the history of the People's Republic of China (PRC). The death of Mao Zedong in September 1976 was swiftly followed by the arrest and eclipse from power of Jiang Qing, Mao's widow, and her cohorts. This rapid turn of events brought an end to the Cultural Revolution—a decade in which economic considerations in the development of China's industries were subordinated to ideological principles. The erratic policies pursued during that decade slowed the growth of the industrial and agricultural sectors and brought the national economy to the brink of collapse between 1974 and 1976. In August 1977, at the Eleventh National Congress of the Communist Party of China, the Central Committee of the Chinese Communist Party announced that the mission for the last quarter of the twentieth century would no longer be that of class struggle, but rather that of socialist modernization, in order to develop China's economy to match "the first ranks of the world by the year 2000." This officially launched the country on the Four Modernizations program, which seeks development in the fields of science and technology, industry, agriculture, and military defense. Although an often uneasy truce prevailed between Hua Guofeng (Mao's handpicked successor) and the strongman of the new era, Deng Xiaoping, the post-1976 leadership was by and large committed to the goals of the Four Modernizations. By June 1981, with Hu Yaobang replacing Hua Guofeng as chairman of the party—a move that had been preceded almost a year earlier by the ascendancy of Zhao Ziyang to the premiership—the political power in China was consolidated in the hands of the pragmatists.

Although debate continues over the types of reforms and changes that ought to be made in the Chinese political and economic systems, one thing is evident: the post-Mao leadership is determined to raise efficiency and productivity in the industrial and agricultural sectors through management reforms and changes in the structuring and operations of industrial and agricultural concerns. This book focuses on the management and structure of industrial organizations. An indication of the types of changes that will likely be introduced throughout China is found in the Sichuan experiments, a series of reforms designed to grant greater autonomy to the enterprises with respect to planning, decision making, and financial matters. The Sichuan experiments were first introduced in Sichuan Province under the auspices of Zhao Ziyang, then first secretary of the party in that province. By 1980 Sichuan-style experiments had been introduced in 6,600 state-owned enterprises throughout the country. Although these account for only 16 percent of all state-owned enterprises in China, their industrial-output

Portions of this book appeared in R.L. Tung, *Management Practices in China*. China: International Business Series (New York: Pergamon Press, 1980). Reprinted with permission.

value constitutes 60 percent of the nation's total. The profits turned over to the state by these 6,600 enterprises amount to 70 percent of China's total. The Sichuan-style experiments have so far yielded encouraging results. Productivity in most of the experimental units has increased substantially as a result of reforms. This has meant higher profits for the state and larger bonuses for the workers.

Besides reforms in the structure and management of industrial enterprises, changes have been implemented in other sectors of the economy. These include the limited use of the market mechanism; competition among enterprises; and technological exchange and economic cooperation with foreign countries, including capitalist economies—practices and policies that were previously dubbed "revisionist" and "capitalist." Although these reforms have given rise to certain problems, those changes that have had a positive impact on the development of the Chinese economy will likely remain.

This book examines various aspects of industrial societal functioning and the operations of industrial enterprises. Specifically, the book seeks to identify

1. the role of ideology in the post-Mao era of socialist modernization
2. the Four Modernizations program and the factors that could affect the success or failure of this colossal effort
3. the Chinese political system and the changes that have been implemented since 1978 to facilitate the early attainment of the goal of socialist modernization
4. a brief overview of legislation enacted since 1979 governing various aspects of societal functioning and the operations of joint-venture concerns with foreign partners
5. the Chinese mentality and outlook toward work, innovation, and achievement
6. the motivational devices used in China to spur workers to heighten performance
7. reforms in the economic system and management of industrial organizations, including case studies of several state- and collectively owned enterprises
8. selected aspects of organizational functioning, such as participative management, the recruitment of workers, promotion within the organization, and the role of the trade unions in China
9. reforms in the structure and management of foreign trade and a discussion of its prospects for the future
10. the outlook for increased productivity in Chinese industrial enterprises.

Further institutional and policy changes are being contemplated in many of these areas. Consequently, certain practices and procedures described in the book may change over the next two to three years. However, the book does incorporate the latest practices and procedures in vogue in the leading enterprises as of mid-1981. These will probably constitute a model for emulation by other enterprises across the country.

To provide the background for understanding these industrial practices in Chinese enterprises, the book also examines the history of growth and industrial development in the heavy- and light-industrial sectors in the PRC since 1949 and analyzes the positive and negative conclusions that can be drawn on the basis of the country's first thirty-one years of performance. This is essential to understanding why China has progressed and developed along certain lines and why the Chinese government perceives the need for change or readjustment in certain areas.

It is imperative for business people engaged in or intending to engage in trade with the PRC to be thoroughly familiar with Chinese business practices and social customs. The book provides practitioners with a basic working knowledge of Chinese business practices and social customs that is essential to the smooth conduct of business with the Chinese.

In addition to the book's appeal to practitioners, it is also of interest to academicians. Based on an examination of industrial practices in Chinese enterprises, inferences could be drawn for research in the field of comparative management and for the development of principles and concepts of organizational theory and behavior. Even though management principles and techniques in the PRC are less sophisticated than those in the West, the changes made in practically all aspects of Chinese societal and organizational functioning over the past thirty-one years represent a large-scale social experiment. Hence, from the researcher's perspective, China's organizational principles and policies represent an interesting case for study.

The information provided in the book was obtained during two study tours to China. The first was a month-long trip to six cities: Beijing, Shanghai, Guangzhou, Anshan, Shenyang, and Dalien (the last three are heavy-industrial cities in northeastern China, in the region formerly known as Manchuria) in July 1979. The 1979 trip included visits to enterprises ranging from heavy-industrial plants (such as the Anshan Iron and Steel Works) to an arts and handicrafts factory. The second trip to China was made in June and July 1980 at the invitation of the Foreign Investment Commission, the highest agency under the Chinese State Council that approves all joint ventures and major forms of investment. The 1980 trip was confined to Beijing, and most of the enterprises visited were in the light-industrial and textile categories.

Since all the visits were arranged by the authorities at the Foreign Investment Commission, this choice of factories perhaps reflects the government's current emphasis on developing the light- and textile-industrial sectors. Up to 1978 there has been imbalances in the allocation of state investments; heavy industry was emphasized at the expense of the light-industrial and agricultural sectors. The information presented on the operations of industrial enterprises and on various aspects of societal functioning is based on interviews with enterprise management and leading members of the respective government bureaus and agencies, and on observations and impressions derived during these two study tours. These are supplemented with relevant library research in the Chinese and English languages.

In considering the industrial practices reported in the book, two points should be borne in mind. First, despite the fact that China is currently more willing than formerly to provide foreign researchers with information on the operations and performance of industrial enterprises, restrictions still exist. After repeated attempts to gain access to less advanced units, I did not receive permission. Hence the factories visited were all advanced industrial units and represent the model that other, less advanced units seek to emulate. In China, new techniques, practices, and procedures are introduced on an experimental basis among the leading enterprises. If these techniques prove effective, they are eventually implemented throughout the country.

Second, although I sought to collect information on the history, organizational processes, and performance of each enterprise for the sake of comparison, some factories were unwilling to provide information on all these variables. It should be noted, however, that, in general, organizational practices are fairly homogeneous across all enterprises.

I would like to thank all those individuals who have given their time willingly and generously to permit the successful completion of this project. So many people have contributed in various but significant ways that I cannot thank them all individually here. However, special thanks are due to Mr. Han Yuanzuo, director of research, Foreign Investment Commission; Mr. Chang Xiyua, director of the Bureau of Planning, Ministry of Commerce; Mr. Wang Liehwang, division chief, Research Institute of International Trade, Ministry of Foreign Trade; Mr. Sun Jen, chief of the Division of Policy Research at the Labor Bureau; Mr. Zhang Yenning, secretary-general of the China Enterprise Management Association, who is also a member and director of bureau, State Economic Commission; Mr. Zhuang Shouchang, chief of secretariat, China International Trust and Investment Corporation; Mr. Tang Gengyao, deputy general manager, General Coordination Department, Bank of China; Mr. Li Jiahua, deputy manager, Research Department, People's Insurance Company of China; Mr. Xu, chief engineer and factory director of the Beijing Internal Combustion Factory; Mr. Wang, deputy director of the Qing Hur Woolen Mill; and the management personnel at the Beijing No. 3 Textile Mill, Jewelry Factory, the Beijing No. 4 Cosmetics Factory, the Beijing No. 1 Carpet Factory, and the Beijing Jade Factory. Special thanks are due to Mr. Chang Mingchi of the Foreign Investment Commission, who arranged most of the visits to the respective ministries and enterprises.

Last, but not least, I would like to thank my husband, Byron, for his moral support and understanding throughout the whole project. I would also like to thank him for his consideration in presenting me with a word processor for the project. The word processor made easier the task of writing the several drafts of the book, and the chore of editing and producing the final version of the manuscript.

Chinese Industrial Society after Mao

1 A Conceptual Framework for Analyzing Management Practices

In order to analyze and understand management practices and organizational processes in a planned economy like that of the People's Republic of China (PRC), it is necessary to examine the impact of broad societal-environment variables (such as the political, socioeconomic, and cultural systems) as constraints on the operations of industrial enterprises. Even in free-market economies such as that of the United States, the role of such societal variables cannot be dismissed. Numerous studies (Thompson 1967; Lawrence and Lorsch 1967; Duncan 1972; Tung 1979) have shown the relationships between organizational environments and organizational processes and performance. In post-Mao Chinese industrial society, where the overriding concern is to increase productivity and improve organizational efficiency, any attempt to understand the operations of Chinese industrial enterprises would be incomplete without an analysis of the internal and external factors that could affect an enterprise's performance and effectiveness.

Management researchers agree that organizational effectiveness is a desirable goal and one that should be assessed and measured. Beyond that, there is little consensus about how organizational effectiveness should be operationalized and measured. Various models of organizational effectiveness have been proposed. These include the univariate effectiveness measures put forward by Thorndike (1949), who identified several of these criteria as productivity, mission accomplishment, organizational growth, and net profit; and the multivariate effectiveness measures as exemplified by the Katz and Kahn (1978) and the Yuchtman and Seashore (1967) models.

It is not the intention here to demonstrate the superiority of one model of organizational effectiveness over another. Most researchers agree that organizational effectiveness is not a unidimensional construct and that it can be examined within a multivariate framework. Multivariate frameworks of organizational effectiveness are superior to unidimensional models in that the former allow for the comprehensive, systematic analysis of the major variables that may affect the outcome variables in the organization, and can indicate the dynamics of the relationships existing among different sets of variables. It is not intended here to present a comprehensive model of organizational effectiveness that would indicate all the complex relationships possible between variables. Rather, a simplified framework will be presented, listing variables that are generally thought to affect organizational outcomes (see figure 1-1).

1

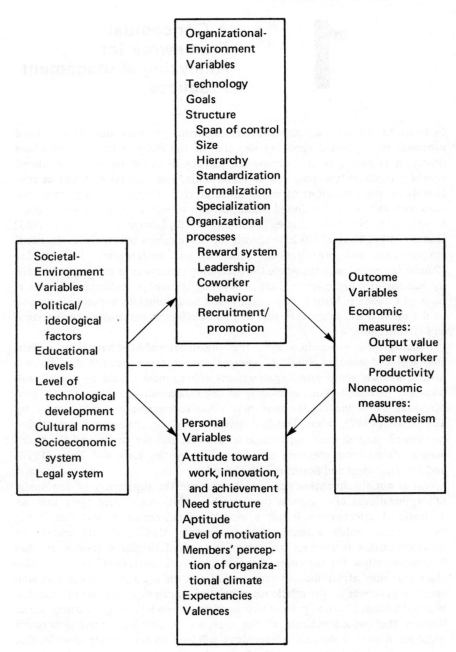

Figure 1–1. A Simplified Framework of Organizational Effectiveness

The variables that may affect organizational outcome fall into three general categories: societal-environment variables, organizational-environment variables, and personal variables.

Societal-environment variables refer to all those factors outside the organization that influence the enterprise's management practices and organizational functioning. These variables include the political/ideological factors, educational levels of the people, the level of technological development, cultural norms, and the socioeconomic system. Farmer and Richman (1965) present a comprehensive list of the variables that make up an organization's macro or societal environment. Only those variables that have a real, direct effect on organizational functioning and performance will be discussed here. Relevant societal variables may have direct or sequential effects on the other three types: organizational-environment variables, personal variables, and outcome variables. For example, a change in ideological orientation might affect the criteria for promotion within an organization and the incentives used for motivating workers to heighten their performance. Likewise, a change in economic structure might affect the allocation of raw-material supplies to an organization and the distribution of finished products. An example of a sequential effect is a reform in the economic system that results in a change in the organization's structure. For example, the Chinese government's decision to grant greater autonomy to certain enterprises in decision making and the conduct of foreign trade necessitates modifications in the enterprise's structure in order to accommodate such changes. Structural changes within the organization in turn modify organizational processes, which influence members' perception of the organizational climate, which ultimately may affect organizational performance.

Organizational-environment variables include the organization's technology, goals, structure, and processes. A distinction is made between organizational *structure* and organizational *processes*. Structural variables include span of control, total size, levels from the top, type of hierarchy, formalization, specialization, and standardization. Process variables include style of leadership, group behavior, and organizational policy relating performance to reward—in short, those factors that directly affect the daily work experiences of the individual (Lawler, Hall, and Oldham 1974).

Personal variables refer to the organizational members' attitude toward work, achievement, and innovation; their positions in the organization; their need structure, aptitude, and level of motivation; their perceptions of the organizational climate and the way in which outcomes (rewards and punishments) are tied to individual effort; and the attractiveness of such outcomes or rewards. In organizational-behavior literature, *organizational climate* is defined as the "psychological atmosphere" created by observable realities within the organization (such as size, structure, and supervisors) that can change the sensory inputs received by individuals within the unit, which in turn interact with the individual's needs to produce a set of behaviors that ultimately contribute to the

composition and nature of the environment (Pervin 1968; Pritchard and Karasick 1973). Members' perceptions of the relation of outcomes to individual
efforts are known as *expectancies;* the concept of "attractiveness of outcomes
or rewards" is referred to as *valences.*

As pointed out previously, there is no consensus among researchers on how
organizational effectiveness should be operationalized and measured. Consequently, surrogate measures of the organizational-effectiveness construct are
used. These measures could be categorized into two groups: (1) indicators of
job satisfaction and (2) economic measures of effectiveness. As suggested by
Negandhi and Prasad (1975), it is important to distinguish rather than aggregate
the two because many economic measures of effectiveness are largely determined by conditions external to the organization (such as the level of technological development or exchange-rate problems) that are generally beyond its
control. Hence it is both inappropriate and insufficient to use universal economic measures of organizational effectiveness alone to explain and compare
management practices and effectiveness across countries at different levels of
industrialization. It is necessary to include other outcome variables (such as job
satisfaction, absenteeism, and turnover) that are determined to a greater extent
by conditions internal to the organization itself. It is argued that job satisfaction
and turnover, two common indicators of organization effectiveness in the United
States, may not be relevant measures of effectiveness in the Chinese context.
Given the tremendous differences in the socioeconomic and political systems,
the notion of job satisfaction as understood and defined in the United States is
alien to Chinese workers. The notion of turnover is likewise irrelevant since the
Chinese worker lacks the mobility of his U.S. counterpart to move from organization to organization.

Most of the aforementioned variables—societal-environment variables,
organizational-environment variables, personal variables, and outcome variables— will be examined in subsequent chapters of the book. On the basis of
such analysis one can better appreciate how broad societal variables influence
organizational practices in China that in turn affect organizational performance.
Additionally, the results of such studies have widespread implications for theories of comparative management, organizational theory, and behavior. The
results of such studies would increase our knowledge and understanding of
why certain management styles are effective in one culture, but not in another.
They would also further our understanding of the relationships among different
sets of variables.

2 The Role of Ideology in post-Mao Industrial Society

The year 1976 marked a milestone in the history of the People's Republic of China. The deaths of Premier Zhou Enlai (Chou En-lai) in January 1976 and of Mao Zedong (Mao Tse-tung) in September 1976 were followed in October 1976 by the arrest of the so-called Gang of Four (The Gang of Four refers to Jiang Qing, widow of Mao Zedong; Wang Hongwen; Zhang Chunqiao; and Yao Wenyuan.) In 1977 the leaders of the post-Mao era declared that the mission for the new era was socialist modernization of the country.

The policies and guidelines espoused by these new leaders are in many ways in direct contrast to those advanced by Lin Biao (at one time Mao's heir ap-parent) and the Gang of Four, who virtually controlled the country from 1966 to 1976. Domestically, the government's stated mission for the new era is no longer class struggle but, rather, socialist modernization in science and tech-nology, industry, agriculture, and military defense. This effort is generally referred to as the *Four Modernizations* program. The aim of the Four Modern-izations is to bring China's economy to the "first ranks of the world" by the year 2000.

On the international front, China's leaders seek to build better and closer relations with other countries (including capitalist economies) by resuming diplomatic relations and engaging in technical, cultural, and economic exchanges with these nations. China's leaders are aware that in order to attain the goals of the Four Modernizations, the country must enjoy relatively stable political conditions, both at home and abroad, and must build up its foreign-exchange reserve through expanded trade and economic assistance from abroad.

In order to accomplish the mission of the new era, China has adopted political and economic reforms and has reinstated policies condemned as "capitalist" and "revisionist" during the years of the Cultural Revolution. Such reforms included resuming diplomatic relations with the United States, the symbol of capitalism; permitting foreign firms to engage in joint-venture invest-ments in China to develop the country's industries and natural resources; and engaging in technical and cultural exchanges with other countries, some of them capitalist. Some of the policies reinstated were the use of material incentives such as bonuses to spur production in both industrial and agricultural sectors; the encouragement of alternative means of ownership, such as collectively owned (as distinguished from state-owned) enterprises and ownership by individual operators; emphasis on technical innovation and development through reinstitution of entrance exams to universities and more rigorous curricula at

5

universities and technical colleges; and the use of expertness as an important criterion for recruitment and promotion of personnel to managerial and technical positions.

As China enters the last two decades of the twentieth century it is appropriate to ask whether idology, which figures so prominently in all aspects of Chinese society and which affected the operations of industrial enterprises in the first three decades of the history of the People's Republic of China, would continue to play a role in the new era of economic development and socialist modernization—and if so, what role?

This chapter addresses some of the most salient issues concerning the role of ideology in post-Mao industrial society. Specifically, these are:

1. Is Maoism (or "Mao Zedong Thought") dead in China? The "Thoughts of Mao Zedong" are an integral part of Marxism-Leninism as interpreted and practiced in China.
2. How do the sayings of Marx, Lenin, and (specifically) Mao offer guidelines and prescriptions for economic development and industrialization of China in the post-Mao era of the Four Modernizations?
3. What is the role of ideology in post-Mao industrial society? Does it continue to serve a purpose in the drive toward the Four Modernizations—and if so, what purpose?

These issues are examined in light of the works of Marx, Lenin, and Mao, as interpreted by the present leaders of China, and the information available on the current operations and management of industrial enterprises.

A distinction should be made at the outset between pure and practical ideology. As Richman (1969, p. 48) defined it, *pure* ideology exists in an abstract and theoretical form, providing people with a "unified and conscious world view." *Practical* ideology, on the other hand, provides a guide for concrete action. Throughout this chapter and the book, ideology will not be treated or discussed in a vacuum. Rather, ideology will be examined as applied and practiced. In other words, only practical ideology will be considered.

Maoism in post-Mao Society

Although foreign press coverage of the events celebrating the thirtieth anniversary of the founding of the PRC was replete with headlines such as "millions hear Mao berated by Deng aide" and allusions to a de-Maoification campaign in China as manifested by the removal of portraits and quotations of the late chairman from many public places, this is a less than accurate interpretation of the status of Mao Zedong in post-Mao China. Mao is still credited as the chief architect in the construction of new China. In Vice-Chairman Ye Jianying's speech delivered on the thirtieth anniversary of the founding of the PRC (the same speech that was reported in some foreign press as berating Mao), Ye stated that "we hold that all our victories were achieved under the guidance of Mao Zedong Thought, without which there would be no New China today" (*Beijing Review*, October 5, 1979, p. 8). On Qing Ming Festival, 1980 (the day on which the Chinese commemorate the dead), a scroll bearing the following message was placed in front of the Monument of the People's Heroes at Tian An Men Square: "Without Chairman Mao, there would be no New China. One should never forget the well-digger when one drinks water. Eternal glory to Chairman Mao Zedong!" (*Beijing Review*, April 14, 1980, p. 3). Perhaps the most significant revelation of the status of Mao in the last quarter of the twentieth century is given by Senior Vice-Premier Deng Xiaoping in an interview with Oriana Fallaci, an eminent Italian journalist. In the interview, Deng remarked that removal of portraits of Mao is not synonymous with de-Maoification. Rather, they were removed because, in Deng's view, excess exposure of any individual is tantamount to disrespect (*London Times*, September 14, 1980). In the same interview Deng pointed out that although Mao Zedong committed mistakes in the later years of his life, he will always be remembered for his contribution to the construction of new China. In evaluating Mao's mistakes and contributions, Deng argued that the latter greatly exceeded the former. Consequently, he emphasized, Mao Zedong will always occupy a special place in Chinese history and the country will continue to follow Mao Zedong Thought in the post-Mao era of the Four Modernizations. The term *Mao Zedong Thought* refers to "the correct part of Chairman Mao's thinking in his lifetime" (*London Times*, September 14, 1980, p. 8). This same message was repeated in a meeting with a group of French journalists on February 12, 1981 (*Beijing Review*, February 23, 1981, p. 6). The distinction between the mistakes made by Mao Zedong and the crimes committed by the Gang of Four, as defined in the Chinese press, will be presented in a later section.

What is strikingly different in the post-Mao era is the lack of physical manifestation of such reverence for the late chairman. There is a more explicit explanation of what constitutes Mao Zedong Thought, a more critical and pragmatic assessment of Mao's sayings as they pertain to socialist and economic reconstruction of the country—for society at large; for operating factories, schools, and communes and handling the forces of production; for China's policies toward foreign technology, equipment, and aid; and for the country's trade and political relations with other countries. There is an open acknowledgment that Mao did make mistakes in his later years, but that mistakes are different from crimes.

Gone are the days so characteristic of the early years of the Cultural Revolution, which began in 1966 as an ideological movement but later developed into a power struggle between moderates and ultraleftists for succession to leadership in view of Mao's failing health and eventual death in September 1976.

In those days almost every Chinese citizen displayed a copy of the little red book containing the quotations of Chairman Mao. The militant youths generally known as the Red Guards rampaged throughout the country seeking to remove any apparent vestige of capitalism or revisionism. In the decade 1966-1976, the policy of using bonuses to spur production in factories was denounced as "vestiges of capitalism" and hence eliminated. All interest payments promised by the government to former industrialists as compensation for the nationalization of private businesses in 1956 were stopped. Intellectuals were despised. Distinctions between physical laborers and mental laborers, such as doctors and university professors, were eliminated. In some hospitals—for example, the Huashan Hospital in Shanghai—the division of labor among doctors, nurses, and attendants was eliminated. All three groups took equal turns in administering medical treatment, nursing, and cleaning the wards. Operations in most factories were seriously disrupted, and there were complete work stoppages in some. Classes at universities and schools were seriously undermined and, in some educational institutions, suspended altogether. Throughout the country, research on science and technology was brought to a virtual standstill. The Red Guards spread the xenophobic idea that all things foreign were bad and should be warded off, and the ultraleftist doctrine that every word and saying of Mao was an indisputable truth that must be carried out verbatim.

China's leaders now say that the fanatical and anarchistic conditions prevailing in China in the decade 1966-1976 were the actions of misguided people who were incited to so act by Lin Biao, the Gang of Four, and their cohorts. The Chinese now acknowledge that Mao Zedong personally led and initiated the Cultural Revolution, which was a mistake in itself because of the harm it did to the country at large. His other mistakes lay in his inability to shift the nation's focus to socialist modernization promptly after the basic transformation of the means of the ownership in 1956 and in his overextension of the scope of class struggle (Huang 1981, pp. 15-23). However, although Mao made mistakes, he did not commit crimes. The Chinese leaders explain through the press that mistakes are fundamentally different from crimes in nature, means, and ends. They differ in nature in that mistakes occur where one's "subjective thinking is divorced from objective reality," whereas crimes refer to actions and behavior that actually endanger society. The means adopted in making a mistake generally fall within the confines of law, whereas the means pursued in committing a crime are in violation of the criminal statutes of the country. Furthermore, a person who makes a mistake generally harbors good intentions, whereas one who commits a crime deliberately wants to visit evil on society. Given the aforementioned differences between mistakes and crimes, the Chinese leaders indicate that in general "mistakes in work are unavoidable" (*Beijing Review*, January 5, 1981, pp. 21-23).

The Chinese are quick to point out that the trial of the Gang of Four in late 1980 did not involve Mao and does not "lead to a negation of Mao Zedong. . . .

The Chinese Communist Party and the Chinese people will always remember Mao Zedong as a founder of the Party and the state. One thing is certain: the Chinese people will never do to Chairman Mao what Khruschev did to Stalin" (*Beijing Review,* January 5, 1981, pp. 3-4).

In an interview with Edgar Snow, a leading Western expert on China, on January 9, 1965, Mao Zedong, commenting that Khruschev's fall from power may have occurred because of his failure to build a personality cult around himself, candidly admitted that a cult of personality had developed in China (Barnett 1968, pp. 35-68). On the same occasion, however, Mao remarked to Snow that future generations would assess historic events according to their own value systems. In the same interview Mao raised the possibility that, given the changing conditions on earth, "A thousand years from now . . . even Marx, Engels and Lenin . . . will possibly appear rather ridiculous." Based on this fairly lengthy interview, Snow concluded that Mao was prepared to allow future generations to evaluate his "political legacy" (Barnett 1968, p. 39). This is precisely what the present Chinese leaders seek to do in the post-Mao era of socialist modernization—to assess the contributions and mistakes made by Mao in his lifetime. One of the agenda items for discussion at the Sixth Plenary Session of the Eleventh Central Committee of the Chinese Communist party, which was held in the second half of 1981, was to assess Mao's contribution to the country and, more specifically, to identify the role of Mao Zedong Thought in the era of socialist modernization.

It seems apparent that as Mao aged and increasingly removed himself from the day-to-day affairs of running the country, a fierce power struggle developed among those under him who wanted to shape the future of the country. As China's leaders now tell us, Mao personally launched the Cultural Revolution—wherein lay his mistake. Beyond the original intentions of the Cultural Revolution—to train successors and provide for smooth leadership transition—it is difficult to conceive that a man such as Mao, who had contributed so much to the economic reconstruction of the country, could deliberately set the country on a course toward economic chaos and destruction, thereby completely reversing the contributions and accomplishments of his early years. It is also hard to believe that Mao in his last years was fully aware of the destructive elements inherent in the policies pursued during the years of the Cultural Revolution. The Cultural Revolution, though perhaps inaugurated with good intentions to ensure continuity after Mao's death, nevertheless was abused by persons close to Mao for their own selfish ends. At least, that is what China's present leaders would have us believe about Mao Zedong's role in the Cultural Revolution.

Far from completely discarding the sayings and teachings of Mao, Hua Guofeng in his "Political Report to the Eleventh National Congress of the Chinese Communist Party" delivered on August 12, 1977, and adopted six days later, announced the historic mission of the Eleventh Congress as follows: "to hold high the great banner of Chairman Mao and carry out his behests . . . bring into full play all positive factors inside and outside the Party at home and abroad . . . and make China a great, powerful and modern socialist country before the end of this century" (*Eleventh National Congress* 1977, pp. 7–8). This document and ensuing speeches by other top-ranking government officials were replete with references to the sayings of Mao and exhortations to carry out the late chairman's behests. A joint editorial of the *Renmin Ribao* and the *Jiefangjun Bao* on February 7, 1977, stated, "We will resolutely adhere to whatever policy decision made by Chairman Mao, we will always follow unswervingly whatever directive of Chairman Mao." Two months later Deng Xiaoping modified this statement by saying that the two "whatevers" should be eliminated. Instead, Deng "put forward the formulation of using the correct, comprehensive Mao Zedong Thought to guide our whole Party, whole army and the whole population" (*Beijing Review,* March 2, 1981, p. 15).

Hence it may be erroneous to say that Mao was berated. However, there are two noticeable and striking differences in the present approach to the study of and adherence to Mao's principles: (1) the development of a correct approach to the study of Marxism-Leninism and Mao Zedong Thought, and (2) a more realistic and pragmatic assessment of Mao's contribution to the socialist reconstruction of the country.

Correct Approach to Marxism, Leninism,
and Mao Zedong Thought

Lin Biao and later the Gang of Four asserted that every sentence and word uttered by Mao was truth, and that "one sentence equals ten thousand." Essentially, this meant taking particular points and sentences out of context. An example of this was the use of Mao's assertion, "For thousands of years, it had been said that it was right to oppress, it was right to exploit, and it was wrong to rebel. This old verdict was only reversed with the appearance of Marxism" (*Beijing Review,* September 29, 1978, p. 16). Mao was here referring to the revolutionary struggle of the proletariat to attain socialism. However, this "right to rebel" was taken out of context by Lin and his followers to mean a campaign against everything—hence the disruptions of factories, schools, and universities, and the stagnation in the growth and development of the forces of production and the economy as a whole. Similarly, Lin and his followers deemphasized Mao's instructions about the need to study technology, to do economic work well, and to develop production. Instead, they drew the absurd conclusions that "politics can override everything else" and "production will go up as a matter of course when revolution is carried out successfully" (*Beijing Review,* October 5, 1979).

To aid people in developing a correct approach to the study of Marxism-Leninism and Mao Zedong Thought, the Chinese press has published a series of articles over the past two years to serve as guidelines. Among the principal guidelines advocated were:

1. It is wrong to mutilate Marxism-Leninism-Mao Zedong Thought into individual sentences independent of one another and to follow these parts independent of the whole context. As Lenin pointed out, "From this Marxist philosophy, which is cast from a single piece of steel, you cannot eliminate one basic premise, one essential part, without departing from the objective truth, without falling prey to a bourgeois-reactionary falsehood" (Burns 1935, p. 673).

2. Advocate the slogan that "practice is the sole criterion for truth." Discussion on this subject was stimulated by an article written by a professor of philosophy at the Nanjing University and published in *Guangming Ribao*. In the article, the professor pointed out that practice, not theory, is the sole criterion for testing truth. In other words, only those things that have been proved in practice to be beneficial to the people and the socialist cause represent the truth that should be upheld. The article also argued that truth does not move in a straight line but changes over time. The thesis advanced here was not new. It was contained in Mao's work "On Practice," written in July 1937 to oppose dogmatism in the Chinese Communist party. During the years 1931–1934, some party members refused to believe that Marxism was not dogma but a guide to action. To correct such erroneous thinking, Mao wrote fairly extensively on the subject, citing Marx, Engels, and Lenin: "Marxists holds that man's social practice alone is the criterion of truth of his knowledge to the external world." Mao pointed out that actions based on ideas that are not in conformity with the objective laws of nature are doomed to failure (*Selected Works*, vol. 1, 1975, pp. 295-296).

3. Since political, economic, and social conditions are not static but change over time, it is fallacious to become complacent and fail to develop Marxism-Leninism-Mao Zedong Thought further to conform to changing objective reality. As Engels wrote, "We can only know under the conditions of our epoch and as far as these allow" (*Renmin Ribao*, October 30, 1979). Zhou Enlai noted that Mao Zedong Thought did not spring up overnight. Rather, it evolved over a number of years as a result of experience and in line with objective conditions. As evidence, Zhou cited the fact that in the summer of 1928 Mao Zedong considered that "work in the cities should be the central task." Not until January 1930 did Mao reverse this stand and shift the focus to the countryside. This reversal came about after Mao's realization that the revolution could succeed only with the support of the peasants, who make up over 80 percent of China's population. ("Excerpts of Selected Works of Zhou Enlai, Volume 1" in *Beijing Review*, March 2, 1981, p. 10).

Although Karl Marx argued for the superiority of communism, his writings remained vague about the specifics and dynamics of the future communist economic system. Marx did point to state ownership of the means of production and to the need to establish some form of planned economy as distinguishing features of the future communist society. However, he did not provide any operational theory or blueprint that would guide the functioning of a communist economic system. Consequently, before Lenin could apply Marxism to Russia in the early twentieth century, he had to study the conditions then prevailing in that country and develop Marxist theory further to fit the objective conditions of Russia. Similarly, when Mao envisioned and worked for the establishment of a communist state in China, he did not simply appropriate the Soviet model without making an inquiry into China's objective conditions. Instead of advocating blind application of the general principles of Marxism-Leninism to China, Mao proposed that some kind of preliminary screening be made so that only those principles applicable to the objective conditions in China would be adopted. It is in the transformation of Marxism-Leninism into a Chinese or Asian form that his closest colleagues saw Mao's major contribution to the development of Marxism-Leninism (Rumyantsei 1969). This is the precise definition of Mao Zedong Thought, which refers to the "sinicization" of Marxism-Leninism to fit China's objective conditions, and to the application and development of Marxism-Leninism in the effort to overthrow feudalism, capitalism, and imperialism and to bring about socialist revolution and construction in China.

On several occasions Mao declared that, given changing conditions, one should not be afraid to replace outdated theses with new ones to conform to new historical conditions. It is reported that Mao once stated that "my personal thoughts are developing, and I, too, am liable to make mistakes" (*Beijing Review*, March 2, 1981, p. 12). Consequently, as China enters the last two decades of the twentieth century, Mao Zedong Thought should be further developed and integrated with the goals of the Four Modernizations. Hence, the development of Mao Zedong Thought to conform to social realities could not and should not be construed as de-Maoification. The development of Mao Zedong Thought and the defense of it are not opposed to each other (*Beijing Review*, September 28, 1979, pp. 3-4; *Renmin Ribao*, October 30, 1979).

China's leaders now call for a renewal of the spirit of the Yanan Rectification Movement. The Yanan Rectification Movement was launched by Mao Zedong in 1942 to liberalize people's minds so that they could "proceed from reality in everything, . . . seek truth from facts and link theory with practice" (*Beijing Review*, October 5, 1979). This liberalization of the mind is fundamental to China's current drive to attain the goals of the Four Modernizations. Although China recognizes the need to learn advanced technology and techniques from abroad, the Chinese are quick to point out that modernization is not synonymous with wholesale Westernization. The Chinese constantly emphasize that modernization will be carried out in the Chinese way (Yao 1979). This essentially means that although the country will learn from the positive experiences of different countries (including capitalist economies), China will adopt only those methods and procedures that suit the country's objective conditions.

Leaders Are Not Gods

A second point of departure in China's current adherence to the principles of Mao is the recognition that Mao Zedong Thought or Maoism is not the product of a single person. In the speech delivered at the thirtieth anniversary of the founding of the PRC on September 29, 1979, Vice-Chairman Ye Jianying stated that Mao Zedong Thought is the product of the collective "wisdom of his comrades-in-arms, the Party and the revolutionary people," rather than Mao's personal wisdom alone. (*Beijing Review,* October 5, 1979, p. 8). The Chinese Communist party (CCP) currently emphasizes that the contributions of others, such as Zhou Enlai and Zhu De, to the development of Mao Zedong Thought should be duly acknowledged. The party, though calling on the people to assess the contributions and limitations of the leaders critically, has deemed it equally fallacious not to recognize the contribution of those who later in their lives committed crimes. As a case in point, the party called on the people to recognize Lin Biao's contribution in the battle of Pingxingguan and the Jinzhou campaign, even though he is generally condemned for his role during the Cultural Revolution (*Beijing Review,* January 29, 1980).

In the same speech delivered at the thirtieth anniversary of the founding of the PRC, Vice-Chairman Ye stated that "leaders are not gods. They are not infallible and therefore should not be deified." Ye went on to say that Mao was not a "prophet" but a great Marxist and that Mao "was the most outstanding representative of the great Chinese Communist Party and the great Chinese people." This is far from a harangue against the late chairman but is merely a more pragmatic and accurate appraisal of his contribution to Chinese society—an attempt to bring Mao down to earth, in line with Mao's own assertion in March 1955 that "our cause depends on the many for its success, and the few [that is, leaders and cadres] play only a limited role. While the few play a role that should be recognized, it is not a role of signal importance" (*Selected Works,* vol. 5, 1977, p. 166). Mao went on to remind leading cadres to guard against arrogance because "things can be made without [leaders and cadres] as history and many facts of life can testify." This attempt to bring Mao down to earth makes better sense in a country bent on economic progress and development. If Mao were deemed a deity, then he would be irreplaceable; with his death, the country's progress would be brought to a virtual standstill. If Mao were considered godlike, then the ordinary citizen could not seek to emulate his accomplishments. As Zhou Enlai once wrote, "If no one could learn from him, then Mao Zedong would be isolated from us, wouldn't he?" (Excerpts from Selected Works of Zhou Enlai", vol. 1, in *Beijing Review,* March 2, 1981, p. 9)

Along with this reevaluation of Mao's contribution to the Chinese revolution and society at large, China's leaders now adhere more strongly to the principle of collective leadership, while downplaying the role of any single individual. This principle is not new. Between the 1930s and 1950s, the CCP seldom gave great publicity to any single individual. In 1949, for example, Mao prohibited the celebration of the birthdays of party leaders and banned the naming of streets, places, and enterprises after party leaders (Editorial, *Renmin Ribao*, February 1, 1979). At the Third Session of the Eleventh Party Central Committee, the party as a whole once again endorsed the principle of collective leadership and decided that to uphold this principle, less publicity should be given to any single individual. In line with this policy, Vice-Chairman Ye Jianying pointed out in his speech on the thirtieth anniversary of the founding of the PRC that "it is not permissible . . . to exaggerate the role of individual leaders" (*Beijing Review*, October 5, 1979, p. 21). Consequently, beginning with the second half of 1979, compared with the previous twelve months, the Chinese press downplayed the dominant role assumed by any single individual. In the second half of 1978 and early 1979, Vice-Premier Deng Xiaoping dominated news on China, at least in the United States, with headlines such as "Deng's New Long March" (*Time*, November 27, 1978). This culminated in his selection as *Time* magazine's fifty-second "Man of the Year" (*Time*, January 1, 1979); *Time* described him as the "prime mover" of the Four Modernizations program. These days, Deng is keeping a much lower public profile. This is far from saying that he has lost or relinquished his power. Rather, this is in line with China's current emphasis on the principle that no one individual should be singled out as the sole or prime mover of the country. This is to prevent the occurrence of another personality cult around any single individual.

In line with this policy of espousing collective leadership, since 1980 the party has called on all leading cadres to "restore the Party's fine traditions," combat bureaucracy, and not seek special privileges. Since the second half of 1980, the Chinese press has carried criticisms of the abuse of special privileges by certain leading cadres. For example, in 1980 the Central Committee of the CCP commended a young chef from one of the restaurants in Beijing for making the party aware that the minister of commerce abused his authority by dining at the restaurant frequently, at considerably reduced prices. Since this incident was reported in the press, Chinese citizens have become more vocal about their discontent with the abuse of power by certain leading cadres (*Beijing Review*, November 3, 1980).

In the second half of 1980 the party decided to abolish the system of lifetime tenure for leading cadres. The problems associated with this system are threefold. First, the country is administered by individuals in their seventies and eighties. Although many of these individuals are still mentally agile, some suffer from failing health and consequently are unable to manage the day-to-day business of running the country. Furthermore, the administration needs new blood. Second, lifetime tenure tends to breed complacency. Third, the system is often associated with concentration of power in the hands of a few people because a given leading cadre often holds several positions concurrently (*Beijing Review*, November 17, 1980). To set an example, Deng Xiaoping stepped down as senior vice-premier of the party in the last quarter of 1980, although he still retains his position in the powerful politburo. This reorganization is in line with the new policy of separating party affairs from day-to-day administration of the government.

In addition, the party has called on the country henceforth to select cadres from among those who fulfill the following three criteria: (1) adherence to socialism; (2) possession of technical competence; and (3) being in the prime of life in order to bring new blood and ideas to the party and the organizations (*Beijing Review,* August 11, 1980).

Marxism–Leninism–Mao Zedong Thought as Applied to Economic Progress and Industrialization

Karl Marx identified the six major historical stages of economic development from primitive communism, through feudalism, to mercantilism, to capitalism, then socialism, and eventually to full communism. Although he argued for the inevitability of the downfall of capitalism and the ultimate triumph of socialism and finally communism, Marx was fairly vague about the future communist economic system. Besides alluding to state or public ownership of the means of production and some form of centrally planned economy as two of the distinguishing features of communist society, Marx failed to provide a detailed blueprint or operational theory that would guide the actual establishment and functioning of such an economic system. Consequently, when Lenin and the Russian Communist party sought to establish the Union of Soviet Socialist Republics, they had to develop an operational system from scratch. The specifics of how Lenin and others developed blueprints for a socialist economic system have been discussed elsewhere and will be omitted here. The present analysis will focus on the adaptation of Marxism-Leninism to the Chinese situation.

In their attempt to convert China to a socialist state, Mao and the party recognized that the political, economic, social, and cultural conditions in China were very different from those of the Soviet Union. Almost until the middle of the twentieth century, China was a semicolonial country. Even as capitalist relations were crystallizing, semifeudal and feudal relations were still very strong. Besides, the country was exploited by foreign imperialist powers. Peasants constituted approximately 90 percent of the gainfully employed population, whereas industrial workers made up less than 1 percent of the total work force. In the first quarter of the twentieth century, the working-class movement in China was very weak.

When the Communist Party of China was organized in 1921, its membership consisted of only a few dozen people. Seamen, railwaymen, and other detachments of the working class took part in political activities between 1921 and 1925. Unlike the case in the Soviet Union, however, these were by far a minority. In China the Communist party was replenished mainly by peasants and by members of the urban petty bourgeoisie and the national intelligentsia. In China it was the antifeudal, anti-imperialist, and national-liberation movement that made up the major elements of the revolutionary process. Schwartz (1951), a noted China scholar, suggested that it was perhaps the Leninist doctrine of imperialism (rather than socialism per se) that held the major attraction for the founders of the CCP; it was this element above all else that first gave Marxism-Leninism its burning relevance to the Chinese intelligentsia. Once Marxism-Leninism attracted followers in China, their theses were developed and applied to the analysis of other aspects of the Chinese economy and society.

Mao was acutely aware of such differences and of the futility of attempting to transplant Marxism-Leninism to China without first modifying and adapting it to suit the objective conditions. As pointed out earlier, this "sinicization" of Marxism-Leninism to Chinese reality is generally referred to as Mao Zedong Thought.

Mao's creativity in adapting Marxism-Leninism to China was acknowledged as early as the 1930s. By 1945 the term "Thought of Mao Zedong" was incorporated into the party constitution. By 1951 the Chinese communists were claiming that "Mao Zedong's theory of the Chinese revolution is a new development of Marxism-Leninism . . . a new contribution to the treasury of Marxism-Leninism" (*Current Background*, July 5, 1951). Mao's major contribution to the development of Marxist theory lies in the fact that he combined the theory and practice of Marxism with concepts and patterns of behavior drawn from the Chinese past in such a fashion as to render it comprehensible and acceptable to the Chinese people. The Chinese communists believe that Marxism-Leninism contains universal truth that holds good for all countries but that must be adapted to the peculiar circumstances of each. A favorite cliché of Chinese communists is, "Marxism is not a dogma, but a guide to revolutionary action." They claim that the very method of Marxist dialectics dictates that theory must be integrated with action, and that action must be planned in light of objective conditions prevailing at a given place and time. Mao emphasized the imbecility of wholesale or unconditional Westernization even in the application of Marxism. Although Mao wanted the Chinese to become modern people as quickly as possible; he did not want them to feel emotionally indebted to foreign sources of knowledge. In a society like that of China, which places heavy emphasis on tradition, the communist leaders were much too wary and intelligent to attempt to abandon Chinese cultural traditions altogether. A number of the principles espoused by Confucius seemed to blend in well with Marxist-Leninist orthodoxy. The long tradition of rule by a Confucian elite, for instance, undoubtedly makes it easier for the Chinese to accept as perfectly normal the continued dominance of the Communist elite. Moreover, Confucius's slogans "hear more and see more," "learn a lot and ask questions," "review what you have learnt in order to learn something new," and "study must go hand in hand with thinking" (*Beijing Review*, April 6, 1979, p. 20) appear to fit in well with China's current emphasis on the idea that "practice is the sole criterion for truth" and on the need to absorb positive experiences from different countries.

Mao was determined to rebuild a "new" China from the ruins of the old. The new China, like its predecessor, was to resume its rightful place among the nations—the preeminent place. In 1938 Mao asserted: "we must not cut off our whole historical past. We must make a summing up from Confucius to Sun Yat-sen and enter into this precious heritage" (Creel 1953, p. 18). On another occasion Mao apparently contradicted himself by declaring: "we wish to eradicate the old Chinese culture; it is inseparable from the old Chinese government and the old economic system. We intend to establish a new kind of Chinese national culture" (Creel 1953, p. 18). The key to understanding this apparent contradiction lies in the fact that Mao, on the one hand, adhered closely to the Confucian emphasis on learning whatever is beneficial from others. Confucius once remarked, "if I am walking along with two others, one must be qualified to be my teacher." After all, Mao was exposed to Confucianism at a very tender age and, like other schoolboys of his day, memorized the books that expounded the views of Confucius, Mencius, Chu Tsi, and other Confucian authorities. Confucianism thus had a lasting influence on Mao's subsequent intellectual development and his outlook on life and society at large. Mao considered this evidence of his use of the dialectical principle, which permits the absorption of good elements from decaying things. His denunciation of Confucius, on the other hand, was based primarily on his belief that Confucianism, which is essentially a backward-looking philosophy, is incapable of solving the country's problems. In Confucian orthodoxy, a past golden age when the virtuous sage-emperors ruled was the great social model held forth for emulation. In direct contrast, Marxists-Leninists look to the future for the perfection of their ideals. The Confucian yearning for peace of mind, stability, and contentment with the status quo was replaced by the forward-looking Marxist philosophy, which emphasizes the struggle for improvement over past and present, socioeconomic change, progress, and development.

Mao was a prolific writer on diverse subjects, ranging from tactics of guerrilla warfare to analysis of class struggles to practically every aspect of societal operations. Most of his writings are contained in the five volumes of the *Selected Works of Mao Zedong,* which were written during different periods of the Chinese revolution and socialist construction of the country. The following is a summary of the major points of Mao Zedong Thought that relate to economic progress, development, and industrialization of China. These points are still adhered to and expanded on in China's current drive to modernize the various sectors of its economy. It is important to bear in mind that China's present leaders explicitly state that Mao Zedong Thought is not the product of a single person. Rather, the term refers to the application and development of Marxism-Leninism in China to fit the country's objective conditions, in order to bring about socialist revolution and reconstruction in China.

Need for Economic Construction

Mao emphasized the need for economic construction, which he considered inseparable from the revolutionary cause. In 1933, in an article entitled "Pay Attention to Economic Work," Mao rebuked those party members who neglected the importance of economic work to socialist construction. Mao chastised these people for failing to "understand that to dispense with economic construction would weaken the revolutionary effort rather than subordinate everything to it" (*Beijing Review*, May 19, 1978, p. 8). Mao was determined to rebuild a new China that would resume its rightful place among nations. He was acutely aware that no nation could become great while plagued by economic underdevelopment and poverty. Mao recognized that upon the completion of nationalization of all private enterprises in 1956, the next step in socialist construction would be socialist modernization. Socialist modernization seeks to transform the economic and technical backwardness of the country to catch up to the modern economies of the world. In 1957, in "On the Correct Handling of Contradictions among the People," Mao wrote that "our basic task has changed from unfettering the productive forces to protecting and expanding them in the context of the new relations of production" (*Selected Works*, vol. 5, 1977, p. 419). In 1958, in an article entitled "Continued Revolution," Mao explicitly pointed out that henceforth the party's efforts should be diverted toward technical revolution. At the end of 1964, in Zhou Enlai's "Report on the Work of the Government to the Third National People's Congress," he officially announced for the first time the Four Modernizations program. This program was reiterated at the Fourth National People's Congress in 1975. The implementation of this program was delayed because of the political instability and economic chaos that prevailed in the country during the years 1966–1976.

This principle of combining the political cause with economic work is now emphasized more than ever before. In fact, as pointed out previously, Huang (1981) wrote that Mao erred, particularly in his later years, by failing promptly to shift the nation's focus to economic construction after the basic transformation of the means of ownership. At the Third Session of the Fifth National People's Congress, held in Beijing in August 1980, Premier Zhao Ziyang stressed the urgent need to carry out political and economic reforms. In his view, reforms in the two areas are inseparable from each other and must be complementary (*Beijing Review*, September 22, 1980, p. 5).

China's leaders now emphasize that the central task in the last quarter of the twentieth century is no longer class struggle because, by and large, the exploiting classes have been transformed into laborers who work in order to earn their primary means of livelihood. According to 1979 statistics, there were only 800 former capitalists remaining in the country who earn more than 300 yuan per month (*Beijing Review*, November 16, 1979, p. 9). Thus the important question to be tackled at this point is that of the Four Modernizations.

Relationships between the Development of Heavy Industry, of Light Industry, and of Agriculture

In several works, such as "On the Ten Major Relationships" (1956), Mao explicitly discussed China's path to industrialization and laid down policies for handling the relationships between the growth of heavy industry, of light industry, and of agriculture. These recommendations were based on a review of the Soviet Union's experiences and China's objective conditions. In the Soviet Union heavy industry was emphasized to the neglect of light industry and agriculture. Between 1913 and 1953 the value of heavy-industrial output increased 46.5-fold, whereas light industry increased only 8.8-fold and agriculture a mere 46 percent. This resulted in shortages of consumer products in the market, an unstable currency, and a setback in the development of heavy industry. Mao exhorted the country to learn from the Soviet experience and also to take into consideration China's objective conditions, namely, that an overwhelming proportion of the population (approximately 80 percent) still depended on agriculture as their principal means of livelihood. Mao wrote that although priority must be given to the development of heavy industry, this does not mean that "the production of the means of subsistence, especially grain, can be neglected. Without enough food and other daily necessities, it would be impossible to provide for the workers in the first place, and then what sense would it make to talk about developing heavy industry?" Consequently, Mao called for "correctly handling" the relationships between heavy industry, on the one hand, and the light industrial and agricultural sectors on the other (*Selected Works*, vol. 5, 1977, p. 286).

Despite China's recognition of Soviet mistakes in the development of the national economy of the USSR, the Chinese fell prey to the same shortcomings in their own national economic-development plans. Until 1978 there were serious imbalances in the appropriation of resources among the three sectors, in that heavy industry was emphasized to the neglect of light industry and agriculture. For instance, between 1966 and 1978 investment in capital construction and heavy industry averaged more than 55 percent of the total annual state budget allocations. Agriculture accounted for a little more than 10 percent, and light industry received a mere 5 percent of the annual appropriations (*Beijing Review*, December 21, 1979, p. 11). These imbalances could be attributed at least in part to a misconception of the goals of socialist production, which will be discussed subsequently. Imbalances in allocations among the various sectors resulted in an increase in the output of the national economy that occurred while the people's standard of living was not improved commensurately. The guiding principle in the first twenty-nine years of the history of the PRC was "production first, living conditions next." For example, between 1949 and 1978 the total value of heavy-industrial output increased some 90-fold, whereas that for the light-industrial sector rose 39.2-fold. Although these rates of growth compare favorably with those of most developing nations, the livelihood of the people was not improved commensurately. In 1978, for instance, the annual average consumption by urban and rural workers was only 175 yuan, compared with 76 yuan in 1952. This is a mere 2.3-fold increase in a period of twenty-seven years (*Beijing Review*, February 23, 1981, pp. 16–20).

China's leaders now reemphasize the importance of adhering to Mao's general policy of developing the economy in the following order: agriculture, light industry, and then heavy industry. Under the current Three-Year Plan (1979–1981) for readjustment of the national economy, state investment in agriculture and light industry have been increased. Heavier investment in agriculture is designed to raise the standard of living of the rural population and thus to lessen the gap between urban and rural areas. In 1980 the per capital income in the urban areas was 781 yuan, whereas that for the rural areas was only 170 yuan (*Beijing Review*, February 23, 1981).

Heavier investment in light industries is designed to serve two purposes: (1) to produce more goods for export in order to generate foreign exchange needed to purchase the equipment and technology necessary to further the goals of the Four Modernizations; and (2) to improve the overall standard of living of the people in the country. Even though wages were increased for three consecutive years (1977, 1978, and 1979), money still has little purchasing power. There is an extreme shortage of consumer goods in the country. In 1979, the first year of the Three-Year Plan for readjustment, the enterprises in China manufactured 5,000 new items of consumer goods to satisfy the growing needs of the people, especially those of the relatively more affluent urban workers. In 1980 retail sales of consumer goods reached 207.1 billion yuan, an 18.2-percent increase over the 1979 figure. The government announced that the retail-sales volume for 1980 was the highest attained since 1949, even after adjusting for the higher prices of commodities. In 1980 the overall price index rose approximately 11 percent. New products added to the list of consumer goods were washing machines, refrigerators, minibikes, and automatic calendar watches (*Beijing Review*, January 14, 1980, p. 3). In the past, the three most wanted consumer items were the wristwatch, the bicycle, and the sewing machine. In 1980 the production of wristwatches, bicycles, and sewing machines reached 22.5 million, 13 million, and 7.6 million respectively. These represented a 30-percent increase over 1979 figures (*China Reconstructs*, May 1981). As income rises, the list of most wanted items has expanded to include television sets, electric fans, tape recorders, refrigerators, and washing machines

(*China Reconstructs,* March 1981). In 1980 the country produced 2.5 million television sets domestically. This attempt to improve the people's livelihood is in line with China's current reevaluation of the goal of socialist production.

The October 20, 1979, edition of the *Renmin Ribao* (*People's Daily*) carried a special editorial entitled "On the Aim of Socialist Production," which indicated that the principal aim of production should be to upgrade the living standards of the people. The editorial pointed out that in the past there had been an erroneous tendency to undertake production primarily for its own sake, while completely ignoring market demand. The editorial explained that the reasons for the persistence of this phenomenon were primarily threefold:

1. During the Cultural Revolution, consumption was viewed as a negative factor, and improving people's livelihood was considered almost synonymous with pursuit of capitalist goals.
2. The mistaken assumption prevailed that production of capital goods could be developed independent of the production of consumer goods.
3. Development of heavy industry was emphasized as the expense of agriculture and light industry.

In the current Three-Year Plan for readjustment of the national economy, due emphasis is given to production for the purpose of improving the people's standard of living (*Beijing Review,* February 23, 1981).

Socialist Modernization

On June 6, 1950, shortly after the founding of the PRC, Mao wrote that it would not be possible to eliminate capitalism and realize socialism quickly because of China's objective conditions (*Selected Works,* vol. 5, 1977, p. 30). China's present leaders emphasize that socialism will develop over a very long historical period and that China will be unable to arrive at full communism for a long time to come because objective conditions are not yet ripe. Before China can attain full communism, the country must "go all out, aim high and achieve greater, faster, better and more economic results in building socialism" (*Selected Works,* vol. 5, 1977, p. 138). Implicit in this policy is the assumption that a major prerequisite for transition to full communism is socialist modernization of the country. Otherwise, how can socialism claim that it is superior to capitalism? In the phase of transition from socialism to communism, it is necessary to unite with intellectuals, industrialists, businessmen, and all other elements that can be united—including foreign interests as long as they serve China—to facilitate the attainment of the goals of socialist modernization. This serves to explain the current emphasis on the policies of: (1) encouraging foreign trade and other forms of economic cooperation with other countries; (2) learning advanced techniques from abroad, including those of capitalist economies; (3) allowing alternative means of the ownership of production, such as collective ownership of enterprises and ownership by individual producers; and (4) using technical competence as an important criterion for determining a person's suitability for a position of responsibility. One notable example of this new policy is the appointment of Rong Yiren, an eminent industrialist in China before 1949, as the chairman of the board of directors of the China International Trust and Investment Corporation (CITIC). CITIC was formed in 1979 as a primary vehicle for inducing foreign investment in China. Among its many functions, it introduces foreign partners to local enterprises in joint-venture endeavors, and services other aspects of foreign investment. The government has also implemented the policy of appointing scientists to scientific advisory groups for a variety of industrial projects (*Beijing Review,* December 8, 1980.

As they strive to achieve the goals of the Four Modernizations, China's leaders do not want to repeat the mistake made by their nineteenth-century predecessors—that of overreliance on foreign sources for the country's development. Though adhering to the principle of self-reliance, China's leaders point out that self-reliance is not synonymous with economic isolationism. In the words of Deng Xiaoping: "by self-reliance we mean that a country should mainly rely on the strength and wisdom of its own people, control its own economic lifelines, make full use of its own resources." Self-reliance is not synonymous with rejection of foreign aid because no country can be self-sufficient in all things. Consequently, it is necessary to engage in economic and technical exchanges "to make up for each other's deficiencies" (Cheng 1974, p. 6). Thus the government does not see any inconsistency in its present policy of engaging in technical and cultural exchanges and trade relations with foreign countries, on the one hand, and upholding the socialist principle of striving for eventual full communism and stressing the principle of self-reliance on the other. After all, Mao emphasized that China must "learn from the advanced countries . . . so as to make fewer mistakes" (*Selected Works,* vol. 5, 1977, p. 155).

Alternative Means of Ownership

In the Draft Constitution of the PRC, dated June 14, 1954, Mao wrote that although "socialist ownership by the whole people is the principle, but in order to realize this principle we should combine it with flexibility. And flexibility means state capitalism, which takes not one but 'various' forms, which is to be realized not overnight but 'gradually.' This makes for flexibility" (*Selected Works,* vol. 5, 1977, pp. 143-144). Thus, in the transition from socialism to full communism, other forms of ownership of the means of production may still exist, as long as they further the goal of socialist modernization. Some

of the other means of ownership allowed are collective ownership by the working people; joint-venture arrangements with foreign firms to develop the productive forces in China; and the granting of business licenses to individual operators.
According to Article 5 of the 1978 Constitution of the PRC:

> There are mainly two kinds of ownership of the means of produc-
> tion . . . : socialist ownership by the whole people and socialist collec-
> tive ownership by the working people. The state allows non-agricultural
> laborers to engage in individual labor involving no exploitation of
> others, within the limits permitted by law and under unified arrange-
> ment and management by organizations at the basic level in cities
> and towns or in rural areas. [*Constitution of the PRC* 1978, p. 10]

Individual operators generally work in the service and handicrafts sectors (*Beijing
Review*, September 15, 1980). In July 1979 the Joint Venture Law was promulgated. Since then, laws pertaining to labor-management relations have been
promulgated, as have corporate and individual income-tax laws affecting joint-
venture enterprises. The Joint Venture Law provides for a minimum of 25-
percent investment, with a maximum of 99 percent. According to Rong Yiren,
chairman of the China International Trust and Investment Corporation, China
would allow 100-percent foreign ownership under special circumstances—for
example, where high-level technology is concerned. Such 100-percent equity
ownership would not, of course, be considered as a joint venture (Rong Yiren,
Speech, November 9, 1979).

Mao Zedong Thought and the Operations of
Industrial Enterprises

Compared with their Western counterparts, Chinese industrial personnel—
managers, technicians (both referred to as *cadres* in China), and workers—are
given precise, detailed descriptions of what is expected of them as members
of a factory, workshop, or work unit. Since late 1978 the state has experimentally granted greater autonomy with respect to decision making to a select
group of enterprises. The state has also allowed the use of free-market mechanisms on a limited scale. The free-market mechanism, however, is always subject
to and controlled by central planning (Lin 1980). After all, China is a planned
socialist economy. Consequently, even with the reforms, the state still sets
minimum production targets, allocates raw materials, and purchases and markets
a fixed percentage of the enterprises' output. In addition, the state also prescribes the overall policies and guidelines that industry should follow in its
operations. The party committee attached to each enterprise and the trade
union to which the employees in a particular enterprise belong make sure that
these policies and guidelines are adhered to in the operations and functionings

of the enterprise (Laaksonen 1975). It should be noted, however, that these political guidelines and principles will not be applied to joint-venture enterprises. New laws governing labor-management relations in joint ventures were promulgated on July 26, 1980. Joint ventures will be run along Western lines. After all, one of the purposes of establishing joint-venture concerns in China is to facilitate the acquisition of advanced technologies, including management techniques, from abroad. However, joint-venture enterprises will be influenced by local conditions to a certain extent. Senior-ranking Chinese officials insist that China will modernize the Chinese way—that is, that the country will not indiscriminately implement Western management techniques regardless of local conditions.

The policies and guidelines adhered to in the current operation of Chinese industrial enterprises include the relevant principles embodied in the Charter of the Anshan Iron and Steel Company; "In Industry, Learn from Daqing (Taching)"; the Thirty-point Decision on Industry; and the Three-Year Plan (1979–1981) for readjustment, restructuring, consolidation, and improvement of China's economy. The key word here is *relevant*. In China the current emphasis is on the slogan "practice is the sole criterion for truth." This means that only those principles and guidelines (as embodied in the Charter of the Anshan Iron and Steel Company, "In Industry, Learn from Daqing," and the Thirty-Point Decision on Industry) that fit in with the objective conditions of the Four Modernizations and that have proved to work in practice will be upheld, whereas others will be abandoned.

China's present leaders are acutely aware of the backwardness of the operation and management of industrial enterprises and are eager to learn new techniques from more advanced nations. Specifically, China is eager to learn the principles and application of cost accounting, quality control, and product innovation and development—in short, techniques that would increase productivity and improve overall efficiency in the operations of the enterprises. The socialist principles and guidelines to be outlined here are not viewed as contradictory to the pursuit of this policy of seeking new management techniques from abroad. Rather, the new management techniques are designed to complement the principles contained in these guidelines and policies, which could be viewed as the philosophy guiding the operations of socialist enterprises. A careful reading of these policies would show that the pursuit of new management techniques from abroad would serve to enhance, rather than contradict, the socialist principles contained in the guidelines discussed.

Charter of the Anshan Iron and Steel Company
(Anshan Charter)

This is a directive issued by Mao Zedong in March 1960, wherein he summarized the lessons drawn from economic construction in the USSR and from China's own experience in socialist revolution and construction, and laid down the fundamental principles to be followed in running socialist enterprises, both large and small. The relevant principles adhered to are:

1. Keep politics firmly in command.
2. Strengthen party leadership.
3. Launch vigorous mass movements, such as socialist-labor emulation drives.
4. Reform irrational or outmoded rules and regulations.
5. Encourage close cooperation among cadres, workers, and technicians.
6. Go all out for technical innovation and technical revolution.

The aforementioned principles are emphasized in China's current drive to modernize its economy. These principles could be used in conjunction with new management techniques borrowed from advanced nations and would serve to facilitate and ensure the successful implementation of such modern procedures through the direction provided by the party leadership in the Chinese enterprises, as well as through the cooperation and understanding of all categories of personnel in the enterprise—namely, administrative cadres, technical cadres, and workers. The party plays an important role in the organization and functioning of an individual enterprise. Party members supervise and coordinate the productive forces within the enterprise and ensure that targets are met and government policies adhered to. In turn, the party transmits the concerns of industry and of workers to the relevant government authorities to guide them in formulating plans and policies.

"In Industry, Learn from Daqing"

In 1964 Mao Zedong issued a directive entitled, "In Industry, Learn from Daqing," wherein he exhorted China's enterprises, whether engaged in heavy or light industry, to emulate the example and spirit of Daqing. Mao attributed the success of Daqing to the tremendous will power, strict discipline, and methods of organization practiced there. In May 1977 the National Conference on Learning from Daqing in Industry was convened, wherein China's leaders once again emphasized the importance of following the practices of Daqing in running socialist enterprises. The relevant principles are:

1. The three-point covenant governing the work and life-styles of the leading cadres. Leading cadres must:
   a. keep to the style of hard work and plain living and not seek special privilege
   b. take part in productive labor, and not sit around like overlords (this principle is modified to mean that leading cadres must "go among the masses" in order to keep themselves abreast of the plight of the workers)

c. observe the rules of the "three honest's" and the "four strict's". The former include honesty in thought, word, and deed; the latter include setting strict standards for work, organization, attitude, and observance of discipline

In light of recent criticisms in the press of the abuse of authority by certain leading cadres, the party has once again called on all cadres to improve their attitudes and life-styles.

2. Selection and commendation of pacesetters in the industry annually. Though engendering a spirit of competition among units and workers, the enterprise should at the same time develop a spirit of cooperation so that the less advanced workers and work units can learn from the more advanced ones and thus make stready progress in their work. This is particularly important in the Three-Year Plan for readjustment, restructuring, consolidation, and improvement of China's economy, the major purpose of which is to raise the level of productivity and improve management techniques in all enterprises.

3. Institute the system of responsibility at each post and eliminate the bad habit of "passing the buck."

4. Cadres should be both "red" (politically sound) and "expert" (possessing the necessary technical expertise to perform the job well).

5. Emphasize training of workers and cadres so as to advance their skills.

6. Emphasize thrift and eliminate waste in production. According to 1979 statistics, 55 percent of the enterprises have failed to match the lowest levels of consumption of raw and semifinished materials previously attained (*Beijing Review,* July 6, 1979, p. 13).

The principles espoused in the foregoing directive would serve to facilitate the acquisition, dissemination, and implementation of advanced management techniques in Chinese industrial enterprises. By incorporating Daqing's spirit of fearlessness, of mustering every ounce of strength to overcome hardship and difficulties, Chinese industrial enterprises could see that even though they are confronted with the mammoth task of developing the country's national economy to the first ranks of the world by the year 2000, the goal is attainable if the people possess the zeal, fervor, and discipline exemplified by the model workers of Daqing.

Although all enterprises are exhorted to emulate Daqing, it should be noted that China has now advanced new guidelines for emulation of advanced models. In 1964 Dazhai (a small mountain village about 400 kilometers southwest of Beijing) was designated as the model in agriculture. Since 1978 the government has discovered that some of the production figures reported by the brigade were grossly inflated. This has led to a reassessment of Dazhai. The government has concluded that although Dazhai had it merits, it also had its limitations. Hence, the government decreed that henceforth "advanced models should never be elevated to the level of awe-inspiring sanctity." Though the achievements of an advanced model will be publicized, its limitations should also be pointed out so that others may separate the wheat from the chaff (*Beijing Review,* April 20, 1981, p. 27). This policy is in line with the current reassessment of the contributions of Mao Zedong and the government's recent statements that "leaders are not gods, and hence should not be deified." Furthermore, the government notes that given the fact that conditions vary throughout the country, it would be erroneous to blindly duplicate the experiences of the advanced models while totally disregarding local conditions.

The Thirty-Point Decision on Industry

This document, drawn up at a national conference in June 1978, is an embodiment of Mao Zedong Thought and the policies and principles of running industry. It summarizes the positive and negative experiences of the first twenty nine years of the People's Republic of China. The thirty-point decision has been implemented experimentally at a select sample of leading enterprises. The main policy guidelines contained in the decision include the system of division of labor and undertaking of responsibility by the factory directors under the leadership of the party committee; reorganization of industry in accordance with the principles of specialization and coordination; application of the principle of "from each according to his ability, to each according to his work"; improvement of workers' and staff members' welfare; and enforcement of strict discipline. In late 1980 there was a call to separate the party committee from administration at the enterprise level. It is argued that the present system (whereby the factory director is under the leadership of the party committee) is unsuitable for improving organizational efficiency. Arguments have been advanced that call for the gradual replacement of this system with one wherein the factory director is in charge of administrative duties under the leadership of the Congress of Workers and Staff or its equivalent in the enterprise (*Beijing Review,* January 26, 1981, pp. 17-20).

As in the previous two documents, the principles contained in the "Thirty-point Decision on Industry" would serve to facilitate the implementation of advanced management techniques learned from aborad through emphasis on the principles of responsibility, coordination of activities, specialization, and exertion of one's best efforts to ensure the attainment of the production targets set for the respective industrial enterprises.

Three-Year Plan (1979-1981) for Readjustment, Restructuring, Consolidation and Improvement of China's Economy

According to Yao (1979), in Hua Guofeng's "Report on the Work of the Government," delivered at the second session of the Fifth National People's Congress on June 18, 1979, Hua revealed some disturbing figures about the state of China's economy. He noted that 43 percent of the major industrial products manufactured by key enterprises had failed to reach the best quality levels previously attained; 55 percent of the enterprises had failed to reach the lowest levels of consumption of raw and semifinished materials previously attained; and 24 percent of the state-owned enterprises were operating at various degrees of losses (*Beijing Review*, July 6, 1979, p. 13). He designated the years 1979–1981 (now extended to 1982) as the three years for readjustment, restructuring, consolidation, and improvement of China's economy. Enterprises in all industries were called on to observe closely the following guidelines and policies:

Readjustment. This includes conscientious efforts to:

1. Rectify the serious disproportions and economic havoc brought about during the Cultural Revolution years.
2. Bring about relatively good coordination in the development of agriculture, light industry, and heavy industry.
·3. Maintain a proper ratio between consumption and accumulation.

Based on his analysis of China's past performance, Xue Muqiao, a noted Chinese economist and an influential figure in China's State Planning Commission, hypothesized that when rates of accumulation exceeded 40 percent, the national economy would decline, and when rates of accumulation surpassed 30 percent, imbalances in economic growth would result. Xue concluded that in order to achieve rapid economic growth, the rate of accumulation should be around 25 percent (Xue 1980).

Restructuring. This requires overall reform of the structure of economic management. Some of the changes to be implemented include the following:

1. Eliminate absolute egalitarianism by making the income of the workers and the profit to be retained by the enterprise commensurate with their contribution to the state.
2. Eliminate overlapping and inefficient administrative organs. In any enterprise, the number of nonproductive personnel should not exceed 18 percent of the total payroll. The excessive levels in the existing structure of industrial management should be eliminated, and the number of cadres at all levels should be reduced.
3. Grant greater autonomy to the local authorities with respect to planning, capital construction, finance, acquisition of raw materials, and the conduct of foreign trade.

Consolidation. Changes in this area include the following:

1. Establish a system of clearly defined responsibility for everyone in the enterprise.
2. Establish a system of specialization of labor and coordination of economic activities across different enterprises to achieve greater economies of scale in production.
3. Consolidate poorly managed enterprises through reorganization and mergers.
4. Establish rules and regulations to govern all aspects of the factory's operations, and ensure strict implementation of these rules and regulations. In all the factories and enterprises I visited, rules and regulations to be followed in the operation of machinery and equipment and in the process of production were prominently displayed throughout the factory so that there could be little question about how things ought to be carried out in the factory.

Improvement. This requires an upgrading of the existing levels of production, technology, and management. According to Chinese statistics, in 1979 the production levels of the large industrial enterprises in the country were only one-fifth to one-tenth of those of the developed nations of the world (*Beijing Review,* July 6, 1979). In order to bring about an improvement in these areas, the following practices were recommended for adoption:

1. Organize and direct socialist-labor emulation drives.
2. Raise the vocational skills of cadres and workers, and the management skills of leading cadres, through education.
3. Learn science, technology, and management techniques from foreign countries.
4. Develop foreign trade in order to finance the import of foreign technology and equipment.

The policies and guidelines laid down in the Three-Year Plan for Readjustment once again urged the Chinese industrial enterprises to discontinue use of inefficient and ineffective procedures, to abandon outmoded rules and regulations, and to adopt practices and procedures that are in line with the country's mission and objective conditions.

The Role of the Press

Any discussion of the importance of ideology would be incomplete without a brief discussion of the role of the press in propagandizing the official policies and guidelines governing all aspects of society. In an illuminating British Broadcasting Corporation documentary entitled "The Incredible Chinese News Machine," aired on September 15, 1980, Cockerell outlined the role played by the Chinese press in keeping the public informed of the latest party lines. There are some 382 newspapers in the country with a total circulation of 70 million copies daily (Zhou 1981, pp. 23-29). The most important newspaper and the one with the largest circulation in China is the *Renmin Ribao* (*People's Daily*), published under the auspices of the Central Committee of the CCP and serves as "the official voice" of the party (Cockerell 1980, p. 355). With a daily circulation of 5.3 million copies, the *Renmin Ribao* is printed in Beijing, in twenty other cities in China, in Hong Kong, and in Tokyo. To ensure that the masses are knowledgeable about the contents of the paper, it is posted on bulletin boards in public places throughout the country. In addition, editorial highlights are broadcast over the radio stations. With its large circulation, the *Renmin Ribao* serves as an important mechanism for keeping the masses informed of official party views on practically all aspects of societal functioning—political affairs, education, culture, art, and literature. The newspaper uses rhetoric that reflects the current party guidelines. Of course, the dominant theme now is the Four Modernizations. The newspaper is replete with sentences like, "The Chinese people's march toward the great goal of the Four Modernizations echoes from the foothills of the Yenshan Mountains to the shores of the Yellow Sea to all corners of the world," and, "We are setting out on our new long march to scale the heights of Science and Technology" (Cockerell 1980, p. 356). The press thus serves as an important outlet for educating and directing the Chinese to adhere to the principles and guidelines that govern all aspects of society.

Discussion

Based on the foregoing examination of the role of "Maoism" in post-Mao society and an analysis of Marxism-Leninism-Mao Zedong Thought as they guide economic progress and development in the country, it can be seen that ideology continues to play a very important role in post-Mao Chinese industrial society. The codes of conduct governing the behavior of cadres and workers and the directives affecting organizational functioning in factories and industrial enterprises are replete with references to official party policies. Cadres and workers are constantly reminded of the importance of "putting politics firmly in command" and of the need to contribute one's best to the organization as dictated by the principle, "from each according to his ability." The basis for advancement in the organization and for selection as a model worker is guided by the dual criteria of "redness" (political and ideological soundness) and "expertness' (technically competent). Remuneration policies in all industrial enterprises are governed by the socialist principle of "from each according to his work; more pay for more work and less pay for less work." Slogans urging all people to "utilize every second and minute to strive towards the goals of the Four Modernizations" and to "go all out for technical innovation and technical revolution" are prominently displayed in factories, schools, universities, and other public places. Workers in all factories engage in at least one political/ideological study session per week. Nowadays, the theme or topic for ideological discussion in most factories is how the individual and the work unit could contribute to the goals of the Four Modernizations.

China's leaders emphasize that although it is important to build the material base for economic development and socialist modernization, a "spiritual civilization" is indispensable (*Beijing Review,* March 9, 1981, pp. 18-20). In fact, in early 1981 the country's leaders called on the populace to pursue the goal of "building a socialist spiritual civilization" in addition to striving toward the goal of the Four Modernizations. The phrase "building a socialist spiritual civilization" was coined by Vice-Chairman Ye Jianying in his speech delivered at the thirtieth anniversary of the founding of the PRC in 1979. The goal of building such a socialist spiritual civilization involves both a practical aspect and an ideological one. The practical aspect involves the building of a solid base for the development of education, science, literature, and art. The ideological aspect involves the engendering of social ethics, traditions, and customs in order to foster communist ideals. The latter includes "dedication to the people's cause and building the socialist motherland" and subordinating one's self-interest to the overall interests of the state and the people. China's leaders do not perceive material and spiritual goals as mutually exclusive. In fact, they emphasize that the pursuit of a socialist spiritual civilization complements and will facilitate the early attainment of the goal of material civilization—the Four Modernizations. The communist ideal of subjugating one's self-interest to that of the state will help people contribute their best efforts (even though it may involve self-sacrifice) to work toward the goals of the Four Modernizations. The key to building a spiritual civilization lies in "ideological and political work and the theoretical education of Marxism and Mao Zedong Thought in a systematic way" (*Beijing Review,* March 9, 1981, p. 20). Consequently, any attempt to portray Chinese industrial society accurately and to understand the operations and management of Chinese industrial enterprises would be incomplete without an examination of the role of ideology as it affects the various aspects of industrial society and economic progress and development.

By any reckoning, the PRC's accomplishments in its first thirty years are impressive. Although economists may disagree over the absolute rates of growth achieved by the PRC during its First Five-Year Plan (1952-1957)—conservative figures as calculated by "hostile economists," to borrow Schurmann's 1968 terminology, ranged from 5 to 6 percent, whereas more optimistic figures ranged up to a high of 11 to 12 percent (Schurmann 1968)—none dispute that China's economic growth and development since 1949 have been remarkable.

Although the country's per capita income is still very low compared with those of developed nations of the world, China has come a long way from the economic chaos that plagued it before 1949. For example, in the twenty four months prior to liberation in 1949, the consumer-price index rose over 4,000 percent. To compound this runaway inflation, there was immense corruption, poverty, political chaos, and technological stagnation (Schurmann 1968). When these conditions are compared with the progress made under the Communist party, one must ask how Mao and his party were able to accomplish such a feat—namely, to bring peace, order, and steady growth to the country—within a relatively short period of time. Althouth the answer to this question may be complex, one key to Mao's success lay in his ability to recognize that China's worst enemy—and, at the same time, its most powerful resource—is its vast population. Depending on a leader's ability to mobilize these human resources, the latter could be converted into one of the richest assets of the country. Mao recognized that the majority of the Chinese people lacked a spirit of cooperation and the ability to pool their resources to strive toward a common goal. According to Dr. Sun Yat-sen, founder of the Chinese Republic in 1911, the Chinese were like a "heap of loose sand" that totally lacked cohesion of purpose and commitment toward a common goal. Mao was convinced that if he could harness these millions of Chinese to share and work cooperatively, then half the battle would be won. What was needed was a philosophy—a universal guiding principle that could serve as a driving force to harness the masses of the people, a theme around which the masses could rally, and a unifying principle that could guide and mobilize the people. Mao found the answer in the Marxist doctrine of class struggle and the Leninist doctrine of anti-imperialism. The majority of the people living in China in the 1940s were workers and peasants who suffered tremendously under the ruling elite. To compound the plight of the workers and peasants, China was an independent nation in name only and was in fact relegated to semicolonial status. Foreign countries wielded tremendous political and economic power in China. In the midst of this immense human degradation and massive disorientation in practically all aspects of Chinese society, the masses of the people saw the burning relevance of the Marxist doctrine of class struggle and the Leninist doctrine of anti-imperialism. This new philosophy provided a focal point around which the masses could rally as a means to deliver them from their miseries.

Marxism-Leninism provided the unifying theme that guided the people to action in overthrowing the feudal and imperialist elements in the country. As China enters the last quarter of the twentieth century, over half its population has been brought up on the socialist principles of Marxism-Leninism. This new generation sees Marxism-Leninism as a way of life, a guiding principle that helps them solve problems, something that provides meaning for existence. Marxism-Leninism thus represent both a means and an end for struggle and progress. As for the older generation, brought up in the conditions of pre-1949

China, many could attest to the tremendous improvement the country has made in nearly all aspects of society under the guiding principles of Marxism-Leninism-Mao Zedong Thought. The ideological principles of Marxism-Leninism have served China well over the past thirty years. Now that China has embarked on a "New Long March," a task that requires tremendous will power, determination, cooperation among the people, and coordination among all sectors of society, there is little reason for China's present leaders to abandon a weapon that has served the country so well in the past, as evidenced by the recent emphasis on the goal of building a "socialist spiritual civilization." Of course, it should be recognized that any policy based on pure ideology and abstract principles is inadequate in the face of the many demands and challenges of the world. An economic policy formulated on purely ideological grounds, without any reference to objective conditions, is destined to failure. However, the brand of ideology espoused and practiced in China so far is not such a "pure" ideology. It has a more pragmatic and practical bent that serves as a guide to action. This practical brand of ideology, which adapts and conforms to changing objective conditions, will continue to be used by China's present leadership as a major driving force in helping the nation unite and work toward the herculean task ahead of the country—the goal of the Four Modernizations.

3 The Four Modernizations

On August 12, 1977, in his "Political Report to the Eleventh National Congress of the Communist Party of China," Hua Guofeng announced that the mission for the last quarter of the twentieth century is: "to bring into full play all positive factors inside and outside the Party at home and abroad, . . . and make China a great, powerful and modern socialist country before the end of the century" (*Eleventh National Congress* 1977, pp. 7–8). This statement officially launched the country on the Four Modernizations program. This colossal task has been aptly described by Beijing as the "New Long March", an echo of the 6,000-mile trek covered by Mao Zedong and his troops in the 1930s, which led to their eventual takeover of China in 1949. The Four Modernizations program seeks development and progress in science and technology, industry, agriculture, and military defense. Through this effort, the country hopes to raise the per capita income of its people to U.S. $1,000 by the year 2000. The per capita income for 1980 stood at U.S. $250 (*Beijing Review,* October 27, 1980, p. 16).

This goal did not come about suddenly. Rather, the implementation of the program was delayed. In 1958, two years after the nationalization of all industries in China, Mao Zedong pointed out in an article entitled "Continued Revolution" that henceforth the party's efforts should be directed toward technical revolution. In the words of Mao, "If in the decades to come, we do not modify radically a situation in which our economy and our technology are greatly retarded to those of the imperialist countries, it will be impossible for us to avoid being abused anew" (*Business Week,* May 20, 1978, p. 40). The Four Modernizations program was officially announced for the first time in Zhou Enlai's "Report on the Work of the Government of the Third National People's Congress," delivered in late 1964. This message was reiterated at the Fourth National People's Congress in 1975. The implementation of this program was delayed because of the political and economic instability that prevailed in China between 1966 and 1976.

China's leaders are aware that in order to attain the goals of the Four Modernizations, it is imperative that China enjoy relatively stable political conditions, both at home and abroad, and that the country build up its foreign-exchange reserves through foreign trade and economic assistance from abroad in order to finance this mammoth program. In order to accomplish the mission of the new era, widespread reforms have been adopted in the political and economic arenas since 1978. Some of these changes have included resuming diplomatic relations with capitalist countries, permitting foreign firms to engage in joint-venture investments in China to develop the country's industries and natural resources, and engaging in technical and cultural exchanges with other countries. Many policies and practices that were denounced as capitalist and revisionist during the Cultural Revolution have now been reinstated, including the use of material incentives, such as bonuses, to spur production in both the agricultural and industrial sectors; encouragement of the establishment and development of collectively owned enterprises and of the individual economy; emphasis on technical expertise, innovation, and development through the reinstitution of entrance exams to universities and more rigorous curricula at both universities and technical colleges; and the use of expertness or technical competence as an important criterion for recruitment and promotion to managerial and technical positions.

This chapter seeks to examine the factors that could affect the success or failure of the Four Modernizations program. These factors appear to be twofold: (1) political stability in China, and (2) China's ability to finance the Four Modernizations program and to absorb these new technologies within a relatively short period of time. Each of these factors will be discussed in greater detail.

Political Stability

In order to attain the goals of the Four Modernizations, it is imperative that the country enjoy relatively stable political conditions. At the Third Session of the Fifth National People's Congress, convened in Beijing between August 30 and September 10, 1980, the leading political figures in China once again endorsed the need for peace at home and abroad to facilitate the attainment of the goals of the Four Modernizations. Most observers of China are generally optimistic about the future political stability of the country, for three primary reasons:

1. the Chinese leaders' determination to abandon the periodic ideological up-heavals that plagued the PRC periodically since its establishment in 1949
2. the adoption of institutional and economic changes designed to raise productivity and improve organizational efficiency
3. a pragmatic reassessment of the country's limitations and weaknesses and a determination to correct these in order to facilitate the smooth development and progress of the Four Modernizations

Each of these will be discussed below.

Determination to Abandon Political and Ideological Upheavals

Since the establishment of the PRC in 1949, the country has been plagued by periodic political and ideological upheavals, such as the Great Leap Forward

Movement of the late 1950s and the Cultural Revolution, which spanned the ten years from 1966 to 1976. Between 1974 and 1976 the country was brought to the verge of economic collapse by the pursuit of erratic policies. During those years China's technical and economic progress stagnated. Intellectuals were denigrated; classes in universities, high schools, and junior schools were seriously disrupted and in some cases suspended altogether. Factories were often placed under the administration of technically incompetent people as political sound-ness ("redness") was used as the predominant criterion for appointment and promotion of people to administrative positions. Material incentives such as bonuses, which can serve as a powerful motivating device to spur workers to heighten production, were abandoned.

In a communique issued at the Third Session of the Eleventh People's Congress in December 1978, the entire Central Committee explicitly pointed out that these political upheavals were counterproductive and should be aban-doned. To guard against the future recurrence of such disruptive ideological upheavals, the government has tried to ensure the succession of pragmatists to top party leadership positions. The appointment of Zhao Ziyang as premier in September 1980, the replacement of Hu Yaobang as party chairman in June 1981, and other changes in the membership of the politburo provide encouraging evidence that China's present leaders may well succeed in this effort.

As a pragmatist and fervent proponent of raising efficiency and productivity, Premier Zhao directed the attention of the Third Session of the Fifth National People's Congress (held between August 30 and September 10, 1980) to the reform of the political and the economic systems. In Zhao's view, reforms in these two areas are inseparable because "the two supplement each other" (*Beijing Review,* September 22, 1980, p. 5). In the area of political reform, Premier Zhao addressed the need to resolve the problems of overconcentration of power in the central government and the system of lifelong tenure for cadres. The session once again endorsed the principle of collective leadership. To pre-vent the recurrence of personality cult around any individual, the contribution of any single individual should be downplayed.

China's leaders, fully cognizant of the heavy price the country paid for the ten-year hiatus between 1966 and 1976, are determined to make up for lost time. The anarchistic, iconoclastic mood of the Cultural Revolution has now been replaced by a more positive, pragmatic, and inquisitive atmosphere among the majority of people in their examination and implementation of ways to modernize as rapidly as possible. In the weekly political study sessions in each of the nation's factories, the current theme is how the work group or individual can contribute to the goals of the Four Modernizations.

Will China's future leadership continue to endorse the goals of the Four Modernizations? Three issues should be examined:

1. Will the Four Modernizations lead toward capitalism and away from social-ism? This issue is of concern to staunch supporters of Marxism–Leninism–Mao Zedong Thought.

2. Is the policy of importing foreign technology synonymous with wholesale Westernization and hence contradictory to the Chinese emphasis on self-reliance?
3. Will future leadership continue to pursue the goals of the Four Modernizations?

On the question of whether modernizations will lead to capitalism, Deng Xiaoping was confident that this kind of problem will not occur in the foreseeable future because for now the primary concern is to free the Chinese people from poverty. "A part of our population may get a little better-off than the rest of the population, but our goal is to let the whole people become better off" (*Beijing Review*, January 14, 1980, pp. 20–21). The goal of modernization, at least, at this point, is not to engage in a zero-sum game wherein some will become better off at the expense of others. Rather, the goal is to improve the standard of living of the people as a whole. Implicit in this policy is the assumption that a major prerequisite for transition to full communism is the socialist modernization of the country. Otherwise how can socialism claim superiority over capitalism?

This brings us to the second issue—the importation of foreign technology. In carrying out socialist modernization with limited resources, China sees the need to unite with intellectuals, industrialists and businessmen, and all other elements that can be united, including foreign elements, as long as they serve China, in order to facilitate early attainment of the goal of socialist modernization.

In striving to achieve the goals of the Four Modernizations, China's leaders do not want to repeat the mistakes made by their nineteenth-century predecessors, that of overreliance and dependence on foreign sources for the country's economic growth and development. Though adhering to the principle of self-reliance, China's leaders constantly point out that self-reliance is not synonymous with economic isolationism and self-seclusion. In the words of Deng Xiaoping, "by self-reliance we mean that a country should rely on the strength and wisdom of its own people" (Cheng 1974, p. 6). Self-reliance does not imply self-seclusion or rejection of foreign aid since no country could be self-sufficient in all respects. Countries need to engage in economic and technical exchanges to complement each other's economies. The government sees importation of foreign technology and equipment as necessary for building the foundations of a strong modern nation as soon as possible; this alone, they believe, can guarantee the country's long-term independence and survival. Building a strong, modern nation is also seen as a prerequisite for the transition to full communism. Thus the government sees no inconsistency in its present policy of engaging in technical and cultural exchanges and trade relations with foreign countries (including capitalist economies), on the one hand, and upholding the principles of self-reliance and striving for eventual communism in the future, on the other.

In an interview with *Time* magazine (February 5, 1979, p. 35), Deng addressed the issue of whether future leadership will continue to pursue the goals of the Four Modernizations. He indicated that the correct way to approach this issue is to analyze whether or not the policies designed to implement the goals of the Four Modernizations will be fruitful. It is highly unlikely that future leadership will discontinue any policies that are able to improve the standards of living of the people. In this answer, Deng struck at the core of the issue. If the Four Modernizations program can in fact bring about an increase in the overall standard of living of the people and make China a strong, powerful nation, then it is highly unlikely that the general populace would tolerate any leader or any policies that would reverse or retard this improvement. After all, once people have a taste of better material conditions, they will probably be unwilling to give up these improvements. As *Fortune* magazine described it, Deng implied that if China could continue to adhere to the goals of the Four Modernizations throughout the 1980s, the program would become so deeply entrenched that it would be difficult for anyone to try to uproot it (*Fortune,* October 23, 1978, p. 104).

Institutional Changes and Economic Reforms

In September 1980 Zhao Ziyang took over as premier of China. From 1975 on, Zaho Ziyang served as first secretary of the Sichuan provincial party committee. As will become evident in subsequent chapters, Sichuan is noted for its pioneering efforts in introducing experimental reforms in the management and operation of enterprises in order to improve efficiency and raise productivity. In October 1978 a fourteen-point experimental program was introduced on a trial basis in six enterprises in Sichuan Province. Shortly afterward, these experimental reforms spread to over a hundred enterprises throughout the province. The fourteen-point experimental program called for granting greater autonomy to individual enterprises in their operations and management. It also allowed enterprises to retain 15 to 25 percent of their profits earned in excess of the target set forth in the state plan. In addition, workers were given fairly hefty bonuses as a reward for their contribution to the enterprise's fulfillment of certain prespecified standards. A study conducted six months after the implementation of these experimental reforms showed that the output value in a hundred experimental units had increased at a rate of 36.7 percent above the average attained throughout the province. These reforms, commonly referred to as the Sichuan experiments, attracted the attention of enterprise management and officials at various levels of the government throughout the country. With Zhao Ziyang's ascendancy to the premiership, it is anticipated that these reforms will be introduced, where appropriate, in more enterprises in a broader spectrum of industries throughout China.

To emphasize the new mission of raising productivity and improving efficiency, in 1980 the government authorized the State Planning and State Economic Commissions to undertake a series of studies designed to reform the structure of economic management in the country. A number of eminent

Chinese economists who had advocated fairly liberal policies in the early 1960s, but had been ostracized during the Cultural Revolution, have been assigned responsible positions in the government. They are now studying proposals for changes in China's economic system based on other countries' experiences (particularly those of Yugoslavia), and in light of China's objective conditions. Some of the changes that have been implemented since 1978 include the granting of greater autonomy to the individual enterprise with respect to certain aspects of its operations; the use of economic means, such as taxes, rather than administrative means; limited use of the market mechanism in conjunction with and subordinate to state planning; and tolerance of competition among enterprises on a limited scale.

Besides implementing changes in the domestic economy, China has also introduced reforms in the operation and management of foreign trade. After all, foreign trade is considered an important aspect of the Four Modernizations. Changes in these area include the promulgation in July 1979 of the Law of the People's Republic of China on Joint Ventures using Chinese and Foreign Investment. Regulations governing labor-management relations in joint-venture concerns and corporate and individual income taxes were promulgated in 1980. Other institutional changes designed to facilitate the conduct of foreign trade and investment within China include the establishment of special economic zones in the provinces of Guangdong and Fujian; the establishment of commissions (such as the Foreign Investment Commission and the Import-Export Commission) and corporations (such as the China International Trust and Investment Corporation) to legislate and induce foreign investment; and the decentralization of foreign-trade activities. These changes are in line with other economic reforms affecting the domestic sector.

Institutional changes and economic reforms are designed to raise productivity, which would result in an increase in living standards for the people. This ties in with Deng's assertion, discussed previously, that if the policies implemented under the Four Modernizations program could bring about a general increase in the living standard of the populace, then most people would tend to oppose policies such as those espoused by the Gang of Four. This would prevent the recurrence of disruptive ideological upheavals in the country.

Pragmatic Reassessment of the Country's Limitations

In 1978 the PRC tried to import too much foreign technology and equipment too soon—before China had the personnel, infrastructure, and ancillary equipment needed to utilize fully the imported equipment and technology. This resulted in waste as much of the imported equipment was left idle, in wait for personnel to be trained and for the infrastructure and ancillary equipment to be built. This led to the government's realization of the need to reorder economic priorities, a reassessment that was contained in the Three-Year Plan (1979–1981, now extended to 1982) for readjustment, restructuring, consolidation, and improvement of China's economy. This period of reassessment could possibly extend to 1983. In fact, one of the primary objectives of the Sixth Five-Year Plan (1981–1985) is to seek readjustment of the national economy.

Readjustment involves bringing about relatively good coordination in the development of agriculture, light industry, and heavy industry, and maintaining an appropriate ratio between consumption and accumulation. Restructuring involves overall reform of the structure of economic management to make it more efficient. Consolidation involves specialization of labor and coordination of economic activities across different enterprises to achieve greater economies of scale in production. Improvement involves upgrading existing levels of education, production, technology, and management, as well as developing foreign trade (Tung 1980).

The policy of reajdustment, though slowing down the rate of growth originally anticipated in 1977, is a more realistic way of developing the country's economy. Chinese officials consider the present retrenchment only temporary in nature. Although it will cause a temporary slowdown in the rate of economic development, it is designed to build a more solid base for the country's subsequent growth. The reason this factor represents a basis for optimism is that the Chinese have demonstrated that they will not overextend themselves beyond their capabilities. In the words of the former U.S. ambassador to China, Leonard Woodcock, this is "a much more realistic, more sensible, and much more helpful path to the future than what was being looked at in the 'Fantasy Land' of 1978" (*Pacific Basin Quarterly,* December 1979, p. 3). Had China harbored unrealistic goals, its efforts to modernize might collapse.

Potential Problems

Despite the fact that most observers of China are fairly optimistic about the future political stability of the country, there are several potential problems. The two major ones are briefly identified as follows.

Popular Dissatisfaction. In order to attain the goals of the Four Modernizations, China has adopted a series of reforms and changes designed to upgrade scientific and technical skills. Reforms in this area include using entrance examinations to screen applicants (at present, because of limited facilities, only 4 percent of the applicants actually gain admission to universities); sending students abroad for advanced training; adopting titles for engineers and technicians; and awarding academic degrees at universities, effective January 1981. Whether the Chinese admit it or not, changes of this nature will result in the development of an elite class. There are already signs of unrest among those who feel disenfranchised under the new system. In September 1979, for example, 400 young people staged a sit-in to protest educational discrimination in China (*China Business Review,* November–December 1979, p. 31). The attitudes and outlook of this emerging elite will almost invariably differ from those of people who are not fortunate enough to be the beneficiaries of such programs. *Fortune* magazine (October 23, 1978, p. 100) discusses the potential conflicts that may erupt between those from the emerging elite and those who grew up during the Cultural Revolution. The latter "matured during years of xenophobia, isolation and anti-intellectualism. Value conflicts separating these generations will thus be severe—one might even say explosive."

This potential problem poses a far greater threat to political stability than does the issue of leadership succession. To alleviate these potential tensions and problems, the government has adopted the following measures:

1.   to advance the educational and technical skills of those who are not fortunate enough to receive a formal university education through other types of programs, such as the tube university (which is broadcasted on television), spare-time colleges, and so on
2.   to imbue cadres with the need to be humble and go among the masses (the decision to abolish the system of lifelong tenure of cadres is a step in this direction)
3.   to assure the people that even though one segment of the population may become better off sooner than the rest, the ultimate goal is the improvement of all
4.   to strive to build a socialist spiritual civilization, as discussed in the previous chapter

Whether or not these measures are sufficient to allay potential tensions and problems remains to be seen.

Problems in Implementing Changes. The former U.S. ambassador to China, Leonard Woodcock, views this as a major hurdle that the Chinese must surmount in order to attain the goals of the Four Modernizations. Despite recent institutional changes, a massive bureaucracy still remains. The middle-level bureaucracy appears to be "hesitant to do anything until they are absolutely sure that the wind that is now blowing is going to continue to be the wind that will blow in that direction for the predictable future" (*Pacific Basin Quarterly,* December 1979, p. 5). Their wariness is justifiable in that some had had bad experiences in the past. This view appears to be shared by some of the Chinese themselves. In an interview with the Beijing bureau chief of *Time* magazine, Richard Bernstein, a young Chinese factory technician noted that although the Four Modernizations "is fine in theory," there are problems in implementation. In the young technician's opinion, many Chinese factories are still under the administration of "retired soldiers" who may not possess the skills essential to run an enterprise. Besides, many would like to maintain the status quo and are averse to change. Bernstein observed that although this young technician's perspective is more pessimistic than that of most Chinese, it is indicative of the "uneasiness" many Chinese experience in these rapidly changing times (*Time*, April 28, 1980, p. 33). The root of the problem appears to be that massive and often radical changes affecting practically all aspects of society are implemented so rapidly that many people find it difficult to keep themselves abreast of the latest changes, much less digest the implications of such changes.

China's Ability to Finance

With respect to the importation of high-technology equipment to aid in the modernization of China's industries, two related questions arise: (1) Will China be able to pay for these projects? (2) Will the country be able to absorb these advanced technologies?

The ability to finance these projects does not appear to be a serious problem for several reasons. First, it is estimated that the Bank of China has lines of credit totaling $26.2 billion (*China Business Review*, January–February 1980). In 1979 the Bank of China entered into a series of short-, medium-, and long-term loan agreements with governmental and nongovernmental financial institutions in the United States, Japan, France, Sweden, Canada, and Italy. In addition, many countries have extended Export-Import (Exim) Bank financing to China. In 1980 China gained admission to international financing institutions, such as the World Bank and the International Monetary Fund (IMF). (These various sources of international financing will be examined in greater detail in chapter 11.) Given their tradition of financial prudence, the Chinese are unwilling to exhaust this full line of credit and are proceeding cautiously. The government's policy on the use of foreign funds is guided by the following principles:

1. China will accept foreign credit as long as it does not impinge on the country's national sovereignty. As Vice-Premier Gu Mu stated, "We are ready to accept loans from all friendly countries provided they will not affect our sovereign rights and the terms are appropriate" (*Beijing Review*, October 12, 1979, p. 3). China's leaders do not want to repeat the mistake made by their predecessors in the second half of the nineteenth century and the first half of the twentieth, when overreliance on foreign credit and assistance resulted in a virtual loss of China's sovereignty.

2. The ability to repay is always considered. Mr. Liu Lixin, a vice-president of the head office of the People's Construction Bank of China, declared that "experience over the years proves that [the use of foreign funds] should be commensurate with our ability to repay foreign loans and to provide ancillary equipment" (*Beijing Review*, August 25, 1980, pp. 23–25).

Ability to repay foreign loans refers to the capacity to repay both principal and interest. As a rule of thumb, the government stipulates that the amount of money repaid as principal and interest per annum should not exceed 20 percent —or at most 25 percent—of the total amount of foreign-exchange earnings for the same year. Given such considerations, according to Mr. Liu, projects requiring the use of foreign funds must meet the following three conditions:

1. The products manufactured by the investments using foreign funds must be competitive on the international market.
2. Where the products manufactured through such investments could not be exported, they must be substitutes for similar products that are normally imported, thus conserving the use of foreign exchange.
3. The rate of return on investment on the project must be higher than the rate of interest on the money borrowed.

Ability to provide ancillary equipment refers to the country's ability to provide fuel, communications, and other services needed to put the project into operation. On the basis of past experience, it is estimated that for every U.S. dollar of imported equipment, the country needs to spend an extra 4 yuan (or U.S. $2.58) on ancillary equipment before the imported equipment can be put into operation. Consequently, if China does not have the capability to provide the ancillary equipment, foreign exchange should not be expended on the purchase of such imports in the first place, since it will only result in waste (*Beijing Review,* August 25, 1980). This stipulation is intended to prevent a repetition of the mistake made in 1978, when China imported too much too soon and found it lacked the personnel to handle all these sophisticated imports.

3. Equipment that could be produced domestically must not be imported. This will conserve the use of foreign exchange to pay for such imports.

4. Only equipment appropriate for the present stage of the country's economic development should be imported. China maintains that it does not need to import the most advanced technology and equipment in all instances. Rather, the country should adopt a more practical technology suitable to China's objective conditions, which include scarce capital resources and a huge labor force. Use of this more practical technology would conserve capital investment and use more labor in the production process. In the words of Mr. Liu, "We must avoid seeking a high level of automation blindly and indiscriminately" (*Beijing Review,* August 25, 1980, p. 25). This policy is more realistic and more suitable to China's objective conditions. China has abundant manpower, but the educational and technical skills of most workers are not high. Consequently, a high level of automation, appropriate for the needs of more advanced nations, may be inappropriate for China's present conditions. The development of labor-intensive industries and the purchase of equipment requiring less capital investment are more in line with the country's objective conditions. As former U.S.

Ambassador Woodcock noted, the Chinese now do not merely refer to the Four Modernizations, but they speak of "Four Modernizations in the Chinese way" (*Pacific Basin Quarterly,* December 1979). By Chinese-style modernization, the country means that the policies to be implemented to realize modernization must take into consideration China's objective conditions: a weak industrial base and a huge population, 80 percent of whose members still depend on agriculture as their principal means of livelihood. Given these differences, China's path to modernization could not resemble that of the Western nations. Rather, its modernization program must take the following into consideration: (1) Provide jobs for the people. Given the country's weak industrial base, shortage of foreign exchange, and abundant labor force, China should seek to develop labor-intensive industries. (2) In order to develop the country's industrial base and conserve foreign exchange, the Chinese should learn science and technology from abroad, rather than import complete plants and equipments. In short, Chinese-style modernization means "build(ing) an independent national economic system by relying mainly on accumulation of funds at home, supplemented by foreign aid. We cannot blindly follow other countries' experiences and patterns, but should assimilate what is useful so as to explore a way of modernization suited to our country" (*Beijing Review,* April 6, 1981, p. 3).

5. A reordering of priorities is needed in the development of the national economy. Projects that "increase China's export capacity, produce fast returns, and earn more foreign exchange" (Liu and Wang 1980, p. 9) should be given priority. Light and textile industries fit these criteria and hence are given priority in the allocation of funds. Ever since the establishment of the PRC in 1949, investment in light industry has been negligible compared with that in the heavy-industrial sector. Despite this disproportion in the allocation of capital resources, the light-industrial sector has contributed significantly to the country's state revenue and foreign-exchange earnings. For instance, in 1977 the value of light-industrial outputs constituted 20.1 percent of the state's revenue and accounted for 21.2 percent of China's exports. Textile products alone accounted for over 20 percent of the total value of the country's exports (Chen 1979, pp. 5, 10). China is making great efforts to increase its exports and thereby to generate foreign exchange to finance these projects. The export items the country is counting on in the short run are textile and light-industrial products. To promote the development of the textile industry, the latter will receive first priority in terms of allocation of energy resources and other raw-material supplies. In addition, experimental reforms designed to stimulate productivity have been introduced in textile mills throughout the country. Besides the practice of awarding bonuses to reflect the quantity and quality of production by the respective workers and work units, these factories are granted certain autonomy in the pricing of items in accordance with quality. In addition, these factories are allowed to "create and promote their brand names and advertise" (Chen 1979, p. 5).

Nonexport items that have potential for generating hard-currency earnings include those in the service industry, such as hotels for the tourism industry and insurance premiums pertaining to China trade. Other sources of hard-currency earnings include return on investments in Hong Kong, remittances by overseas Chinese, and income from shipping operations. Chinese investments in Hong Kong have increased sharply over the past several years. Also within the past few years, China's merchant marine has expanded more rapidly than have those of other countries. As of June 1979, approximately 70 percent of China's foreign trade was handled by its own merchant marine. This percentage is higher than that for any merchant fleet in the world. In 1978 income from shipping operations increased by 33.5 percent. It is projected that income from shipping operations will increase commensurately with the expansion of China's merchant-marint fleet. The latter is designated as one of the priority sectors in the current Three-Year Plan (Chen 1979).

In the long run China is looking to the export of energy resources, such as oil and coal, as a major earner of foreign exchange. Energy has been designated as a top-priority sector in terms of allocation of resources in the Three-Year Plan for Readjustment not only because of its foreign-exchange-earnings potential, but also because of its importance in fueling economic growth. The government estimates that approximately 20–30 percent of the country's industrial production suffered from the serious shortages of energy supplies resulting from the irrational economic policies pursued between 1966 and 1976. According to a spokesman for the Ministry of Power Industry, in the country's current retrenchment program, none of the contracts between China and foreign nations in the energy sector have been canceled or suspended. In fact, many new contracts are currently under negotiation (*Beijing Review,* April 6, 1981).

Many of the reported figures on the size of business contracts that China has concluded with foreign firms or agencies are inflated. Additionally, mere letters of intent have been publicized as contracts. The former U.S. ambassador to China, Leonard Woodcock, explained that these two factors account for some of the ridiculously high dollar figures reported in the media of contracts China has entered into with foreign firms: "They sum up to a total of over $600 billion which is, of course, absurd. Say, for example, a project will cost $1.7 billion by completion. But what is agreed on is only the first phase, which may be $15 million or $5 million or whatever" (*New China,* Winter 1979, p. 19).

Besides paying for imports in hard currency, China has entered into other forms of economic arrangements with foreign firms in order to conserve foreign exchange. These alternative forms of economic arrangements include compensatory trade, cooperative production, and processing. Such arrangements are designed to reduce China's need to borrow from abroad or expand its own foreign-currency reserve (CIA, December 1978; *Beijing Review,* December 21, 1979; *China Business Review,* November–December 1979). These alternatives will be examined in greater detail in chapter 11.

In light of the foregoing factors, the question of China's ability to finance appears not to pose much of a problem. One dark cloud over the horizon in this respect appears to stem from the deteriorating international economic situation and capital markets in the 1980s, largely as a result of the energy crisis and inflation. The deteriorating international economic situation has led to balance-of-trade deficits for a number of advanced nations, thus forcing them to slow down or curtail their imports. This trend is accompanied by a worsening of capital markets. Besides high interest rates, long-term capital financing will become more scarce and will be made available only to those with excellent credit ratings (Tomlinson 1980, pp. 61–66). Fortunately, China enjoys an excellent credit rating and has an impeccable record of credit-worthiness. In any case, this bleak financial picture will probably lead to a depressed marked for China's nonenergy products, as well as a much closer scrutiny by international bankers of China's intermediate balance-of-payments situation.

China's ability to absorb advanced technologies appears to pose a more serious problem because education levels in China are still low. Despite massive improvements since 1949, it is estimated that in 1979 only 70 to 80 percent of the country's workers had attained a junior- or middle-school education; two-thirds of the workers had attained only the rank of second- or third-grade workers (in China, workers are divided into eight grades according to their skill levels, with the eighth grade being the highest); and only 3 percent of the labor force is currently employed as technicians or engineers (*Beijing Review,* February 18, 1980). The statistics for rural areas are even more dismal. China is undertaking massive efforts to develop the educational and technical skills of its people as rapidly as possible.

Besides these problems of educational levels and technical skills, China has a weak infrastructure. The country has recognized the infrastructure as "the vanguard industries in the national economy" (*Beijing Review,* August 25, 1980, p. 24). Consequently, in the coming years China will assign priority to the development of its infrastructure, including port development, construction of railways, and the building of the merchant-marine fleet to support the growth of the economy and to meet the demands of expanded foreign trade.

The foregoing analyses of the internal political situation in China and China's ability to finance and absorb foreign technology suggest that the Chinese are cognizant of the factors that might hinder the country's progress toward the goals of the Four Modernizations. More encouragingly, China is taking measures to counteract these potential threats. This in itself is a positive feature. Whether China's economy will actually match those of the world's advanced nations by the year 2000 is open to question. Despite the country's deficits for two consecutive years, 1979 and 1980, advances have been made in the light-industrial and agricultural sectors. To many, the important question is not whether China is actually able to attain the goals of the Four Modernizations by the year 2000, but whether the country will remain committed to these goals. In the eyes of many people, commitment to the goals of the Four Modernizations would constitute a significant achievement for a country that has stagnated both economically and technologically for almost 150 years prior to 1949. This in itself would mark a significant turning point in China's history, which will very likely have a tremendous impact on the future course of world events. As Napoleon Bonaparte once remarked: "China? There lies a sleeping giant. Let him sleep, for when he wakes he will move the world." China, the once sleeping giant, has been awakened from its slumber and is now charging at full strength toward the goals of the Four Modernizations.

4

China's Economic Growth and Development since 1949

This chapter seeks to trace the history of the industrial sector in China from 1949 to the first quarter of 1981, and to assess the positive and negative experiences in China's industrial development over the past three decades. Although the focus both of this chapter and of the book as a whole is on Chinese industrial society, no discussion of China's economic development would be complete without a brief examination of the agricultural sector. After all, more than 80 percent of China's people still depend on agriculture as their principal means of livelihood. Therefore, this chapter will also briefly examine development in the agricultural sector.

The Rehabilitation Years, 1949–1952

The year 1949 marked the end of the civil war in China and the establishment of the People's Republic of China. The same year witnessed the beginning of socialist reconstruction of the country—a colossal task that involved rebuilding the country from the ruins of economic and technological stagnation, massive social disorientation, and political chaos brought about by several decades of imperialist exploitation, external wars, internal strife, and the ineffective economic policies of the Kuomintang government. For example, in the twenty-four months prior to October 1949, the consumer-price index rose approximately 4,000 percent (Schurmann 1968).

The government of the PRC acted swiftly to embark on a series of national economic policies designed to set the country on its feet again. These economic policies were embodied in what is commonly referred to as the Rehabilitation Years (1949–1952) and the First Five-Year Plan (1953–1957).

Policies adopted during the Rehabilitation Years brought encouraging results. Within eighteen months of the establishment of the PRC, inflation was curbed. Prices on essential commodities such as grain, salt, cooking oil, fuel, and cloth were controlled. In 1949 the government took over the Bank of China, and in 1953 the Political Council (the forerunner of the present-day State Council) published the new banking regulations. A new currency was established, which today remains as one of the most stable currencies in the world. The year 1950 saw the passage of the Agrarian Reform Law. The land that was nationalized was redistributed among the poor and middle peasants. According to Chinese sources, during the three years of economic rehabilitation the industrial sector achieved

49

an annual growth rate of 30 percent, and that for the agricultural sector exceeded 10 percent per annum (*Beijing Review,* June 29, 1979, p. 21).

First Five-Year Plan, 1953–1957

The First Five-Year Plan marked the movement toward collectivization and nationalization of urban and rural means of production. Shortly after 1949 there were a number of joint state-private enterprises. The number of joint state-private enterprises increased to 1,700 by 1954. By 1956 the nationalization of all private enterprises in the country was almost completed. To compensate the national capitalists (that is, the industrialists and entrepreneurs who engaged in joint state-private enterprises with the government) for surrendering their interests in the joint state-private enterprises, the government agreed to pay them a 5-percent annual interest on their shares in the joint enterprises for a period of ten years. Concurrent with the policy of nationalization of industry, the government embarked on the road of collectivization in other parts of the industrial and agricultural sectors. Many small shops and individual operators were organized into cooperatives. Table 4–1 presents the extent to which nationalization and collectivization had been accomplished in the industrial and agricultural sectors and in commerce.

To ensure stable growth and development of the economy, the government realized that it was first necessary to develop a strong industrial base in the country. After all, industries constitute an important part of any modern economy, Consequently, during this period some 10,000 industrial enterprises and

Table 4–1
Extent of Socialist Transformation of Industry, Commerce, Handicrafts, and Agriculture, by 1956

Sector	Extent of Transformation	Percentage
Industry	Output value of state-owned industry	67.5
	Output value of state-private industry	32.5
Wholesale trade	Sales of state-owned and state-private enterprises	97.2
Retail trade	Sales of state-owned enterprises	68.3
	Sales of state-private enterprises and cooperatives	27.5
Handicrafts	People having joined cooperatives	91.7
	Output value of handicraft cooperatives	92.9
Agriculture	Peasant households having joined elementary and advanced cooperatives	96.3
	Peasant households having joined advanced cooperatives	87.8

Source: *Beijing Review,* December 26, 1977, p. 13.

mining operations were established, including 156 key projects (*Beijing Review*, July 21, 1980, p. 18).

The policies and reforms implemented during the Rehabilitation Years and the First Five-Year Plan yielded promising results. Within eight years China, for the first time in decades, was set on the path of growth again. Economists may disagree over the absolute rate of growth the PRC achieved during its First Five-Year Plan. Estimates ranged from a low of 5–6 percent to a high of 11–12 percent (Schurmann 1968). According to the Chinese Statistical Bureau, the annual growth rate achieved during the First Five-Year Plan averaged 18 percent and 4.5 percent for the industrial and agricultural sectors, respectively.

Second Five-Year Plan, 1958–1962

This period is commonly referred to as the Great Leap Forward. Between 1958 and 1962 all sectors of the economy were exhorted to "go all out, aim high, achieve greater, faster, better and more economical results in building socialism." During the Second Five-Year Plan, the development of heavy industries was emphasized at the expense of the light-industrial and agricultural sectors. In 1959 alone, 500 new factories were commissioned (Herdan 1976). The grand design collapsed. China had attempted to accomplish too much too soon. In 1959 agricultural production declined drastically. This led to the government's call for readjustment, as embodied in the Three-Year Readjustment Period (1963–1965). Readjustment brought forth encouraging results. In 1965 and 1966 the Chinese economy had recovered sufficiently to register fairly rapid growth (*Beijing Review*, June 29, 1979, p. 22). In 1966 the country embarked on the Cultural Revolution, which spanned the next decade and brought the country to the brink of economic collapse by 1974. The Cultural Revolution years coincided with the country's Third Five-Year Plan (1966–1970) and Fourth Five-Year Plan (1971–1975).

China's leaders now acknowledge that only the First Five-Year Plan succeeded, whereas the next three Five-Year Plans either collapsed or were rendered inoperable by unstable political conditions. As Mao Zedong declared in 1955: "we need three five-year plans basically to accomplish socialist industrialization and socialist transformation. We must strive to secure this length of time for peaceful construction" (*Selected Works*, vol. 5, 1977, p. 214). Unfortunately, the necessary fifteen years of peace and tranquillity, unhampered by political and ideological upheaval and turmoil, never materialized.

Three-Year Plan for Readjustment, 1979–1981

In 1978 the PRC tried to accomplish too much too soon. In that year China overextended itself by embarking on a number of large-scale construction projects and importing a lot of foreign technology and equipment, although the country had barely recovered from the economic chaos brought about by the Cultural Revolution. These projects proved too much for China to handle, both financially and technically. For instance, much advanced technology and equipment was imported before China had the personnel, infrastructure, or ancillary equipment needed to utilize the imported equipment fully. This resulted in waste, as much of the imported equipment lay idle, waiting for personnel to be trained and for the infrastructure and ancillary equipment to be built. This led to the government's realization of the need to reorder economic priorities. In Premier Zhao Ziyang's view, it would be unrealistic to assume that China's modernization program could be accomplished rapidly. Rather, the country should strive for moderate but continuing and steady growth (*Beijing Review*, February 9, 1981, p. 14). This reassessment was contained in the Three-Year Plan (1979–1981, now extended to 1982) for readjustment, restructuring, consolidation, and improvement of the country's economy. This period of reassessment could possibly extend to 1983. Restructuring involves bringing about relatively good coordination in the development of agriculture, light industry, and heavy industry, and maintaining an appropriate ratio between consumption and accumulation. Restructuring involves overall reform of the structure of economic management to increase efficiency. Consolidation involves specialization of labor and coordination of economic activities across different enterprises to achieve greater economies of scale in production. Improvement involves upgrading existing levels of education, production, technology, and management, as well as developing foreign trade (Tung 1980).

Despite the encouraging results achieved in the light-industrial and agricultural sectors in the first two years of readjustment (1979 and 1980), certain problems remained. These are primarily twofold: (1) There have been state deficits for two consecutive years. In 1979 the state deficit amounted to 17,060 million yuan (*Beijing Review*, September 8, 1980, p. 5). In 1980 the deficit was 12,100 million yuan instead of the projected 8,000 million yuan. (2) Prices of commodities have risen. On November 1, 1979, the retail prices of pork, beef, mutton, poultry, and eggs increased some 30 percent (*China Reconstructs*, January 1980). In 1980 the retail prices of foodstuffs increased another 13.8 percent over 1979, and the average retail-price index rose 6 percent. To cover expenditures, the central bank issued new currency amounting to 7,600 million yuan instead of the budgeted 3,000 million yuan (*Beijing Review*, March 16, 1981). Deficits and inflationary trends led to the government's call for continued readjustment in 1981. The government states that the focus in 1981 and the Sixth Five-Year Plan (1981–1985) will be on readjustment of the national economy.

Continued readjustment will necessitate a general slowing down in the implementation of reforms designed to restructure the management of the economy and industrial enterprises (*Beijing Review*, March 9, 1981, p. 30). According to Xue Muqiao, a noted Chinese economist, this does not mean an abandonment of the reforms that have been introduced in the economic system and management of enterprises since 1978: "That the pace of reforms will be stepped down does not signify a change in orientation, or backtracking. Moreover, some current reforms do not interfere with readjustment but help it" (*China Reconstructs,* April 1981, p. 10). Xue noted that some of the reforms designed to restructure the system of economic management will continue to be pursued during the period of readjustment. These reforms include the granting of greater autonomy to industrial enterprises, and the financing of construction projects through bank loans rather than state allocations. Xue argued that the present emphasis on readjustment is designed to rectify the problems inherent in the implementation of some of the reforms, such as indiscriminate distribution of bonuses and unauthorized price raising, and to build a more solid base for future economic development. In the words of U.S. economist Richard J. Seltzer: "pragmatic readjustment policy entails a period of slower but more balanced and selective development. Its goal is to lay the basis for more rapid growth later in the 1980s" (*China Reconstructs,* April 1981, p. 10). The Chinese refer to this as the policy of "one step back, two steps forward" (*Beijing Review,* July 21, 1980, p. 15). Through continued readjustment the state hopes to (1) eliminate state deficits in 1982 by balancing state expenditures with revenues; (2) discontinue the policy of indiscriminately issuing paper currency to cover financial expenditures; and (3) check inflationary trends through stabilization of commodity prices, especially those of essential items, which account for approximately 70 percent of consumer spending. The government seeks to accomplish these goals through the implementation of the following policies:

1. Reduce expenditures through cutbacks on capital construction projects. In 1981 the government suspended or canceled work on twenty-five capital construction projects, including the second phase of the Baoshan Iron and Steel complex near Shanghai, once designated as the cornerstone of the Four Modernizations.
2. Impose tighter controls on the issuance of bank loans.
3. Improve people's livelihood "within the limits of present capability."
4. Assign heavier emphasis to the development of agriculture, light industries, the energy sector, and the country's infrastructure such as transportation and communication networks.

Whether these measures are sufficient to eliminate state deficits and reduce inflationary trends remain to be seen.

Development in the Industrial Sector

In 1949 there were only 120,000 industrial enterprises throughout China. These were mainly engaged in light industries, were usually small in size, and were concentrated in the coastal regions. Heavy industry was negligible. In a thirty-year period, the number of industrial enterprises increased more than threefold. In 1980 there were approximately 400,000 state-owned enterprises in the country, with fixed assets of 320 billion yuan. (*Note:* the Chinese billion, like the British billion, is equal to a million million, *not* a thousand million as is the case with the U.S. billion.) This is approximately twenty-five times the value of fixed industrial assets in pre-1949 China (*Beijing Review,* October 5, 1979, p. 10).

Chinese industrial enterprises are of two main types: state-owned enterprises and collectively owned enterprises. *State-owned enterprises* represent "public ownership by the whole people . . . under which the state owns the means of production on behalf of all the working people" (*Beijing Review,* February 11, 1980, p. 14). State-owned enterprises constitute the backbone of the country's economy. *Collectively owned enterprises* represent "public ownership under which the means of production are owned collectively by the working people in the enterprises and communes." Under this form of ownership, "the means of production and products belong to the laborers of the collectives concerned." Collectively owned enterprises supplement China's economy. In 1978 the fixed assets of state-owned enterprises made up 91.8 percent of the total fixed industrial assets in the country. In the same year, a full 80.7 percent of the country's total industrial-output value came from state-owned enterprises. In 1978, 71.5 percent of the nation's industrial workers and staff workers (30.41 million people) were employed in state-owned enterprises; 12.15 million worked in collectively owned enterprises (*Beijing Review,* February 11, 1980, pp. 13–16). Besides these two forms of ownership, the 1978 Constitution of the PRC authorized the development of the individual economy, provided there is no exploitation of others and the activities engaged in are legal in nature. According to the Chinese Statistical Bureau, by 1980 there were 810,000 people licensed to transact business as individual operators throughout the country, primarily in the retail trade and service sectors (*U.S. News & World Report,* March 23, 1981, p. 58; *Beijing Review,* May 25, 1981, pp. 3–4).

In the past, state-owned enterprises were considered superior and hence were emphasized. During periods of political and ideological upheavals, the collectively owned enterprises and the individual economy were dubbed "tails of capitalism" and were discouraged or outlawed. The Chinese government now states that the superiority of an ownership system is not judged nor measured by the extent of public ownership, but in terms of economic results. The government contends that these three types of economy should be allowed to coexist because each plays a different role in the national economy and each supplements the others. For the development of large, modern industries, the establishment of state-owned enterprises may be most appropriate. In the countryside, however, collective ownership may be more appropriate. Also, collectively owned enterprises can be established with minimal capital investment and can provide an important source of employment for the huge Chinese population. In addition, because of their smaller size, such enterprises are usually more flexible. Consequently, they may be more adept at revamping their complete product lines within a relatively short period of time to meet changing market needs. Individual enterprises, on the other hand, "make good use of the labor power within families," and play an important role in the retail trade and service sectors, areas that were previously neglected in the national economy (*Beijing Review,* December 8, 1980, p. 14). All three forms of ownership are under the management of the Industrial Administration Bureaus, which belong to the Ministry of Commerce.

The Development of Heavy Industry

In establishing the base for China's heavy-industrial sector, iron and steel were designated as key since they provide the raw materials for the development of other industries. Emphasis on the development of the iron and steel industries in the first twenty-nine years of the PRC's history accounts for the rapid growth of these industries. The output of steel expanded 218-fold, from 158,000 tons in 1949 to 34,480,000 tons in 1979. The output of pig iron increased 145-fold, from 252,000 tons in 1949 to 36,730,000 tons in 1979. Besides the construction of a number of large integrated iron and steel works in the major industrial cities of Beijing, Shanghai, Anshan, Wuhan, and Paotow, the government also improved and expanded existing facilities in these cities. In addition, many small- and medium-sized iron and steel factories were established throughout China to facilitate the development of industries in the hinterland. In 1978 work began on the construction of the Baoshan Iron and Steel complex in Shanghai. The project was expected to cost the country U.S. $5 billion at completion. This is the largest project to utilize imported technology and machinery (primarily from Japan) since the establishment of the PRC in 1949.

Under the current Three-Year Plan for Readjustment (1979–1981), heavier emphasis is placed on the development of light industries and agriculture to correct past imbalances in the allocation of resources. This calls for a reduction in the allocation of investment in the iron and steel industries. In 1979, the first year of this reduction, output for both metals continued to rise. In 1979 steel output was 34.43 million tons, an increase of 2.65 million tons over 1978; output for pig iron was 36.69 million tons, 1.9 million tons above that for 1978. The government attributed this increase in output, despite reduced investment, to more efficient utilization of existing facilities (*Beijing Review,* February 18, 1980, p. 3). In 1980 the emphasis shifted to increasing the quality and the varieties of iron and steel products while reducing production costs. In early 1981 the government, continuing its policy of readjustment, canceled a number of capital construction projects, including the Baoshan Iron and Steel complex.

Rapid expansion of the iron and steel industries provided the economic base for development of China's machine-building industry. Before 1949 the machine-building industry in China consisted almost solely of production of electric-motor pumps and other simple machines. In 1979 China had more than 400 machine tool plants, 40 of them large. These produced more than 1,000 different kinds of products, including tractors; motor vehicles; equipment for metallurgical, mining, chemical, petroleum, and power industries; farm machinery; ships; scientific instruments; and meters. Over 80-percent of the machinery installed and used in China's basic industries is supplied domestically. In 1979 China exported some 200 different kinds of machines to some 70 countries in the world (*Beijing Review,* October 5, 1979, p. 38). The 1949 figures for the major products in the machine-building industry are compared with those for 1981 in table 4–2.

To fuel the growth of industry in China, the government sees the need to develop the energy sector. The principal sources of energy used in the country are coal, hydroelectric power and crude oil, with the majority of industries relying on coal as the primary source of energy. Until 1949 China had approximately twenty large- and medium-sized coal mines, which were poorly equipped and employed outmoded mining techniques. Compounding these problems, miners were demoralized by the lack of concern on the part of the mine owners and operators for workers' health and safety. Because of these unfavorable conditions, production of coal was very low. In 1949 the total output was only 32.43 million tons (Cheng 1974, p. 24). After the establishment of the PRC in 1949, more mines were opened. These employed more advanced techniques and equipment for mining coal. At the same time, greater attention was paid to the miners' health and safety. This boosted morale. As a result, within thirty years coal production increased 19.12-fold to 620 million tons in 1979. In 1979 China had confirmed coal deposits of about 600,000 million tons, making it one of the world's largest coal producers. Another 200,000 million tons were recently confirmed in a 150,000-square-kilometer area in Shanxi Province. Coal deposits are conveniently located throughout the country to provide a ready source of energy supply to nearby industries.

In 1979 there were approximately thirty large coal mines, each with a daily output capacity of over 10,000 tons. The medium-sized to small mines are generally placed under the administration of the cities, communes, and counties, whereas the large mines come under the direct administration of the central government. In 1979 China had twenty coal-science research institutes, eight mining colleges, and thirty secondary technical schools, all of which were engaged in training technicians for geological prospecting and for coal-mine design and construction (*China's Foreign Trade* 1979, pp 2–4). China plans to develop its coal industry further by signing contracts with foreign countries for the construction of large coal mines.

Prior to the discovery of crude oil in Daqing (Taching) in northeastern China, geologists had designated China as an oil-resource-poor nation. In September

Table 4-2
Output of China's Major Industrial Products, 1949–1981
(in millions)

	1949	1952[a]	1978	1979[b]	1980	1981 (est.)
Coal	32.43 tons[c]	66.49 tons	618 tons	635 tons	620 tons	620 tons
Crude oil	0.121 tons	0.436 tons	104.05 tons	106.15 tons	105.95 tons	106 tons
Electricity	4,310 kwh	7,260 kwh	256,550 kwh	256,550 kwh	300,600 kwh	312,000 kwh
Pig iron	0.252 tons	1,929 tons	34.79 tons	36.73 tons	38.02 tons	
Steel	0.158 tons	1,349 tons	31.78 tons	34.48 tons	27.16 tons	35.00 tons
Timber	5.67 cu.m.	11.20 cu.m.	51.62 cu.m.	54.39 cu.m.	53.59 cu.m.	
Cement	0.66 tons	2.86 tons	65.34 tons	73.90 tons	79.86 tons	78.00 tons
Chemical fertilizer (counted on the basis of 100% effectiveness)	0.006 tons	0.039 tons	8.693 tons	10.65 tons	12.32 tons	
Machine tools	0.0016	0.0137	0.1832	0.140	0.134	12.3 tons
Power-generating equipment	—	0.006 kw	4.838 kw	6.212 kw	4.193 kw	N.A.[d]
Motor vehicles	—	—	0.1491	0.189	0.222	N.A.[d]
Tractors	—	—	0.1135	0.126	0.098	0.160
Bicycles	0.014	0.08	8.54	10.09	13.02	0.0975
						14.84

Source: The PRC's State Statistical Bureau (reprinted in *Beijing Review*, May 12, 1980, p. 3; *Beijing Review*, May 11, 1981, p. 24).
[a]1952 was the year preceding the First Five-Year Plan (1953–1957).
[b]1979 was the first year of the Three-Year Plan (1979–1981) for readjustment, restructuring, consolidation, and improvement of China's economy.
[c]*Tons* refer to metric tons.
[d] Not available.

1956 crude oil was discovered in Daqing. This success prompted the government to engage in further exploration projects in other parts of the country. By 1979 China had built twenty-six oil fields with a total annual-output capacity of over 100 million tons of crude oil. This makes China the eighth-largest oil-producing nation in the world (*China Reconstructs,* January 1980, p. 15). The government now seeks to explore new sites rather than merely expand the production capacities of existing fields. New sites under exploration include the offshore continental shelves and the inland basins in the country's interior. Where possible, foreign technology and machinery are used. In late 1979 there were some 400,000 people engaged in geological work, using over 10,000 drills and other modern machinery.

Another important source of energy in China is hydroelectric power. In 1949 production capacity was 4,310 million kilowatt-hours (kwh). In 1979 hydroelectric output totaled 278,900 million kwh, a 64.71-fold increase.

The manufacture of chemical fertilizers for agricultural use was very low in 1949—only 6,000 tons. In 1979 production totaled 9.57 million tons, representing a 1,595-fold increase over a thirty-year period.

The Development of Textile and Light Industries

The first cotton mill was established in China in the 1880s, and the industry developed slowly over the next five decades. In 1949 there were only 5 million spindles, and the industry employed 750,000 workers. Annual outputs of cotton cloth, woolen piece goods, and silk were 2.5 billion meters, 5 million meters, and 50 million meters, respectively (*China Reconstructs,* May 1981, p. 6). Approximately 70 percent of the country's light industries were then concentrated in a few coastal cities. In 1949, for example, approximately 47 percent of the country's cotton-textile equipment was located in Shanghai.

The textile and light industries developed more rapidly between 1949 and 1978, compared with the five decades from the 1890s to 1949. In 1949 all textile machinery was imported. The workers in the mills referred to their products as "old thousand countries," indicating that the machinery came from many different lands. There were a few textile-machinery plants, but their activities were confined to servicing rather than production. In 1954 China produced its first complete set of cotton-textile equipment, from spinning to dyeing to printing. By the late 1950s the country was producing complete sets of equipment for cotton, wool, linen, silk, and knitwear. In the 1950s a substantial portion of the raw materials used in the textile industry was imported. Now China supplies approximately 80 percent of the raw materials used in the industry (*China Reconstructs,* May 1981). In 1980 China produced 13.3 billion meters of cotton cloth.

In 1978 the total value of light-industrial production was seventeen times that of 1949 (*China Reconstructs,* February 1980, p. 11). Output of bicycles increased 610-fold, from 14,000 units in 1949 to 8.54 million units in 1978 and 13 million in 1980. Since most of the products manufactured in the textile and light industries are consumer goods, and there was a tremendous upsurge in the country's population in the twenty-five years following 1949, it may be more meaningful to examine these statistics in terms of output per capita. Output of bicycles per capita increased 64 times, from 1 per 7,124 people in 1952 to 1 per 112 people in 1978. Production of sewing machines per capita increased 12 times, from 1 per 2,308 people in 1957 to 1 per 197 people in 1978. Output of wristwatches per capita increased 8.8-fold from 1 per 627 people in 1965 to 1 per 71 people in 1978. Machine-made-paper output increased 6.6 times, from 0.7 kilos in 1952 to 4.6 kilos per capita in 1978. Processed sugar increased 2.7 times, from 0.9 kilos in 1952 to 2.4 kilos per capita in 1978. Cotton-cloth production rose 1.7-fold, from 6.7 meters per capita in 1952 to 11.5 meters per capita in 1978, and 13 meters per capita in 1980 (*China Business Review,* September–October 1979, p. 27).

The country's export of textile and light-industrial products also increased substantially over the years. In 1953 only 50 kinds of textile and light-industrial products were exported. In 1978 over 700 different kinds of textile and light-industrial products were exported to some 150 countries. The amount of foreign exchange generated by the export of textile and light industrial products increased at an average annual rate of 16.2 percent. In 1978 profit and taxes paid by light-industrial enterprises comprised one-sixth of the country's total national revenue, or 18,000,000,000,000 yuan.

To promote the development of textile and light industries, the government erected plants and factories throughout the country according to proximity to raw materials, fuel, transportation, and local markets. For instance, sugar refineries were established in the Heilongjiang and Inner Mongolia regions where most of the country's sugar beets are grown. In Tibet, which had no industry prior to 1949, the government established woolen mills, paper mills, and leather factories (Cheng 1974, p. 26). In Xinjiang there were only a few handicraft textile workshops in 1949; by 1980 the region had dozens of modern mills, with 240,000 spindles for cotton and another 16,000 spindles for wool (*China Reconstructs,* May 1981).

Despite these impressive gains in the textile and light-industrial sectors since 1949, in the first twenty-nine years there were imbalances in the allocation of resources for heavy as opposed to light industries. Under the First Five-Year Plan (1953–1957), for instance, a full 46.5 percent of state appropriations went to heavy industry and capital construction, whereas light industry received a mere 5.9 percent of capital investment. Between 1966 and 1978 state investment in capital construction and heavy industry consistently accounted for more than 55 percent of the annual total state-budget allocations, whereas light industry received a mere 5 percent of annual appropriations (*Beijing Review,* December 21, 1979, p. 11). These imbalances in the allocation of resources could be attributed at least in part to the misconception of the goals of socialist production, as discussed in chapter 2.

In the current Three-Year Plan for Readjustment (1979–1981), greater emphasis is placed on the development of textile and light industries to correct for past imbalances in the allocation of capital investment. The reasons for this shift in emphasis are primarily threefold:

1. It is an effort to improve the overall standard of living of the people. The October 20, 1979, edition of the *Renmin Ribao* carried a special editorial, entitled "On the Aim of Socialist Production," which indicated that the primary purpose of production was to meet the ever growing material and cultural needs of the working people and of society at large. In the past production was undertaken primarily for its own sake, largely ignoring consumer demand. Even though wages were increased for three consecutive years (1977–1979), money did not have much purchasing power. There was an extreme shortage of consumer goods. In 1979, the first year of the Three-Year Plan for Readjustment, 5,000 new commodities were added to the list of consumer goods. These included washing machines, refrigerators, mini-bikes, and automatic calendar watches (*Beijing Review*, January 14, 1980, p. 3). In 1981 China plans to manufacture 23.6 million wristwatches and 8.6 million sewing machines (*China Reconstructs*, December 1980, p. 15).
2. It is intended to produce more goods for export in order to generate foreign exchange to purchase much needed equipment and technology to further the goals of the Four Modernizations.
3. Textile and light industries, though accounting for almost half of the total volume of retail trade, usually require less capital investment, yield higher profits, and are able to realize a quicker return on investments. As a case in point, the amount of profit and taxes paid to the state between 1949 and 1978 by the textile industry in Shanghai alone was 77.3 times the total state investment in that sector (*Beijing Review*, June 29, 1979, p. 8).

To highlight the importance of the textile and light industries, the government sponsored the largest national exhibition of light-industrial products in September–October 1979 to acquaint the people with the variety of products manufactured in this sector and to familiarize them with the reasons and need for greater emphasis on the growth of this sector in the current Three-Year Plan for Readjustment. The growth of light industry responded favorably to this shift in investment allocations. In 1979, the first year of readjustment, total industrial-output value increased 8 percent over 1978. For the first time in the history of the PRC, the rate of growth of light industry (9 percent) exceeded that of heavy industry (7.4 percent). In 1980 the output value of the light-industrial sector increased 17.4 percent over that for the preceding year, whereas that for heavy industry increased by a mere 1.6 percent (*Beijing Review*, March 16, 1981, p. 14). In the same year, light industry accounted for a full 46.7 percent of total industrial-output value. This represented a 3.6-percent increase over 1979 (*Beijing Review,* January 26, 1981, p. 7). The taxes and profits turned over to the state by this sector as a percentage of net fixed assets also increased. In 1979 the government estimated that for every 100 yuan of net fixed assets in the light industrial sector, the state received 36.3 yuan in taxes and profits. This compares with 35.5 yuan in 1978 and 31.5 yuan in 1977 (*Beijing Review,* September 22, 1980, p. 33).

The Development of the Handicraft Industry

Traditionally, the handicraft industry played a very important role in China's economy. In the 1930s agriculture and the handicraft industry made up some 90 percent of the country's economy. In 1954 the handicraft industry still accounted for approximately 20 percent of the country's total industrial-output value. Under the First Five-Year Plan (1953–1957), with the move toward collectivization and nationalization, approximately 90 percent of the independent artisans throughout the country were organized into cooperatives.

In China's drive toward the goals of the Four Modernizations, the handicraft industry will continue to play a role in the country's economy. In 1980 the Ministry of Light Industry extended four times as much in loans to this sector as in 1979 (*Beijing Review,* December 15, 1980, p. 5). In 1980 approximately 40 percent of the arts and handicrafts cooperatives were mechanized—that is, used some tools and equipment in the process of production.

There are several reasons for encouraging the continued development of the handicraft industry. First, the handicraft industry provides an important source of employment for the country's huge labor force, as it is highly labor intensive. According to government estimates, for every 1 million yuan of fixed-asset investments in heavy, textile and light, and handicraft industries, approximately 94, 257, and 800–1,000 new jobs are created, respectively. Second, since Chinese handicraft products have a good market overseas, the industry provides an important source of foreign-exchange earnings. In 1979 export items from this sector generated 1,000 million yuan in foreign-exchange earnings. Finally, the handicraft industry generally requires low capital investment and is able to realize a quick return on investment. For example, between 1973 and 1978 the state invested 62 million yuan in this sector (approximately 2.3 percent of total state allocations). In 1979 the output industrial value of this sector reached 2,600 million yuan, a 41.9-fold return on the state's investment (*Beijing Review,* September 15, 1980, pp. 16–20; December 15, 1980, pp. 4–5).

On the basis of the foregoing survey of industrial growth and development in the PRC from 1949 to 1979, an assessment of its positive and negative experiences or features can be made, as follows.

Positive Experiences

By any reckoning, the PRC's accomplishment in its first thirty years is impressive. Even though the country's per capita income is still very low compared with that of developed nations (in 1980 it stood at U.S. $250), China has come a long way from the disorientation and economic chaos that plagued the country prior to 1949. On the eve of the establishment of the PRC in 1949, China suffered every conceivable sort of economic and social ill—runaway inflation, political chaos, technological stagnation, famine, disease, and starvation (Schurmann 1968). When these conditions are compared with the progress made under the Communist party, one is tempted to ask how the Communist party was able to accomplish such a feat within a relatively short period of time. Although the answer to this question may be complex, two keys to success were (1) the incredible organizational skills of Mao Zedong and other Chinese Communist party leaders and (2) the role of ideology in spurring people to action. Ideology is here discussed as a means to an end, not an end in itself.

As pointed out in chapter 2, Mao recognized that China's worst enemy, and at the same time its most powerful resource, was its vast population. If these human resources could be mobilized, they could be converted into one of China's richest assets. Mao was convinced that if he and his party could harness these millions of Chinese to work toward a common goal, then half the battle would be won. What was needed was a theme around which the masses could rally. As pointed out in chapter 2, Marxism-Leninism provided such a focal point, representing for the people a means to deliver them from their miseries.

Of course, Marxism-Leninism by itself could not have brought about this remarkable transformation without the leadership skills of Mao Zedong, Zhou Enlai, and other leaders of the Chinese Communist party (CCP). Mao, Zhou, and the other CCP leaders succeeded in arousing the spirit that lay dormant in the masses. Although Marxism-Leninism is a new philosophy, certain of its principles are not new to the Chinese mentality. Notions such as the existence of a utopia, the perfectability of humankind, and unswerving loyalty to one's family were expounded by Confucius and leading Confucian scholars through the ages. Confucius stressed filial piety, and Mao and his party merely broadened the concept of one's immediate family to that of the state. The loyalty hitherto rendered to one's parents was henceforward transferred to the family-state. Both Confucius and Mao believed in the perfectability of humanity and the existence of a utopia. People unfamiliar with the inspiring force behind the European Enlightenment thought that Mao borrowed this explicit faith in mankind from the European philosphers. In fact, Confucius's notions of the benevolent and wise philosopher-king and of the perfectability of man had a tremendous influence on the leading thinkers of the European Enlightenment, as evidenced in the writings of Voltaire.

Mao's faith in humanity accounts for his sincere conviction that the common man could rebuild a new and strong China. His faith in human perfectability gave him the courage and mission to remold human attitudes and values into utopian ones. For Confucius, the utopia had existed in the past, in the times of Emperors Yao and Shun, who ruled China before the establishment of the first imperial dynasty. Confucius urged the Chinese rulers of his day to emulate the principles espoused by Yao and Shun. For Mao, there also existed a stage of "primitive communism" in the past. This was described in the Marxist analysis of economic progression through the ages. In direct contrast to the Confucian yearning for a golden age in the remote past, Marxism-Leninism preaches that the utopia lies in the future. Thus Mao urged the people to work toward the future utopia—the stage of full communism. From the foregoing it is evident that the principles of striving for a golden age of perfection were already deeply ingrained in the social consciousness of the Chinese people. Mao and his party had to reactivate and reorient this spirit to suit the needs of modern times. However, the very existence of such principles among the Chinese people made Mao's work much easier and helps to account for the relative smoothness and rapidity with which the value systems of the Chinese were reoriented under the Communist regime.

In a television interview hosted by David Frost in later 1979, Dr. Henry Kissinger, former U.S. secretary of state, was asked to provide capsule portraits of world figures into whom he had a unique insight, including Mao Zedong and Zhou Enlai. In describing Mao, Kissinger used the words "colossal personality; emanating global power; intoxicated with revolution." Kissinger described Zhou as an "intellectual, electric, compassionate; maybe the most intelligent person I have met." These capsule portraits capture the essence of the attraction these two leaders hold for the Chinese people and others throughout the world. These brief descriptions summarize the spirit and essence of these two men better than any lengthy political rhetoric.

For the first time in modern history, China had capable leaders who possessed the fervor, determination, and above all the competence to organize and mobilize the people to follow the government's directives on socialist construction, policies guided partly by ideological principles but based largely on a comprehensive analysis of the objective conditions that prevailed. The leadership provided by Mao, Zhou, and others, along with the tenets of the Marxist doctrine of class struggle and the Leninist doctrine of anti-imperialism, as translated into guides for concrete action, provided the motivating forces for mobilizing the masses to work toward the goals of socialist construction. These two factors explain, to a great extent, the reasons for the success achieved by China within a relatively short period of time. These principles of organization, of the party's role in organizing and mobilizing the masses, were effected all the way down to the party committee at the enterprise level.

With the deaths of Mao and Zhou in 1976, the question arose whether progress and development would continue without these two great leaders? The answer up to now appears to be in the affirmative. The post-1976 Chinese government has demonstrated strong leadership abilities. With the consolidation of top leadership in 1980, it appears that power is more deeply entrenched in the hands of the pragmatists who are most likely to advance policies and programs designed to stimulate China's economic growth. Zhao Ziyang, the new premier, is generally credited as the architect of the highly successful Sichuan experimental program, the goal of which is to increase productivity and further economic development.

As for the second positive factor that spurred the people to action, ideology, its role in post-Mao society was examined in chapter 2.

Negative Experiences

On the basis of an analysis of China's industrial progress and development from 1949 to 1978, the negative experiences appeared to be primarily fourfold:

1. disproportionate allocation of resources among heavy industries, light industries, and agriculture
2. imbalances in the ratios between accumulation and consumption
3. periodic political and ideological upheavals
4. overcentralization of authority in the hands of the state and overreliance on administrative means for running the economy

Each of these is discussed in greater detail in this section.

Disproportions in the Allocation of State Investment. In several works, such as "On the Ten Major Relationships" (1956) and "On the Correct Handling of Contradictions among the People" (1957), Mao discussed China's path toward industrialization and formulated policies for handling the relationships between the growth of heavy industry, of light industry, and of agriculture. These recommendations were based on a review of Soviet experiences and of China's objective conditions—namely, that an overwhelming proportion of the population still depended on agriculture as their principal means of livelihood. On this basis Mao formulated the general policy of "taking agriculture as the foundation, and industry as the leading factor for the development of the national economy." Mao called for drawing up the national economic plan in the following order of priority: agriculture, light industry, and heavy industry. Mao wrote:

The emphasis in our country's construction is on heavy industry. The production of the means of production must be given priority, that's settled. But it definitely does not follow that the production of the means of subsistence, especially grain, can be neglected. Without enough food and other daily necessities, it would be impossible to provide for the workers in the first place, and then what sense would it make to talk about developing heavy industry? Therefore, the relationship between heavy industry, on the one hand, and light industry and agriculture, on the other, must be properly handled. [*Selected Works,* vol. 5, 1977, p. 286]

Despite its recognition of the Soviet Union's mistakes, China also fell prey to the same shortcomings in its own national economic-development plans. As pointed out previously, until 1978 there were serious disproportions in the allocation of capital resources so that heavy industry developed much more rapidly than did light industry or agriculture. These disproportionate allocations resulted in an increase in the output value of the national economy, while the people's standard of living was not improved commensurately. China's leaders now reemphasize the importance of adhering to Mao's general policy of developing the economy in the order of agriculture, light industry, and heavy industry. Under the current Three-Year Plan for Readjustment (1979–1981), state investment in agriculture and light industry has been increased. Heavier investment in agriculture is designed to raise the standard of living of the rural population and thus to lessen the gap between urban and rural areas. Higher investment in light industries is designed to serve two purposes: (1) to produce more goods for export, in order to generate foreign exchange to finance the Four Modernizations program, and (2) to improve the overall standard of living of the people.

Past imbalances in the appropriation of resources could be attributed at least in part to misconceptions about the goals of socialist production. In the past production was undertaken primarily for its own sake, regardless of consumer demand. China's leaders now emphasize that the goal of socialist production is to improve people's livelihood. In the words of an economic commentator from Hainan: "we advocate that under the socialist system, anyone who becomes wealthy is honorable. . . . The wealthier a person becomes, the greater his contribution to the State and society" (*China Business Review,* November–December 1979, p. 54). In the Three-Year Plan for Readjustment, due emphasis is given to production for the purpose of raising the overall standard of living of the people.

Imbalances in the Ratios between Accumulation and Consumption. In the past, because of misconceptions about the goals of socialist production, there were imbalances in the ratios between accumulation and consumption. During the First Five-Year Plan, the average rate of accumulation was 24.2 percent of the national income. This rate climbed to 30.8–40 percent over the Second Five-Year Plan. During the Three-Year Readjustment Period (1963–1965), it dropped to 22.7 percent; but it rose rapidly to 31–34 percent during the Cultural Revolution

(1966–1976). Economic performance and people's livelihood fluctuated commensurately with the varying ratios of accumulation over these different periods (see table 4–3).

During the First Five-Year Plan, the country estimated that total industrial and agricultural output value increased at the rate of 10.9 percent per annum, whereas national income grew at the rate of 8.9 percent per annum and workers' wages increased by 7.4 percent per annum. During the period of the Great Leap Forward, total industrial and agricultural output increased at merely 0.6 percent per annum, whereas national income actually declined by 3.1 percent per annum. During those years people's livelihoods were adversely affected. During the Three-Year Readjustment Period (1963–1965), total industrial and agricultural output value rose at an average annual rate of 15.7 percent, and national income climbed 14.5 percent per annum. Between 1974 and 1976 China suffered severe financial losses. The government estimated that from 1974 to 1976 the state lost 100,000 million yuan, 28 million tons of steel, and 40,000 million yuan in revenue (*Beijing Review,* July 21, 1980, p. 18). Based on these statistics, Xue Muqiao, a noted economist and an influential figure in the country's present economic reforms, concluded that in order for the economy to develop rapidly, the rate of accumulation should remain around 25 percent. The present period of readjustment is necessitated by the fact that in 1978 the rate of accumulation was hovering at around 36.5 percent. This created imbalances in the national economy. Xue argued that under no condition should the rate of accumulation exceed 30 percent because of the negative effects of high rates of accumulation. Further, if the rate of accumulation were to exceed 40 percent, it would result in economic decline (*Beijing Review,* March 9, 1981, pp. 30–31). The government hopes to lower the rate of accumulation to the desired 25 percent.

Periodic Political and Ideological Upheavals. Ideology has been cited as a positive factor in spurring people to action. However, in its extreme form, when ideology becomes an end in itself rather than a guide to progress, ideology can prove detrimental to economic growth and development. The way in which periodic political and ideological upheavals can affect the operations and productivity levels of industrial enterprises are best exemplified by two important aspects of organizational functioning: (1) the application of the dual criteria of "redness" and "expertness" in the selection of model workers and in promotion to managerial positions in the organization; and (2) the types of incentives used to motivate workers to heighten performance.

Since the founding of the PRC in 1949, the government has laid down the policy that only those who are judged to be both "red" (politically and ideologically sound) and "expert" (technically competent) can be nominated as advanced workers or promoted to the top ranks of management. Controversy has centered on how these principles ought to be applied in practice. Specifically, the question has arisen as to what the criteria are for redness and expertness. In

Table 4-3
Some Major Economic Indicators, 1953–1979

Period	Percentage of Accumulation in National Income	Average Growth Rate of Industrial and Agricultural Production (%)	Average Growth Rate of National Income (%)	Rate of Increase of Financial Revenue (%)	Rate of Labor Productivity Increase in State-Owned Enterprises (%)
First Five-Year Plan (1953–1957)	24.2	10.9	8.9	11.0	8.7
Second Five-Year Plan (1958–1965)	30.8	0.6	-3.1	0.2	-5.4
Period of Readjustment (1963–1965)	22.7	15.7	14.5	14.7	23.1
Third Five-Year Plan (1966–1970)	26.3	9.6	8.4	7.0	2.5
Fourth Five-Year Plan (1971–1975)	33.0	7.8	5.6	4.2	-0.3
Fifth Five-Year Plan					
1976	31.1	1.7	-2.3	-4.8	-8.6
1977	32.3	10.7	8.3	12.6	8.1
1978	36.5	12.3	12.3	28.2	12.3
1979	33.6	8.5	6.9	-7.9	6.4

Source: *Beijing Review*, March 23, 1981, p. 25.

periods of political and ideological upheavals, such as the Great Leap Forward and the Cultural Revolution "redness" has been emphasized. In those years, those who engaged in political demagogy were nominated as advanced workers and promoted even though they might not have possessed the necessary technical skills. This led to inefficiency and chaos in the management of enterprises. These occasional upheavals were usually accompanied by a marked decrease in production. With the fall of the Gang of Four in October 1976, and the present leaders' endorsement of the Four Modernizations, most factories and enterprises have adopted a more pragmatic approach to the application of the principle of "redness" versus "expertness". The use of examinations to determine the candidate's level of technical competence, emphasis on training and acquisition of technical skills, and institution of more rigorous curricula at the universities and colleges lead one to believe that the Chinese authorities now place greater emphasis on "expertness" to determine a person's suitability for advancement and promotion in an organization. Most enterprises now deem that "redness" is a necessary but insufficient criterion for nomination as an advanced worker or for promotion to management.

A second way in which ideological upheavals could affect productivity is in the types of incentives used. In China two types of incentives are used to motivate workers to heighten performance: (1) material incentives, such as salary and bonuses; and (2) nonmaterial incentives, or moral encouragement. In normal times the two types of incentives are used jointly. In times of political and ideological upheavals, moral encouragement has dominated and almost completely supplanted material incentives. For example, during the Cultural Revolution it was claimed that those who were armed with Mao Zedong Thought did not need material incentives to make them work. Consequently, bonuses were abolished during those years. Periods of political upheavals have usually coincided with sharp declines in production levels in industrial organizations. In 1977 bonuses were reinstated in most enterprises.

As discussed in chapter 2, to guard against the future occurrence of such disruptive ideological upheavals, the government has issued guidelines to assist people in developing a correct approach to the study of Marxism-Leninism. Some of the principal guidelines advocated were: (1) it is wrong to mutilate Marxism–Leninism–Mao Zedong Thought into individual sentences independent of one another and to observe these parts independent of the whole context; and (2) practice is the sole criterion for truth. This means that only those things which have been proved in practice to be beneficial to the people and the socialist cause represent the truth that should be upheld. Furthermore, this approach argues that truth does not move in a straight line, but changes over time.

Overcentralization of Authority. Because China is a planned socialist economy, all economic activities and undertakings are subject to a centrally developed and administered plan. Formerly, the state set production goals and targets for the enterprises, allocated resources and raw materials to them, laid down broad policies and guidelines to be followed in their operations and management, and distributed or marketed their output.

With 400,000 industrial enterprises operating in the economy, and literally hundreds of thousands of products being manufactured, it has become virtually impossible for the state to devise a plan comprehensive enough to encompass all minute details and yet flexible enough to accommodate all contingencies. This practice has often led to problems, such as bottlenecks in operations and overstocking of inventory.

In the past production plans were formulated without much regard for market forces. Thus certain commodities were produced that had no immediate market, whereas other products that were in demand were produced in insufficient quantities. Furthermore, state-owned enterprises have not been treated as independent accounting units and hence have not been responsible for their own profits and losses. This policy has tended to stifle initiative and creativity and to foster the development of a spirit of unhealthy complacency among certain managers and workers in the industrial enterprises.

Under central planning the state has relied primarily on administrative fiat to run industrial enterprises. In the past directives were filtered down from the central government through a fixed hierarchy of organizational levels, which were often cumbersome and redundant in their activities. As a result, the flow of information was often delayed and distorted through the administrative channels. Moreover, the process usually took so long that by the time a certain directive got through, the objective conditions might have changed. This caused much frustration and was costly to both enterprise and state in terms of time, resources, and money, because delayed time often meant reduced profits.

The government now recognizes the limitations inherent in the past economic structure and is determined to rectify the situation. Many of the changes were laid down in the Three-Year Plan (1979–1981) for readjustment, restructuring, consolidation, and improvement of China's economy. The changes include the following: (1) decentralization of authority to allow industrial enterprises greater autonomy with respect to decision making, planning, and handling of financial matters; (2) limited use of the market mechanism in conjunction with, and subject to, central planning; (3) elimination of overlapping and inefficient administrative organs; and (4) use of economic means such as taxes. Detailed discussion of these reforms is provided in chapter 9.

Although the emphasis in this book is on industrial society, any analysis of economic development in China would be incomplete without a brief discussion of progress and development in the agricultural sector, because approximately 80 percent of China's people still depend on agriculture as their principal means of livelihood.

The Agricultural Sector

Development in the Agricultural Sector

During the First Five-Year Plan (1953–1957), the government was largely able to implement its policy of collectivization in the agricultural sector. The three-level system of ownership of the means of production was introduced. These three levels are the commune, the brigade, and the team, with the last as the basic accounting unit. As in the industrial sector, farms are classified into two general categories: state farms, which are owned by the whole people; and collectively owned farms, which belong to the people's communes. In 1979 there were 2,048 state farms employing some 4.8 million workers and staff members. In the same year, there were 50,000 collectively owned farms in the country (*Beijing Review*, April 21, 1980).

Between 1949 and 1979 China was able to expand its agricultural production, particularly in the areas of grain, cotton, sugar, and pigs. For example, grain production increased 2.7-fold, from 113.2 million tons in 1949 to 330 million tons in 1979. In 1980, because of bad weather and other factors, grain production declined by 15 million tons to 315 million tons (*China Reconstructs*, May 1981). The output of cotton increased 5.39-fold, from 444,500 tons in 1949 to 2.4 million tons in 1979. In 1980 cotton production increased by another 10 percent. The production of sugar expanded 11.5-fold, from 20,000 tons in 1949 to 2.3 million tons in 1979. The number of pigs increased 5.43-fold, from 57.75 million heads in 1949 to 313.83 million heads in 1979. Moderate increases were also reported in cash crops, animal husbandry, fishery, and rural industry. Over the thirty-year period a number of water conservation projects of various sizes were built for irrigation purposes. Prior to 1949 most agricultural work had been done manually, without the assistance of farm machinery or the use of chemical fertilizers (*Beijing Review*, March 24, 1980). Table 4–4 presents the 1978 statistics reflecting the conditions of agricultural production. Despite these gains, many problems remain in the agricultural sector. The principal ones can be briefly outlined as follows:

Vicissitudes of Agricultural Growth. Between 1949 and 1957 China was able to make fairly impressive gains in the development of the agricultural sector. For example, in 1952 total grain output reached 154 million tons, a figure higher than that for any year prior to the establishment of the PRC. Between 1952 and 1957 agricultural output increased at an average annual rate of 4.5 percent. Unfortunately, the growth trend established from 1949 to 1957 failed to continue. In the late 1950s the agricultural sector suffered losses resulting from inexperience in running collective farms and natural disasters. Just as the agricultural sector had recovered sufficiently to register growth in the Three-Year Readjustment Period (1963–1965), the country embarked on the Cultural

Table 4–4

Conditions of Agricultural Production in 1978

Total power of agricultural machinery	160 million horsepower
Number of large- and medium-sized tractors	557,000
Number of walking tractors	1,370,000
Number of large- and medium-sized reservoirs holding 170,000 million cubic meters	Over 80,000
Area of land under irrigation	46,670,000 hectares
Chemical fertilizer used per hectare	525 kilograms

Source: *Beijing Review,* March 24, 1980, p. 15.

Revolution. Between 1966 and 1976 China implemented policies that were not conducive to the growth of the agricultural sector. For example, the system of fixed production quotas was abandoned; the practice of calculating work points so that remunerations could be made on the principle of "more work, more pay" was abolished; rural fairs were banned; private plots were confiscated; and peasants were discouraged from engaging in household sideline production. The slogan in those days was "the poorer you are, the more honored you will be" (*China Reconstructs,* August 1979, pp. 20-24). These policies had an adverse effect on the development of the agricultural sector.

Rapid Increase in the Population. Between 1957 and 1978 the population of China increased by 300 million, whereas the amount of cultivated land actually decreased because some of the land was used for capital construction. Consequently, despite the increases in grain production, the average per capita share of grain for 1978 was the same as that for 1957 (*Beijing Review,* March 24, 1980, p. 15).

Disproportions in the Allocation of Resources among Sectors. As pointed out earlier, in the first twenty-nine years of the PRC, heavy industry was emphasized at the expense of the light-industrial and agricultural sectors. This severely retarded growth in the agricultural sector. For example, in 1979 the assets of a production brigade averaged less than 10,000 yuan. In some communities the production brigade barely possessed the means required for simple reproduction (*Beijing Review,* March 24, 1980). Consequently, rural income remained low. In 1979 the per capita income for industrial workers was 705 yuan, whereas that for peasants was only 83.4 yuan.

Reforms in the Agricultural Sector

Since 1979 a series of reforms has been introduced in the agricultural sector (*Beijing Review,* March 24, 1980, pp. 14-20). The principal ones are as follows:

1. As with reforms in the industrial sector, state farms were granted greater autonomy with respect to production, planning, and handling of financial matters. The government recognizes the need to run farms according to economic laws and principles.

The system of treating state farms as independent accounting units, implemented in 1955, had a favorable impact on the development of the agricultural sector. From 1949 to 1965 the number of workers employed on state farms increased from 3,000 to 2.38 million. The amount of arable land expanded from 30,000 hectares in 1949 to 3.15 million hectares in 1965. Profits also increased. However, the policy of economic accounting was abandoned between 1966 and 1976. In that period the agricultural sector suffered losses totaling 3,500 million yuan. Most state farms operated in the red between 1966 and 1978. In 1979 the policy of treating state farms as independent accounting units was reinstituted, and the state farms responded favorably to this change. In the same year state farms showed a profit of 300 million yuan (*Beijing Review*, April 21, 1980, p. 7).

2. Eliminate absolute egalitarianism by reinstituting the policy of calculating work points and distribution of bonuses according to the principle of "from each according to his ability; and more pay for more work."

3. Develop rural industries. In order to stimulate growth in rural communities, the government has encouraged the establishment and development of commune-run enterprises. In 1979 it was estimated that China had 1.5 million commune-run enterprises, an average of approximately 30 enterprises per commune. Commune-run enterprises engage in a wide range of industries, including processing, excavation, transportation, building, and repair. In 1978 the total production value of these commune-run enterprises reached 49,000 million yuan, a 25-percent increase over the preceding year. In 1979 the output value of the rural industries amounted to one-third of the communes' total income. Profits derived from rural industries provide funds for the development of agriculture. In 1978 the rural industries were able to generate profits amounting to 2,600 million yuan. This amount, equal to 60 percent of the total state investment in the agricultural sector for that year, was channeled for use in agricultural development. In addition, rural industries provide an important means of employment. In 1979, 28 million people were employed by the commune-run enterprises (*Beijing Review*, September 28, 1979; February 4, 1980).

The government now emphasizes the need to diversify the agricultural economy. In the past, the emphasis was on grain production even in places where conditions were not suitable for growing grain. The government now encourages the development of animal husbandry, fish farming, and other sideline productions to suit local conditions. The current slogan is "'one pattern' will not do!." Essentially, this means that it is not practical to impose a uniform policy regardless of varying local conditions (*Beijing Review*, November 3, 1980). Table 4-5 illustrates the extent to which a production brigade in Henan province, located approximately 600 kilometers south of Beijing, has diversified its economy between 1975 and 1979.

Table 4–5
Diversification of Economy in the Liuzhuang Production Brigade, Henan Province

Year	Total Income (Yuan)	Percentage of Income from Agriculture	Percentage of Income from Industries and Sideline Occupation	Total Labor Force	Percentage Engaged in Agriculture	Percentage Engaged in Industries and Sideline Occupation
1975	546,642	58.0	42.0	580	74.28	21.73
1976	710,185	41.4	59.6	580	55.69	40.52
1977	1,160,791	34.8	65.2	587	51.11	45.14
1978	1,264,139	27.5	72.5	585	48.89	47.35
1979	N.A.	N.A.	N.A.	580	45.69	50.52

Source: Adapted from *Beijing Review*, February 11, 1980, pp. 21–22.

In early 1979 the government lifted the ban on rural fairs. In the past all commodities were distributed through the state shops or marketing cooperatives. By late 1979, however, some 1,500 stalls were erected in the outskirts of Beijing. These sell more than eighty kinds of farm produce. The seller must pay the state a daily fee ranging from 0.30 to 3 yuan, depending on the amount of goods sold. In their first six months of operation (March–August 1979), the total transactions at the rural fairs on the outskirts of Beijing exceeded 2 million yuan. Rural fairs have returned to most of the large- to medium-sized cities. In 1980 there were some 2,300 peasant markets throughout the country, selling agricultural and sideline products. Peasant markets operate during the daytime, whereas the state-owned commercial departments and individual operators conduct business in the evenings. (*Beijing Review,* September 1, 1980).

The prices of commodities sold at these markets are negotiated between the buyer and seller. In general, most prices are slightly higher than those charged at the state-run stores (*Beijing Review,* November 23, 1979).

4. Increase state investment in the agricultural sector. Consistent with the objectives of the Three-Year Plan for Readjustment, the state has decided to increase investments in the agricultural sector by approximately 18 percent between 1983 and 1985. Besides direct allocations, the state will double the funds available for agricultural loans between 1980 and 1985. These will be available in the form of long-term, low-interest agricultural loans with ten-, fifteen-, and twenty-year repayment schedules. In the first quarter of 1979, the credit extended to communes by banks and credit cooperatives totalled 3,940 million yuan. This represented a 73-percent increase over the corresponding period for the preceding year (*China Reconstructs,* August 1979).

5. Reduce the price gap between industrial and agricultural products by lowering the selling prices of the former and raising the purchase price of agricultural commodities. Although the purchase price of grain was doubled and that for oil seeds increased by 2.4 times between 1950 and 1978, a wide disparity still existed between the selling price of industrial commodities and the purchase price of agricultural outputs (*China Reconstructs,* January 1980). This accounts in part for the slow growth in the agricultural sector and the widening income gap between urban workers and peasants. To correct this situation, the state hopes to reduce the price gap by raising the purchase price of agricultural outputs and lowering the selling price of industrial commodities. In 1979 the purchase price for grain produced in fulfillment of state quota was increased by 20 percent; the purchase price for grain produced in excess of state quota was raised 50 percent. The state has also promised to raise the purchase price on other agricultural products in the future. In order to make certain industrial commodities more accessible to the pocketbooks of those in rural communities, the state has concomitantly lowered the selling prices of industrial products, such as farm machinery and chemical fertilizers, by some 10–15 percent. In 1980 the state allocated more than 10 billion yuan for the specific purpose of

raising the purchase price of agricultural products and lowering the selling price of industrial products (*China Reconstructs,* January 1981).

6. Improve agricultural output through planned land reclamation and mechanization of existing farms. In the late 1950s the government proposed to realize farm mechanization by 1980. In 1980 Mr. Yang Ligong, minister of agricultural machinery, noted that because of the backward state of the economy, this was an unrealistic goal. However, the country will continue to mechanize where possible. Mr. Yang stated that in places where conditions are ripe for the widespread use of machinery, such as Liaoning, Jilin, and Heilongjiang provinces, mechanization will be accomplished at an earlier date. As with industrial management, the country insists that farm mechanization will be done in the Chinese way. This would take into consideration the objective conditions in the rural communities—low levels of technological and economic development and an abundant population (*Beijing Review,* August 18, 1980, pp. 5–6).

7. Allow diversity and flexibility in responsibility for production and management of communes. For example, in the more backward areas, where the collective economy is underdeveloped, the system of fixing farm-output quotas on the household basis will be used. Under this system the production team remains as the basic accounting unit. (Each production team comprises twelve to twenty households.) However, the plots of land come under the management of the individual household. At harvest time the individual household turns over a fixed amount of its output to the production team and is allowed to retain the surplus. The government notes that the kind of responsibility system to be adopted in a particular area or community must be appropriate to local conditions and the peasants' wishes. The government is prepared to implement alternative systems of responsibility as long as these are conducive to raising productivity and increasing the standards of living of the agricultural communities (*Beijing Review,* March 16, 1981; *China Reconstructs,* January 1981).

Through the implementation of these reforms, the country hopes to speed up growth and development in the agricultural sector.

Discussion

Many of the measures designed to correct the negative experiences encountered in the first thirty years of China's history—to rectify imbalances in the appropriation of resources among various sectors of the country's economy, to adjust imbalances between the ratios of accumulation and consumption, to prevent the occurrence of ideological upheavals, to decentralize the authority of the central government, and to reform the agricultural sector—have only recently been implemented, on an experimental basis. Hence it is too early to tell whether these measures will be carried through to the finish, and whether they will be effective in speeding up China's economic growth and development in the coming decades. Nonetheless, the very fact that the government is willing to acknowledge that deficiencies did exist in the past system and to recognize that changes ought to be made is a healthy and encouraging sign. One of the prerequisites for change and improvement lies in the recognition of problems and the perceived need for change.

5 China's Political System

In China, political considerations have a pervasive influence on all aspects of society. Political and economic considerations, for instance, are often inextricably intertwined. Consequently, in order to comprehend fully the complexities of Chinese industrial society, it is imperative to examine China's political system and the role played by the Chinese Communist party in influencing various aspects of Chinese society, including the operations and management of industrial enterprises.

This chapter presents a brief overview of the Chinese political system. Specifically, it examines (1) the organs of political power in China, to show the extent to which politics governs all aspects of societal functioning; (2) the political task for the 1980s; (3) the principles guiding political life; and (4) the reforms that have been made in the political system since 1978.

Organs of Political Power

Article 20 of the 1978 Chinese Constitution designates the National People's Congress (NPC) as "the highest organ of state power." The State Council, which is the executive branch of the National People's Congress, is the highest administrative organization in the government of China. The NPC and the State Council operate at the central-government level. There are three levels below the State Council:

1. the level of the provinces, autonomous regions, and municipalities directly under the central government (the last of these refers to the municipalities of Beijing, Shanghai, and Tianjin)
2. the level of the counties, autonomous counties, and cities
3. the level of the communes, towns, and districts

At the various levels below the State Council, the local people's congresses at the corresponding levels are "local organs of state power" (Article 35, Constitution of the PRC). The hierarchical levels in the political structure are depicted in Figure 5-1.

According to the Chinese Statistical Bureau, at the end of 1978 China had 22 provinces (including Taiwan), 5 autonomous regions, and 3 municipalities directly under the central-government administration. Below this level, there

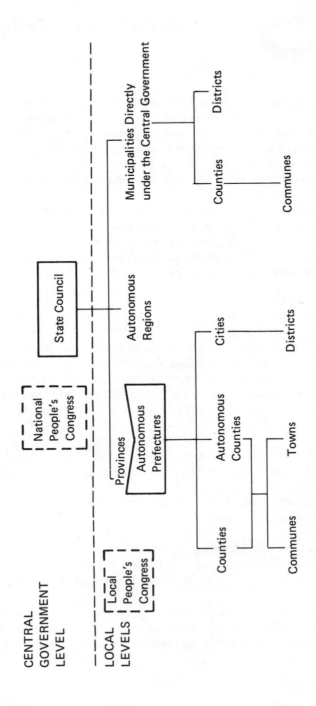

Source: Adapted from *Beijing Review*, May 18, 1979, p. 21.

Figure 5-1. Organs of Political Power in the People's Republic of China

are 29 autonomous prefectures, 2,138 counties, 190 cities, and 50,000 communes (see table 5-1). Autonomous regions, prefectures, and counties refer to
places inhabited by China's minority nationalities. In June 1979, the Jinuo
people were designated as a minority nationality, bringing the country's total
number of minority nationalities to fifty-five. Minority nationalities account for
approximately 6 percent of the country's population. Members of the Han
nationality make up the remaining 94 percent of the country's population.

Table 5-1
Administrative Division of China

	Prefectures	Counties	Cities
Provinces			
Anhui	9	70	11
Fujian	7	62[a]	6
Gansu	10	74	4
Guangdong	9	97	11
Guizhou	7	79	5
Hebei	10	139	9
Heilongjiang	9	76	13
Henan	10	111	14
Hubei	8	73	6
Hunan	11	90	10
Jiangsu	7	64	11
Jiangxi	6	82	8
Jilin	5	48	10
Liaoning	3	53	11
Qinghai	7	38	1
Shaanxi	7	92	5
Shandong	9	106	9
Shanxi	7	101	7
Sichuan	14	181	11
Yunnan	15	122	4
Zhejiang	8	65	3
Autonomous regions			
Guangxi Zhuang	8	80	6
Inner Mongolia	4	43	5
Ningxia Hui	2	17	2
Tibet	5	71	1
Xingjiang Uygur	13	80	7
Municipalities directly under central government			
Beijing		9	
Shanghai		10	
Tianjin		5	
Totals	210	2,138	190

Source: Adapted from *Beijing Review,* May 18, 1979, p. 23.
[a]The county number includes Jinmen County, which is presently independent of the
People's Republic of China.

Because of the sheer size of the provinces and autonomous regions, these are divided into prefectures to facilitate administration. Prefectures do not represent a separate level of political power. Each prefecture encompasses several counties and cities. The people's congresses, at both the national and the local levels, are made up of deputies (*Beijing Review,* May 18, 1979, pp. 18-23). At the grass-roots level of the communes, towns, and municipal districts, deputies are elected through secret ballot. All citizens eighteen years of age or over are eligible to vote. All citizens (regardless of sex, race, religion, educational level, or period of residence) who have reached the age of eighteen may seek election as deputy. However, a small number of people, such as criminals, who have been deprived of their political rights by law, may not stand for election. Nominations for election to the office of deputy are made by the Chinese Communist party, the other eight political parties, people's organizations (such as neighborhood committees), or any elector or deputy (provided the nomination is seconded by at least three others). The list of candidates is generated after repeated discussions among the various groups. In the past the number of candidates that stood for election was equal to the number of deputies to be elected. In 1979 this practice was changed so that the number of candidates standing for election would exceed the actual number of deputies to be elected. In direct elections the number of candidates standing for election should exceed the actual number of deputies to be elected by 50-100 percent (*China Reconstructs,* February 1980).

The local people's congress at the grass-roots level elects the deputies to the people's congress at the next-higher level, which in turn elects the deputies to the people's congress at the next-higher level. The method of direct election of deputies is practiced all the way up to the county level (*Beijing Review,* June 29, 1979, p. 9).

Deputies elected to the National People's Congress serve a term of five years. There are 3,497 deputies to the Fifth National People's Congress. Of these, 10.9 percent are from minority nationalities, and 21.2 percent are women. The deputies come from diverse occupational and social backgrounds. A breakdown of the occupational or social backgrounds of the 3,497 deputies is as follows: 26.7 percent are workers; 20.6 percent are peasants; 15 percent are intellectuals; 14.4 percent are People's Liberation Army personnel; 13.4 percent are revolutionary cadres; 8.9 percent are patriotic personages; and 1 percent are returned overseas Chinese (*Beijing Review,* May 18, 1979, p. 19).

The functions and powers of the NPC are contained in Articles 22, 23, 28, and 36 of the 1978 Chinese Constitution. These include the authorities to amend the Constitution; enact laws; supervise the enforcement of the Constitution and other enacted legislations; confirm the appointment of the premier of the state Council on the recommendation of the Central Committee of the Chinese Communist party; confirm the appointment and removal of other members of the State Council on the recommendation of the premier of the

State Council; elect and dismiss the president of the Supreme People's Court and the chief procurator of the Supreme People's Procuratorate; examine and approve the national economic plan, the state budget, and accounts; confirm administrative divisions under the State Council; decide on questions of war and peace; and exercise other functions and powers as the National People's Congress sees fit.

The NPC meets annually. The Standing Committee of the NPC is its permanent organ, which undertakes the functions of the NPC when it is not in session. The Standing Committee has a membership of 175 delegates. The chairman of the Standing Committee of the Fifth National People's Congress is Ye Jianying. The Standing Committee has several functions:

1. Conduct the election of deputies to the NPC.
2. Convene the sessions of the NPC.
3. Interpret the Constitution and laws, and enact decress.
4. Supervise the work of the State Council, the Supreme People's Court, and the Supreme People's Procuratorate.
5. Amend and override inappropriate decisions made by the local people's congresses at the levels of the provinces, autonomous regions, and municipalities directly under the central government.
6. When the NPC is not in session, decide on the appointment and dismissal of members of the State Council on the recommendation of the premier of the State Council.
7. Appoint and dismiss vice-presidents of the Supreme People's Court and deputy chief procurators of the Supreme People's Procuratorate.
8. Appoint and dismiss plenipotentiary representatives in foreign countries.
9. Ratify and abrogate treaties with foreign nations.
10. Institute and confer state titles of honor.
11. Grant executive pardons.
12. When the NPC is not in session, proclaim a state of war in the event that the country is attacked.
13. Exercise other functions and powers vested in it by the NPC.

The State Council is the executive branch of the NPC. The State Council is responsible and reports to the NPC or to the Standing Committee when the NPC is not in session. The membership of the State Council comprises the premier, the vice-premiers, the ministers, and the ministers in charge of the various commissions under the State Council.

Below the national level, the local people's congresses at the various levels are the local organs of state power. The local people's congresses are empowered to engage in the following activities:

1. Elect and recall deputies to the people's congresses at the corresponding levels.

2. Supervise the enforcement of the Constitution and other enacted legislations and decrees.
3. Draft local economic- and cultural-development plans.
4. Examine and approve local economic plans, budgets, and accounts.
5. At the county level and above, the deputies have the authority to elect and dismiss the presidents of the people's courts and the chief procurators of the people's procuratorates at the corresponding levels.

For the local people's congresses at and above the county level, there are corresponding standing committees. Since 1979 local revolutionary committees (the provisional institutions set up during the Cultural Revolution) have been abolished in most places and have been replaced by the local people's government. The leading members of the people's government are the governor and deputy governor (at the provincial level); chairman and vice-chairman (for the autonomous regions); mayor and deputy mayor (at the city level); heads and deputy heads (at the county level); and directors and deputy directors (at the commune level) (*Beijing Review,* July 13, 1979, p. 10). The local people's congresses and their respective standing committees are the local organs of state power, and the local people's governments are the administrative organs at the corresponding levels. Local people's governments are responsible and report to the local people's congress at the corresponding level.

Besides the local people's congresses at the various levels, the cities are organized into neighborhood committees. In 1954 regulations were promulgated regarding the establishment and functioning of urban neighborhood agencies and committees. In early 1980 the Standing Committee of the NPC reemphasized the importance of adhering to such regulations. Figure 5-2 presents the hierarchical levels in the organization of Beijing Municipality. The hierarchical levels and structure of the neighborhood committees in other cities are similar, although the number of districts and the size of the neighborhood agencies may vary.

Beijing Municipality is divided into ten districts (*Beijing Review,* November 3, 1980, pp. 19–25). Each district is made up of an average of three to five neighborhood agencies. Altogether there are eighty-five neighborhood agencies in Beijing Municipality, each with an average of more than 50,000 residents. Since it is difficult to oversee the activities of 50,000 residents, neighborhood committees are established to help the neighborhood agencies perform their duties. The neighborhood committee is an organ of political power but operates under the leadership of a neighborhood agency. The members of the neighborhood committee are elected from and by the residents of each neighborhood group. A member of the neighborhood committee serves a term of one year. Each neighborhood committee is headed by a chairperson and one

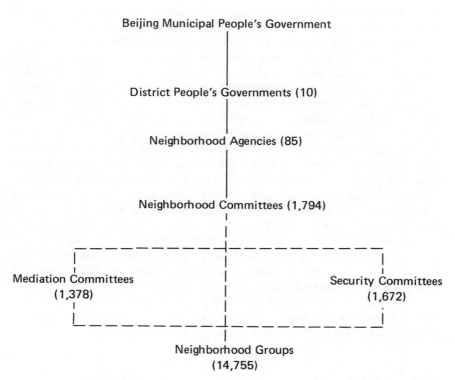

Beijing Municipal People's Government

District People's Governments (10)

Neighborhood Agencies (85)

Neighborhood Committees (1,794)

Mediation Committees   Security Committees
(1,378)   (1,672)

Neighborhood Groups
(14,755)

Source: *Beijing Review,* November 3, 1980, p. 19.

Figure 5-2. Organization of Beijing Municipality, Including Adjacent Suburbs

to four assistants, chosen by the members of the neighborhood committee. The committees perform a variety of functions:

1. They run public-welfare programs, such as neighborhood health clinics.
2. They encourage residents to adhere to government legislation.
3. They help solve domestic problems.
4. They gather local residents' opinions and demands and relay these to government agencies.
5. They assist in the mediation of conflicts.

In addition to the neighborhood committee, there are two others: the security committee and the mediation committee. These operate under the leadership of the neighborhood committee and receive guidance from the public-security organs and the people's courts. The security committee assists in the recovery of lost or stolen property, explains newly enacted legislations to neighborhood residents, and helps juvenile delinquents to reform. The mediation committee helps resolve conflicts between and among families, or within a particular family.

Party branches or party committees are set up at all enterprises, people's communes, offices, schools, detachments of the People's Liberation Army, and neighborhood committees. (In this book, unless otherwise stated, *party* refers to the Chinese Communist party, which is the leading party in the country.) At the enterprise level, there is a party committee that has as its primary function ensuring that state targets are understood and met by the respective production units. The party committee at the enterprise level also provides political and ideological leadership to the members of the enterprise. The director of the factory is under the leadership of the party committee. In late 1980 the government called on the party committee to relieve itself of administration of production functions at the enterprise. The role of the party committee will be further discussed in chapter 9. On the basis of the foregoing analysis, it can be seen that the country has an elaborate political mechanism that permeates all levels of society and affects practically all aspects of its functioning.

Discussion of the Chinese political system often centers solely on the Chinese Communist party. In fact, however, there are eight other political parties in China. These are discussed in the following section.

Political Parties in China

The Chinese Communist party (CCP) is the leading political party in the country. The National Congress, the highest leading organ in the party, is convened once every five years. The chairman of the Central Committee is the head of the armed forces in China. When the Congress is not in session, the Central Committee serves as the highest authority in the party. Below the national level, the party congresses at the various levels are the leading political organs. Party congresses are convened by the party committees at the various levels. Local party congresses at the county level and up convene once every three years. Party branches and party committees are set up in factories, schools, neighborhoods, and detachments of the People's Liberation Army.

All citizens may apply for membership in the CCP provided they fulfill the following criteria:

1.   They are at least eighteen years old.
2.   They conscientiously study Marxism–Leninism–Mao Zedong Thought.
3.   They serve the people wholeheartedly.

4. They unite with all elements, both inside and outside the party, that can be united.
5. They go among the masses and maintain close ties with them.
6. They engage in criticism and self-criticism.
7. They uphold unity in the party.
8. They are honest and truthful, abide by state laws and party discipline, and do not divulge state or party secrets.
9. They set a good example by exerting their best efforts to fulfill the tasks assigned by the party.

A person who meets these criteria may apply for membership. He or she must be recommended by two full party members. The applicant's qualifications will be reviewed and discussed at a general meeting of the party branch. After approval by the next-higher level of party committee, the person is admitted as a probationary member for one year. If his or her conduct and behavior during the probationary period is judged satisfactory, the person is then promoted to full-fledged membership (*Eleventh National People's Congress* 1977, pp. 128-130). In China there are only 35 million Communist party members.

Teenagers under the age of eighteen may become members of the Communist Youth League. The Communist Youth League, established some sixty years ago, has a present membership totalling 48 million (*Beijing Review*, March 3, 1980, p.3). It is generally regarded as a breeding ground for future CCP members. Children between the ages of nine and fifteen may join the Chinese Young Pioneers Association. At the school level, the organization is referred to as a brigade; at the classroom level, it is referred to as a detachment (*Beijing Review*, September 8, 1978). Members of the Chinese Young Pioneers Association are educated in communist ideals.

Besides the Chinese Communist party, there are eight other political parties (*Beijing Review*, December 14, 1979, pp. 19-27; *China Reconstructs*, February 1980, pp. 2-9). A brief description of each of these parties follows.

1. The Revolutionary Committee of the Kuomintang was founded in Hong Kong on January 1, 1948. Its original membership was derived from a faction of the Kuomintang party that disagreed with the policies pursued by the then leading members of the Kuomintang party.
2. The China Democratic League is made up of intellectuals who worked in the fields of culture and education. The forerunner of the China Democratic League was the League of Chinese Democratic Parties and Organizations, which was established in 1941. In 1944 this was reorganized into the Democratic League.
3. The China Democratic National Construction Association was established in 1945. Its original membership consisted of capitalists and entrepreneurs.

4. The China Association for Promoting Democracy was founded in 1945. Its original membership consisted of intellectuals from the educational and cultural circles in Shanghai.
5. The China Peasants' and Workers' Democratic Party was established in 1947. Its membership consisted of intellectuals working in medicine and public health.
6. The China Zhi Gong Dang, reorganized in 1947, derived its membership from returned overseas Chinese.
7. The Jiu San Society was formerly known as the Society for Science and Democracy. Its members are generally employed in the fields of culture and education.
8. The Taiwan Democratic Self-Government League was established in Hong Kong in 1947. Its original members were from Taiwan.

On the eve of the establishment of the People's Republic of China, these eight political powers formed a united front under the leadership of the Chinese Communist party. In 1949 these parties drew up the Common Program, wherein they agreed to serve socialism and accept the leadership of the Chinese Communist party. In 1950 Mao Zedong advanced the policy of "long-term coexistence and mutual supervision" with these political parties. This principle was enforced primarily through the consultative mechanism among the parties. From 1949 to the mid-1960s, the Chinese Communist party met regularly with these political parties to discuss major issues. The eight political parties also participated in politics. Between 1966 and 1976 their activities were suspended. After 1977 they resumed their activities. In mid-October 1979 each of these political parties convened its own national congress to revise its party constitution and elect leading members. At the end of 1979, the Central Committee of the Chinese Communist party resumed its former practice of holding consultations with leaders of the other political parties on major political issues once every two months. In December 1980 Hu Yaobang, then general secretary of the Central Committee of the Chinese Communist party, reiterated in a public statement that all political parties in China should be allowed to operate independently and should be treated on a equal footing with the country's leading party. Approximately 6.9 percent of the 3,497 deputies to the Fifth National People's Congress come from these eight political parties. In 1980 the other political parties recruited a total of 5,253 members. This was the first time since 1957 that the other political parties were able to register such considerable increases in membership (*Beijing Review,* May 25, 1981, p.6).

Guiding Principles of the Chinese Communist Party

At the First Session of the Fifth National People's Congress, held on March 5, 1978, a new Chinese Constitution was adopted. This is commonly referred to as the 1978 Chinese Constitution. Since its establishment in 1949, the PRC has revised its Constitution three times. The first two revisions were made in 1954 and 1975. The latest revision was made to reflect the new mission for the post-1976 era: that of socialist modernization of the country in industry, agriculture, science and technology, and military defense—commonly referred to as the Four Modernizations program. The 1978 amendment was designed to facilitate the early attainment of this goal.

The philosophy guiding the administration of China, as prescribed in the 1978 Constitution, is primarily threefold: proletarian dictatorship, democratic centralism, and socialist democracy. These three principles are spelled out in Articles 1, 3, and 17 of the 1978 Constitution. Each is discussed in this section.

Proletarian Dictatorship

Article 1 of the Constitution states: "The People's Republic of China is a socialist state of the dictatorship of the proletariat led by the working class and based on the alliance of workers and peasants." *Dictatorship of the proletariat* means that the working class will exercise leadership over the state through the Chinese Communist party (CCP) (*Beijing Review,* March 1, 1979, p. 9). Since 80 percent of China's people still depend on agriculture as their principal means of livelihood, it is imperative that the working class join forces with the peasants. This is what is meant by "the alliance of workers and peasants." The functions and aims of the dictatorship are primarily twofold: (1) to suppress those elements within the country that resist socialism, and (2) to protect China from external aggression.

Democratic Centralism

Article 3 of the Constitution states: "The National People's Congress, the local people's congresses at various levels and all other organs of state practise democratic centralism." Though encouraging democracy, China must ensure unity and enforce discipline among its 1 billion people. This dual policy of allowing democracy on the one hand, and centralizing authority, on the other, is referred to as the principle of *democratic centralism.* At the Eleventh National Congress of the CCP, held in 1977, the party prescribed the authority relationships that should prevail among the various elements of society: "the individual is subordinate to the organization; the minority is subordinate to the majority; the lower level is subordinate to the higher level; and the entire Party is subordinate to the Central Committee" (*Eleventh National Congress,* 1977, p. 104).

Socialist Democracy

Article 17 stipulates: "The State adheres to the principle of socialist democracy, and ensures the people the right to participate in the management of state affairs and of all economic and cultural undertakings, and the right to supervise the organs of state and their personnel." All citizens other than those who have committed crimes against the state (such as murder, rape, other serious criminal offenses, or counterrevolutionary activities) are guaranteed certain fundamental rights. These rights are stipulated in the 1978 Constitution and can be summarized as follows:

1. The right to participate in state administration. All citizens eighteen or over are eligible to vote and may seek election as deputies to the local people's congresses, as discussed in the previous section. Citizens have the right to supervise the deputies they have elected and to file complaints against any individual who holds public office (Articles 44 and 55).

2. Citizens are entitled to "freedom of speech, the press, correspondence, assembly, association, procession, demonstration, and the freedom to strike, and have the right to 'speak out freely, air their views fully, hold great debates and write big-character posters' " (Article 45). The "right to speak out freely, air their views fully, hold great debates, and write big-character posters" (abbreviated as *si da* in Chinese) refers to the practice of criticizing others by writing big-character posters. This practice reached its height during the Cultural Revolution. Although the original intention of *si da* was to expose corrupt practices, big-character posters were sometimes abused as a way of making false allegations against others anonymously. In addition, the party believed that state secrets were sometimes divulged through such channels. At the Fifth Plenary Session of the Eleventh Central Committee of the CCP, held in late February 1980, the *si da* clause was deleted from Article 45. Henceforth, big-character posters could be put up only in the organization to which the author belongs or on a wall in Yuetan (Moon Altar) Park. This is the site of the new Democracy Wall. Authors of big-character posters on this new Democracy Wall must abide by the provisional stipulations that went into effect on December 8, 1979 (*Beijing Review,* December 14, 1979, p. 6). Under these stipulations, the authors must register their names, pseudonyms, addresses, and organizations to which they belong with the registration center at the site. The government states that although the contents of the posters will not be examined, the authors are liable for the political and legal implications of the posters. Specifically, authors are prohibited from disclosing state secrets, falsifying charges, or libeling others through the content of the posters. Those who violate these stipulations or stir up disturbances at the site will be punished by law. The government justified its actions by explaining that although *si da* does provide a means for airing opinions, it is not the only means. The government argues that deleting *si da* from the Constitution does not mean eliminating democracy because citizens

can continue to voice their opinions through other channels, such as speaking to the local people's congresses at the various levels; writing to the Central Committee of the CCP and to party newspapers; and talking to the representatives at the special offices set up at the various levels of the party or to government organizations whose primary function is to address citizens' complaints and concerns. Moreover, *si da* has often been abused in the past to make false allegations against other individuals anonymously and to disclose state secrets (*Beijing Review,* April 28, 1980, p. 4). The government spokesman points out that this practice is in line with international law because "no country in the world allows a person to make false charges and libel others" (*Beijing Review,* December 14, 1979, p.7). The former U.S. ambassador to China, Leonard Woodcock, was of the opinion that the deletion of the *si da* clause from the Constitution has been played up by Western journalists as a "step backwards for democracy in China." In his view, this move "has in no way impeded the continued loosening within their own system" (*Pacific Basin Quarterly,* December, 1979, pp. 5–6).

In addition to the freedoms referred to in Article 45, citizens have the right to observe a religion or to "propagate atheism" (Article 46).

3. Citizens have the right to work and take adequate rest. In old age or in the event of sickness and disability, they are entitled to assistance from the state (Articles 48–50). These benefits are discussed in chapter 8.

4. "Citizens have the right to education" and the "freedom to carry on scientific research" (Articles 51 and 52).

5. Women should be accorded equal treatment with men in all aspects of "political, economic, cultural, social and family life. Men and women enjoy equal pay for equal work" (Article 53).

The State has established the following mechanisms to guarantee and protect these fundamental rights to the citizens:

1. Establish local people's congresses and people's organizations (such as neighborhood agencies), as discussed previously.
2. Set up special offices at different levels of the party and government administration to address complaints citizens may have about particular individuals who hold public office. Citizens could also write directly to the Central Committee of the CCP. Alternatively, the citizen may choose to air his or her view through *Renmin Ribao* (*People's Daily*) or other party newspapers.
3. Promote the system of "democratic management" at factories, communes, government organizations, and detachments of the People's Liberation Army. At the enterprise level, workers participate in management primarily through the Congress of Workers and Staff.

The three principles of espousing proletarian dictatorship, democratic centralism, and socialist democracy were further expounded in a document entitled

"Guiding Principles for Inner-Party Political Life," which was adopted at the Fifth Plenary Session of the Eleventh Central Committee of the CCP, held in 1980 (*Beijing Review,* April 7, 1980, pp. 11-19). The twelve principles contained in the document are briefly summarized as follows:

First, adhere to the party's political and ideological lines. The Party's political line for the last quarter of the twentieth century calls for working toward the goals of the Four Modernizations. At the Third Plenary Session of the Eleventh Central Committee of the Chinese Communists Party, the country's leaders declared that the primary mission for the party, and for the country as a whole, for the last quarter of the twentieth century is no longer that of class struggle, but rather socialist modernization. This shift in focus has led to confusion in the minds of some people. Since 1949 many people have assumed that under socialism political work is synonymous with class struggle. Consequently, some fear that shifting the focus from class struggle to socialist modernization may lead to an abandonment of socialism. To correct this line of thinking, China's leaders now emphasize that politics is not confined to class struggle and that the pursuit of economic objectives does not necessarily lead to an abandonment of socialism. Rather, the establishment of a sound economic base is viewed as a prerequisite to the eventual attainment of full communism.

According to Marxist theory, classes exist only in a certain phase in the historical development of production. Since 1949 the exploiting class has largely been transformed through education into workers who earn their means of livelihood primarily through their own labor. In late 1979 the country estimated that there were only 800 former capitalists remaining in the country who earned more than 300 yuan a month (*Beijing Review,* November 16, 1979, p. 13). The government argued that based on its success in transforming former capitalists into laborers, the country should divert its attention to other important aspects of socialism. According to Marx, Engels, and Lenin, increasing productivity is also central to the pursuit of socialism. As Marx and Engels wrote in the *Communist Manifesto,* after the working class has seized political power from the capitalists and nationalized the basic means of production, it should seek to develop the productive forces as quickly as possible. In a speech delivered at an All-Russian Conference of Political Education Workers of Guberni and Uyezd Education Departments, on November 3, 1920, Lenin stated that once political power has been consolidated in the hands of the proletariat, the main content of politics should "shift . . . to economic policy." Chinese Premier Zhao Ziyang explained the important role of modernization and economic work by arguing that as long as the two principal tenets of socialism (public ownership of the means of production, and distribution of income according to the principle of "to each according to his work") are adhered to, China "should adopt whatever system, structure, policy and method that are most effective in promoting the development of the productive forces and in bringing the superiority of the socialist system into play" (*Beijing Review,* November 23, 1979, p. 3).

The party's ideological line calls for adherence to four basic principles: (1) following the socialist road, (2) practicing proletarian dictatorship, (3) accepting the leadership of the CCP, and (4) following Marxism–Leninism–Mao Zedong Thought (*Beijing Review*, March 30, 1981, p.7). In addition to the four basic principles, Hu Yaobang, the former general secretary of the party Central Committee who took over as chairman of the party in June 1981, has called on the party to focus its attention on the following four points: (1) improve socialist democracy and the legal system; (2) maintain close ties with the masses; (3) improve the political life of the party by adhering to the twelve "Guiding Principles for Inner-Party Political Life"; and (4) offer guidance and nurture the country's youth, the future citizens of China (*Beijing Review*, February 23, 1981, p. 9).

Though emphasizing the need to build the base of "material civilization," the party has also called on the country to pursue the goal of "building socialist spiritual civilization." This phrase was coined by Vice-Chairman Ye Jianying in his speech delivered at the thirtieth anniversary of the founding of the People's Republic of China in 1979. The country's leaders emphasize that although it is important to build a strong material base for economic development and progress, success in this area does not necessarily result in a spiritual civilization, which is also fundamental to human existence (*Beijing Review*, March 9, 1981, pp. 18–20). China's leaders do not perceive the pursuit of the dual goals of material and spiritual civilizations as contradictory or mutually exclusive. In fact, they emphasize that the pursuit of a "socialist spiritual civilization" complements and will facilitate the early attainment of the goal of material civilization—the Four Modernizations. Building a spiritual civilization involves the communist ideal of subordinating one's self-interest to that of the state and the common good. This spirit is more conducive to economic progress and development since the people will identify more closely with state goals and thus will work wholeheartedly toward the attainment of the Four Modernizations. The key to building a spiritual civilization depends on ideological and political work. In early 1981 the Propaganda Department of the Central Committee, in conjunction with three ministries under the State Council issued a decree calling on all the people in the country to support the movement of the "Five Stresses and the Four Points of Beauty." The *Five Stresses* call on the people to pay attention to socialist decorum, manners, hygiene, discipline, and morals. The Ministry of Education announced that beginning in the fall of 1981, children at all primary schools must take a course in ideology and socialist decorum. The *Four Points of Beauty* call for beautification of the mind, language, behavior, and the environment. Beautification of the mind means developing a strong moral character and upholding socialism and the party's leadership. Beautification of behavior means engaging in productive activities and assisting others. Beautification of the environment refers to personal hygiene and protection of the physical environment (*Beijing Review*, April 13, 1981, p. 5).

In order to facilitate the early attainment of socialist modernization, it is imperative that the party strengthen its leadership to unite and goad the people toward the goals of the Four Modernizations. To prevent the development of another personality cult around any single individual, the party must uphold the principle of collective leadership. To this end, the party has specifically prohibited the following activities: the naming of places, enterprises, and streets after leading party members; the celebration of the birthdays of party members; the construction of memorial halls for living persons; and the staging of elaborate welcome and send-off ceremonies for leaders on official business, except for diplomatic reasons (*Beijing Review,* April 7, 1980, pp. 13-14). Funeral services for leading cadres should be kept simple and economical. In addition, the publication of biographies or collective writings should be treated cautiously (*Beijing Review,* August 25, 1980, p. 3). Though downplaying the significance of any single individual, the party emphasizes the importance of adhering to the principle of collective leadership at all levels, from the Central Committee down to the grass-roots level. The principle of collective leadership essentially involves adoption of the following practices (*Beijing Review,* April 14, 1980; November 3, 1980):

1. All major issues should be decided through the process of collective decision making and not by any particular individual.

2. Democratic centralism should be practiced, whereby the minority interest is subordinate to that of the majority.

3. The significance of and contribution by any single individual should not be overestimated, as was discussed in chapter 2. Portraits of leading party members should not be displayed in excess. This was the reason given for the removal of most portraits of Mao from public places. The portraits of Marx, Engels, Lenin, and Stalin were also removed from Tien An Men Square in Beijing on August 21, 1980. A spokesman explained that these portraits "will be put up only when necessary" (*Beijing Review,* September 1, 1980, p. 6).

4. An individual should not hold too many posts concurrently. At the Third Session of the Fifth National People's Congress held in August–September 1980, it was decided that there should be a division of work between the party and the government, for two primary reasons: (1) to prevent overcentralization of power in the hands of a few, a practice that tends to hinder the implementation of socialist democracy: If the party supersedes the government, then the local people's governments do not have the autonomy to make decisions. (2) To improve the quality of work: A person who holds both party and government positions concurrently has to assume too much responsibility. Consequently, the quality of his or her work may be affected. Through division of work between party and government, the quality of work in both arenas can be improved. This division of work is designed not to weaken the party, but to strengthen it so that party members can concentrate on political and ideological work. The important role of ideology in China's current dirve to attain the goals of the Four Modernizations was discussed in chapter 2.

In line with this decision to divide work between the party and the government, the party decided that henceforth, leading members of the party Central Committee should not concurrently hold posts in the government, and that the first secretaries of party committees at various levels should not concurrently hold posts as mayors or as heads of provincial, municipal, or county people's governments (*Beijing Review,* January 12, 1981). In line with this policy, Deng Xiaoping resigned as vice-premier while continuing to serve as vice-chairman of the CCP.

5. The policy of lifelong tenure for leading cadres should be abandoned. Lifelong tenure can breed complacency among some cadres. In addition, the party needs new blood. Consequently, cadres in the prime of their lives should be promoted to leading positions whenever possible. In late 1980 Song Renqiong, Director of the Organization Department of the party Central Committee, announced the party's decision to introduce fundamental changes in the cadre system. Changes include the institution of examinations to select cadres; the establishment of provisions for their retirement; and the implementation of systems for supervising, rewarding, punishing, removing, rotating, and transferring cadres. This point, coupled with the previous one, serves to explain in part some of the recent changes in the membership of the State Council.

6. Though unity is emphasized, all party members should be allowed to disagree and to explain the reasons for their disagreement. In this way more alternative solutions to a problem can be presented and discussed. This should improve the quality of the solutions to a problem.

7. Though the need to uphold the principle of collective decision making is emphasized, collective leadership does not imply an abandonment of personal responsibility. The party advocates the implementation of a system of division of labor, whereby each person is responsible and held accountable for his or her post. In practice this means that decisions on all major issues should be reached through the process of collective decision making in the party committee. After a decision has been made, an individual or a number of individuals will be assigned to carry out specific activities designed to implement the decision. These persons will be held responsible for its orderly implementation: "Collective responsibility must not be interpreted as nobody's responsibility" (*Beijing Review,* February 23, 1979, pp. 23–24).

Party discipline must be observed. Besides adhering to the party's political and ideological lines, a party member must not divulge state or party secrets. Party members should be exemplary in their observance of legislation, communist morality, and discipline in work. Of course, this ideal may not be met in practice. This accounts for the recent reforms in the political structure and the calls for the party to combat bureaucracy and feudalistic ideas. These will be discussed subsequently.

Party members are expected to promote unity and prevent the formation of cliques and factions within the party. All party members must be truthful and honest in thoughts, words, and deeds. Party members should be tolerant of dissenting viewpoints. The principle of the "three not's" should be upheld. The "three not's" mean (1) not seizing on and magnifying another person's shortcoming; (2) not attaching labels (such as "bourgeois" or "revisionist") to other people; and (3) not persecuting or falsifying charges against another person.

Party members are expected to engage in criticism and self-criticism. At the same time, all party members should be allowed to voice their discontentment with any senior party official. They should promote democracy through the process of election by secret ballot. The revolutionary committees set up between 1966 and 1976 as interim organs of state power have largely been replaced by the local people's governments. The representatives to the revolutionary committees were not democratically elected. The 1978 Constitution stipulates that the people's congresses at the various levels should be elected by the people. With the implementation of the new electoral law on January 1, 1980, direct elections are now held at the grass-roots level up to the county level. The electoral law provides for the election of deputies and also for the supervision, recall, and replacement of deputies.

The party should seek to overcome unhealthy tendencies such as "factionalism, anarchism, extreme individualism, bureaucracy and privilege-seeking." The latter two have been the subject of much discussion in the Chinese press since 1980.

Bureaucracy is generally regarded as a "manifestation of the poisonous vestiges of feudalism" (*Beijing Review,* June 30, 1980). Bureaucracy exhibits itself in one of several forms: lifetime tenure, development of a personality cult around a single individual, privilege seeking, or imposing one's wishes on the masses. In order to eliminate such unhealthy tendencies, the party has called on its members to adhere to the following guidelines:

1. Engage in self-criticism to evaluate one's shortcomings.
2. Do not seek special privileges for oneself or for members of one's family. Privileges include securing promotion in the organization and gaining permission to study abroad.
3. Leading cadres are not above the law.
4. Uphold the principle of collective leadership.
5. Downplay the significance and contribution of any single individual.
5. Implement a system for recruitment, supervision, rotation, retirement, and removal of leading cadres.

As a result of public discussion, cases in which leading cadres have abused the powers of their position have been exposed. For example, the minister of commerce, Wang Lei, often dined lavishly at the Feng Ze Yuan Restaurant in Beijing, but paid only the price of ordinary meals. A chef at the restaurant brought this to the Central Committee's attention. After investigation, the

Central Committee issued a circular praising the chef for bringing the case to the party's attention. Minister Wang admitted his indiscretion and wrote a letter to the restaurant apologizing for his midsconduct; he also paid back the money he owed for his meals (*Beijing Review,* November 3, 1980).

In the past, when leading cadres went on inspection tours of the country, the community would often spend a lot of money on banquets and sight-seeing tours to entertain the visiting dignitary. In mid-1980 the party issued a statement that this practice should be stopped. The party stated that when cadres from the Standing Committee of the National People's Congress go on inspection tours of the country, they should not be treated with so much fanfare. Instead, the community need only "send someone to show them around and give them a briefing" (*Beijing Review,* August 11, 1980, p. 6).

Party members should adopt a correct attitude toward those who have committed mistakes. The contributions and mistakes of individuals should be assessed, and family members or relatives of a convicted person must not be implicated.

Cadres must maintain close ties with the masses and seek their opinions. The party stated that although the leading cadres are responsible for making important decisions about various aspects of organizational functioning, such decisions should take into consideration the suggestions and opinions of the workers and the people. If the leading cadres were to isolate themselves and make decisions based only on their own subjective judgments, "they cannot produce anything good" (*Beijing Review,* February 23, 1979, p. 23). The local people's congresses at the various levels of the government, and the Congress of Workers and Staff at the enterprise level provide forums for people to provide input into important decisions.

Cadres must be both red and expert—politically sound and technically competent. The party has espoused this principle since the establishment of the PRC. However, there have been variations in its application. During periods of ideological upheaval such as the Great Leap Forward and the Cultural Revolution, redness was emphasized to the neglect of expertness. Those who engaged in political demagogy were often promoted to senior positions in organizations even if they did not possess the technical competence to organize and administer. The party now stresses the importance of recruiting cadres who possess the necessary technical expertise. In 1980 Song Renqiong, director of the Organization Committee of the Party Central Committee announced the party's decision that henceforth cadres will be selected from among those who fulfill the following three criteria: (1) committed to the socialist cause; (2) technically and professionally competent; and (3) in the prime of life. Song stated that organizations should, when possible, recruit administrative cadres (those who do not engage in productive labor) from among university graduates (*Beijing Review,* August 11, 1980).

To advance the technical skills of existing cadres, since 1979 China has ordered that all cadres in the industrial and agricultural sectors be trained, in rotation, over the next five years. In 1979, for instance, some 460,000 cadres from enterprises and industrial organizations enrolled in programs in business administration and technology. At the end of the program, the cadres must pass an examination testing their technical competence. Those who fail the exam have to repeat the program. These training programs range from two weeks to four months in duration and are generally taught by professors from local universities and colleges (*Beijing Review,* February 25, 1980).

From the foregoing analysis of changes in the political system since 1979 and of the principles governing the behavior of party members, it can be seen that the political infrastructure of China in the last quarter of the twentieth century is designed to facilitate the attainment of the goals of socialist modernization.

6 China's Legal System

Although China has shared with most other Southeast Asian countries a traditional distaste for law and legal concepts, the Chinese realize that law constitutes an important part of any modern society. Since the establishment of the PRC in 1949, the government has enacted laws governing various aspects of societal functioning. In January 1957 Mao Zedong addressed the need to legislate and the importance of abiding by the law. "Laws form part of the superstructure. . . . They are designed to . . . protect the interests of the working people, the socialist economic base and the productive forces." Mao noted that complying "with the law does not mean being bound hand and foot," for only by acting in accordance with the law can the social order be preserved (*Selected Works,* vol. 5, 1977, p. 379). However, between 1966 and 1976 many laws and decrees were suspended because the role of law in society was misrepresented. In that period law was interpreted as an instrument of class struggle. Consequently, there was no separation of powers between the state and the judicial system, and the former superseded the latter.

In 1977, when China embarked on the goal of socialist modernization, the government realized the deficiencies inherent in the existing legal system and was determined to rectify the situation. In order to attain the goals of the Four Modernizations, China needs a relatively long period of political peace and stability, both at home and abroad, so that efforts can be concentrated on economic construction. In order to preserve peace and order within society, the legal system must be strengthened. Henceforth, the government decided, all organs of the state would have to be subject to the law. This is designed to prevent individuals from putting themselves above the law, as happened during the Cultural Revolution. In addition, enacting a series of laws governing all aspects of society would safeguard China's economic base. Any act that undermines the country's economy and endangers the national interest—such as disruption of state planning, misappropriation of state funds, or embezzlement—is considered a criminal offense and is punishable by law (*China Reconstructs,* December 1979, p. 2). Moreover, since China has decided to expand its foreign-trade activities and engage in various forms of economic cooperation with foreign countries, including the establishment of joint-venture concerns within China, it is imperative that China enact a series of laws that will facilitate the establishment of such relationships and govern the conduct of foreign investment.

Seven new laws were promulgated in 1979 alone and went into effect on January 1, 1980:

1. the Organic Law of the local people's congresses and the local people's governments
2. the Electoral Law for the National People's Congress and the local people's congresses
3. the Criminal Law
4. the Law of Criminal Procedure
5. the Organic Law of the people's courts
6. the Organic Law of the people's procuratorates
7. the Law on Joint Ventures with Chinese and Foreign Investment

Laws governing other aspects of societal functioning and the conduct of foreign investment, such as the Nationality Law, the Marriage Law, the Income Tax Law for Joint Ventures, the Individual Income Tax Law, Regulations on Labor Management in Joint Ventures, and so on, were promulgated in 1980. Laws pertaining to contractual relations and other aspects of corporate functioning are currently being drafted. The government decreed that all laws enacted since the establishment of the PRC will remain in force as long as they do not contravene the 1978 Constitution and the legislation promulgated after 1977.

This chapter examines several aspects of the legal system as they affect Chinese industrial society. Specifically, this involves a brief overview of (1) the legislation governing various aspects of societal functioning; (2) the judicial system and organs in China, including an examination of the role of lawyers in China; and (3) the methods used to reform criminals.

Legislation Governing Various Aspects of Societal Functioning

In this section each of the aforementioned seven laws, as well as other laws governing various aspects of Chinese industrial society, is discussed briefly.

Organic Law of the Local People's Congresses and the Local People's Governments; Electoral Law

The 1978 Constitution guarantees that all citizens have the right to take part in government administration by standing in for election as deputies to the respective local people's congresses, and by supervising the work of the deputies whom they have elected to office. This is designed to implement the principle of socialist democracy. The Organic Law of the local people's congresses and the local people's governments, and the Electoral Law, stipulate the relationships between the various levels of the local people's congresses, and between the local people's congresses and the local people's governments; who may stand for election; and how elections should be conducted at the various levels of government.

By the end of 1980 elections had been held in 1,319 of the 2,757 units at the county level. In most places voter turnout for the elections exceeded 90 percent (*Beijing Review*, February 9, 1981).

Criminal Law; Law of Criminal Procedure; Organic Law of the People's Courts; Organic Law of the People's Procuratorates

The 1978 Constitution guaranteed citizens certain rights, as discussed in the previous chapter. Article 9 of the Constitution further stipulates: "The State protects the right of citizens to own lawfully earned income, savings, houses and other means of livelihood." The Criminal Law is designed to protect these rights of the citizens. In addition, the Criminal Law seeks to protect the state from counterrevolutionary and other criminal activities. The law contains 192 articles, spelled out in thirteen chapters (*Beijing Review*, July 13, 1979). The highlights of the Criminal Law are contained in appendix L.

Article 10 of the Criminal Law defines an offense as

> any act which endangers state sovereignty or territorial integrity; jeopardizes the dictatorship of the proletariat; sabotages the socialist revolution or socialist construction; disrupts public order; encroaches upon property owned by the whole people or that owned collectively by the working people; encroaches upon the legitimate private property of a citizen or on a citizen's right of person, democratic rights or other rights; or any other act which endangers society and is punishable by law; but no act which is markedly trivial and results in insignificant harm shall be deemed an offence.

Eight categories of criminal offenses are identified: counterrevolutionary activities, violation of public security, disruption of the socialist economic system, infringement of the rights of citizens, encroachment on property, disruption of public order, offenses against marriage and the family, and malfeasance (*Beijing Review*, August 17, 1979). Counterrevolutionary offenses include all activities that undermine the socialist system and the political stability of China (*Beijing Review*, July 13, 1979, p. 11). Given the traditional Chinese respect for elders, the sanctity of family life, and the obligation to care for youth, the state considers any failure to care for the elderly, the young, or the sick; maltreatment of members of one's family; or interference with another person's freedom of marriage through violent means to be criminal offenses punishable by law.

Malfeasance refers to the abuse of power by government officials, including accepting bribes; divulging state secrets; willfully passing a wrong judgment; inflicting corporal punishment on an imprisoned person; illegally releasing a convict; and illegally opening, concealing, or destroying correspondence and other telegraphic communications (*Beijing Review*, August 17, 1979).

All offenses committed by any person (with the exception of those protected by diplomatic privileges and immunity) within Chinese territory will be
dealt with according to the Criminal Law. "Chinese territory" includes Chinese
vessels and planes. The Chinese legal system does not recognize rights of extra-
territoriality (*Beijing Review,* August 17, 1979). A person judged to be mentally
incompetent cannot be held criminally liable.

In China penalties are classified into two major categories: principal and
supplementary. *Principal penalties* include the imposition of the death sentence,
life or fixed-term imprisonment (from six months to fifteen years), public
surveillance for between six months and three years, and detention for a period
of under six months. Criminals who are subject to public surveillance are not
permitted to travel or to change their place of residence. In addition, they are
not eligible to vote or to stand for election. *Supplementary penalties* include the
imposition of fines, deprivation of political rights, confiscation of property, and
deportation in the case of foreigners (*Beijing Review,* August 17, 1979). The
death sentence can be imposed only by or with the approval of the Supreme
People's Court in cases where the criminal act results in serious harm to the state
and the people. These include cases of homocide, arson, and intentional flood-
ing. The death penalty may not be imposed on individuals under the age of
eighteen or on women found to be pregnant during the trial. In China there is a
provision for the death penalty with two years' reprieve. If the convicted person
shows sufficient repentance within the two-year period, the penalty may be
changed to life imprisonment (*Beijing Review,* November 3, 1980).

The Criminal Law is applied only where the individual(s) have actually committed a criminal offense. Violations of the law that are noncriminal in nature
are dealt with according to the civil code and other economic laws.

The Law of Criminal Procedure contains 164 articles and sets forth the
judicial procedure to be followed in the application of the Criminal Law. The
law stipulates the functions and relationships between the public-security organ,
the different levels of procuratorates, the different levels of the people's courts,
and the Supreme Court. Essentially, the public-security organ is responsible for
apprehending the violator and conducting preliminary investigations. The
people's procuratorate approves the arrest and initiates the prosecution. The
court tries the case and hands down the sentence on the convicted. According to
the Law of Criminal Procedure, trials should be open to the public, except in
cases where state secrets are likely to be disclosed, in trials of minors, and in
those involving "intimate private life."

In local people's courts, cases of the first instance are tried before a bench
consisting of a judge and jurors (known as *assessors* in China). The jurors have
the same powers as the judge. Jurors are selected from citizens aged twenty-three
and over who have the right to vote and stand for election. While performing
their duties, the assessors receive full pay from their place of employment. If
they are unemployed, the court will provide them a subsidy (*China Reconstructs,*

December 1979). The convicted has the right to appeal to the next higher level of the local people's court. In China the court of second instance is the court of last instance.

The judicial authority is exercised by the local people's courts, the special people's courts, and the Supreme People's Court. In 1980 China had over 3,100 local people's courts at the various levels. The roles, functions, and powers of the people's courts and the people's procuratorates, and their relationships to the local people's congresses, are detailed in the Organic Law of the People's Courts and the Organic Law of the People's Procuratorates. Local people's courts are established at four different levels: (1) the *basic courts,* at the level of the district or county; (2) the *intermediate courts,* at the level of the municipality or prefecture; (3) the *higher courts,* at the level of the province and autonomous regions; and (4) the *Supreme People's Court,* at the national level. The Supreme People's Court is the highest judicial organ in the country. In addition, there are special people's courts that deal with the military, rail-transport, water-transport, and forestry sectors.

There is a corresponding level of people's procuratorates at each of the four levels of local people's court. As defined in Article 1 of the Organic Law, people's procuratorates "are organs of the state supervising the administration of justice." The procuratorates are empowered to "supervise and ensure the correct enforcement of the Constitution and the law and safeguard the unity of the state legal system" (*Beijing Review,* December 28, 1979, p. 16). The people's procuratorates at the various levels are responsible and report to the local people's congresses and their standing committees at the corresponding levels. The 1978 Constitution provides that the people's procuratorate at the higher levels supervise, but not exercise leadership, over the procuratorates at the lower level (*Beijing Review,* December 28, 1979).

The public-security departments are headed by the Ministry of Public Security at the national level. At the various lower levels there are local public-security bureaus.

At all levels each court is made up of two divisions: *criminal* and *civil.* Courts at the intermediate and higher levels also have a third division, the economic section. The economic division is empowered to impose economic sanctions on those enterprises and government organizations that violate the state's economic regulations. Given the country's traditional distaste for arbitration, for the time being only major cases that cannot be resolved through mediation or the consultative mechanism between the parties concerned are referred to the economic courts. Such cases include breaches of contracts that result in heavy economic and political losses; serious cases of fraud or work of inferior quality; failure to take appropriate precautionary measures to safeguard workers' health or to dispose of industrial wastes; theft or embezzlement of workers' wages and state funds; and serious cases of neglect of duty that result in heavy loss to public property (*Beijing Review,* August 10, 1979). Each court at all levels has a president, two or more vice-presidents, one chief judge, an associate judge for each division, and other judges. The presidents of the courts at the various levels are elected by the local people's congress at the corresponding level. The other members of the court are appointed and removed by the standing committees of the congress at the corresponding level. Each court has a judicial committee whose task is to "sum up judicial experience and discuss difficult or major cases" (*China Reconstructs,* June 1980). The local people's procuratorates deal only with violations of the Criminal Law. Infractions of the law that are non-criminal in nature are handled by the discipline-inspection departments of the CCP and the various organs of the government.

In addition to the local people's courts at the various levels, all enterprises and other organizations establish their own legal departments or recruit the services of legal advisors to deal with contractual arrangements and other legal matters. Consequently, special judicial administrative organs are established for these purposes (*Beijing Review,* October 19, 1979).

In 1979 the State Council reestablished the Ministry of Justice. The ministry is responsible for supervising and training judicial cadres; handling the judicial administrative work of the local people's courts at all levels; supervising institutes of politics and law attached to the various government agencies; supervising the work of lawyers and notary publics; drafting legislation; managing judicial funds and incomes; sponsoring research on jurisprudence, including the publication of law books, journals, and periodicals; educating the masses about the law and the legal system; and handling legal matters arising in the international arena (*Beijing Review,* October 19, 1979). Given the sheer size of the country's population, the generally low educational levels of the people, and the traditional Chinese dis-taste for law and legal concepts, the task of educating the masses about the law is by no means simple. Soon after the promulgation of the laws on July 1, 1979, the government embarked on a nationwide campaign to familiarize people with the new laws. This included publication of the text of the laws, accompanied by explanations and commentaries, in all major newspapers in the country; a twenty-minute special program every other day on the Central People's Broad-casting Station; other publications; and public meetings to discuss the content of the law (*Beijing Review,* July 20, 1979). Some Western observers are skeptical about the extent to which this legalization drive will actually take root in the country (Li 1980).

Given the country's determination to play in increasingly large role in the international arena, the International Law Society of China was established in 1980. Its major function is to promote the study of international law and facilitate its development in China (*Beijing Review,* March 17, 1980).

Law on Joint Ventures

The Joint Venture Law allows a minimum of 25 percent and a maximum of 99 percent foreign investment. A full text of the law appears in appendix A. This law is discussed in greater detail in chapter 12. In addition to the passage of the Law on Joint Ventures, regulations pertaining to the operations and conduct of foreign investment in China, such as the Income Tax Law on Joint Ventures, the Individual Income Tax Law, Regulations on the Registration of Joint Ventures, Regulations on Labor Management in Joint Ventures, Regulations on Special Economic Zones, and Provisional Regulations for Exchange Control have also been promulgated. These laws are designed to facilitate the establishment of various forms of economic cooperation with foreign countries, and to provide for their smooth operations. The texts of these laws are contained in appendixes B, C, D, E, F, G I, and J.

To assist further in the development of foreign trade, most organizations in China that engage in foreign commerce have established legal departments or expanded their legal activities. For example, the China Council for the Promotion of International Trade has expanded its legal services to provide lawyers for Chinese and foreign parties to resolve such legal matters as trade and maritime disputes (*China Business Review,* November–December 1979).

Patent and Copyright Law

One of the purposes of engaging in trade and economic relations with foreign countries is to acquire advanced technologies. In order to allay the concerns of some foreign firms about transferring technology to China, the country has decided to draw up a set of patent and copyright laws. These laws are currently in the drafting stage. After the enactment of the patent law, China may accede to the Paris Convention and the International Copyright Convention. In 1979 some 2,000 U.S. trademark registrations were processed or approved in China. At the end of 1979 China sought admission to the World Intellectual Property Organization (*China Business Review,* November–December 1979).

Customs Regulations

Since 1977 travel to and from China has been made easier. This has led to an increase in smuggling and other illegal activities. In 1979, 13,400 cases of smuggling were uncovered, a 41 percent increase over the 1978 figure. In April 1980 the government adopted the following measures to curb smuggling:

1. Strengthen the work of customs by reestablishing the General Administration of Customs.
2. Improve decrees and regulations pertaining to customs. Based on the results of investigations, the government discovered that some enterprises in the country have actually collaborated with the smugglers. To check this unhealthy tendency, the state decreed that individuals and enterprises involved in smuggling will be fined and their goods confiscated. In cases involving

serious infractions, the individuals and enterprises will be punished according to law. To prevent collusion with smugglers, the directive further stated that commercial enterprises may trade only in the commodities specified in their licenses. Furthermore, they are prohibited from purchasing goods in the marketplace at high prices. Industrial and mining concerns may sell their surplus products only after fulfilling the requirements of state purchasing plans and honoring their contractual agreements with other organizations and agencies (*Beijing Review*, February 16, 1981, p. 5).

3. Provide better supervision and control of the tariff system for imports and exports.
4. Install devices to help detect the unlawful entry of goods (*Beijing Review*, May 19, 1980).

The Marriage Law

The Marriage Law was enacted in 1950, soon after the establishment of the PRC. However, between 1966 and 1976 this original Marriage Law was virtually ignored, so that many young people grew up in ignorance of the law. The new Marriage Law, which went into effect on January 1, 1981, reaffirms the principles of free marraige, monogamy, equality between men and women, and protection of mothers and children (*China Reconstructs*, March 1981). Anyone who interferes with another person's freedom of marriage through violent means is punishable under the Criminal Law.

Some of the provisions added to the new Marriage Law include the following:

1. To slow the rate of population growth in the country, the legal marriage age for men has been raised from twenty to twenty-two, and for women from eighteen to twenty.
2. The principle of family planning is included in the new law. The Marriage Law stipulates that "both husband and wife have the obligation to practise family planning." Each couple is encouraged to have only one child. Those who subscribe to the one-child policy are given a certificate to that effect. In addition, the child receives a monthly health subsidy. Children who come from families that subscribe to the policy have priority in gaining admission to kindergartens and are exempted from tuition fees from kindergarten all the way through to middle school (*Beijing Review*, October 5, 1979, p. 29). Couples who have more than two children may be penalized (*China Reconstructs*, March 1981). All these measures are designed to help attain the goal of zero population growth by the year 2000.
3. The obligation to support one's parents is written into the law. The law states that "children have the duty to support and assist their parents."

4. The provision for divorce has been revised. The 1950 Marriage Law states that "divorce *may* be granted if mediation fails." The 1981 law states that "in cases of complete alienation of mutual affection, and when mediation has failed, divorce should be granted." Though making divorce easier, the state does not approve irresponsible desertion of one's spouse. Adultery and abandonment are not automatic grounds for divorce. A divorce is not permitted when the wife is pregnant or within one year after the birth of the child. There are reports that the divorce rate has increased since the promulgation of the new law. In general, however, divorces are still fairly uncommon in China. Statistics indicate that for Beijing's Xicheng District, the ratio of marriage to divorce is 100 to 0.6 (*Beijing Review*, March 16, 1981).

For a full text of the Marriage Law see Appendix K.

Lawyers in China

In China's current drive to improve the country's legal system, lawyers again have an important role to play in society.

The system of people's lawyers was introduced on an experimental basis in the mid-1950s in Beijing and Shanghai. This system was subsequently implemented in other major cities. By June 1957 China had 19 lawyers' associations, 800 legal advisory offices, 2,500 full-time lawyers, and 300 part-time lawyers. But the system was discontinued after only two years because of the traditional Chinese distaste for law in general and because of the misunderstanding of the role of defense lawyers (*Beijing Review*, November 17, 1980).

With the enactment of new legislation since 1979, the government once again sees the need to implement a lawyer system. In April 1979 the Commission for Legal Affairs of the National People's Congress Standing Committee established a task force to draft regulations governing the conduct of lawyers. The work of the task force was subsequently transferred to the Ministry of Justice after the latter was established in September 1979. The provisional regulations governing the work of lawyers will be implemented on January 1, 1982.

Lawyers in China are defined as "state legal workers" and are paid by the state. Lawyers generally perform the following functions:

1. They act as legal advisors to the government organizations, enterprises, people's communes, and other people's organizations.
2. They take part in litigation in both criminal and civil suits. In 1978 lawyers first reappeared as advocates in court in Beijing.
3. They explain legal matters and provide legal services to the public by drafting legal documents and so forth (*Beijing Review*, November 17, 1980).

One of the major difficulties in implementing the lawyer system is, of course, the shortage of legal personnel in China. According to the vice-minister of justice, Wang Yuechen, there were only 3,000 lawyers in the country at the end of 1980: 1 lawyer for every 300,000 people. The government has tried to rectify this situation by establishing law institutes at most universities and technical colleges. In 1981 the country enrolled 2,500 students in the law institutes or departments. The Central Cadres' Training School in Political Science and Law will train the teaching staff for law institutes at various places. In addition, the government has organized spare-time colleges and sponsored short-term training programs throughout the country to provide formal legal training to every judicial worker at or above the level of an assistant judge by the year 1983. China's goal is to have 1 lawyer for every 10,000 people in the cities and 1 for every 50,000 people in rural areas by 1985 (*Beijing Review,* August 10, 1979; December 8, 1980).

In addition to the lawyer system, China has reinstituted the notary-public system, under the administration of the judicial departments. The main items notarized are births, marriages, deaths, academic transcripts, citizenship status, and agreements of trust. Since 1977 notary offices in Beijing alone have notarized over 4,700 contracts pertaining to foreign trade. An editorial in the *Renmin Ribao* in late January 1980 proposed that the notary-public system be further improved through raising the educational levels of the notary publics and enacting legislation governing their conduct (*Beijing Review,* February 4, 1980).

Methods for Dealing with Offenders

China espouses the principle of "revolutionary humanitarianism"—that is, combining punishment of criminal offenders with leniency. Essentially, this means that the imposition of penalties is designed not to inflict punishment on the offender, but to reform the individual through a combination of "punishment and public surveillance and ideological remoulding, and combining productive labor with political education" *(Beijing Review,* June 9, 1980, p. 18). In imposing penalties, including the death sentence, the basic objectives is to "educate and save more offenders." Consequently, if offenders demonstrate "sufficient repentance or render meritorious service" during their imprisonment, their penalties can be reduced. In the case of the death penalty, the sentence may be changed to life imprisonment.

One can get a better idea of this policy of combining punishment with leniency by looking at Chinese prison life. The following is an eyewitness account by two reporters from *China Reconstructs* of prison life in a jail on Yuxin Road in the southern part of Beijing (*China Reconstructs,* September 1979, pp. 49–51). All prisoners follow a strict regimen: wake up, 6:30 a.m.; breakfast, 7:00 a.m.; work, 7:30–11:30 a.m.; lunch, 11:30–noon; noon break, noon–2:00

p.m.; work, 2:00–6:00 p.m.; supper, 6:30–7:00 p.m.; free activities, 7:00–7:30 p.m.; study, 7:30–9:30 p.m.; go to bed, 9:30 p.m.

The prisoner's day is centered around work. The government considers work an important means of rehabilitating prisoners. "The prisoners gradually acquire the habit of respecting work and detesting idleness. Work also helps prisoners learn a productive skill." Consequently, by the time they leave the prison, many have acquired skills equivalent to the third or fourth of the eight grades of skill established in China. Government regulations prohibit discrimination against former criminals in terms of employment. The prisoners receive nominal pay for their work—5 to 10 yuan per month. In the first quarter of 1979, 75 percent of the prisoners received bonuses.

The government also seeks to rehabilitate prisoners through ideological education. Every day each prisoner engages in two hours of study. Ideological education is conducted by the prison staff and may take the form of "patient talks," a method commonly used in China to help an individual reform. This literally means that a staff member sits down and talks to the individual for hours in a friendly manner, trying to help the person understand why he went wrong and how to make amends. According to Jiao Kun, deputy director of the Beijing Bureau of Public Security, statistics over the first thirty-one years of the history of the PRC show that this method of combining physical work and ideological education has been successful in reforming criminals (*Beijing Review*, February 23, 1981, p. 23). To support this premise, Jiao cited the following statistics. In 1965 the crime rate was the lowest ever since 1949. During the Cultural Revolution, when laws were suspended, the crime rate went up. In 1977 the system of reforming criminals through ideological education and physical labor was reinstituted. In 1980 the number of criminal cases was only one-third that of 1977.

Although the overall crime rate has gone down, the incidence of juvenile delinquency in China has been on the increase. Jiao Kun attributed this to the disruption of education during the Cultural Revolution. In that period youths were encouraged to "rebel and make revolution." Minors or criminals under the age of eighteen generally are sent not to prisons, but to reformatories. The following is an eyewitness account by a reporter from *Beijing Review* of the Xicheng District Reformatory in Beijing (*Beijing Review*, November 2, 1979, pp. 18–26).

The reformatory is run like a school, and the inmates are called students. In the reformatory the student engages in four days of study and two days of manual labor a week. The objectives are threefold: (1) to make the students abide by strict discipline and live as members of a collective; (2) to help them break away from their former partners in crime; and (3) to help them analyze the objective and subjective causes of their mistakes.

The methods for reforming them include helping them analyze the causes of their mistakes and educating them on how they can improve in the future. The students also engage in self-criticism, and punishment is meted out when neces-sary. According to the statistics of one reformatory, of the 1,028 people who went through the program, the relapse rate is only 15 percent. The 85 percent who have been reformed through such programs have taken jobs as workers, peasants, soldiers, technicians, and teachers. For Beijing as a whole, in 1980 more than 75 percent of the juvenile delinquents had mended their ways through these reformatories.

From the foregoing analysis of China's current legalization drive—even though concerns have been raised about the success of the campaign in a country with a traditional distaste for law and legal concepts—it can be seen that China is making great efforts to build up a strong level system that will ensure peace and stability and will facilitate economic intercourse with foreign countries, in order to aid in the attainment of the goal of socialist modernization.

7

Chinese Mentality and Outlook toward Work and Industrial Progress

China's leaders are aware that industrialization and modernization are crucial to the long-run survival of the country, and that technology and capital are of profound importance in the development of the Chinese economy. At the same time, they know that China is deficient in both elements. The Chinese leadership realizes that the country abounds in one resource—manpower. Depending on the leaders' ability to mobilize it, this resource may be converted into one of the country's richest assets. However, in order for manpower to be utilized, it must be organized and raised to an acceptable level of technical competence.

Consequently, an examination of the reasons for the recovery and fairly rapid growth of the Chinese economy after 1949, as well as a projection of whether such trends will continue into the future, entails a study of the ways and means by which leaders organize the entire population, encourage them to engage in productive activities, and seek to raise their educational and technical levels. This chapter seeks to examine, first, the party's attempt to imbue or indoctrinate the masses with an attitude conducive to industrial progress, and, second, the government's policy on raising educational levels. Specifically, a critical analysis and appraisal of the Chinese worker's attitude toward achievement, innovation, and technical revolution will be made. Although the majority of the Chinese people still derive their principal means of livelihood from the farm, it is in the industrial sector that the most rapid strides have been made over the past three decades. Besides, this study is concerned with industrial practices, progress, and development. Consequently, only the attitudes of the industrial workers, and not those of the farming population, will be considered.

Before studying these attitudes, a word is needed about attitude change in general. We all know that a person's total outlook vis-à-vis work, politics, social values, and so forth is hard to change. Thus one must ask how the Communist party was able to change or reorient the attitudes and outlook of a billion people within a relatively short period of time. As will be evident at the end of the discussion on attitude change, the word *reorient* is perhaps more appropriate than the word *change,* because the latter implies the introduction of something entirely new, whereas the former conveys the idea of setting something on the right track again.

The founders of the PRC emphasized the imbecility of wholesale or unconditional Westernization, even in the application of Marxism-Leninism. Mao Zedong wanted the Chinese to become modern people as quickly as possible. At the same time, he did not want the Chinese to feel emotionally indebted to foreign sources of knowledge. In a society like that of China, which places heavy emphasis on tradition, the leaders were much too intelligent and cautious to abandon China's cultural traditions altogether. A number of the principles espoused by Confucius seemed to blend in very well with Marxist-Leninist orthodoxy. The long tradition of rule by a Confucian elite, for instance, undoubtedly makes it easier for the Chinese people to accept as normal the continued dominance of the Communist-party elite.

China's present leadership is opposed to a downright denunciation of Confucius and Confucian principles. The general assessment is that although Confucianism is essentially a conservative philosophy, there are good elements that can be absorbed from it (*Beijing Review*, April 6, 1979). Hence a number of the principles promulgated by Confucius—the perfectability of man; the existence of a utopia; filial piety (broadened to include the concept of the family-state); the need for the ruler to maintain good working relations with the people; the need to "hear more and see more," "learn a lot and ask questions," and "review what you have learned in order to learn something new"—are kept alive to this day, although they may be modified or reoriented. However, the very existence of such principles among the Chinese made the CCP's work much easier and helps to account for the relative smoothness and rapidity with which the value systems of the Chinese were reoriented under the new regime.

Attitude toward Achievement

In *The Achieving Society* (1961), McClelland demonstrated his hypothesis that there is a fairly high correlation between the achievement drive of different peoples and their respective countries' rate of growth. This finding has important implications for countries concerned with economic growth. According to McClelland's hypothesis, people with a high need for achievement (nAch), in contrast to those with low nAch, tend to be more favorably disposed toward hard work and doing jobs well, particularly nonroutine jobs. In addition, they have a greater propensity to undertake challenging assignments, "take calculated rational risks, to innovate and to be quite favorably disposed to change in the direction of greater economic and technical progress" (Richman 1969, p. 281). Given this premise, if a country is able to raise the nAch of its population, it enhances the probability of improving managerial effectiveness and industrial progress on a national scale. In *The Achieving Society*, McClelland identified several methods for measuring the nAch score. These include an analysis of children's readers, thematic-apperception tests (TATs), and questionnaires to study adolescent boys and their mothers.

McClelland subsequently applied this hypothesis to several Southeast Asian countries, including the PRC, Taiwan, and India. From an analysis of Chinese children's readers (for children between the ages of eight and ten), McClelland (1963) concluded that the nAch in the PRC between 1950 and

1959 (mean = 2.24; z score = +0.32) was significantly higher than that for pre-1949 China (mean = 0.86; z score = -0.90) and for Taiwan between 1950 and 1959 (mean = 1.81; z score = -0.25). The nAch score for China in the late 1920s was substantially below the world average, whereas the score in the 1950s had surpassed it. The nAch score for Taiwan in the 1950s was higher than that for the 1920s, although it was still below the world average (McClelland 1963, p. 12).

Although it may be true that the communists are more concerned with raising the achievement level of the population, the low nAch score for China in the 1920s should not be interpreted to mean that the Chinese then were little concerned about achievement or that the achievement motive was alien or foreign to China.

In the first place, the Chinese have always stressed achievement, as witnessed by the existence of the Civil Service Examination System in ancient China and the considerable success that Chinese who left the country before the 1920s achieved in other parts of the world. In ancient China children were constantly encouraged to take the Civil Service Examinations held regularly at the provincial and national levels. From a very tender age children were told constantly that once they passed these exams, their status in society (along with their family's) would rise tremendously.

The reason for China's low nAch score in the 1920s can be attributed in part to three factors:

1. In ancient China those persons who had a high nAch drive were typically more concerned with political power than with economic growth and development. This is understandable since the merchant class occupied a low social status in ancient China. Even today in Taiwan, bright young intellectuals often seek positions in the government rather than in business. McClelland's measures focused on economic achievement. According to McClelland (1961, p. 43), achievement is "defined in terms of concern about success in competition with some standard of excellence," and a person who is supposedly high in achievement motivation "is interested in getting ahead in the world." McClelland himself admitted that achievement should not be restricted to the economic sense. "One theoretical possibility is that high nAch leads to excellence in all forms of activity and not just in the economic sphere" (McClelland 1961, p. 70). He conceded that "perhaps all the boys with high nAch in a Buddhist society will become monks and not businessmen" (1961, p. 239). However, since it was easier to measure achievement in terms of economic growth because of more abundant and readily available data, and because risk taking and other entrepreneurial behavior are in general closely associated with the achievement motive, McClelland confined his use of the term *achievement* to the economic sense.

2. There are methodological problems associated with the nAch score. Clarke (1973, p. 41) argued that one should distinguish between the need for achievement and the value of achievement. The former is measured by projective

techniques and is dependent "upon the cue-characteristics of the testing conditions, the experimenter's personality, and the testing materials." The achievement value (vAch), on the other hand, is a cognitive-evaluative construct derived from self-report measures. Several studies have shown the vAch score "to be a highly consistent and generalized construct for college and high school populations." (To my knowledge, there has been no assessment of vAch of the Chinese residing in the PRC.) Other researchers (Cofer and Appley 1965; Atkinson and Feather 1966) also pointed to the problems inherent in the nAch score and in projective techniques in general. These problems are greatly compounded when a researcher applies the techniques to a cross-cultural setting. McClelland's technique, though objective, was culture bound. The methodological problems associated with cross-cultural surveys will not be examined here.

3. As Richman (1969, p. 285) pointed out, for some countries there may be a fairly significant margin of error between the nAch score derived from children's readers and the actual existence of achievement drive among the population. Since this drive is not alien to the Chinese mentality, what the communists had to do when they came to power was to harness the energy of the population toward economic activities by emphasizing that economic development is essential to China's survival in the industrial world. In fact, the 1978 Chinese Constitution contains several provisions that emphasize the importance of economic work and progress. Article 11 stipulates:

> The state adheres to the general line of going all out, aiming high and achieving greater, faster, better and more economical results in building socialism, it undertakes the planned, proportionate and high-speed development of the national economy, and it continuously develops the productive forces, so as to consolidate the country's independence and security and improve the people's material and cultural life step by step.

Article 48 guarantees all citizens the "right to work." Article 10 stipulates:

> Work is an honorable duty for every citizen able to work. The State promotes socialist labor emulation, and putting proletarian politics in command, it aplies the policy of combining moral encouragement with material reward, with the stress on the former, in order to heighten the citizens' socialist enthusiasm and creativeness in work.

In China's current drive to attain the goals of the Four Modernizations, the achievement drive is emphasized more than ever. The following are some of the policies the government has instituted to advance this goal:

1. the reinstitution of entrance examinations to college and universities, so that only the best and the brightest will be admitted
2. the use of exams to determine a candidate's suitability for a job opening

3. the use of mass-scale education programs on the television and the institution of spare-time and factory-run colleges to provide alternative means of education to those who are not fortunate enough to gain admission to the universities

4. the use of examinations at most factories to determine a candidate's suitability for promotion to the level of technician or engineer.

5. the nomination of advanced workers, units, and factories to serve as models for emulation by the less productive ones

6. The practice of awarding bonuses and certificates of merit to those who fulfill and overfulfill their production quotas

7. the indoctrination of kindergarten children with the "five loves"—love of the motherland, the people, labor, science, and public property (*Beijing Review,* January 7, 1980, p. 18)

8. the inclusion of the need to "study diligently" as one of the ten-point rules for primary- and middle-school students.

Each of these policies will be discussed in greater detail.

All these policies and programs attest to the government's emphasis on the need for achievement, for progress, and for development among people from all age brackets and walks of life. The efforts of the Chinese leaders in this direction apparently have borne fruit. Although Confucius postulated that human nature could be perfected, his doctrine had fatalistic overtones—not every person was capable of approaching perfection. The Communist party replaced this with the more positive attitude that all people, including the simplest, most ignorant peasant, could become masters of their own destinies. In 1945 Mao Zedong wrote that "we must persevere and work unceasingly, and we too, will touch God's heart" (*Selected Works,* vol. 3, 1975, p. 271). Here, Mao was referring to the ancient parable of the old man who believed he could remove the two giant mountains that obstructed his way. He believed that even if he could not finish the task in his lifetime, his posterity would one day be able to accomplish it. The heavens were moved by the old man's faith and sent two angels down to carry the mountains away on their backs. Mao's treatise "On Practice" reemphasized the philosophy espoused by an eminent scholar of the Sung dynasty: "Since the beginning of time, 'success' is only attained through constant practice" (*Selected Works,* vol. 1, 1975, p. 237).

This changed attitude is reflected in the fact that all workers constantly engage in study sessions to identify solutions to problems, such as supply bottlenecks, technical difficulties, quality control, and development of new products. On his visit to China in early 1966, Richman was struck by the fact that nearly everyone had a writing pad and pen at hand to take notes: "Practically every Chinese citizen one encounters in a Chinese city is studying and reading something *related* to his job . . . they are frequently trying to improve their occupational skills and job performance" (Richman 1969, p. 212).

The same held true in the late 1970s. During my visits to various cities in 1979 and 1980, I noticed that most elevator operators, post-office clerks, sales clerks at department stores, factory workers, and school-age children were all reading books to help them learn a foreign language, in most instances English. It is generally acknowledged that English is now the official second language in China. Many practice their new language skills on the tourists. In fact, some tourists observed that sales clerks appeared to be more interested in practicing their English-language skills than in selling products. On several occasions, when people learned that I was a professor at a university in the United States, they came up and asked me for the definition of a word, the correct usage of a phrase or term, or the proper pronunciation of a word. Many told me that they regularly follow the fifty-minute English-language program scheduled on the television networks five days a week. In my visits to factories, the engineers and technicians were keenly interested in how their operations compared with those in the United States, and welcomed recommendations and suggestions for improvements in the management of their enterprises.

Another remarkable change that has come about in China since 1949 is the positive attitude toward physical labor and toward women's participation in the work force. Manual laborers, once despised in ancient China, are told that there is nothing contemptible about their jobs and that they too can make significant contributions to the progress of society. In 1959 a night-soil collector (a member of an occupational group that was despised in pre-1949 China) was selected as one of the National Congress of Labor Heroes. During the meeting, Liu Shaoqi (then chairman of the state) greeted the night-soil collector with the following remarks: "We all should do our best to serve the people under party leadership. We are both public servants—you, as a night soil collector, and me as the chairman of the State. There is merely a division of labor between the two of us" (*Beijing Review,* May 26, 1980, pp. 21–22). This changed attitude is witnessed by the fact that intellectuals and management personnel are also required to engage in activities involving physical labor. Although the extent to which intellectuals and management personnel actually engage in physical labor varies with periods of political upheavals—for example, during the Cultural Revolution a university professor might be assigned to clean toilets, whereas now the university professor is only required to clean the window in his own office—the point is that physical labor is no longer regarded as despicable.

Another change is the attitude toward woman working outside of their homes. Prior to 1949 women from respectable families did not work. After 1949 women were encouraged to participate in productive labor. By 1957, 70 to 80 percent of the agricultural cooperatives had women as chairmen or vice-chairmen (*Beijing Review,* March 16, 1981).

Another way in which the Chinese government seeks to raise the achievement drive of the general populace is to link education to job requirements. Richman (1969), who did some fairly extensive comparisons of industrial development in China and India, concluded that although the latter country had a larger percentage of people who received an education beyond the high-school level, nevertheless the typical Indian university graduate is more frustrated because he is often unable to find a job where he can use his skills. Richman found that there was a greater incidence of unemployment among high-school and university graduates in India, as compared with China. This situation is due largely to the failure of India's educational system to produce the types of people required by industry. In other words, there is a considerable mismatch in India between education, on the one hand, and industrial requirements and manpower utilization on the other. "Such a lack of opportunities tends to constrain the achievement drive on a wide-spread scale" (Richman 1969, p. 290).

In China, by contrast, education is more closely tied to technical needs. Thus the Chinese student is taught what is immediately required in industry and, consequently, feels that what he has learned has not been wasted is thus a happier and more satisfied worker. In China all graduates of universities or colleges, secondary technical schools, and workers' training schools are employed. Since 1949 the government has established the system of assigning jobs to college graduates under a unified plan drawn up by the State Planning Commission. According to a senior spokesman responsible for placement of graduates from the Beijing Institute of Post and Telecommunications, priority is given to the needs of the state in assigning jobs. However, the students' "specific conditions such as their political ideology, vocational proficiency, health, and whether they have any difficulty in their families" are also taken into consideration (*Beijing Review*, October 27, 1978, p. 18). The graduate has the right to decline a particular job assignment, but those who do so without a good reason would have to wait for future employment, which may take quite a long time. In practice, most of them accept the government assignment, since they have been imbued over the years with the need to subordinate their private concerns to those of the state. Upon graduation each student is given a three-week vacation before assuming his or her job assignment. During this period the student receives a stipend similar in amount to what he or she receives while attending college. In addition, the government pays for relocation costs to the place of employment, if relocation is required.

According to Kang Yonghe, director of the State Bureau of Labor, the unemployed or those "waiting for employment" (the term used by the Chinese government to describe the unemployed) are primarily middle-school graduates in the towns and cities and youths who were sent down to work in the countryside during the Cultural Revolution but now want to return to the cities (*Beijing Review*, February 11, 1980). To train workers further in skills needed in industry, the government has established labor-service companies that provide the trainees with technical skills that will help them find a job. For example, there is presently a demand for workers in the service-trade sectors. Consequently, many of the labor-service companies offer programs to prepare people for

trades. At the end of 1980 China had 831 labor-service companies
ucts, February 1981). The issue of employment will be dis-
ın a subsequent chapter.

ıner way in which the need for achievement drive is reinforced in China
ьy making people see the link between studying hard and attaining a desired
outcome. A worker knows that whatever efforts he or she applies to improving
his or her occupational skills and job performance will be rewarded or duly
acknowledged by both superiors and peers. Under the current system of promotion by means of tests of competencies, workers with no formal education at
a university or college, who have acquired their knowledge through self-study
or evening schools, are eligible to sit for such examinations. If they pass, they
too are promoted.

Attitude toward Innovation

Like their counterparts in the United States, Chinese workers are encouraged
to innovate. A common slogan in the factories is "go all out for technical innovations and technical revolution." In fact, Article 12 of the 1978 Constitution
stipulates:

> The State devotes major efforts to developing science, expands scien-
> tific research, promotes technical innovation and technical revolution
> and adopts advanced techniques wherever possible in all departments
> of the national economy. In scientific and technological work we
> must follow the practice of combining professional contingents with
> the masses, and combining learning from others with our own creative
> efforts.

In the Kailuan coal mines, designated as a leader in the industry, it was
reported that the mining engineer of one of the collieries worked in the pits
for more than two months to study why rock falls occurred frequently at a
particular seam. This resulted in the design of a new roof-control method that
prevents such fallouts (*Kailuan Story* 1977, p. 14).

In a study trip to China in the early 1970s, Meisner (1972, pp. 728–729)
reported that there is a staff member in each workshop in the factory who
gathers "suggestions for innovations" and "opinions on technical questions."
This was in line with Richman's findings in his 1966 tour of thirty-eight factories. The same holds true for the factories I visited in July 1979 and in June–
July 1980. Management, technicians, and workers constantly take part in
sessions to discuss alternative methods for solving problems and for improving
efficiency. In a number of factories, the chief engineer concurrently holds
the position of factory director. This indicates the importance assigned to
the solution of technical problems in the operations of the enterprise. In my

conversations with the factory directors, they were often keenly interested in learning how similar problems would be solved in the United States. The factory directors usually ended briefings on the operations of their enterprises with a hearty request for their "foreign friends" (a term favored by the Chinese) to offer suggestions for making improvements.

In China the notion of suggestion boxes is apparently taken seriously by everyone involved in an enterprise. A bicycle factory in Tientsin that had to decide whether to increase the cost of production by 3.5 fen (cents) in order to give the bicycle a smoother ride received, according to Richman (1969, p. 53), more than 300 suggestions for practicing economy. All these suggestions were discussed and analyzed in after-work study sessions. Richman noted that this appeared to be a common practice in all the industrial enterprises he visited. The practice of soliciting and discussing suggestions and comments from all levels of workers in the enterprise is still followed in post-1977 industrial society.

Of course, overemphasis on discussing, analyzing, and implementing every single innovative suggestion from the workers may have its own disadvantages. It takes time, and implementing new techniques may be expensive. However, given the facts that (1) the Chinese industrial enterprise, compared with the large and well-established U.S. enterprise, is still in its infancy; (2) the average Chinese worker has only fairly recently become aware of the fact that he too can help in overcoming problems; (3) China has abundant labor power; and (4) the leaders of the country are consciously seeking to stimulate and raise the creative and innovative abilities of the working population—then perhaps at this stage in China's economic development, the benefits far outweigh the costs incurred in holding study sessions on workers' suggestions.

To further encourage innovation among the people, the government adopted the following two policies: (1) grant awards for inventions and technical innovations; and (2) encourage scientific and technical research projects in the research institutes associated with the enterprises, the Chinese Academy of Sciences, and the universities. At the National Science Conference held in 1978, a resolution was passed to encourage all large industrial and mining enterprises to establish their own research institutes and to expand existing research facilities. Medium-sized and small factories and mines were also encouraged to set up research institutes, when possible. Another resolution passed at the conference was to give scientific research personnel adequate time to engage in research. At least five-sixths of their work day should be devoted to research work. In addition, they should be given the opportunity to upgrade their skills. Research workers who have attained the level of assistant research fellow, lecturer, engineer, or higher should be allowed a certain period of time off for advanced study every two to three years (*Beijing Review*, April 7, 1978).

In 1979 the State Council promulgated "Regulations for Awards on Inventions," which are designed to encourage scientific research and technical innovations. The awards are administered by the State Scientific and Techno-logical Commission (*Beijing Review*, February 2, 1979, p. 8). This policy is not new. The late Premier Zhou Enlai drafted several regulations pertaining to awards for scientific and technological inventions, and the system of granting awards for inventions was practiced prior to 1966. In those days Mao Zedong used to write personal inscriptions on the certificates of invention. Besides the use of moral encouragement to reward those who made significant contributions in science and technology, material awards are also given. These include mone-tary rewards of 1,000 yuan, 2,000 yuan, 5,000 yuan, and 10,000 yuan (depend-ing on the significance of the inventions), as well as certificates and medals. For very important inventions, special prizes are given. Monetary rewards for scientific invention are tax exempt. From April 1979 to early 1981, the State Scientific and Technological Commission approved 165 scientific inventions in the fields of industrial technology, agriculture, and medicine (*Beijing Review*, April 6, 1981).

The inventions become the property of the state, and hence enterprises throughout the country can have access to them. Since 1980 factories and units that want access to these inventions have had to pay a fee. At the end of 1980 the Physics Institute of the Chinese Academy of Sciences contracted twenty-one new technologies to nineteen Chinese enterprises. The terms of the contract range from fee payment based on profits to royalties based on sales. For fee payment, the terms are usually a fee of 20 percent on profits in the first year, decreasing to 10 percent in the second year and to 5 percent in the third year. Royalty payments are usually 5 percent of sales in the first year, decreasing to 2-3 percent in the second year (*China Business Review*, November–December 1980).

In May 1980 the State Council approved "Reward Measures for People Reporting Mineral Deposits." This decree is designed to encourage people to discover mineral deposits for use in the Four Modernizations program. These awards are to be given to nongeologists and range from 10 to 5,000 yuan, depending on the size and economic value of the deposit. For small mineral deposits, monetary rewards range from 10 to 100 yuan. For medium-sized deposits, the rewards range from 100 to 400 yuan. For large deposits, the rewards range from 400 to 800 yuan. For precious metals and valuable min-erals urgently needed by the government, such as uranium, chromium, dia-monds, and gold, the award ranges from 800 to 5,000 yuan (*Beijing Review*, June 23, 1980).

After the promulgation of these various measures, some people expressed concern that giving monetary rewards will lead to inequities in society. An editorial in the *Renmin Ribao* addressed this issue by stating that awarding inventions is in line with the socialist principle of "to each according to his work." Furthermore, rewarding individuals for scientific inventions will provide an incentive for others to follow suit.

During the Cultural Revolution, research on science and technology came to a virtual standstill. Many of the research institutes were closed. In 1977 these were reopened and were encouraged to resume research. As pointed out previously, Article 12 of the 1978 Constitution stipulates that the state "expands scientific research, promotes technical innovation and technical revolution." The scientific community responded favorably. In 1978 the government announced that results were achieved in more than 600 major scientific and technological research projects throughout the country. Some of these included the development of the first integrated-circuit computer capable of performing 5 million calculations per second, and the production of new materials, including copper-clad plate steel (*Beijing Review,* July 6, 1979, pp. 40–41). In the 1950s and the 1960s most research projects focused on the physical sciences. This resulted in the development of the atomic and hydrogen bombs and of satellites. In the Five-Point Guideline on Science and Technology issued in early 1981, the government decreed that henceforth the primary objective of research projects is to accelerate the pace of economic development, and that scientific research "should be in consonance with the growth of the economy and social needs" (*Beijing Review,* April 20, 1981, pp. 6–7). Given the present emphasis on development of the light-industrial, textile, and agricultural sectors, the government has called on the research institutes to engage in projects that would further this goal. In the light and textile industries, some 3,887 innovations were introduced in 1979 and 1980. These primarily involved increasing the variety of products available and improving the quality of existing products (*Beijing Review,* April 6, 1981).

Though emphasizing the need for innovations and technical inventions, China has constantly called on the people to practice frugality in order to conserve scarce resources and facilitate industrial progress. In 1955 Mao wrote: "We must encourage diligence and thrift in running the household, running the cooperative, and building the country. Our nation must first be diligent, and second, thrifty" (*Selected Works,* vol. 5, 1977, p. 229). To practice frugality, the government has launched a program to recycle industrial wastes. In Shanghai alone, by the end of 1978 some 19,000 people were employed for the specific purpose of collecting and recycling industrial wastes. In the same year approximately 90 percent of the enterprises in Shanghai had established the system of collecting wastes and selling them periodically (*Beijing Review,* February 23, 1979). The government also emphasized the need to conserve energy. In China the heat-energy utilization rate is around 30 percent. This is low compared with that of other advanced nations. To encourage more efficient utilization of energy, the People's Bank of China in Shanghai has been extending loans to enterprises for the purpose of installing energy-saving devices (*Beijing Review,* November 10, 1980). In most enterprises, "practising thrift and eliminating waste" in the production process is used as a criterion for evaluating the performance of a factory or work unit, which in turn constitutes a basis for awarding bonuses.

China's Educational Policy

As pointed out previously, China recognizes the need to upgrade its educational standards in order to attain the goals of the Four Modernizations. In fact, senior-ranking officials readily concede that education should be considered the "fifth modernization." The 1978 Constitution contains several provisions that spell out the role of education in Chinese society. Article 13 stipulates: "The State devotes major efforts to developing education in order to raise the cultural and scientific level of the whole nation . . . "; Article 51 states: "Citizens have the right to education. To ensure that citizens enjoy this right, the State gradually increases the number of schools of various types and of other cultural and educational institutions and popularizes education."

This policy of upgrading educational standards did not come about suddenly. China has always emphasized the need for education. In 1950 Mao Zedong wrote, "restoring and developing the people's education is one of the important tasks at present." In 1952 the numbers of students enrolled in primary schools, secondary schools, and colleges were 51 million, 3.1 million, and 191,000, respectively. These figures represented a fairly rapid increase within a three-year period from the establishment of the PRC. In 1949 student enrollments in primary schools, secondary schools and colleges stood at 24 million, 1.26 million, and 117,000, respectively. By 1965 these respective figures had climbed to 116 million, 14.418 million, and 674,000. In the same year approximately 84.7 percent of school-age children were enrolled in primary schools (*Beijing Review,* February 3, 1978). Although the educational level of the average Chinese is low compared with the average in the advanced nations, the majority of the population is literate. Within thirty years of the establishment of the PRC, some 126.8 million previously illiterate people were taught to read and write. In 1980 the literacy rate in the rural areas was estimated at 70 percent, whereas that for the urban areas is much higher. This is a significant improvement over pre-1949 China.

This section seeks to examine the policies that have been implemented since 1977 to raise the educational and technical skills of the people.

Guiding Principles

China's educational policy is governed by two guiding principles, the first of which emphasizes the moral, intellectual, and physical development of students. In 1956 Mao Zedong wrote that the country's educational policy "must enable everyone who receives an education to develop morally, intellectually and physically and become a worker with both socialist consciousness and culture" (*Beijing Review,* February 3, 1978). Besides the intellectual development of students, China sees the need to breed a generation of young people who are physically fit and morally upright. The latter principle is emphasized in the current campaign to build a socialist spiritual civilization, which stresses the need for ideological education. In a forum sponsored by the Ministry of Education in May 1977, it was proposed that ideological education "should aim at helping the student cultivate the habit of studying diligently, observing discipline, loving labor and being ready to help others." Ideological education should be carried out through positive examples; open discussions; after-class activities; and study of Marxism–Leninism–Mao Zedong Thought, the principles and policies guiding the Four Modernizations, and communist ethics (*Beijing Review,* June 15, 1979, pp. 7–8).

The second principle governing China's educational policy is that of *open-door schooling,* which means combining education with productive labor. In 1958 Mao Zedong wrote that "education must serve proletarian politics and be combined with productive labor." During the Cultural Revolution this policy was interpreted to mean that "the wider the door opens, the better" and "the more time a student spends on labor, the better." In light of this interpretation, an inordinate proportion of the students' activities were diverted to physical labor, thus allowing little time for the acquisition of new knowledge and technical skills. The government's present policy is that although the principle of open-door schooling is basically correct, it should be practiced in moderation. In primary and secondary schools the principal focus should be on the acquisition of knowledge and technical skills. This should be supplemented with physical labor commensurate with the student's age. In combining labor with education, the students acquire respect and love for labor and the ability to combine theory with practice. Combining study with work also has its economic significance. In Jilin Province, for instance, the output value of commodities produced by primary- and middle-school students amounted to 140 million yuan in 1978. These could be used to improve facilities in the schools (*Beijing Review,* August 10, 1979).

Kindergartens and Primary Schools

The government compares the young children in the country "to the sun at 8 or 9 in the morning (i.e. at its best)." Consequently, China sees the need to educate the youth of today to be the future leaders of tomorrow who will assume the responsibility of making China a strong and powerful nation (*Eleventh National Congress,* 1977, p. 106–107). In late 1980 there were an estimated 988,000 nurseries and kindergartens throughout China, providing care and education to some 35 million preschoolers. This represents a 760-fold increase over 1949, when there were only 1,300 kindergartens. Despite this impressive increase, the government recognizes the need to build more facilities, since the 1980 figure of 35 million preschoolers accounted for only 30 percent of all preschool-age children in the country (*Beijing Review,* March 9, 1981). This 30-percent figure, however, should not be interpreted to mean that the remaining 70 percent are neglected. In China, although most mothers work, it is common to find three generations living under one roof. Consequently, young children are often cared for by their grandparents. In the future the government proposes to train more kindergarten teachers to run more preschool institutions. Since 1977 five colleges have reinstituted programs specializing in preschool education. Throughout the provinces, institutes for training kindergarten teachers have been established. In addition, existing kindergarten teachers are encouraged to attend special training programs to upgrade their technical skills.

In China there are two kinds of kindergartens: those run by educational departments, government organs, and enterprises; and those run by the neighborhood committees in the cities and in the communes. Most enterprises have a nursery or kindergarten adjacent to the workshops. In the Beijing No. 2 Cotton Mill, which employs some 8,200 workers, there is a two-story building that has been set aside as a kindergarten for 263 children. The children in this kindergarten are divided into three grades: grade 1 for children aged three to four; grade 2 for those aged four to six; and grade 3 for children aged six to seven. Most of the children (189 out of 263) board at the nursery, and the rest use the facilities only in the daytime. In 1980 monthly charges per child amounted to 13 yuan (10.5 yuan for room and board, 2 yuan for child care, and 0.5 yuan for miscellaneous expenses) plus 50 percent of actual medical expenses incurred. Children who come from families that subscribe to the one-child policy enjoy free child care and medical benefits (*Beijing Review,* January 7, 1980).

Although the facilities offered at the kindergartens run by the different organizations may vary, the services offered are fairly uniform. In early 1981 the Ministry of Education established minimal standards for the subjects to be taught; the diet for preschoolers; the size of their desks, chairs, and beds; and the recommended number of hours of study for children in each age group. The subjects to be taught at kindergartens include 30–45 minutes of daily lessons in sports, Chinese language, general knowledge, arithmetic, music, and drawing. Audiovisual equipment and toys are used as teaching media. Besides general knowledge, the children also receive ideological and moral education. All preschoolers are taught the "five loves": of the motherland, the people, labor, science, and public property (*Beijing Review,* March 9, 1981). In my visits to the nurseries and kindergartens, I found it amazing that toddlers could recite long passages describing their devotion to their motherland. The plays staged by preschoolers revolve around the themes of cooperation and the need to help others.

As with Chinese enterprises, certain primary and secondary schools are designated as *key schools.* Key schools come under the direct administration of the Ministry of Education and receive priority in the allocation of resources. They must comply with certain standards and are expected to set good examples for other schools. In 1978 there were twenty key schools in the cities of Beijing, Tianjin, Shanghai, Yenan, Daqing, and Dachai. Nonkey schools are referred to as *ordinary schools* and are encouraged to emulate the standards and curricula of the key schools. Those that excel in their performance may later be designated as key schools. In 1979 there were 949,000 primary schools (a 2.7-fold increase over 1949) with a total enrollment of 146.24 million students (six times the enrollment for 1949). In 1949 only 20 percent of school-age children attended schools. In 1980 over 90 percent of school-age children attended primary school.

Although situations vary, a child typically enters primary school at the age of seven. Under some special circumstances children are admitted at six or six-and-a-half. Primary-school education programs span a period of five years. In the fall of 1980 the Beijing Municipal Bureau of Education extended the program to six years. This change is designed to provide a more solid educational base for children. The bureau pointed out that the five-year program was inadequate if primary-school students were to master 2,400 characters (300 more characters than were required during the Cultural Revolution) in their first three years. In addition, since 1977 extra courses in mathematics and general knowledge have been added to the curricula. With the implementation of the six-year program, the entrance age to grade 1 has been lowered from seven to six-and-a-half (*Beijing Review,* December 8, 1980). Subjects taught at all primary schools include Chinese, arithmetic, general knowledge, foreign language, politics, physical exercise, music, and drawing. General knowledge and foreign language are taught from the third grade up. Foreign language is taught at some of the urban primary schools. In late 1979 the principal foreign language taught was English. The school year extends for nine-and-a-half months every year. Students in grade 4 and above engage in manual labor for half a month every academic year. In some of the primary schools that I visited, students manufactured chalk for classroom use and assembled components for nearby factories.

On two separate occasions in the 1950s and 1960s, the Ministry of Education introduced rules governing the conduct and behavior of primary- and middle-school students. However, most rules were suspended during the Cultural Revolution. As a result, some young people acquired bad habits and attitudes. As pointed out in chapter 6, the incidence of juvenile delinquency has been on the increase. This prompted the government to take remedial action. In 1979 the Ministry of Education approved two sets of rules, one for primary schools and the other for middle schools. Although the two sets of rules are not identical, they share common elements. Effective September 1, 1979, all primary- and middle-school students must abide by the following points:

1. Love the motherland and the people.
2. Protect and care for collective and public property.
3. Study diligently.

4. Pay attention to hygiene, and participate in sports and other physical exercises.
5. Participate in physical labor, and lead a simple and frugal life.
6. Obey the law, and observe discipline.
7. Respect their teachers, be polite, and develop close ties with their classmates.
8. Be modest, honest, and prepared to make amends for their mistakes (*Beijing Review,* January 7, 1980).

At the same time, the government has called on parents to assume greater responsibility in bringing up their children to be law-abiding and moral citizens.

Since 1978 the textbooks used in primary and secondary schools have been revised. Textbooks from the United States, England, Japan, France, and West Germany were used as references in the revision process. The new texts emphasize modern science, technology, and the conduct of experiments, and combine theory and practice. "Political jargon has been done away with" (*Beijing Review,* September 29, 1978). In mathematics, for example, set theory, algebra, and statistics are taught. In foreign-language texts, the emphasis is on teaching the student to listen, speak, read, and write the language.

Besides the acquisition of general knowledge, primary and secondary schools also stress moral and ideological education. Children between the ages of nine and fifteen may belong to the Chinese Young Pioneers Association. The latter serves as a training ground for future CCP members. Members of the Young Pioneers are encouraged to develop morally, intellectually and physically.

Middle Schools

In 1979 China had 162,000 regular middle schools (a 40-fold increase over 1949) with an enrollment of 65.48 million (a 63-fold increase over 1949).

Again, although there are variations across the country, the typical secondary school is run along the following lines (*Beijing Review,* January 7, 1980). The age for admission is twelve. The program spans five years, although proposals have been made to extend it to six. The first three years are designated as junior middle school and the latter two as senior middle school. Subjects include politics, Chinese language, mathematics, physics, chemistry, biology, foreign language (English is by far the most common), history, geography, basic farm knowledge, hygiene, physical education, music, and drawing. All secondary school students engage in nine months of study and one month of physical labor.

Vocational Schools

In 1979 China had 1,700 secondary technical schools with an enrollment of 530,000 students (a 6.9-fold increase over 1949). In China the policy of "walking on two legs" has been implemented in various arenas. In the field of education, this policy means establishing both regular senior middle schools and vocational schools. In 1965 the ratio between students in regular senior schools and those in vocational schools was 48 to 52. In 1979 the ratio was 86 to 14 (*Beijing Review,* September 1, 1980). The reason for the change was that most vocational schools were disbanded during the Cultural Revolution. In late 1979 the government decided to reintroduce vocational schools on an experimental basis in several major cities in order to better serve the needs of industry. Technical and polytechnic schools were established in these cities, and 1,900 students enrolled in these technical schools. The curricula at technical schools include the subjects taught at regular middle schools plus a technical subject. The students also combine regular classwork with industrial or farm work (*Beijing Review,* January 7, 1980). Besides the establishment of technical schools, nineteen different technical subjects were introduced in the regular middle schools to train students for the particular industrial and agricultural needs in their localities.

The results obtained in these experimental units proved encouraging. Consequently, in the second half of 1980 the State Council decided to expand technical-education programs to other parts of the country. The reason behind the establishment of technical-education programs is to equip students with technical skills that will prepare them for their jobs upon graduation. Graduates of regular middle schools typically do not possess the technical skills they need on the job. Consequently, most have to undergo further training for two to three years. The reform means that students from vocational schools would be better prepared for their jobs. The types of technical subjects offered at the various schools are geared to the industrial and agricultural needs of the particular locality. Furthermore, the government encourages all trades and professions to run their own vocational and technical schools. In the future the government may convert some of the regular middle schools to vocational, technical, or agricultural schools, in line with the policy of linking education with technical needs. Upon graduation these students are free to find their own jobs or to wait for assignment through the labor department (*Beijing Review,* November 17, 1980).

This policy of reinstituting vocational schools has been well received. In 1980, 36,000 students applied for admission to the ninety-seven senior-middle-school vocational programs in Beijing. Because facilities were limited, only 4,000 students were admitted. This is a three-year training program. Upon graduation these students will be designated as junior or intermediate specialists with a middle-school education. This will enhance their chances of finding suitable employment. The vocational programs in Bejing offer technical training in thirty-five different subjects, including foreign trade, commerce, and the service trades. These vocational programs are jointly sponsored by forty-five senior middle schools and fifty-one enterprises.

The institution of vocational/technical schools would further alleviate another problem. Most middle-school graduates aspire to gain admission to the university and acquire a college education. However, China has only a limited number of institutions of higher learning. In 1979 such institutions were able to accept only 270,000 to 300,000 students, about 4 percent of the total number of middle-school graduates in the country. The minister of education, Jiang Nanxiang, predicts that this situation will not likely change within the next few years (*Beijing Review,* July 13, 1979). Consequently, besides preparing middle-school graduates for institutes of higher learning, the middle schools should also train workers for the country's many enterprises and communes. This is referred to as "one red heart and two preparations" (*Beijing Review,* June 1, 1979). "Red heart" refers to devotion to the country and readiness to serve the cause of socialist modernization. "Two preparations" means that although most aspire to obtain a college education, given the limited facilities at institutes of higher learning, the middle-school graduate should be prepared to forego a university education. The establishment of vocational and technical schools would help prepare those who do not gain admission to a university to work in industry.

Institutes of Higher Learning

The Chinese government estimated that between 1949 and 1979 the country's institutes of higher learning produced some 2,946,000 graduates. This is sixteen times the number of graduates produced by all institutes of higher learning from 1929 to 1949. In 1979 there were 598 universities and colleges, with a total enrollment of 850,000 students (a 7.3-fold increase over 1949). These colleges and universities offer studies in some 800 specialties, 500 of them in the fields of science and engineering (*Beijing Review,* January 7, 1980).

During the Cultural Revolution, education at most colleges and universities was seriously disrupted. Between 1966 and 1971, for instance, colleges and universities throughout the country suspended the enrollment of new students. After 1971 universities began enrolling a limited number of students. With China's current pursuit of the goals of the Four Modernizations, the importance of a college education has again been emphasized.

Since 1977 the Chinese government has introduced a series of reforms with respect to the enrollment of students. In selecting candidates for admission, the applicant's moral, physical, and intellectual qualifications are taken into consideration. Moral and physical qualifications are the preconditions. Moral qualification is defined as supporting the leadership of the Communist party, loving the motherland, studying hard, loving labor, and observing discipline. To meet the physical qualifications, in general, applicants should be under twenty-five years of age (applicants to foreign-language programs should be under twenty-three), single, and senior-middle-school graduates. The government has made special provisions to enroll precocious students in institutes of higher learning.

Of the 700 freshmen enrolled at the Chinese University of Science and Technology in the fall of 1977, 92 were under the age of sixteen (*Beijing Review,* April 14, 1978).

After reviewing the applicant's moral and physical qualifications, the final selection is based on the scores obtained in the qualifying entrance examinations. Since 1977 all applicants have to sit for college entrance exams. In July 1978 an estimated 6 million people sat for the nationwide three-day examination. Examination centers are established throughout the country, but the examination questions are uniform. Students are examined on their general knowledge plus their ability to analyze and solve problems. Applicants for admission to the arts program are examined on the following subjects: politics, Chinese language, mathematics, history, geography, and a foreign language. Applicants for admission to medicine, the physical sciences, engineering, and agriculture must demonstrate proficiency in the following subjects: politics, Chinese language, mathematics, physics, chemistry, and a foreign language. Priorities are given to applicants from particular communities in certain specialized fields. For example, in the institutes of mining, petroleum, and geology, priority is given to workers and staff members already employed in these fields, and to senior-middle-school graduates in mining areas. Similarly, the institutes of forestry and agriculture give priority to senior-middle-school graduates from the forest and farming communities, medical colleges give priority to "barefoot doctors" (paramedics), and teachers' colleges give priority to those already teaching in the countryside. Candidates who are currently employed in the enterprises are generally given fifteen days off with full pay to prepare for the exams. Special consideration is also given to minority nationalities (*Beijing Review,* June 1, 1979).

In China certain institutions of higher learning are designated as key universities and colleges. These receive priority in the allocation of instructors and other personnel, equipment, and funds. There are 100 key universities and colleges throughout the country, in which students with better qualifications are enrolled. In Beijing, for instance, out of a total of 128,000 applicants who sat for the qualifying entrance examinations, only 5,900 were admitted to the key universities, and 5,000 were admitted to the regular universities (*Beijing Review,* October 12, 1979).

Until recently, no college student had to pay tuition. In addition, approximately 75 percent of the students receive a monthly stipend from the state for living expenses, between 6.5 and 22 yuan per month, depending on the individual's family income. Students enjoy free room and board in university dormitories and are entitled to free medical benefits. The course of study generally lasts four years. In some universities this has now been extended to five.

Although the need for study is emphasized, students are given ample time to engage in sports and other physical activities. At Qinghua University in

Beijing, one of the oldest universities in China, there are two popular slogans: "work for the motherland in good health for fifty years," and "8 − 1 > 8." The latter slogan refers to the practice of engaging in one hour of physical exercise every afternoon. The equation means that the hour spent in sports will actually improve the quality and performance of work throughout the day (*China Reconstructs,* May 1980).

Reforms in Higher Education

Although the number of graduates of institutions of higher learning have increased substantially over pre-1949 China, the government realizes that this is far from sufficient. For example, in September 1979 some 4.6 million middle-school graduates applied for admission to the colleges and universities. Of these, only 270,000 were admitted. Given the limited facilities, the government projects that the situation will not ease in the near future. It estimates that the annual enrollment of new students in regular universities will not exceed 300,000 in the next few years. If this situation were allowed to continue, it would result in acute shortages of highly skilled personnel by 1985. The government has tried to rectify this situation through two principal reforms: (1) enrolling day students, and (2) adopting diverse methods of education.

Enrollment of Day Students

In the past all students lived in university dormitories. In 1979 the teacher/administrative staff-to-student ratio was 1 to 1.5. The reason for this low ratio is that when students live in the dormitories, the government must provide personnel to run the dormitories. Another disadvantage of this system is the high cost involved. For every student who lives in the dormitory, the government has to provide an extra 30–40 square meters of living quarters. In 1980 the government proposed that some institutes of higher learning experiment with the system of enrolling day students. Thirty-six institutes of higher learning in Beijing were included in the experimental programs. They were able to enroll 14,400 day students while occupying only 89,000 square meters of floor space. This translated to an average of 7 square meters per student, only a fraction of the 40 square meters per student required under the live-in system. Besides conserving building space, the practice of enrolling day students also cuts down the number of personnel needed to staff and run the dormitories (*Beijing Review,* July 28, 1980).

Introduction of Diverse Methods of Education

In the past students did not have to pay tuition fees. In September 1980 the government introduced on an experimental basis the system of requiring some of the students to pay tuition. This system was introduced in Beijing, Shanghai, Tianjin, and certain cities in Liaoning and Henan provinces. For the academic year beginning in September 1980 the universities and colleges in Beijing enrolled an additional 2,000 students who paid tuition. They paid a tuition fee of 20–25 yuan each term and lived at home instead of at the university. These students use the same facilities as others, but their classes are usually held in the evenings, after normal university hours (*Beijing Review,* September 29, 1980). Upon graduation, students in these programs receive a certificate but must seek employment on their own, whereas those enrolled in the daytime programs are assigned jobs by the government. Based on the results of examinations held at the end of the first academic year, it appeared that these students' standards were almost equal to those of students attending the regular universities.

Other channels of education include the "Tube University," correspondence and night colleges (or spare-time colleges), and self-study.

Tube University. China's Central Broadcast and Television University (the Tube University for short) was established in 1979. It is the largest educational undertaking in China in terms of student enrollment. In 1980 there were 600,000 students formally enrolled in the program. These were admitted after passing a qualifying entrance exams. Students enrolled in the Tube University follow the lectures on the television, turn in their homework assignments, and sit for regularly scheduled exams under the supervision of special counselors. Tuition is free. Besides the 600,000 students formally enrolled in the program, countless others follow the lectures regularly on television.

Most of the students enrolled in the Tube University are technicians, workers, and staff members in industrial enterprises. Eighteen basic and specialized courses are offered. These include English, mathematics, physics, and chemistry. Lectures are given thirty hours a week and are taught by professors from a number of key universities. At the end of the academic year students sit for an exam, which is graded by the central university. In the first year of operation, 80 percent of the students passed. Upon the conclusion of their three-year program, these students sit for an examination and are awarded a Tube University diploma (*China Reconstructs,* February 1980; March 1981; *Beijing Review,* January 5, 1981).

Correspondence and Night Colleges. China first introduced the system of correspondence and night colleges in the early 1950s, but in 1966 they were suspended. Since 1978 such colleges have again gone into operation. In early 1980 China had seventy-two colleges and universities offering correspondence courses and an additional thirty institutions of higher learning sponsoring night programs. In 1980 enrollment in these programs amounted to 240,000 students, or 24 percent of the number of students enrolled in the regular universities.

Most of the students in these colleges are cadres, workers, and staff members with a senior-middle-school education. To gain admission to these programs, students must pass a qualifying entrance exam. The admission scores obtained by students enrolled in these programs are almost equal to those of students attending the regular universities. The textbooks used in the correspondence and night colleges are similar to those used at regular universities. Instructions at most of the night colleges begin at 6:00 p.m., so that many students must go directly from work to classes.

The government encourages the establishment of correspondence and night colleges because students can be trained at one-tenth the cost and with one-sixth the manpower required at regular universities. The Ministry of Education estimates that by 1985 students from correspondence and night colleges will constitute one-third of the total college-student body in the country (*China Reconstructs,* October 1979; *Beijing Review,* May 19, 1980).

The government has decreed that all large- and medium-sized cities and large enterprises throughout the country should establish spare-time colleges. In 1979 there were twenty spare-time colleges run by the trade unions (*Beijing Review,* August 31, 1979). In mid-February 1981 the Beijing Municipal Council of Trade Unions established a new spare-time college program, in which 885 students were enrolled. These were selected from a total of 3,580 applicants on the basis of scores obtained at the entrance exam and recommendations by their respective factories. Students attend classes three half days and two evenings every week. The program runs for four to five years. Tuition is paid by the factory or production unit to which the student belongs, and the student receives full pay while attending college. The spare-time college offers courses in environmental protection, electronic engineering, Chinese language, mathematics, accounting, statistics, economic law, and enterprise management (*Beijing Review,* March 16, 1981).

Self-Study. The government also encourages self-study. In major cities, such as Beijing, any person, regardless of age and official educational level, will be granted a diploma and considered a college graduate if he or she passes the required examinations. The Beijing Municipal Government has established an examination committee for the specific purpose of administering exams to self-study students and awarding diplomas to the successful candidates (*Beijing Review,* December 8, 1980).

Besides the enrollment of day students and the introduction of diverse methods of education to increase the number of graduates of institutes of higher learning, the government has also introduced changes in other areas that are designed to raise general educational levels within the country to meet the needs of the Four Modernizations. Since 1977 the government has adopted the following reforms to further this goal.

Adjust the Imbalance between Arts and Sciences

As indicated previously, China's institutes of higher learning offer specializations in some 800 subjects. However, over 500 of these subjects are in the areas of science and engineering. In 1979 approximately 57.8 percent of all students enrolled in institutes of higher learning majored in science and engineering. Although science and engineering are undoubtedly important to the cause of modernization, specialization in the arts and social sciences—such as economics, law, finance, and industrial management—is also important. For example, although there are thousands of communes in China, until 1980 there was not a single institute of higher learning that offered a course in commune administration.

Postgraduate Education

Since 1978 China has reintroduced the system of postgraduate education. In early 1980 "Regulations for Awarding Academic Degrees" were passed by the Standing Committee of the National People's Congress. Effective January 1, 1981, academic degrees at the bachelor's, master's, and doctoral levels can be conferred. Academic degrees obtained from universities abroad will also be recognized. In addition, the regulations provide for the awarding of honorary doctorate degrees to outstanding Chinese and foreign scholars (*Beijing Review,* January 5, 1981).

Scholarly and Scientific Exchanges with Overseas Countries

On January 31, 1979, the United States and China signed an accord to promote scientific and scholarly exchanges between the two countries. Since then, sister relationships have been established between many universities in the respective countries. These provide for student, faculty, and other types of academic exchanges. As of December 1979 China had entered into similar agreements with eight other countries, including Australia, Canada, the Federal Republic of Germany, France, Italy, Japan, Sweden, and the United Kingdom (*China Business Review,* November–December 1979). Since 1979 China has sent an estimated 5,100 students to further their education in forty-five different countries. Of these, 3,900 fall into the category of visiting scholars, 560 are engaged in postgraduate studies, and 660 are enrolled in undergraduate programs. An overwhelming majority of these students (4,600) are studying the physical and natural sciences. The remainder are majoring in foreign language (380) and the social sciences (110). With the government's realization of the need to correct imbalances between the physical sciences and the arts, this trend may change. Vice-Premier Fang Yi, the minister in charge of science and education, has indicated that China will continue to send students abroad to receive advanced training (*Beijing Review,* December 15, 1980).

Training Cadres, Workers, and Staff Members

According to a 1979 survey of twenty-six provinces, municipalities, and autonomous regions in China, it was estimated that approximately 81.4 percent of the country's workers and staff members had attained only a junior-middle-school education. In the same survey it was estimated that approximately 70 percent of the industrial workers were below the third grade (of eight) in terms of technical skills and that only 3 percent of the total work force had attained the level of engineers or technicians. In order to modernize, China must train a large contingent of skilled workers.

In 1978 Yuan Paohua, the vice-minister in charge of the State Economic Commission, proposed the following measures to raise the educational and technical skills of China's work force (*Beijing Review,* September 8, 1978):

1. Implement a system for examining the technical skills of workers. Results of such examinations will be used as criteria for wage increases and promotions.
2. Each enterprise must establish a training program. The types of training programs will be elaborated on subsequently. In all enterprises, veteran workers and new workers should enter into a contract, either implicit or explicit, whereby the former will agree to train the latter. (In ancient China the skills of the veteran workers were closely guarded secrets that were passed on only to members of one's immediate family.) In addition, all new workers must undergo a training program after their recruitment.
3. Train more engineers and technicians.
4. Encourage workers to develop a scientific approach to problem solving. Enterprises are encouraged to learn relevant techniques from advanced nations and to promote greater cooperation and information exchange among enterprises within a given industry.
5. All middle-aged and young workers are encouraged to learn a foreign language.

To realize the goal of raising educational and technical skills among all levels of enterprise personnel, the country has embarked on mass-scale training programs.

One of the principal vehicles for training workers and staff members is through the establishment of spare-time schools or colleges. Spare-time colleges and schools were first established in the early 1950s. In 1965 there were 410,000 workers enrolled in spare-time colleges and another 6.5 million in spare-time schools. In the 1950s and the first half of the 1960s, these spare-time schools succeeded in teaching many workers to read and write. In 1949 approximately 80 percent of the workers were illiterate, but by 1966 most had learned how to read and write. The activities of the spare-time colleges and schools were seriously disrupted during the Cultural Revolution.

Since 1977 spare-time schools and colleges have been reinstituted. Spare-time colleges include the Tube University and the correspondence and night colleges discussed previously. Spare-time schools are generally sponsored by the factories and mines at the grass-roots level or by the trade unions at the higher levels. At a national conference on workers' education in early 1980, the country decided to train 30 million young workers out of the total work force of 100 million workers. These 30 million young workers will attend various spare-time schools and training programs sponsored by the enterprises and other government agencies. A few of these schools and training programs are jointly sponsored by Chinese and foreign enterprises. All levels of enterprise personnel are enrolled in these spare-time education programs. Courses offered include general knowledge, science and technology, management, foreign languages, and other specialized subjects relevant to the particular enterprise (*Beijing Review*, February 18, 1980; October 13, 1980). Shangdong Province proposes to train all its workers under thirty-five years of age within the next three to five years to reach a minimum educational level of senior-middle-school or technical-secondary-school graduate (*Beijing Review*, April 6, 1979). By late 1980, 52 percent of the enterprises in Tianjin had established spare-time training programs. Approximately 23.5 percent of Tianjin's workers and staff members are enrolled in these programs (*Beijing Review*, October 13, 1980).

Throughout the country, commercial departments have also established training programs for their service workers. Workers in the various service sectors receive training at the respective cities that specialize in the particular trade. For example, workers are sent to Shanghai for training in television repair, tailoring, and window decoration. Workers in the field of commercial photography are sent to Beijing for training. In Guangdong workers are trained in optometry and the Cantonese culinary arts (*Beijing Review*, October 6, 1980).

In particular, China recognizes the need to train a large contingent of cadres who will be able to run the enterprises more efficiently. There are two types of cadres in Chinese enterprises: administrative and technical. In 1978 the government decided to train leading cadres in all enterprises, in rotation, between 1979 and 1982. In the first two years all party-committee secretaries, directors, chief engineers, deputy directors in charge of production in large- to medium-sized enterprises, and leading cadres in administrative departments in transportation and industry will be trained. The duration of the training program varies. Upon completion of the training program, the cadres must sit for an exam to determine whether they have mastered the contents of the programs. In 1979, for instance, ninety-eight directors from large and medium-sized textile mills throughout China attended a three-month training program sponsored by the Shanghai Textile Institute. Courses taught included socialist political economy and enterprise management. Among the subjects covered under enterprise management were planning, quality control, financial and cost accounting (*Beijing Review,* June 23, 1980). Besides full-time training programs, enterprises also offer on-the-spot training programs and spare-time courses. In addition, some cadres are sent overseas to further their technical skills.

China Enterprise Management Association

To further the goal of developing enterprise management, the China Enterprise Management Association (CEMA) was established. The following information on CEMA was obtained in an interview with Mr. Zhang Yenning, secretary-general of the China Enterprise Management Association and member and director of bureau, State Economic Commission.

CEMA was established on March 3, 1979, as a nongovernmental agency that is funded by the government. Its membership is open to cadres, administrators, university faculty members, researchers, and factory technicians. CEMA reports to the State Economic Commission. The president of CEMA is Yuan Baohua, vice-chairman of the State Economic Commission.

CEMA sponsors workshops, seminars, and vocational training for management personnel. Its functions are primarily fourfold:

1. It promotes technical-information exchange among large- and medium-sized enterprises throughout China for the specific purpose of raising the productivity of China's 400,000 enterprises.

2. To train managers, deputy general managers, and engineers, CEMA sponsors workshops and seminars and invites foreign experts to give lectures. The seminars range from one week to two months in duration. In the training programs the cadres learn advanced management techniques and how to implement these successfully in their enterprises. CEMA is interested in all functional areas of management, particularly financial management, quality control, production, accounting, and general management.

China plans to introduce the use of computers wherever applicable and possible. Consequently, the government has invited experts to teach the use of computers. In September 1980 the World Bank sent a team to China to teach the application of computers to financing.

3. CEMA disseminates knowledge through publications. By July 1980 CEMA had published six periodicals, which are used as teaching materials in training programs for management personnel. These periodicals are not published regularly. The agency's magazine, *Enterprise Management,* is published quarterly. CEMA has signed an agreement with *Business Week* to publish a periodical entitled *Modern Management.* The first issue appeared in August 1980, followed by one more issue in 1980. In 1981 there were quarterly publications of *Modern Management.*

4. CEMA sponsors exchange programs in the field of management. Organizational specialists from China will undertake study tours abroad, and foreign experts are also invited to visit Chinese factories. The first U.S. association CEMA contacted was the American Management Association. In October 1979 and March 1980, the president and vice-president of the American Management Association visited China. CEMA also plans to establish contacts with more research-oriented associations.

CEMA has members from over twenty-nine provinces. Membership is on either an enterprise or an individual basis. The 60 enterprise members consist of large- and medium-sized enterprises. The 130 individual members include eminent scholars in economics and management. CEMA is responsible only for enterprises above the county level. Enterprises below that level are managed by the municipalities.

CEMA has established local enterprise-management associations in Liaoning Province and in the cities of Lanzhou, Shanghai, and Tianjin. In the future, local associations will be set up in Hunan Province and the city of Guangzhou. These local enterprise-management associations are under the direction of CEMA.

CEMA emphasizes that the development of enterprise management in China will be done in the "Chinese way." This essentially means that China will learn the experiences of the United States, Japan, and Western Europe. Some technology transfer will take place that can be applied directly to the operations of certain Chinese enterprises. Also, foreign technology and techniques will be assessed in light of China's objective conditions to determine their suitability for the country's use and the modifications that need to be made. Some machinery and equipment from abroad may not be appropriate for China. In that case the country will use the foreign experience only as a reference. For example, the Tianjin Bicycle Factory invited Japanese experts to study its operations, give lectures, and offer recommendations and suggestions for improvement. The Japanese offered suggestions on how to improve the assembly line, which were reviewed in light of existing conditions in the factory. These included an assessment of the factory's personnel and equipment. Necessary adjustment were made to suit existing conditions. As a result, the operations of the factory have been greatly improved.

CEMA sees the major impediments to China's modernization program as primarily fourfold:

1. Management skills at the various enterprises differ, and at some enterprises these skills are low. For example, in the Petroleum and Chemical Corporation, management is quite advanced.
2. There are idle capacities on existing machinery. China will try to make fuller use of these machines in the future.
3. The technical skills of the administrative personnel are not high. Some general managers of medium-sized enterprises have no professional training.

These factories plan to sponsor training programs for their general managers. Management in rural areas are trained by local authorities, and some are trained by CEMA. CEMA provides lecturers for such training programs.

4. China lags seriously behind the advanced nations in science and technology. Consequently, it has much catching up to do. China hopes to effect these changes by the end of the twentieth century, although Mr. Zhang declines to comment on whether China will be able to surpass the United States or Japan by the year 2000.

Books and Other Publications

Besides the aforementioned means of raising the educational and technical standards of China's people, another method is the dissemination of information through books, journals, and other publications. In early 1980 China had 1,200 newspapers and periodicals, compared with 750 in 1976. Circulation reached 112 million copies in 1978, and was up by another 44.8 percent in 1979 (*Beijing Review,* April 27, 1979; February 4, 1980). In one month alone Beijing's 105 bookstores sold 400,000 copies of a self-teaching book series to middle-school students. Popular subjects include mathematics, physics, and chemistry. Foreign textbooks are also popular (*Beijing Review,* January 21, 1980). Most of the people are eager to advance their knowledge through books and other publications. In fact, one U.S. advertising agency, Benjamin Company of New York, has decided to capitalize on this popularity by employing books as a medium for advertising. Benjamin Company plans to distribute to libraries, schools, enterprises, and government agencies millions of Chinese and English books (primarily in the form of cheap paperbacks) that contain advertisements on the back and inside covers or in special bound-in inserts. The president of the company noted that "with 25 'readings' anticipated on each sponsored book available through the various Chinese library networks, the advertiser can anticipate remarkable exposure for his message" (*The Washington Post,* March 30, 1981). This proposal has met with the approval of the Publishers Association of China, which intends to give the campaign its full support since there is still a shortage of reading material, particularly books in the English language, in the country.

Discussion

On the basis of the foregoing analysis of the industrial workers' attitude toward work, achievement, and technical innovation, and of China's educational policy, it appears that although the country has made considerable headway, much remains to be done. However, the very fact that China recognizes the importance of education in the socialist modernization effort is encouraging, for without a large contingent of skilled workers and technicians, all the advanced technologies and capital in the world will not warrant its attainment.

8 Motivational Patterns in Chinese Industrial Enterprises

A study of motivational patterns in Chinese industrial enterprises is interesting from the viewpoints of both the practitioner and the academician.

From the practitioner's perspective, the normalization of diplomatic relations between the United States and the PRC signaled a new era of expanded trade between the two countries. The trade figures between China and the United States for 1979, the first year of normalization, more than doubled those for the preceding year. Many U.S. firms are eager to get a piece of the action in the Chinese market because of the vast potentials such a large country holds for a firm's future profitability. China's commitment to the goals of the Four Modernizations presents opportunities for U.S. businesses to involve themselves in the development and subsequently to reap the fruits of modernization of a hitherto largely untapped market of 975 million people (Kraar 1975).

A further stimulus to trade relations between the United States and the PRC was provided by the enactment of the China Joint Venture Laws on July 1, 1979. This law offers foreign firms the opportunity to set up factories and manufacturing facilities in China. In order to benefit fully from such joint-venture relationships, the non-Chinese partner must have a basic understanding of how Chinese enterprises are run and how Chinese workers are motivated.

From the academician's viewpoint, although Chinese management theories and techniques are fairly underdeveloped compared with those of the advanced nations, China does provide an interesting case for study and comparison. China's experiences might be regarded as a large-scale social experiment. Under the Communist party the Chinese have become fairly effectively organized and mobilized to develop the productive forces available (Kraar 1975).

This chapter examines how Chinese industrial enterprises motivate their workers to increase productivity. In the *Social Psychology of Organizations* (1978), Katz and Kahn identified three basic types of motivational patterns:

1. *rule enforcement,* wherein organizational members accept role prescriptions and organizational directives because of their legitimacy
2. *external rewards,* wherein incentives tied to desired behaviors or outcomes are instrumental to achieving specific rewards

An abridged version of this chapter previously appeared in R.L. Tung, "Patterns of Motivation in Chinese Industrial Enterprises," *Academy of Management Review* 6 (1981): 487–494. Reprinted with permission.

3. *internalized motivation,* wherein organizational goals are internalized and become part of the individual's own value system

The methods of motivating workers in Chinese industrial enterprises can be analyzed according to these three basic motivational patterns.

Rule Enforcement

In comparison with their Western counterparts, Chinese industrial personnel—managers, technicians (collectively known as *cadres* in China), and workers—are given exact, detailed prescriptions for what is expected of them as members of a factory, workshop, or work unit. Since late 1978 the state has granted greater autonomy in decision making to a select group of enterprises on an experimental basis. The state has also allowed the use of free-market mechanisms on a limited scale. The free-market mechanism, however, is always subject to and controlled by central planning (Lin 1980). After all, China is a planned socialist economy. Consequently, even with the reforms, the state still sets minimal production targets, allocates raw materials, and purchases and markets a fixed percentage of the enterprises' output. In addition, the state prescribes the overall policies that industry should follow in its enterprises. The party committee attached to each enterprise and the trade union to which employees in a particular enterprise belong both make sure these policies are clearly understood by all concerned and are adhered to in the operations of the enterprise (Laaksonen 1975). It should be noted, however, that these political guidelines and principles will not be applied to the joint-venture enterprises. New laws governing labor-management relations in joint ventures were promulgated on July 26, 1980. Details of these regulations are given in appendix F. Joint ventures will be run along Western lines. After all, one of the purposes of establishing joint-venture concerns in China is to facilitate the acquisition of advanced technologies from abroad, including Western management techniques. However, joint-venture enterprises will be influenced by local conditions to a certain extent. If, as senior-ranking officials insist, China will modernize in the Chinese way, then it will not implement Western management techniques indiscriminately.

The policies adhered to in the current operation of Chinese industrial enterprises include the *relevant* principles embodied in the Charter of the Anshan Iron and Steel Company; "In Industry, learn from Daqing"; the thirty-point Decision on Industry; and the Three-Year Plan (1979–1981) on readjustment, restructuring, consolidating, and improvement of China's economy. The key words here are *where relevant.* In China the current emphasis is on the slogan "practice is the sole criterion for truth." This means that only those principles that have proved to work in practice should be upheld. Since political, economic, and social conditions change over time, it is fallacious to adhere to archaic principles that do not fit prevailing conditions. These policies and guidelines were discussed in chapter 2.

External Rewards

Two types of incentives are currently used in China to reward workers for their labor and to motivate them to heighten their performance. The state "applies the policy of combining moral encouragement with material reward, with the stress on the former, in order to heighten the citizens' socialist enthusiasm and creativeness in work" (*Constitution of the PRC,* 1978, Article 10).

China's leaders, both past and present, have never questioned the superiority of nonmaterial incentives or moral encouragement. However, they were not naive enough to assume that the human desire for material gains could be eliminated all at once (Richman 1969; Riskin 1975; Oh 1976). Consequently, throughout the PRC's history, particularly in periods of political stability and economic progress, one sees the dual use of material incentives and moral encouragement.

The principal forms of material incentives used are wages (based either on hourly work or on piecework), subsidies, bonuses, other welfare benefits provided to workers, and direct linkage of the enterprise's or work unit's performance with the amount of profits to be retained for its own personal use (Lin 1980). The latter ties in with the notions of competition and democratic self-management of enterprises. Each of these will be discussed in detail.

Wages, Subsidies, and Bonuses

Most of the information provided on the wage system, unless otherwise stated, was obtained through an interview with Mr. Sun Jen, chief of the Division of Policy Research at the Labor Bureau. China's wage policy is governed by two principles. On the one hand, the state is opposed to a wide wage spread. In the first half of 1980 the lowest-paid worker earned approximately 35 yuan per month, and the highest-paid official, including the premier, made approximately 450 yuan, a differential of only twelve times. (Before devaluation of the Chinese currency on January 1, 1981, 1.55 yuan was approximately equal to U.S. $1.00. Since devaluation the rate is 2.8 yuan to U.S. $1.00.) On the other hand, China is opposed to absolute egalitarianism. It espouses the socialist principle of "from each according to his ability, to each according to his work" and "more pay for more work, less pay for less work." The state believes that absolute egalitarianism may dampen people's enthusiasm for socialism.

Since the 1950s the Chinese wage system has been reformed several times. In 1956 the unified-wage-scale system was adopted. Wage scales are divided into those for cadres and those for workers. *Cadres* refer to the administrative staff, engineers, and senior technicians in government organizations and industrial enterprises. Cadres are governed by a twenty-five-grade wage scale. The wage system for 1980 is presented in table 8–1.

This twenty-five-grade wage system applies to government organizations and to some industrial enterprises. The levels of cadres in enterprises correspond to those in government organizations but are not identical because of the differences in size. In industrial enterprises the wage system is generally more complicated because of the variations in organizational size and operating conditions. Mr. Sun of the Labor Bureau indicated that this twenty-five-grade wage system represents a functional wage scale. Each function generally has several levels of wage scales. For example, the position of factory director spans several grades. This accounts for the variations in salaries received by directors at different factories. The differential between the wage received by a grade 1 cadre (the highest grade) and grade 25 (the lowest grade) in the twenty-five-grade wage system is approximately twelve times. In practice, the lowest grade for cadres is grade 23. Grades 24 and 25 are mainly service staff personnel, not really cadres.

The premier of China receives the wage accorded a grade 1 cadre. In 1956 a grade 1 cadre earned 640 yuan per month. Since then, the leaders in the country have voluntarily reduced their wages on three separate occasions to bring about a more equitable distribution of income. In 1980 the leaders of China earned an average of 404 yuan. The wages for chief engineers are in the high 200-yuan category, and that for managers start in the low 100-yuan. In 1980 in Beijing, the monthly wage for a cadre of grade 23 is 49.5 yuan.

The wages for workers are governed by an eight-grade wage system differentiated according to variations in skills from unskilled (grade 1) to highly skilled (grade 8). The exact number of grades for workers varies across industries. These variations are not determined by the enterprises themselves, but are stipulated by the state according to the different fields of production. Enterprises are divided into several sectors: heavy industry, light industry, and the commercial sector. In certain fields of production, enterprises are governed by a ten-grade wage system, whereas in others there are only six grades. In general, workers in heavy-industrial enterprises earn higher wages than those employed

Table 8–1
Monthly Wage under the Twenty-Five-Grade Cadre System
(in Yuan)

Grade	1	...	8	...	17,	18,	19,	20,	21,	22,	...	25
Wage	450	...	270	...	98,	86,	78,	70,	62,	56,	...	38

in light-industrial enterprises. Workers in the latter, in turn, are generally higher paid than those in the commercial sector. Although variations exist, the wage range is fairly uniform across enterprises in different industries and across different parts of the country.

The differential between grades 1 and 8 under the eight-grade system is 2.8–3.1 times, with an average of 3 times. The wage range varies according to the different fields of production. For example, in a medium-sized heavy-industrial enterprise in Beijing, the range from the lowest- to the highest-grade worker is from 33 to 99 yuan. There is usually a 17-percent difference between each grade. In light-industrial enterprises the range is from 31 to more than 80 yuan. Enterprises in the commercial sector are governed by a ten-grade wage system, with a range from 30 to 80 yuan. The average wage for a worker in China in the first half of 1980 was 55–60 yuan per month.

For wage purposes, government organizations and state-owned enterprises in the country were originally categorized into one of twelve districts. This number has now been reduced to eight. The actual amount of wages paid in each district depends on the price of commodities in the region. In general, there is a 3-percent wage difference between each of these areas. For instance, in remote areas, where prices are high, living conditions are spartan, and transportation is inconvenient, local subsidies are given. These subsidies generally amount to several dozen percent of the monthly wage. These remote areas are referred to as high-wage-scale areas.

In 1980 the average per capita wage in the urban areas is 781 yuan (an increase of 76 yuan from 1979), and the per capita wage in the rural areas is 170 yuan. Although a substantial income gap exists between the urban and rural sectors, the 1980 figure is already double that for 1979. In 1979 the per capita income for rural areas was only 83.4 yuan (*Beijing Review,* February 23, 1981).

Prior to 1979 there was a stipulation that the wages of workers in collectively owned enterprises could not exceed those of workers in state-owned enterprises. In June 1979 this ban was lifted in order to stimulate production in the collectively owned enterprises, in accordance with the principle of "more work, more pay" (*Beijing Review,* June 29, 1979, p. 3). Most collectively owned enterprises in the big cities have already followed this principle. In collectively owned enterprises wages are differentiated on the basis of the worker's skill. The principle of "more work, more pay" is also practiced. In chapter 9, which presents case studies of several enterprises, both state-owned and collectively owned, comparisons of wages can be made.

In the early 1950s wage increases were determined by local authorities. In 1956 this system was replaced by the unified wage system. From then on the central authorities made all major decisions about wage increases. Wage increases are decided by the state in accordance with the national economic plan. Wage increases are of two general types: fixed increases and other increases. Fixed increases refer to increases in wages pertaining to promotion in an organization.

For example, an apprentice must be promoted to the level of first-grade worker in two to three years' time. Similarly, a first-grade worker must be promoted to the second-grade level within one year. Since 1977 it has been proposed that promotions from apprentice to first-grade worker and from first to second grade should be based on examinations. The government promotes the use of the examination system. As of mid-1980, however, this practice has not been implemented in all enterprises throughout the country. In Mr. Sun's words, "even in some enterprises where they were implemented, they were not carried out satisfactorily." Besides fixed wage increases, the government also accords other increases. The state increased wages in 1956, 1959, 1960, 1971, 1977, 1978, 1979, and 1980. The wage increases in 1956, 1963, 1977, and 1979 covered a fairly large segment of the work force. In 1977, for instance, 46 percent of workers and staff members were given a wage or wage-grade increase, and another 20 percent had their wages upgraded to some extent. In 1978, 2 percent of the workers who were outstanding in their respective fields were given a wage increase. In November 1979, 40 percent of the country's workers and government employees were given promotions and wage increases. In some areas, such as health, education, science, and technology, approximately 42–48 percent of the workers received wage increases.

The government has commissioned a number of leading economists to study the relationships between wage increases and rises in productivity. In the First Five-Year Plan (1953–1957), productivity increased 64 percent, and wages were raised by approximately 33 percent in the same period. In the Second Five-Year Plan (1958–1952), productivity increased by 50 percent, and wages were raised by some 25 to 33 percent (*Study in Socialist Productivity*, vol. 2, 1978). Based on their analysis of wage and productivity figures over the 1950s and the early 1960s, a number of economists concluded that in order to stimulate economic growth, the ratio of increase in productivity to increase in wages should be approximately 2 to 1. The present policy of raising workers' wages commensurate with increases in productivity is designed to stimulate economic growth.

To be eligible for a wage increase, the worker's political standing, attitude toward labor, achievements, and skills must be democratically appraised by their colleagues. Based on such assessments, a list of workers deserving pay increases is drawn up. This list must be endorsed by the leadership of the respective units before the wage increase goes into effect. In the process of determining eligibility for pay increases, the party committee does a great deal of ideological education among the workers, familiarizing them with the country's present political and economic situations and explaining to them why a wage increase has been possible, why more people could not get an increase, and why a bigger pay increase is not possible at this stage. Workers are also given a better understanding of the various criteria used and how to apply them correctly. This ideological education tends to lessen the feelings of inequity and animosity that workers may otherwise have.

In China wages are paid for hourly or time work or for piecework. Time work is the major form used in the country. Time-rate wages are measured directly by the duration of labor and are therefore paid according to work done over a certain period of time and up to a certain level in quality. Workers in most enterprises across the country work eight hours a day, six days a week. In 1979 a system of shorter workdays or shorter workweeks was introduced on an experimental basis. In the second half of 1980, for instance, the Ministry of Coal Industry decreed that the "four-shift six-hour day" system should apply to underground workers in all coal mines throughout the country (*Beijing Review,* August 4, 1980). Other variations of the shorter work week have been introduced in other industries, as evidenced in the case studies presented in chapter 9.

Subsidies or extra allowances are given to those performing jobs under harsh working conditions or jobs requiring higher labor intensity. In the coal mines, for instance, workers who toil underground are paid more than those working on the surface. The differential is paid in the form of a subsidy. This ensures a steady number of workers willing to work underground.

Under the piecework system the worker is paid in direct proportion to the quantity of work done or items produced. The piecework system is suited to many different kinds of work, especially work involving physical strength, such as loading, unloading, and transportation. Since 1949 the piecework system has been introduced and then abolished on three separate occasions. In 1956 approximately 42 percent of the work force was paid under the piecework system (Riskin 1975). In periods of ideological upheavals, the piecework system was denounced as capitalistic. Past performance figures indicated that production increased in the aforementioned job categories each time the piecework system was in vogue, and declined whenever the system was revoked. In 1978, when the piecework system was reintroduced for teams of stevedores at the Whampoa Harbor in Guangzhou, loading and unloading were done more promptly and efficiently. Based on a 1979 survey of occupations that had introduced the piecework system, it was estimated that labor efficiency had increased by 18.4 percent as a result of the implementation of the new system (*Beijing Review,* July 21, 1980).

Besides time work and piecework, workers receive overtime pay and bonuses for extra work done. In the Shanghai General Rug Plant, for instance, workers were paid 1.5 yuan over and above their basic pay for each eight extra hours of work in which they could produce one more square foot of rug (Miller 1979, p. 41).

Like the piecework system, bonuses have been introduced and canceled on three separate occasions (Richman 1969). The current practice of using bonuses was reinstated in the spring of 1978. Under the current system, bonuses generally average 25–35 percent of the workers' basic wage (Miller 1979). In a survey of ten factories in Beijing that had introduced the bonus system, it was found that profits increased by 18.9 million yuan after the implementation of the system. Bonus payments in these factories totaled 438,000 yuan, or 2.32 percent of the total profits generated (*Beijing Review,* April 20, 1979). In China practically all enterprises use bonuses. In 1978 a fourteen-point experimental program was introduced in a select sample of enterprises in Sichuan province. These reforms gave the enterprises greater autonomy in managing their own affairs, including the right to retain a certain percentage of profits for distribution as bonuses to workers or for expansion of production facilities. By 1980 this type of experiment had been introduced in some 6,600 enterprises throughout China. In a 1980 survey of these experimental units, it was found that in 1979 the average bonus received by workers in the experimental enterprises was 120 yuan. This figure represents approximately twice the average workers' monthly wage (*Beijing Review,* April 6, 1981). This system of giving bonuses has been warmly received by both cadres and workers because it helps them see the relationship between hard work and more money. During her visit to China in May 1979, then U.S. Commerce Secretary Juanita Kreps was told by Chinese officials that a full 12 percent of China's payroll now goes for incentives. Raymond Vernon, a professor of international business at Harvard who was on the trip, indicated that although this percentage is higher than that in the United States, "it makes sense" because unlike their U.S. counterparts, Chinese workers cannot switch jobs at their own discretion. Consequently, they need incentives to make them committed to their jobs (Miller 1979, p. 41).

To ensure that bonuses will produce the desired results, since 1979 several factories have adopted the system of economic accounting on a trial basis. Economic accounting is designed to overcome the unhealthy tendencies associated with the practice of everyone receiving the same renumeration regardless of relative contribution. This practice has now been replaced by the slogan that "even among brothers, accounts should be settled without ambiguity" (*Beijing Review,* August 31, 1979). In the past, only top management was concerned with the fulfillment of state quotas. Lower-level cadres and workers were concerned only with the amount of output, not with costs and profits. This led to inefficiency and to a waste of manpower and materials. The system of business accounting is practiced at two levels of the organization—at the enterprise level and at the workshop level. Under the guidance of the production plan drawn up by top management, the workshops sign contracts among themselves setting forth the rights and duties on either side. A workshop that fails to fulfill the terms of a contract will assume liability for any loss and make adequate compensation. A workshop that makes more profit will be allowed to retain a portion of this profit for distribution to its workers as bonuses. This system of economic accounting, which ties in with the policy of linking the enterprise's or workshop's performance directly with the amount of profits retained for its own use, has produced encouraging results.

Since November 1978 the State Council has authorized all state-owned enterprises to establish an enterprise-fund system. Under this system, any enterprise that fulfills all its state quotas could retain a portion of its profits to be set aside in the enterprise fund. This fund could be used for distribution as bonuses or for expanding welfare benefits to workers. Within six months of the implementation of the system, enterprise funds throughout the country amounted to 1,700 million yuan (*Beijing Review,* July 20, 1979).

Despite changes in the wage structure, Sun Jen, chief of the Division of Policy Research at the Labor Bureau, concedes that several problems still remain:

1. There is no regular wage increase. Between 1966 and 1976 there were very few increases. During those years production levels declined, and the government did not have enough money for wage increases. With the changes in the economic system, Sun believes that productivity should increase in the future. This would alleviate the problem of sporadic wage increases.
2. The wage system is not comprehensive. Although the criteria for wage increases are identified, it is not clear what weight should be assigned to each respective criterion.
3. There are shortcomings in the wage system. Although the government has encouraged the implementation of the principles of "from each according to his work" and "more work, more pay," these principles are not always applied correctly in practice. In some factories a worker cannot receive higher wages even if he is very good.

Sun is quick to add that the government is aware of the limitations inherent in the present system and seeks to rectify the situation.

In addition to wages and bonuses, workers enjoy very generous sickness, injury, disability, maternity, retirement, death, and other benefits (Weinbaum 1976; Hsu 1977). In 1977 the welfare bill amounted to 17 percent of the total amount paid out in wages for state-run enterprises. This was borne in full by the state.

Sickness, Injury, and Disability Benefits

Workers are entitled to sick leave with pay. For absences of less than six months the worker receives full pay in the first month and 70–100 percent of wages from the second month onward. Where a worker is absent from his or her job for more than six months because of illness, he or she is entitled to 50–80 percent of wages for the entire duration of the sickness. The benefits for workers and staff members in industrial and commercial enterprises are slightly different. In the first six months of absence from work as a result of illness, workers receive 60–100 percent of wages. Thereafter they are paid 40–60 percent of wages. The state pays all medical and hospital expenses. When members of the worker's family fall ill, the state pays half their medical and hospital expenses. For example, if a member of the worker's family requires an appendectomy, the worker pays 2.5 yuan (1979 figure), and the state pays the balance of 2.5 yuan.

When a worker sustains an injury or becomes chronically ill, he or she is admitted to a workers' sanatorium on the recommendation of the factory's trade union and after an examination by a hospial. Since 1979 over 60 workers' sanatoria run by provincial and municipal trade unions have been reopened. In addition, there are 800 small sanatoria operated by large- and medium-sized enterprises (*Beijing Review*, July 13, 1979). Workers' sanatoria are usually located in scenic resorts with mild climates. A worker who sustains injury while at work enjoys free medical benefits, pays for only two-thirds of food expenses while in the hospital, and receives full pay while recuperating. If a worker sustains permanent injury that prevents him or her from working for the rest of his or her life, he or she receives monthly payments equal to 80–90 percent of wages. In addition, the factory or the trade union will provide special assistance by sending others to help with housework (*China Reconstructs*, May 1981).

Retirement Benefits

The retirement age for male workers is sixty and for women workers, fifty. Women cadres and teachers retire at fifty-five. Those who work under adverse conditions, such as underground in mines, in high temperatures, or at high altitudes, may retire five years earlier.

Upon retirement the worker receives a certificate acknowledging his or her contribution to the state and is given monthly pension payments. The actual amount of pension paid varies depending on the number of years on the job and on whether or not the individual is a model worker. In 1978 the State Council stipulated that pensions may range from 60 to 90 percent of a worker's monthly pay. Upon retirement, one son or daughter of a retired worker may be employed in the parent's work unit, provided he or she is qualified for the job. Before a worker retires, the work unit helps the individual solve the various difficulties that may arise after retirement. Approximately 70 percent of the trade unions in Beijing's enterprises have organized special committees to take care of their retired employees. These committees organize study sessions to familiarize the retired with the party's principles and policies, hand out retirement funds, distribute relief funds to those in financial difficulties, and make funeral arrangements. Some retired workers with professional skills are invited to serve as advisors in workshops for youth. At major festivals the committee organizes factory leaders to visit the retired employees. In 1979 approximately 20,000 retired workers wanted to return to the countryside to spend the remaining years of their lives. The state gave each of them an allowance of 300 yuan to assist in relocation (*Beijing Review*, July 21, 1980). Retired workers enjoy free medical care. In addition, it is written into the 1981 Marriage Law that children have an obligation to support their parents if the latter require assistance.

The state also pays for funeral expenses. In general, the funeral allowance is around 240 yuan. For workers who die at work, the state pays the family of the deceased an amount equivalent to three months' worth of the worker's wage. For the deceased's dependents, the state pays a monthly amount equivalent to 25–50 percent of the deceased's wage until the minors become financially independent or until the parents of the deceased die. If the worker dies of ordinary illness, the funeral expenses borne by the state are equivalent to two months' worth of the worker's wage. In addition, the dependents receive a lump-sum payment equivalent to six to twelve months' worth of the deceased's wage. In general, this lump sum amounts to 400–700 yuan (*China Reconstructs,* May 1981).

Other Benefits

Other benefits include housing, generous maternity benefits, transportation subsidies, and day-care facilities for workers' children. Where possible, the factory provides accommodation for the workers. Rents generally require less than 5 percent of the worker's income. There is an extreme shortage of housing for workers in China, but the government is taking measures to correct the situation. A visitor to China notices the large number of construction projects for workers' housing under way in all major cities. In 1979 the government allocated 3,000 million yuan for urban housing construction. In 1979, 4 million people in urban areas and industrial and mining centers were assigned new housing. More houses are under construction; in Beijing, housing starts in 1980 increased by 83 percent over 1979. In addition to constructing houses with state funds, the government has encouraged enterprises to build houses with enterprise funds. Since 1980 the state, in a move unprecedented in the history of the PRC, has allowed individuals to purchase houses in many provinces, municipalities, and autonomous regions. In the city of Shenyang in northeastern China, 139 families registered to buy houses within ten days of the announcement by the State Bureau of Urban Construction that henceforth individuals could buy houses. The average price of a house is 7,000–8,000 yuan. This may be paid in a lump sum, or buyers can assume a 15-year mortgage at an annual interest rate of 1–2 percent. In addition, for the first time in the history of the PRC, the government has allowed individuals in some cities to build houses for their own use (*Beijing Review,* October 20, 1980).

Some factories provide free transportation for their workers to and from their residences. Others pay a transportation allowance of 2 yuan per month.

Maternity leaves extend fifty-six days after the birth of an infant. For families who subscribe to the one-child policy, the mother is given six months leave after the birth of the child. When she returns to work, the mother can leave the infant in the day-care center adjacent to the workshop. Some day-care facilities attached to the enterprises charge a fee of 4–5 yuan per month per child, but others provide free services. Children who come from one-child families are admitted free. A mother who chooses to breast-feed the infant is given time off from her job daily for that purpose. Since the day-care centers are adjacent to the workshops, the mothers can walk over during lunch hours and spend time with their infants. This system of providing child-care facilities at the place of work has attracted attention from some U.S. firms. For example, the Photo Corporation of America International, the world's third largest manufacturer of color photos, employing over 2,700 people worldwide, has introduced this system. According to a company spokesman, this system generates good public relations, promotes good human relations within the company, and above all is cost efficient. Since the implementation of the system, the turnover rate in the company has declined because employees feel more comfortable knowing their children are well cared for while they work. Reduced turnover translates into savings of around $40,000 a year for the company—$30,000 for training new employees, plus $10,000 for recruitment advertising. Furthermore, the system is well received in the community, as demonstrated by the fact that although the whole community has an unemployment rate of 2–3 percent, in 1978 alone there were over 3,500 walk-in applicants (*Seattle Post-Intelligence,* December 17, 1979).

Those workers who are temporarily displaced by the restructuring of enterprises under the Three-Year Plan for Readjustment (1979–1981) will continue to receive their full salaries. Meanwhile, they will be assigned to odd jobs such as maintenance and planting trees around the factory. In addition, they will receive special training in an occupation that is needed in society. The government views this as a form of "intellectual investment." These people will also receive priority in job assignments to other enterprises (*China Reconstructs,* April 1981).

Workers in collectively owned enterprises enjoy the same welfare benefits. For such enterprises, the costs of such programs are borne by the individual enterprise, not the state. The benefits paid are commensurate with the income of these enterprises (*China Reconstructs,* May 1981).

Although workers in China enjoy generous welfare benefits, wages in China remain low. At a meeting with visiting overseas Chinese in late 1974, Deng Xiaoping noted that in order to develop the national economy, the wages of workers would have to remain low (*Beijing Review,* February 28, 1975, p. 5). Because of this situation, Yu Guangyuan, an economist and vice-president of the Chinese Academy of Social Sciences, admitted that the government still needs to educate workers about the importance of subordinating self-interest to that of the state and about the need to "adopt a correct attitude towards the relations between overall and local interests and between long-term and immediate interests" (*Beijing Review,* May 12, 1980). Since wages in China are very low compared with those in the advanced nations, it is worthwhile to examine briefly the budget of an average urban family in order to illustrate the real purchasing power of the average Chinese worker's salary. The following is a breakdown of the monthly expenses of an average family in Shanghai (*China Reconstructs,* March 1980). The husband and wife together earn 146 yuan per month. They support two older people and two young children. The couple spends 14 yuan on rent, water, electricity, and gas; 12 yuan on nursery fees; 21 yuan for lunch at the factory cafeteria for both husband and wife; 58 yuan on food for meals at home; 10 yuan for cigarettes, candy, and fruit; and 16 yuan for miscellaneous expenses. Deducting total expenditures from the combined incomes still leaves a small sum for savings. As pointed out previously, the government emphasizes thrift and frugality. Consequently, although incomes are low, most people manage to save a certain percentage of their monthly incomes. In 1979 it was estimated that the average city dweller had over 200 yuan in savings in the bank. In the first half of 1980 savings deposits in urban areas recorded an increase of 4,000 million yuan, a 1,100-million-yuan increase over the previous record high set in 1979 (*Beijing Review,* July 28, 1980).

To maintain the policy of low wages, the government must stabilize the prices of essential commodities. Although the prices of meat and other non-essential commodities rose by some 30 percent in late 1979, shortly after the government lifted the ban, the prices of essential commodities have remained fairly stable over the past thirty years. In 1978 a kilogram of rice retailed for 0.304 yuan, compared with 0.296 in 1952. A kilogram of wheat flour sold for 0.370 yuan in 1978, compared with 0.344 yuan in 1952; a meter of cotton cloth retailed for 0.840 yuan in 1978, compared with 0.867 yuan in 1952 (*China Reconstructs,* January 1980). The prices of essential commodities are still subject to state control. Even with the controls, the government expressed concern over the development of inflationary trends. The government announced that the inflation rate in 1980 was 6 percent but promised to eradicate inflation under the 1981 National Economic Plan. The success of these efforts remain to be seen.

Internalized Motivation

In China internalized motivation is almost synonymous with moral encouragement. The state emphasizes that all types of material incentives must be used in conjunction with moral encouragement, with emphasis on the latter (Richman 1969; Riskin 1975; Oh 1976). Moral encouragement involves the principle of "fight self"—that is, the individual must seek to emulate the ideal communist, one who is prepared to sacrifice his or her self-interest for the general welfare and progress of all others and the state. It also involves the application of the principle of "from each according to his ability," whereby every worker must do his best, regardless of wage. The principal means of moral encouragement used are socialist labor emulation drives, commendations for pacesetters, and political indoctrination or education.

Socialist Emulation Drives

The first socialist labor emulation drive was launched in Harbin in northeastern China shortly after the city's liberation in 1947. Since the early 1950s socialist emulation drives have been implemented widely across the country. From time to time certain factories, work units, and individuals are designated as advanced factories, units, and workers. These then serve as models for emulation by other factories, work units, and workers. Riskin (1975) noted that although socialist emulation drives do not involve the distribution of material awards, nevertheless the worker sees the direct link between working hard and achieving a desirable outcome. Awards meted out to advanced workers include honorific titles, certificates, medals, banners, attendance at meetings held in their honor at the national level, vacations, travel privileges, and opportunities for career advancement. The new minister of textiles was a model worker in the textile industry in the 1950s.

Socialist labor emulation drives are designed to serve two major purposes: (1) to develop friendly competition between factories, workshops, and individuals so that they will surpass past performance records and set new highs; and (2) to help the less advanced units and workers catch up with the more advanced ones. The latter notion is foreign to U.S. enterprises. In China the most productive unit or person is not supposed to flaunt its superiority and remain aloof from the less productive units and workers. Rather, the aim of emulation campaigns in China is to develop a spirit of cooperation and support so that the advanced units and workers can help the less productive ones improve their performance.

In early 1978, at an industrial conference in Harbin, a turners' group issued a challenge to its counterparts in the city to participate in a friendly emulation campaign. The campaign was carried out under the direction of the Harbin trade union headquarters. The 944 turners' groups were divided into 54 competition zones for purposes of inspection and exchange of information and experience. The results from each of the 54 competition zones were appraised and compared twice a year. The competition proved successful. By the end of 1978 approximately one-third of the turners' groups in Harbin had fulfilled their respective production quotas two months ahead of schedule, and 63 of them were cited by the city authorities as advanced groups (*Beijing Review,* June 8, 1979).

Most factories have emulation committees that meet periodically to appraise and compare the performance of the different workshops and workers. In the Shenyang Heavy Machinery Factory, for instance, the emulation committee meets once a month to appraise and compare the various workshops and work groups on the six norms of output, quality, consumption of raw and semifinished materials, safety, record of attendance, and cleaning up. The work group that fulfills the six norms well is commended. Upon approval at the factory level, the work group is cited as a red-banner or advanced unit. The recommendations and approvals are publicized throughout the factory. The names of advanced work groups or workers, with little red flags pinned beside their names, are displayed on emulation charts throughout the workshop. At the end of the quarter, the performances of the work units are summarized. The work groups or individuals that have performed consistently well over the past months are commended. The photos and names of these pacesetters are displayed in show windows strategically situated at the factory entrance.

In enterprises throughout the country one finds colorful charts drawn on blackboards or huge posters, complete with statistics indicating the targets set and the results attained in the emulation campaigns between the various workshops, work groups, and individuals. Little red paper flags are pinned besides the winner's name. This practice of publicizing the productivity rates of each worker generates a lot of peer pressure among the less productive workers to improve performance.

Commendation as Pacesetters at National Meetings

The outstanding achievements of certain advanced workers and work units are sometimes publicized nationally through the media (radio, television, and newspapers) so that workers and units from other parts of the country can seek to emulate, learn from, and catch up with these advanced units and individuals. In fact, the first five to ten minutes of the thirty-minute news broadcast every evening on China's Central Broadcasting Station is devoted to the profile of an advanced worker.

In addition, national conferences are held to honor the pacesetters from different industries. In May 1977, for instance, a national conference on "Learning from Daqing in Industry" was held, honoring the pacesetters from Daqing. At the conference enterprises across the country were exhorted to learn from the outstanding examples set by the cadres and workers in their performance of their duties. On September 28, 1979, the State Council held a meeting to commend 118 advanced enterprises and 222 national labor models. At the same time, 10,000 youths, women, and workers from different walks of life met in Beijing, where they were praised and commended by leading party officials as pacesetters. Three months later, on December 28, 1979, 340 people were honored as national model workers, and another 351 groups won the title of national advanced units. These awards were presented at the Great Hall of the People in Beijing. Leading CCP members attended the meeting and personally handed out the awards. During the presentation of awards, Li Xiannian spoke of the need to work toward the goals of the Four Modernizations and stated that henceforth the basic criterion for evaluating a worker's performance would be "contributions to the Four Modernizations" (*Beijing Review*, January 7, 1980, p. 8).

As pointed out previously, although it exhorts all individuals and enterprises to emulate the pacesetters and advanced units, the government has recognized the need to be critical of the experiences of these advanced units. In early 1981, in the case of Dazhai (formerly designated as a model in the agricultural sector), the government noted that henceforth "advanced models should never be elevated to the level of awe-inspiring sanctity." In emulating the achievements of an advanced model, one should still be aware of its limitations and shortcomings. Furthermore, since China is a vast country with different levels of technological and economic developments, it is not advisable to impose uniform practices and structures, regardless of the region's peculiar conditions (*Beijing Review,* April 2, 1981, p. 27).

Political Indoctrination

China's leaders recognize that moral encouragement by itself may not work unless it is accompanied by effective political indoctrination (Laaksonen 1975; Riskin 1975; Oh 1976; Stein and Stein 1978). As the government noted: "there is absolutely no doubt about the unity of politics and economics, the unity of politics and technique. This is true now and will always be true" (*Beijing Review,* May 11, 1979, p. 14). At each factory, the party committee and the trade union organize political-discussion sessions for the workers. Workers are required to attend political-study sessions and are evaluated on their political consciousness. Of course, the content discussed at the present political study sessions differs from that of the Cultural Revolution years. In those days meetings for "revolutionary mass criticism" and other political study sessions were held during working hours, disrupting factory operations. In the Shoudu Brewery Factory, which manufactures "Five Star" beer, a popular brand in China, it was estimated that in 1974 alone the factory lost some 13,500 work hours because of the many political study sessions. At present, workers at most factories discuss how they could make their own contributions to the goals of the Four Modernizations. In the Shoudu Brewery it was estimated that when material incentives (reintroduced in 1977) were combined with the correct dose of ideological indoctrination, the productivity and subsequently the net profits for the factory showed marked increases. In 1976 the factory brewed 12,050 tons of beer using 189 kilograms of grain, generating a net profit of 917,000 yuan. This compared with 14,244 tons brewed with 183 kilograms, producing a net profit of 1,066,000 yuan in 1977; and 19,758 tons brewed with 179 kilograms of grain, generating a net profit of 1,334,000 yuan in 1979 (*Beijing Review,* May 12, 1980). These figures indicate that where ideological indoctrination is practiced in moderation and is used in conjunction with material incentives, it can stimulate workers to raise productivity.

The purpose of political indoctrination is to heighten the workers' sense of responsibility as masters of the country and to foster within them the spirit of working selflessly. As pointed out in chapter 2, the government recognizes the role of ideology in speeding up the goals of the Four Modernizations. This has prompted the leadership to call on the country to build a "socialist spiritual civilization" wherein personal interests are subordinated to those of the state. Deng Xiaoping noted that building such a "socialist spiritual civilization" implies more than developments in education, science, and culture. These are, of course, important to the work of the Four Modernizations. In order for a "socialist spiritual civilization" to flourish, the population must be imbued with communist principles and ideals such as "unity, hard work and plain living, eagerness to acquire an education, attaching importance to the development of science, paying attention to personal hygiene and being polite and courteous" (*Beijing Review,* March 9, 1981, pp. 17–19). In response to the call to build a "socialist spiritual civilization", approximately 100,000 youths in Shanghai have responded by organizing themselves into 400 voluntary service teams to provide free repair of bicycles, radio sets, and household appliances, and other services such as tailoring and barbering. In the words of one of the youths who participated in such voluntary services, "Life will be more meaningful if one gives more than he takes!" (*Beijing Review,* March 2, 1981, p. 7).

Discussion

The material incentives in vogue in Chinese enterprises are essentially similar to those in capitalist societies—that is, in return for their contribution to the organization's goals, the employees earn the means of livelihood.

The nonmaterial incentives used in China, however, are somewhat foreign to the Western mentality. Most observers of the Chinese industrial scene are amazed at the considerable success of nonmaterial incentives in motivating workers. There are several possible reasons for the relative success of moral encouragement in Chinese industrial society:

1. In accordance with Maslow's theory of the hierarchy of human needs, once the basic physiological needs have been satisfied, the worker seeks to attain higher level needs. In China the basic physiological needs for all workers are taken care of by the state—social-insurance benefits for workers cover sickness, retirement, disability, death, and so on. Consequently, the workers will aspire to fulfill higher-level needs. Of course, it could be argued that the living standard of the Chinese worker is still far below that of his Western counterpart; however, the next two factors outlined, coupled with the fact that the worker's lot has improved substantially (compared with pre-1949 China) should be taken into consideration in evaluating the needs of a Chinese worker.

2. Money does not have too much purchasing power in China. Although the amounts and kinds of consumer goods available to residents have increased over the past two years, they are still limited by Western standards. In addition, China's leaders constantly emphasize the need to practice frugality. Even though

the Chinese are currently willing to spend more on clothing and other so-called luxury items, they are still very cautious about such purchases lest they be criticized by their peers as being too affluent or capitalistic in outlook. This attitude may be changing in light of the revised aims of socialist production. Until 1978 production was undertaken primarily for the sake of increasing production. The revised aim of production is to improve people's livelihoods. Despite this revision, the government still frowns on the development of wide gaps between people in terms of accumulation of wealth or consumption of consumer goods. In China criticism by one's peers, subordinates, and superiors exerts considerable pressure on an individual to act and behave in accordance with the party line.

3. Effective political indoctrination and education (Laaksonen 1975; Oh 1976; Stein and Stein 1978). As elaborated previously, the Communist party carries out very effective indoctrination and mass-education campaigns to ensure that the people will confirm to the party's policies and guidelines.

Up to now China has relied on a combination of rule enforcement, material incentives, and moral encouragement to spur workers to heighten performance on the job and to increase productivity. There is every indication that this trend will continue. With Zhao Ziyang, a proponent of incentive programs, taking over as premier of the country in September 1980, there may be a heavier emphasis on the use of material incentives. However, it would be naive to assume that China will abandon either rule enforcement or moral encouragement, since both methods have served the country well in the past, as evidenced by the fairly rapid economic strides made since 1949. After all, approximately 60 percent of China's population is under thirty years of age. This younger generation has been imbued, almost since birth, with the need to respect and obey official party policies and to become a true communist, inflamed with the zealous love for one's motherland. Consequently, firms that intend to set up manufacturing operations in China should know about these methods in order to put them to good use. With the introduction of advanced technology appropriate for this stage in the country's economic development, combined with the use of these three types of motivational devices, it is likely that productivity rates in the country will surge ahead in the years to come. This is encouraging from the foreign investor's point of view, as well as in terms of growth and expansion of trade between China and other countries.

Reforms in the Economic System and Management of Industrial Organizations

At the Third Plenary Session of the party's Eleventh Central Committee, held in December 1978, a decision was made to reform China's economic system and the management of industrial organizations in order to facilitate the early attainment of the goals of the Four Modernizations. This chapter focuses on reforms in the structure and management of industrial enterprises. Reforms in organizational processes—recruitment of workers, criteria for promotion, management-worker relations, decision-making processes, and so on—will be presented in chapter 10.

Case studies of several enterprises, both state-owned and collectively owned, are presented in this chapter. Since the visits to these enterprises were made from June to July 1980, the structures and situations described are those that prevailed in the summer of 1980. Further changes are being contemplated by the government. In fact, changes have been introduced so rapidly that it is both frustrating and challenging to try to keep up with the reforms that are being introduced almost every month in the management of industrial organizations. Some management personnel in China candidly admit that they too find it hard to keep up with all the changes taking place. Wherever possible, I have tried to incorporate the latest reforms that have been introduced up to the spring of 1981.

Why the Need for Reform?

The present system of economic management was modeled on that of the USSR. Its principal characteristic is the use of a highly centralized administrative apparatus to direct economic activities and run enterprises. Although reforms were made in 1954, 1958, 1964, and 1970, these were largely confined to adjusting or shifting the locus of power between central and local authorities. The economic relations between the state and the enterprise changed little (*Beijing Review*, February 4, 1980, pp. 21-22). Prior to 1953 China was divided into six administrative regions: the north, northeast, northwest, east, central-south, and southwest. Under each region were numerous provinces and municipalities. At that time all industrial enterprises were under the administration of the six big regions, except for those in northern China, which were under the direct control of the central government. This system was abolished in 1954, and administration of all major industrial enterprises was transferred to the respective industrial ministries of the Central People's Government. Under this system the State Planning Commission drafted annual plans for each sector of the economy: industry, agriculture, transportation, the postal sector, and telecommunications. Thus all power was concentrated in the hands of the central government. In 1958 the power of the local authorities was broadened. Approximately 87 percent of the enterprises that were formerly under the direct administration of the central government were transferred to the management of the respective provinces, municipalities, and autonomous regions. The number of materials that were thereafter subject to unified distribution by the central government was reduced by 75 percent, resulting in a tremendous development of local industry. However, many enterprises established overambitious targets, resulting in an actual decline in productivity. Hence in June 1959 the more important industries were once again placed under the direct control of the respective ministries at the national level.

In 1964 local authorities were once again given greater authority to allocate the distribution of materials and to handle their own financial matters and investments. In 1970 the powers of the local authorities were further enlarged. Some 2,000 civilian industrial enterprises, undertakings, and construction units that were previously under the direct control of the central authorities were again transferred to the provincial level for management.

Throughout these reforms, although the locus of power oscillated between central and local authorities, the enterprises continued to be run by administrative means. Lacking the power to act on their own, they operated according to state plan and directives prescribed by the administrative organs above them (*Beijing Review*, February 4, 1980, pp. 21-22). All economic activities and undertakings, and all relations of production, are subject to a centrally derived and administered plan. The enterprise had little initiative to contribute beyond the minimum stipulated in the state plan. In the words of Fang Weizhong, a vice-director of the State Planning Commission, "enterprises are bound hand and foot and employee initiative and enthusiasm are stifled" (*Renmin Ribao*, September 21, 1979; also cited in *China Reconstructs*, March 1980, p. 64). This practice of overcentralizing planning activities in the hands of the State Planning Commission has often led to inefficiencies—bottlenecks, overemphasis on quantity of production at the expense of quality of products and services, and disregard of market forces. Ignoring market forces has led to overproduction of goods that are not needed immediately and underproduction of commodities that are in great demand.

Though the government recognizes the problems inherent in this system and sees the need for change, the leadership is undecided about how this should be accomplished. At present, the debate on reforms in China's economy centers around three basic approaches (*China Reconstructs*, March 1980, pp. 64-65). The first perspective called for a return to the "classic type of centralized planned economy" that prevailed during the First Five-Year Plan (1953-1957).

A second view held that a "regional planned economy" should be introduced, wherein the provinces, municipalities, and autonomous regions would be given maximum autonomy in the management of their own financial affairs. The local authorities would draft, implement, and be held responsible for their own economic plans. A third approach called for the separation of state administrative organs from economic entities. Under this system, state plans would serve only as a guide to action, and directives from the central government would be minimized. The enterprises would be granted greater autonomy in decision making and financial matters. At the same time, economic means such as the imposition of taxes and the use of the market mechanism would be introduced and allowed to operate alongside and under the supervision of central planning. This system would roughly parallel the Yugoslav and Hungarian models (Jiang 1980).

So far, most leading members of the government feel that reforms should be made along the lines of this third approach. However, though recognizing the need for change and the importance of learning the principles of economic management from the advanced nations (including those of capitalist economies), the leadership has emphasized that reforms in the Chinese economic system should be made in accordance with socialist principles and in light of China's objective conditions. In the words of the authoritative *Beijing Review* (June 15, 1979, p. 17): "Any management system and method must be tested in practice. If they impede the development of the productive forces, they must be reformed no matter who had approved them." This ties in with China's present slogan that "practice is the sole criterion for truth," which essentially means that only those principles that work in practice should be upheld.

Reforms in the Economic System

The principal reforms that have been implemented since 1979 include granting greater autonomy to individual enterprises, simplifying the administrative organizations, using economic means, developing different forms of ownership, electing workshop directors, allowing competition among enterprises, increasing outlets for circulation of commodities, encouraging intercity and interprovincial cooperation, strengthening centralization and unification of management, consolidating badly run enterprises, increasing specialization in industries, and emphasizing quality control.

Greater Autonomy to Enterprises

In the past the state has assigned production plans to enterprises "in the form of a mandate"; allocated raw materials, equipment, and personnel through the unified distribution system; and purchased and distributed all manufactured products. In addition, all profits made by the enterprise were handed to the state. Conversely, all losses incurred were borne by the state. Under this system, all the major decisions were made by state authorities who were far removed from the physical operations of the factory and hence might be out of touch with the problems actually encountered in the production process. The enterprises, which were "right on the production front," had little or no input into the major decisions affecting their operations (*Beijing Review,* April 6, 1981, p. 22).

The government is aware that running the country through administrative fiat, rather than economic means, is not conducive to raising productivity—hence the need to grant greater autonomy to the enterprises. Enterprises will be given greater powers of decision making with respect to planning, production, selling products, and handling financial matters. Under the new system enterprises still must fulfill the production targets set forth in the state plan. After fulfilling state quotas, however, they can if they so choose, utilize excess capacity to manufacture products for sale in the open market. The enterprise is allowed a certain flexibility in the pricing of producer goods (not consumer goods) thus marketed. The enterprise is also permitted to retain a certain percentage of total profits—generally around 10 percent, but higher in some factories. The enterprise has the discretion to use these funds for distribution as bonuses or for expansion of production facilities. Reforms along these lines were first introduced in six enterprises in Sichuan Province in 1978.

It was reported that in early 1978 Zhao Ziyang (then the first secretary of the party for Sichuan Province) and other provincial leaders commissioned a task force to study the causes of low productivity rates in Sichuan. The task force was impressed with the operations and performance of certain collectively owned enterprises. These were less rigid in structure than the state-owned enterprises, exercised greater autonomy in decision making, and were more adaptable in adjusting their product lines to suit changing market needs. In most instances it took less than six months to revamp their complete product line. Zhao and his colleagues decided to introduce these practices experimentally in a select sample of state-owned enterprises. These became known as the *Sichuan experiments.* The experimental units were accorded the following "eight rights" (*Beijing Review,* April 6, 1981, p. 24):

1. They had the right to retain a portion of the profit. Three alternative profit-sharing plans were implemented. In 355 of the 417 experimental units, the enterprise could retain 3-5 percent of profits made in the process of fulfilling the state plan. For profits on production manufactured in excess of the state plan, the enterprise could retain 15-25 percent, depending on the type of industry. An alternative profit-sharing plan was implemented in 57 of the experimental units. Under this plan the 57 enterprises retained a sum proportionate to their gross earnings. A third alternative was introduced in the

remaining 5 enterprises, which were treated as independent accounting units
and could retain all profits after paying the state income tax, industrial and
commercial taxes, and a tax on fixed assets. Under all three profit-sharing
alternatives, the enterprises could use the profits for distribution as bonuses
or for improving workers' welfare.

2. They had the right to use their own funds to expand existing production
   facilities. The enterprise could retain all profits derived from such expanded
   facilities in the first two years of operation.
3. They had the right to retain 60 percent (as opposed to the previous 40 percent) of the depreciation fund for fixed assets.
4. After fulfilling the state plan, the enterprise could draw up subsidiary production plans. The latter might involve processing work for other factories
   or manufacturing more products needed by the market.
5. They were given the right to market products manufactured by the factory
   that the state did not purchase.
6. They received the right to export their products and to retain a portion of
   the foreign exchange thus earned. This foreign exchange could, in turn, be
   used for the import of foreign technology, equipment, and raw materials.
   Recent guidelines have called for the importation of foreign equipment and
   raw materials only where absolutely necessary.
7. They had the right to distribute bonuses at their own discretion, within the
   guidelines stipulated by the state. In 1980 the state decreed that bonuses
   could not exceed two months' worth of the average worker's wage.
8. They received the right to impose penalties on workers, factory directors,
   and party secretaries who through negligence incurred severe economic
   losses for the state.

At first the reforms met with opposition because people were reluctant to
change. Some argued that such reforms could adversely affect the state's revenue.
In the course of these debates it was reported that one secretary of the Sichuan
provincial party committee declared: "should the State financial revenue drop
due to our failure to do a good job in experimentation, I will be the first to have
my salary reduced" (*Beijing Review,* April 6, 1981, p. 23).

In 1980 these reforms were implemented on an experimental basis in some
6,600 enterprises throughout China. Although these constitute only 16 percent
of all the state-owned enterprises in the country, their output value accounts for
60 percent of the nation's total. Moreover, the profits handed to the state by
these 6,600 enterprises amount to 70 percent of the nation's total.

These reforms have produced encouraging results to date. In 1979, for
instance, the production values in 84 of the experimental units in Sichuan
Province rose by 14.9 percent over 1978. The profits turned over to the state
increased by 24.2 percent. In 1980 the output value of the 417 experimental
units increased 9.6 percent, and profits rose 7.4 percent (*Beijing Review,* April

6, 1981, p. 26). In Shanghai, in the textile mills that implemented the reforms, the output value increased 14.1 percent in the first half of 1980, compared with the same period in 1979 (*China Reconstructs,* March 1981, p. 5).

Though enjoying greater autonomy in management of their own affairs, these enterprises also have had to assume added responsibilities. Beginning in 1981 these enterprises will be treated as independent accounting units and will assume full responsibility for their own profits and losses. Instead of turning over a portion of their profits to the state, they will pay a corporate income tax. Instead of receiving state appropriations, these enterprises will have to contract loans with banks to obtain financing for projects. After paying taxes and principal and interest on loans, the enterprise has the discretion to use its profits as it sees fit. The bonuses to be distributed to its employees and the size of the enterprise welfare fund will be directly related to the profits earned by the respective enterprises.

Although the Sichuan experiments have yielded encouraging results so far, in early 1981 the State Council decided to confine these reforms temporarily to the existing 6,600 experimental units, for two primary reasons. First, at China's present stage of economic development, where serious imbalances still exist in certain sectors of the economy, it may be premature to revamp the entire economic structure. Second, in the process of reform, conflicts of interest between the state and the enterprise are inevitable. In cases of conflict, the interests of the enterprise must be subordinate to those of the state. This is in accordance with the principle of democratic centralism. For instance, the Sichuan No. 1 Textile Mill wanted to purchase 3,000 more spindles with its own funds. The state ruled against this because although it would have the advantage of increasing production in the enterprise, it would not be in the province's general interest since the spinning and weaving capacities in the province as a whole already exceeded its printing and dyeing capacities. Consequently, Sichuan No. 1 Textile Mill had to abandon its expansion plans (*Beijing Review,* April 6, 1981, p. 29).

Simplify the Administrative Organizations

In his "Report on the Work of the Government" delivered at the Second Session of the Fifth National People's Congress on June 18, 1979, Hua Guofeng specifically addressed this subject. He instructed that henceforth the number of administrative personnel in any enterprise should not exceed 18 percent of the payroll. Jin Chuan, head of the Machine-Building Bureau in Sichuan, noted that in some work units in the province there were as many as twenty party-committee members and other administrative cadres. An excess of administrative personnel at all levels leads to a situation wherein there is "too much talking and not enough working. . . . There were too many people to sign names and not enough people working" (*Beijing Review,* July 13, 1979, p. 20).

In the past these excessive administrative levels were necessary to some extent because of the elaborate mechanisms whereby the state assigned, allocated, and distributed all the means of production. With the granting of greater autonomy to the individual enterprise, many of these administrative organs could be eliminated and the number of cadres at all levels reduced.

During the Cultural Revolution, revolutionary committees were established in most enterprises, schools, and other organizations. These were the provisional leading organs in the factories and schools. Since late 1978, with the exception of mines and certain factories in which government administration is integrated with management (such as the Anshan Iron and Steel Company), most state-owned enterprises have abolished the revolutionary committees (*Beijing Review,* October 20, 1978). In their place a system of division of responsibility has been adopted, with the factory director (the chief executive officer in Chinese enterprises) under the leadership of the party committee. The leading organs in most enterprises consist of a party committee and a working committee, with the latter under the leadership of the former. In accordance with the party constitution, the party committee is elected by Communist party members once every two years. Each party committee is headed by a party secretary. The size of these committees varies depending on the size of the enterprise. The party committee usually meets once a month to discuss and decide on all important matters relating to finance, production, technology, and the workers' livelihood. The decisions are then implemented by the factory director. The working committee is headed by the factory director and is made up of deputy directors and responsible technical and administrative cadres. The working committee is in charge of day-to-day production and administrative work. In emergencies the director has the authority to take immediate action before reporting to the party committee. The functions of the party committee with respect to the operations and management of the enterprise are primarily threefold: (1) to ensure that state plans, decisions, and directives from the leading organs are properly interpreted and implemented; (2) to support the leadership provided by the factory director; and (3) to supervise and check on the work of the working committee.

Changes are now contemplated that would separate the party committee from the administrative organization in an enterprise. It has been proposed that the party committee should engage in political and ideological work and should no longer assume administrative duties, whereas the factory director should be responsible for the operations and management of the enterprise. However, the party committee will continue to play a supervisory role to ensure that party policies and state laws are adhered to and that production targets set forth in the state plan are fulfilled.

In the second half of 1980 five factories in Beijing implemented, on a trial basis, the policy of allowing the factory director to assume full responsibility for running the enterprise under the leadership of the Congress of Workers and Staff. The latter comprises workers, technicians, and management personnel who are elected by the workers. The Congress of Workers elects the director, reviews the list of deputy directors proposed by the director, and decides on important issues relating to production and management policies, such as the drafting of annual production plans and regulations governing an enterprise's operations (*Beijing Review,* November 17, 1980, p. 3).

Since 1978 all enterprises have been called on to abide strictly by the rules and regulations. In all the enterprises I visited, rules and regulations to be followed in the operation of machinery and equipment and in the production process were prominently displayed on large charts throughout the factory so that the workers would have little question about how things ought to be done.

Use of Economic Means

In the past China relied primarily on administrative means to manage the country's economy. In the future, however, due emphasis will be given to the law of value and the role of the market.

The law of value stipulates that commodities should be exchanged in proportion to their values. In the first thirty years of the PRC, because of Stalin's influence, the law of value was denounced as a capitalist principle and hence ignored. This meant that the principle of "doing things at any cost" was followed, and the principle of "gaining maximum economic results with a minimum expenditure of labor" was labeled "revisionist." The present government, recognizing the limitations inherent in the former policy, stipulates that planning should be done in accordance with the law of value, which "requires an approximation of prices to values instead of a variance of the former from the latter" (Sun 1980, p. 157).

Closely allied with the law of value is the role of the market mechanism. Leading Chinese economists (Xue 1979; Sun 1980) whose opinions hold sway in the new era of socialist modernization argue that the market mechanism is compatible with socialist planning, as exemplified by Yugoslavia. In this model, since the aim of production is to improve people's livelihoods, production targets are set according to consumer needs. The Yugoslav government permits limited competition, free trade between departments and enterprises, and floating of prices of nonessential commodities within a certain range.

Since China is a vast country, it is impossible for the state plan to be all encompassing. In *A Study in the Problems of the Socialist Economy* (1979), Xue Muqiao notes that because of the large number of products and because production demands are constantly changing, it is impossible for the state to regulate the Chinese economy through plans alone. Xue pointed out that at present only several hundred of the several hundred thousand commodities manufactured in China come under the direct control of the State Planning Commission. The output value of these several hundred commodities accounts for over half the nation's total. Out of this number only several are "worked out with minute exactitude while the rest are only roughly estimated." In light of these factors, Xue argues that state plans should serve only as a guide. The production unit or the enterprise should then work out the specifics of the plan itself (*Beijing Review*, October 26, 1979, pp. 14–20).

Since 1979 "free" markets have been allowed to operate in the cities and villages. These are regulated and controlled by the government and are limited in scale. The government argues that the market mechanism will not replace central planning but will supplement the latter and play a subordinate role. In 1979 the means of production, such as machines and rolled steel, manufactured in excess of state plans could be bought and sold in the market. Formerly, these were allocated by the state. Manufacturers responded favorably to this change. In 1979 steel mills produced 2 million tons of rolled steel in excess of the state target, which were sold in the open market. In the same year enterprises under the First Ministry of Machine Building were allowed to sell the products manufactured in excess of state quotas on the market. The products sold through these channels accounted for approximately 14 percent of the total output value of these enterprises.

Despite arguments that socialist planning is compatible with the market mechanism and that the antithesis of planned economic development is not the market, but spontaneity and anarchy in production (Jiang 1980), China still must wrestle with some of the inherent contradictions involved in combining socialist planning with the market mechanism. For example, all enterprises want to manufacture items that are in great demand and that generate a handsome profit. A case in point is electric fans. This resulted in duplication of efforts in many enterprises (*China Reconstructs*, March 1981).

Besides the introduction of the law of value and the market mechanism, Xue Muqiao (1979) advocated the adoption of the following economic measures:

1. Taxes should be imposed to regulate the production of various categories of commodities. Higher taxes could be levied in order to curb the production of certain less desirable commodities, whereas taxes could be waived on the production of desired commodities.
2. The state could also use price policy to regulate the production of certain categories of commodities. Prices on desired commodities could be raised and prices on less desirable commodities lowered.
3. The government should grant loans at reduced interest rates to those enterprises and industries that it seeks to develop.
4. The government should give priority in the allocation of resources and raw materials to those industries and enterprises that it seeks to develop (*Beijing Review*, October 26, 1979, p. 18).

Besides the aforementioned economic means, the state is actively promoting the use of the contract system between various sectors of the economy—for example, between suppliers and producers, between suppliers and distributors, among enterprises, and between the state and enterprises. Under the contract system, the terms and conditions of agreement are agreed on by both parties voluntarily. The use of such contracts means that each party can check on the performance of the other to ensure that the terms and conditions of the contract are being met and carried out.

The contract system has been implemented on a trial basis in the area of loans for capital construction in the light and textile industries and in tourism in Beijing, Shanghai, and Guangdong Province. Instead of the allocation of state funds, the enterprise will contract a loan with the People's Construction Bank of China. Both parties to the agreement undertake economic and legal obligations. If the borrowing enterprise completes the project on time or pays back the principal with interest ahead of schedule, the money accrued from profit and other sources can be kept by the enterprise for its own use for the rest of the period stipulated in the contract instead of being turned over to the state immediately. Conversely, if the borrowing enterprise does not repay the principal and interest on time, the enterprise will be required to pay the sum from its circulating and improvement funds. In addition, interest will be doubled. This system is designed to encourage the enterprises to make careful calculations, to exercise strict budgeting, and to try to get as much done with as little money as possible.

The contract system has also been proposed and implemented on a trial basis in other contexts. It is hoped that the adoption and use of the contract system will lessen the burden on the administrative organs at various levels, ensure that economic activities are conducted more smoothly and efficiently, and encourage enterprises and individuals to assume greater responsibility for fulfilling or overfulfilling their targets.

Other Means of Ownership

In the past it was believed that state-owned enterprises were superior because they represented ownership by the whole people. In the Draft Constitution of the PRC, dated June 14, 1954, Mao Zedong wrote that even though "socialist ownership by the whole people is the principle, in order to realize this principle we should combine it with flexibility" (*Selected Works*, vol. 5, 1977, pp. 143–144). Hence in the transition phase from socialism to communism, other forms of ownership of the means of production should be encouraged as long as they further the goal of socialist modernization.

Since early 1979 the state has encouraged the development of alternative forms of ownership of the means of production. These include the establishment of collectively owned enterprises, the individual economy, and joint-venture concerns with foreign firms. In late 1979 there were an estimated 200,000 collectively owned enterprises in urban areas of China. Approximately 56,800 of these units are engaged in the manufacture of consumer products. These vary in size from several thousand workers down to a dozen (*China Business Review*, September–October 1979, p. 51). By July 1980 it was estimated that some 400,000 business licenses had been issued to individual operators (*Beijing Review*, November 10, 1980, p. 20).

Election of Workshop Directors

Each factory is made up of several workshops, and each workshop has its own workshop director. In the past workshop directors were appointed from among party members. At the Ninth National Congress of Chinese Trade Unions in October 1978, Deng Xiaoping announced the party's decision henceforth to select leading cadres at the grass-roots level (workshop directors, section chiefs, and heads of work groups) through a democratic election process. Since then the practice of electing workshop directors through secret balloting has been adopted at most factories. In the Xinhua Printing House in Lanzhou, for instance, the factory adopted this method for electing workshop directors, section chiefs, and leaders of the various shifts. During the election the party committee advised the workers not to choose people simply because they were amiable. Rather, the emphasis should be placed on electing those who had the ability to provide leadership to the workers, coupled with good management and technical skills, so that they could spur production in the enterprise. Anyone who possessed these qualifications was eligible for election, including nonparty members, those who came from bourgeois families, and those who had committed mistakes in the past. Persons in the latter two groups had to give a good account of themselves politically, be technically competent, and have a good working relationship with the workers in order to become eligible. The list of candidates was drawn up after nominations by the workers, consultations among the representatives, discussions by all workers, and further consultations among the representatives. The candidates gave "campaign speeches" and were grilled by the workers on how they intended to carry on management functions and handle problems in the factory if they were elected. On election day nine workshop heads and seventy-seven section and shift leaders were elected by the workers through secret ballot. The tenure of office is two years. Under the leadership of these technically competent persons, production increased. For the first time in many years the enterprise was able to make a profit.

Where it was not feasible to institute elections, the government advocated the use of opinion polls at regular intervals (at the end of every year, for instance) to provide workers with a means of examining and evaluating the work of the leading cadres in the enterprise.

The advantages of electing cadres at various levels through secret balloting appear to be threefold:

1. Since the workers take part in the election of the cadre, they are more likely to accept the elected person's leadership over them. This would ensure a better working relationship between the leader and the led, which is conducive to efficiency.
2. Because the workers have an input into important decisions, they have a better understanding of the problems relating to the decision at hand and of the processes involved in solving the problems. This better understanding is usually accompanied by a higher commitment to the objectives they help formulate. This principle is very similar to the management-by-objectives technique practiced in the United States.
3. This procedure emphasizes the need for achievement. Henceforth those who work hard know that they also stand a chance of being promoted. This serves as a powerful motivating device for encouraging workers to heighten performance.

In 1980 China's leaders decided that the system of lifetime tenure of cadres should be replaced by appointment of cadres for a fixed term. Veteran cadres now can be dismissed if they lack technical competence or fail to do a good job, even though they may not have committed serious mistakes (*Beijing Review*, November 10, 1980).

Allow Limited Competition among Enterprises

Most of the information provided in this section, unless otherwise stated, was obtained in an interview with Chang Xiyua, director of the Bureau of Planning, Ministry of Commerce. In the past the government emphasized emulation without competition among enterprises. Emulation refers to the practice whereby less advanced units seek to catch up with more advanced ones by learning from them. Competition was prohibited because it was viewed as a capitalist concept. The present slogan is to "protect [that is, promote and not eliminate] competition". Enterprises are now encouraged to compete for better economic results by improving management, raising productivity, and increasing the efficiency of operations. This new policy will help reduce the negative consequences associated with the policy of "everybody eating from the same big pot." The latter slogan refers to the egalitarian treatment of all workers and enterprises, regardless of performance. This practice tended to breed complacency and irresponsibility among some enterprises and workers because they know that no matter how poorly they performed, they would be accorded the same treatment as the more productive units and workers.

Competition is now permitted under two circumstances. First, it must not be destructive; that is, it must not result in exploitation. Competition must be carried out to encourage mutual improvement among the enterprises. Enterprises that consistently suffer losses as a result of poor management may be merged with successful ones, or the workers in such enterprises may select a new management team to run the factory (*Beijing Review*, February 9, 1981, p. 3). Second, competition must be carried out under the direction of the state plan. Competition will not be permitted among factories that manufacture essential commodities, such as petroleum. However, for factories manufacturing nonessential items—electric fans for example—competition may take one of several forms.

One form of competition allows the manufacturer to market any units produced in excess of the state plan. For example, if the state specifies that a factory produce 100 fans, the manufacturer must first fulfill this plan. If it overfulfills the plan, then it can market the excess units itself. A second form of competition occurs among manufacturers from different provinces that produce the same commodities. In the past there were interprovincial barriers. For example, Shanghai fans could not be sold in Beijing even though they were lower priced and of higher quality. Under the policy of protecting competition, however, the Shanghai manufacturer may now sell in Beijing, provided it fulfills the state plan. If the state plan stipulates that 50 percent of the units manufactured by the factory are for export, 20 percent are for sale in Shanghai, and the remaining 30 percent are for sale in other parts of the country, then the manufacturer must adhere to this plan. However, after fulfilling this plan, the manufacturer has the discretion to market any surplus units it produces.

Another means by which competition is carried out is illustrated by the following hypothetical situation. The Ministry of Commerce may sign a contract with a particular manufacturer in Shanghai because of the price and quality of its products. The ministry can refuse to sign a contract with a Beijing manufacturer producing the same products if its products are of inferior quality, even though the latter has a production plan.

Although competition is encouraged, socialist labor emulation is still practiced in China. China now seeks to stimulate workers' initiative through the dual principles of emulation and economic competition. Emulation is not related to economic benefits, whereas competition is directly tied to monetary rewards. Competition refers to higher quality and lower prices of commodities. Through competition, the more successful units will earn more profits for distribution to their workers. Most factories and workers responded favorably to the introduction of competition. For instance, in 1979 in Beijing the amount of industrial commodities judged to be of "good quality" was nearly double that for the preceding year.

With the introduction of competition, the government has noticed the development of some unhealthy tendencies, such as the falsification of results to make an enterprise look good, and concern over an enterprise's own interests at the expense of the state or society at large. To rectify this situation, the country has adopted the following measures:

1. On October 17, 1980, the State Council promulgated provisional regulations governing socialist competition. Their major provisions are:
    a. Though competition is allowed, enterprises are required to fulfill state plans.
    b. Contracts may be signed between and among enterprises for the purchase and sale of commodities and raw materials. These contracts are protected by law.
    c. Trial implementation of competitive bidding on construction and other projects by contractors is instituted.
    d. An enterprise may sell products manufactured in excess of state plans.
    e. Floating of prices on certain nonessential items within a fixed range specified by the state is permitted.
    f. Interprovincial and intraprovincial barriers to the free movement of commodities are eliminated.
    g. Although technical exchange and cooperation among enterprises are encouraged, the enterprise must pay for the transfer of know-how of major innovations and inventions (*Beijing Review*, November 17, 1980, pp. 4–5.

    Besides the provisional regulations governing socialist competition, China is currently drafting other economic laws, such as contract laws and the law of the market to regulate the economy.
2. It has attempted to improve the quality of state planning. In the past plans were too rigid and attempted to be all encompassing. By allowing enterprises to work out the specifics of the plans, the government is freed from working out the details and can concentrate on improving the quality of the overall plan.
3. The State Council has imposed economic and administrative sanctions against violators. For example, black marketeers will be punished according to the law.

Increase Outlets for the Circulation of Commodities

In the past all products were produced and distributed by the Ministry of Commerce at the national and provincial levels. The government realizes the problems inherent in this practice and plans to utilize more channels for the distribution of commodities, and to promote closer and more direct ties between producers and users of products.

For circulation purposes, commodities are classified into two categories: consumer goods and producer goods. In the future the former will be handled primarily through commercial channels, whereas the latter will continue to be allocated and purchased by the state. In the past the State Planning Commission and the State Bureau of Supplies were responsible for the planned allocation of some 256 commodities. In the future the number of commodities subject to planned allocation will be reduced to fewer than 68.

In China producer or industrial commodities are referred to as the *means of production* and include raw materials and industrial capital goods, equipment and supplies. Producer commodities are not bought and sold but are allocated by the state. An enterprise that requires a particular producer commodity must first apply for a distribution quota from the appropriate authorities. Consequently, it has often taken a long time for the enterprise to obtain its supplies, even as the manufacturer of the commodity had an excess of inventory supply because it was not authorized to sell the products itself. Zhao Ziyang compared this rigid system to a "silkworm which wraps itself up in a cocoon" (*Beijing Review,* April 6, 1981, p. 21). According to Chang Xiyua, in the future the Ministry of Commerce will purchase only part of the commodities. The remainder of the industrial commodities will be marketed by the enterprises themselves. The manufacturers can engage in retail or wholesale selling themselves, or they can do the wholesale selling through the Ministry of Commerce or other marketing channels.

Since 1979 cities such as Shanghai have implemented several new methods for marketing producer goods (*China Reconstructs,* May 1981). In July 1979 the Zhaojiabang market was established in a 8,000-square-meter site in Shanghai. Over 40,000 commodities are traded in this market, ranging from merchandise selling for a few cents to machine tools worth thousands of yuan. Transactions are carried out on the basis of cash, credit, or barter. The market publishes bulletins listing the kinds of products available for sale and the prices of these items. Besides buying and selling, the market also provides technical information, installation, and repair facilities. In the first eighteen months of operation, over 530 million yuan of commodities were transacted at the Zhaojiabang market. In addition, the Zhaojiabang market sponsored five national fairs in 1980. Some 2,500 representatives from 600 enterprises throughout the country took part in the fairs. Over 10,000 contracts were signed at these fairs, representing transactions worth some 6,000 million yuan.

Besides these traders' markets, there is the Shanghai Commission Company, which is a "notions wholesale market." The Shanghai Commission Company was first established in 1964 but suspended its operations from 1966 to 1976. In 1980 the company acted as an intermediary by putting buyers and sellers together for 1,500 enterprises from twenty-eight provinces, municipalities and autonomous regions. In 1980 the volume of business transacted under the auspices of the Shanghai Commission Company amounted to 130 million yuan. Jiangsu and Zhejiang provinces also have notions wholesale markets that transacted business worth some 17 million yuan in 1980.

These new marketing channels have also been introduced in rural areas in Shanghai. For example, Shiliupu, a port on the Huangpu River, was converted into a traders' market. In 1980 over 38 million yuan of commodities were transacted in Shiliupu.

In the future the Ministry of Commerce plans to purchase and market commodities through four different methods:

1. There will be only one channel of distribution for essential commodities such as textiles and petroleum. The purchase and sale of such items will be conducted through state-owned enterprises.
2. The Ministry of Commerce can purchase according to the State plan.
3. The Ministry of Commerce can order from manufacturers by issuing order plans. These plans are for reference only. The ministry and the manufacturer will jointly decide the quantity to be bought, and the two will then sign a contract. If the manufacturer fails to produce the quantity specified in the contract, economic sanctions will be imposed.
4. The Ministry of Commerce can engage in selective purchasing. The Ministry of Commerce at various levels can choose what it wants to buy from the manufacturers, without any plans.

The first three methods of purchasing and marketing will apply to more than a hundred kinds of commodities. The fourth channel will apply only to small commodities.

The Ministry of Foreign Trade can also sell some commodities that are unsuitable for export or products manufactured in excess of export quotas. These can be sold in the open market.

Encourage Intercity and Interprovincial Cooperation

China is a vast country, with differences in the levels of economic and technological development between the various parts of the country. Some regions are rich in raw materials, whereas others have a fairly heavy concentration of skilled workers. To make the best use of these resources, the government encourages intercity and interprovincial cooperation through the establishment of joint ventures on a voluntary basis. Through such cooperative arrangements, the technical superiority of some enterprises in certain parts of the country can be combined with the natural-resource supplies from other parts of the country. For example, Hubei Province in south-central China has an abundant supply of raw cotton. However, it does not have the technical skills to develop the textile industry. Under the present policy, Hubei would ship its raw cotton to textile mills in Shanghai and Qingdao, where the textile industry is highly developed (*Beijing Review,* July 21, 1980).

The present forms of economic integration include cooperation between advanced and less advanced factories, between different trades, between urban and rural sectors of the economy, between different forms of ownership, and between enterprises and institutes of higher learning (*Beijing Review,* September 29, 1980; *China Reconstructs,* February 1981). A case in point is the cooperative arrangements between Xianning and Shanghai. Xianning, which is located in Hubei province, has abundant natural resources but lags behind in terms of management and technology. Since June 1979 Xianning has entered into a series of cooperative arrangements with Shanghai to accelerate the speed of development of local industries. These arrangements included the following:

1. One hundred forty experienced workers and technicians from Shanghai were invited to sponsor training programs for workers in Xianning. Each experienced worker or technician from Shanghai has the responsibility for training three or four workers over the two-year cooperative agreement.
2. Direct communication channels would be established between Xianning enterprises and those in Shanghai. The Shanghai technicians would put forward suggestions for improvement. In a nine-month period Shanghai technicians introduced some 900 suggestions, 600 of which were adopted.
3. Joint-venture projects would be established with Shanghai factories.

Within nine months of the establishment of such cooperative arrangements, 140 technological processes were improved, and 130 pieces of machineries were built or renovated in Xianning (*Beijing Review,* March 17, 1980, pp. 7-8).

Strengthen Centralization and Unification of Management

Though allowing enterprises greater autonomy to conduct their own affairs, the government must ensure some degree of uniformity in practice throughout the country. In his "Report on the Readjustment of the 1981 National Economic Plan," Vice-Premier Yao Yilin announced the government's decision to centralize and impose unified management over eight different aspects of the country's economy (*Beijing Review,* March 16, 1981, pp. 14-20):

1. All enterprises, departments, and localities must abide by the principles and policies formulated by the central government.
2. The State Planning Commission will regulate all funds pertaining to capital construction. All capital construction projects under the jurisdiction of the provinces must be approved by the State Council on the recommendation of

the State Planning Commission. Capital construction projects undertaken by the ministries and commissions must also come under the unified management of the State Planning Commission.

3. Major financial matters, including methods of financing and taxation, will be subject to the unified administration of the central government.

4. Controls on the extension of credits will be tightened. All levels of government will have to adhere to the unified systems for credit and cash management.

5. All enterprises, departments, and localities must adhere to state plans pertaining to the allocation of essential materials.

6. Controls on prices will be tightened. Unauthorized and disguised price increases will be prohibited.

7. Indiscriminate issuance of bonuses and other fringe benefits will be prohibited.

8. Controls over foreign exchange will be tightened, and the conduct of foreign trade will be subject to unified management. The Provisional Regulations for Exchange Control of the PRC are contained in appendix I.

Consolidation of Enterprises and Specialization in Industries

Pursuant to the guidelines on the Three-Year Plan (1979–1981) for readjustment, restructuring, consolidation, and improvement of China's economy, enterprises that consistently perform badly and lose money will be consolidated or merged with more successful ones. To increase efficiency, the government has also decided to establish specialized companies. On the basis of statistics from twenty-eight provinces, municipalities, and autonomous regions, some 19,300 enterprises had been reorganized into 1,900 specialized companies or general plants by the end of 1980 (*Beijing Review,* April 27, 1981, p. 5). In Nanjing, for instance, in July 1980, thirty-eight radio factories and research institutes were merged to form the Nanjing Radio Corporation, which now employs 30,000 workers. The corporation operates under unified management, but production is organized according to each member factory's specialty. Major decisions are made by the board of directors in consultation with the factory director, deputy directors, chief engineer, and chief accountant of the respective member factories. Although the management of the corporation is in charge of overall production, each member factory retains a certain amount of autonomy in running its own affairs and is treated as an independent accounting unit responsible for its own profits and losses (*Beijing Review,* August 11, 1980, p. 4).

Quality Control

Under the Four Modernizations program Chinese enterprises place heavy emphasis on quality as well as quantity. Most enterprises have appraisal sessions once a month to compare the performance of the various workshops and work groups on the six criteria of output, quality, consumption of raw and semifinished materials, safety, record of attendance, and cleaning up. Those workshops or work groups that fulfill the six norms well are commended. Upon approval at the factory level, the work group or workshop is cited as a red-banner or advanced unit. These recommendations and approvals are publicized throughout the factory.

In addition, the state designates certain months as "quality months" to encourage workers to upgrade the quality of their products. For instance, September 1977 was designated as quality month among the workers and cadres of industrial and communications departments throughout the country. During this quality month many enterprises established or restored quality-inspection departments or quality-control systems. Discussion sessions focused on how to improve quality. "Quality first!" is now an important slogan in most enterprises.

In my 1980 visit to factories in Beijing, I noted that many of them have implemented the "total quality control" (TQC) system. Everywhere in the factory one notices the words TQC, colorful charts, and statistics displaying the targets set for the various workshops and work groups and the actual results. The Beijing Internal Combustion Engine Factory, for instance, has published a 126-page manual explaining the TQC system and how it should be applied. All workers in the factory have attended a seven-day training program on the TQC system—how to implement the system and how to read the statistics contained in the manual.

In some factories superior and inferior products were exhibited for comparison. For example, the Fourth Ministry of Machine Building organized a national quality contest for black-and-white television sets. After the contest those factories that produced better-quality products were commended, and those that manufactured inferior-quality goods were criticized. The State Economic Commission announced that such mass contests were fruitful because the quality of products improved after the campaigns.

Under the current Three-Year Plan for Readjustment (1979–1981), though state allocations to heavy industries have been reduced, factories in this sector have been encouraged to upgrade the quality of their products to make fuller and better use of existing equipment and facilities, and to expand the variety of products manufactured. As noted earlier, despite the reduction in state investments in the heavy-industrial sector for 1979, iron and steel output continued to increase.

In order to improve the overall standard of living of the people, the government has encouraged enterprises producing consumer goods to manufacture commodities of higher quality and greater variety.

Though reforms of the system of economic management have largely yielded encouraging results, the government has noticed the development of certain problems arising from the implementation of such reforms. In a speech delivered to the Sichuan provincial party committee, Zhao Ziyang emphasized the need to rectify this situation (*Beijing Review,* May 5, 1980, pp. 5-6). Specifically, Zhao addressed the following issues:

1. Because of inexperience, some enterprises that have been granted greater autonomy in handling their financial matters may squander the funds at their disposal. The state must provide guidance to ensure the proper use of the funds at the enterprise's disposal. The state must see to it that "the funds are not spent blindly."
2. Further adjustment must be made in the pricing policy of commodities. The processing industries, for instance, are able to reap greater profits than those engaged in the production of raw materials, fuel, and agricultural machinery. The prices of these commodities must be readjusted in order to ensure a more equitable distribution of profits.
3. To ensure greater economies of scale in production, small enterprises in the same trade should be merged to form specialized companies.
4. Given the differences in the levels of technological and economic development between various parts of the country, the major industrial cities such as Shanghai and Beijing should assist industries and enterprises in the less developed regions to improve their levels of performance.
5. Bonuses should be distributed in accordance with the principle of "more work, more pay." The government is opposed to indiscriminate issuance of bonuses.

In summarizing the issues, Zhao pointed out that "economic work should be done in a flexible way along with strict discipline." He argued for the need to combine "economic levers" with "administrative measures" in order to ensure orderly growth in the economy (*Beijing Review,* May 5, 1980, p. 6).

Ministry of Commerce

The perspectives provided in this section are based on an interview with Chang Xiyua, director of the Bureau of Planning, Ministry of Commerce, in July 1980.

History and Overview

After the establishment of the PRC in 1949, the Ministry of Trade was set up to be responsible for both domestic and foreign trade. In 1952 the Ministry of Trade was split into the Ministry of Commerce and the Ministry of Foreign Trade. The former is in charge of domestic trade, and the latter oversees China's foreign trade.

In China there are three ministries in charge of domestic trade:

1. The Ministry of Commerce is in charge of supply in urban areas and of daily-use industrial articles.
2. The Ministry of Food is responsible for grain and edible oil.
3. The All China Federation of Cooperatives of Supply and Marketing is in charge of marketing in rural areas and agricultural management.

The Ministry of Commerce reports directly to the State Council and has six bureaus under it:

1. the bureau of daily-use articles, including the bureau of textiles
2. the bureau of small metal and electric articles
3. the bureau of chemical raw materials
4. the bureau of sugar, tobacco, and wine
5. the bureau of fuel, petroleum, and coal for nonindustrial use (for domestic consumption)
6. the bureau of food (also known as the food corporation), in charge of pigs, cows, sheep, poultry, and eggs

These six bureaus operate at the central-government level. Under them are the bureaus of commerce at the levels of the provinces, regions, and counties. Each bureau at the provincial, regional, or county level has its own special corporations, each of which is responsible for certain groups of commodities, paralleling the functions performed by the six bureaus at the national level. The number of corporations in each region varies. In some regions there are five or six corporations, in others seven or eight. Some bureaus may have as many as ten corporations. These corporations are in charge of the state-owned enterprises, which form the backbone of the country's economy. The Industrial Administration Bureau manages the collectively owned enterprises and individual operators and also issues the business licenses.

Besides these three ministries, there are two organizations that are responsible for domestic trade, the China Medical Bureau and the Marine Products Bureau. The former is responsible for medical supplies in the country, and the latter is in charge of aquatic products.

The Role of Domestic Trade in the Four
Modernizations Program

Chang indicated that domestic trade will continue to expand under the new era of socialist modernization, for two primary reasons. First, China has a long history of feudalism, without capitalism. Industrial commodities are not highly developed. In addition, productivity is still very low. With the Four Modernizations program, China will expand the production of goods for domestic consumption. Second, in the past China pursued the policy of self-sufficiency. This essentially meant that each enterprise, regardless of size, attempted to undertake all steps in the production process. This was not conducive to economies of scale in production. In the future the country will establish some specialized companies. As discussed previously, the government now encourages economic cooperation and integration among enterprises and provinces.

The proportion of goods produced for export is very low, averaging approximately 7-8 percent of total production. In 1979 the gross national product reached 600 billion yuan, but exports accounted for only 40 billion yuan.

The expansion of foreign trade will benefit the domestic market because the two sectors are highly interdependent. Export commodities are produced by domestic enterprises. Consequently, increases in export will stimulate the development of the domestic economy. In addition, certain equipment could be imported to improve the efficiency of domestic operations.

Case Studies

In this section the case studies of several enterprises, both state owned and collectively owned, are presented. The information presented here is based on interviews with enterprise management and on observations and impressions derived during the study tour of industrial enterprises in Beijing in June–July 1980. The following points should be borne in mind when reading the cases.

First, the visits to these enterprises were made in June–July 1980. Consequently, the structures and situations described are those that prevailed in the summer of 1980. Certain reforms have been adopted since then. Where possible, I have tried to incorporate the latest reforms that have been introduced. Although I visited enterprises in other parts of the country in July 1979, given the many changes that have been introduced in the management of industrial organizations since the second half of 1979, it may not be appropriate to include the enterprises visited in 1979 in the present sample of case studies.

Second, despite the fact that China is currently more willing than formerly to provide foreign researchers with information on the operations of industrial enterprises, restrictions still exist. After my repeated attempts to gain access to less advanced units, permission was not granted. Thus the factories visited were all advanced industrial units, representing the model that other, less advanced units seek to emulate. As noted previously, China introduces new techniques, practices, and procedures on an experimental basis among the leading factories. If these techniques prove effective, they are eventually implemented throughout the country. The State Council announced in early 1981 that for the time being the Sichuan experiments will be confined to the existing 6,600 experimental units.

Finally, although I sought information on the history, organizational structure, organizational processes, and performance of each enterprise, some factories were unwilling to provide information on all the variables. It should be noted, however, that in general organizational practices are fairly homogeneous across all enterprises.

The Beijing Internal Combustion Factory

The information provided in the case is obtained through an interview with Mr. Xu, the chief engineer, and other top management personnel in the Beijing Internal Combustion Factory. Mr. Xu concurrently holds the position of factory director.

History and Overview

Prior to 1949 this factory operated as a repair workshop for the Kuomintang army. In April 1949 the People's Government took over the factory, and it is now a state-owned enterprise. Shortly after liberation, while continuing to serve as a repair workshop for agricultural machinery, the factory also began production of two types of plows. Under the First Five-Year Plan (1953-1957), the factory began production of the combine harvester, which is drawn by horse. The factory underwent rapid development during the period generally referred to as the Great Leap Forward (1958–1962). In that period several buildings were added to the existing factory structure. In the 1960s the factory began to manufacture internal-combustion engines. The factory's major product lines are the 4115 diesel engine and the 492 petrol engine. The 4115 model is fitted onto tractors manufactured in Tianjin and Sijachuang. Each of these cities has its own tractor factories. The 492 gasoline engine is primarily fitted onto jeep model number 212 and truck model number 130 manufactured in Beijing. In 1980 the factory occupied a total floor space of 510,000 square meters. The factory uses more than 3,000 machine tools and pieces of equipment in the production process.

In 1980 the factory employed more than 10,000 workers, 500 technicians, and 1,600 cadres. Approximately 40 percent of the workers and cadres are female.

Organization Structure

In 1979 the structure of the factory was reorganized according to the general guidelines provided under the Three-Year Plan for readjustment, restructuring, consolidation, and improvement of China's economy. The reorganized factory is made up of eight sections, fourteen workshops, and one institute of internal-combustion research (see figure 9-1). The eight sections are enterprise administration, quality control, personnel management, production management, workers' livelihood, civil engineering, technology, and scientific research. There are several subsections under each of these sections. For example, under production management there are four subsections: economic planning, production planning, financial planning, and safety. Under enterprise administration there are also four subsections: supply, purchasing, corporation supply, and transportation.

The fourteen workshops below the eight sections are: (1) the forging workshop, which has an annual production capacity of 12,000 tons; (2) the foundry workshop, which has an annual production capacity of 10,000 tons; (3) the cast-aluminum workshop; (4) the processing-aluminum workshop, which has an annual production capacity of 300 tons; (5) the workshop that manufactures dyes for repair parts and tools; (6) the 4115 diesel-engine workshop; (7) the 492 gasoline-engine workshop; (8) the workshop that undertakes processing and manufactures small machine parts; (9) the tooling workshop, which manufactures special tools and parts; (10) the special-machines and special-tools workshop; (11) the workshop that manufactures braking parts; (12) the power-saws workshop; (13) the maintenance workshop; and (14) the welding workshop.

The administrative organization headed by the factory director exercises leadership under the supervision and direction of the party committee. As noted previously, in the second half of 1980 five enterprises in Beijing experimented with the policy of placing the factory director under the leadership of the Congress of Workers and Staff. It is not known whether the Beijing Internal Combustion Factory is one of these five experimental units. Each of the eight sections is headed by a deputy director. In the Beijing Internal Combustion Factory there is one factory director and seven deputy directors. The factory director is also the chief engineer, who is responsible for quality control, technical knowledge, and the techniques of the eight sections. Prior to reorganization each deputy director was responsible for one kind of work. Moreover, the deputy directors did not have the authority to make decisions but had to report everything to the director, who alone had the authority to make major decisions. After reorganization each deputy director was given responsibility for several workshops. The deputy director can now make decisions.

Each workshop is in turn divided into three or four teams. Some workshops have as many as five or six work teams. On the average there are ten persons to a team. Each team is headed by a supervisor or section chief. In 1980 the factory had a total of fifty-six supervisors.

In each workshop there is an administrative group that is responsible to the factory. In each workshop there are also several other groups, each responsible for a functional activity such as planning and control, financial planning, or inspection.

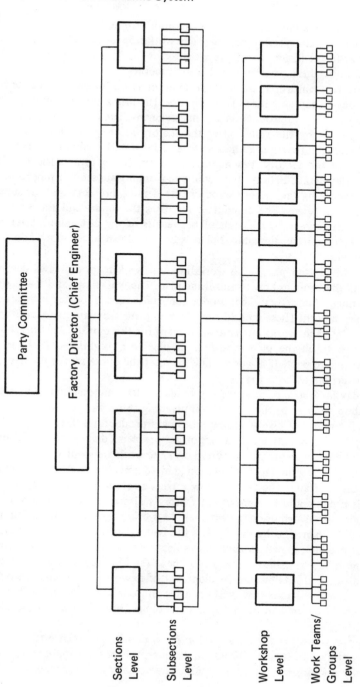

Sections Level

Subsections Level

Workshop Level

Work Teams/ Groups Level

Figure 9–1. Organizational Structure of the Beijing Internal Combustion Factory

Each workshop is under the administration of several deputy directors. The actual number of deputy directors for each workshop depends on the size of the workshop. In the larger ones, there are three or four deputy directors. In the smaller workshops, there are only two deputy directors.

Since the reorganization, the factory director is no longer responsible for running the day-to-day activities of the factory. His primary responsibility is to study policies relating to production and management. The production plans for the factory are set by the state. After the factory receives the state plan, the economic-planning subsection gathers data and information about the production capacity of the factory, raw-materials supply, and contracts signed with customers. After detailed study, the economic-planning subsection reports to a committee comprising the factory director, the deputy directors, and the supervisors of the work teams. The committee discusses the report and draws up the plan for the whole year on the basis of the results of the discussion. After approval by the committee, the annual plan is handed down to the workshops for implementation.

Upon receiving the plan, each workshop and work team evaluates its own capacities and then studies how to fulfill the plan. The workshops and teams sign contracts among themselves. The production subsection allocates production plans for every month. These monthly production plans stipulate the quantity to be produced by each workshop and work team for the month. All workshops and units must fulfill the plan regardless of objective conditions. There is no flexibility in this respect. If a worker fails to meet the quota set for the day, he must work overtime without pay.

Every day at 4:00 p.m., the factory holds a telephone conference wherein each workshop reports to the production-planning subsection the results of its production for that day. Every Friday morning a production meeting is held in the factory. At this weekly meeting, important problems that arise in the course of production and accidents that occurred over the week are studied.

Since March 1979 the factory has been granted greater autonomy to manage its own financial affairs. The factory now retains a certain percentage of profits earned. This profit could be used at the factory's discretion to expand production facilities, for distribution as bonuses to workers, or for improving the workers' welfare benefits. In the past, if the factory wanted to manufacture a new type of product, it had to apply to the state for financing. This is referred to as a "sample fee to manufacture prototypes." The factory now retains a certain portion of its profits for the development of new products. Since then the factory has developed two new diesel engines and one gasoline engine. Part of the profits could be used to import new technology from abroad to help make prototypes.

In the past funds for the construction of workers' living quarters had to be allocated by the state. It was difficult to get approval for such applications, and it was usually a long time before the funds were actually appropriated. With the granting of greater autonomy to handle financial matters, a certain percentage of the profits is now set aside for the construction of houses for workers. There is an extreme housing shortage in China. In the past two years the factory has used several hundred thousand yuan to construct two new buildings for the workers. These are six-story buildings. Most workers choose to live in the factory quarters, but they have the right to live elsewhere if they so choose.

Part of the profits could also be divided among the workers and cadres as bonuses on the basis of "more work, more pay." Both cadres and workers are happy because they can now see the direct link between hard work and reward.

With greater autonomy, the enterprise could now increase the quantity of its production. In the past the factory manufactured only the amount specified in the state plan. This was inefficient because many of the machines had idle capacity. Now that excess quantities can be sold through the corporations and commodity fairs, the factory has an incentive to expand production capacities.

Quality Control

In 1979 the factory implemented the Total Quality Control (TQC) system. The TQC system was introduced to the Beijing Internal Combustion Factory by a local university professor and a team of Japanese technicians. The government is now trying to implement the system throughout China. The factory has published a 126-page manual on the TQC system, explaining the operation and implementation of the system. All workers in the factory undertake a seven-day training program on how to read the charts used in the TQC system. The factory now uses computers to assist in production scheduling.

The quotas set forth in the TQC system are established by the factory under the guidance of the state plan and its customers. Workers can have an input into the establishment of quotas and can offer suggestions on how to improve performance. Suggestions are discussed but will be implemented only after they have been compared with performance levels specified in the charts. There are suggestion boxes, but only a very few suggestions are being offered.

Rules and regulations on the operations of machinery and in the production process are clearly posted throughout the factory. Although safety standards are posted throughout the factory, not all workers adhere to them.

Educational Levels of the Workers

Most workers are middle-school graduates. Consistent with government policy, the enterprise is trying to raise the educational levels of its cadres, technicians, and workers. The vocational-training program for the cadres lasts three or four months. At the end of the training program, cadres sit for an examination. Those who fail must repeat the program.

The factory has an Internal Combustion College that is under the administration of the municipal government of Beijing and is similar to formal universities. The college offers four-year programs for its students. The students are engaged in full-time study and must pass an entrance exam to qualify for admission. Exams are held twice during the academic year. Before graduation the students also must pass a comprehensive exam. This college is *different* from the institute of internal-combustion research identified under the new organization structure for the factory.

Evaluation of Workers' Performance

Every month the performance of each workshop is evaluated. Each workshop and work team is evaluated on the seven criteria of quantity, quality, absenteeism rate, maintenance of machine tools, safety in production, environmental cleanliness, and workers' attitude toward work. The latter is defined as "whether the worker cares to make comments and offer suggestions on how to improve performance." Marks are assigned to each criterion. These marks add up to 100 points. On the basis of these seven criteria, each workshop receives a total score. The marks obtained for the various workshops are compared and the workshops rank ordered.

Besides group comparisons, the performances of the individuals within each work group are also compared. In every work team an individual (usually the head of the team) is responsible for calculating the marks of each individual for comparison. Every worker is assigned a mark, and the marks are compared and rank ordered. Individual bonuses are meted out on the basis of the scores received by the individuals.

Besides the monthly evaluation, there is an overall assessment of each worker's enthusiasm twice a year, once in June and once in December. The evaluation is done by the worker's superiors and outside consultants. The worker's enthusiasm is assessed on the following criteria: (1) quantity, (2) quality, (3) fulfillment of plan, and (4) whether the worker offers comments and suggestions for improvement in the study-session meetings held after work. There is a special subsection in the factory that is responsible for gathering proposals and suggestions offered by the workers. These proposals will be studied. On the basis of the results of these biannual appraisal sessions, which are referred to as socialist labor emulation drives, model workers are selected.

Productivity

In 1979 the factory manufactured a total of 50,700 engines, of which 30,200 were gasoline engines and 20,500 were diesel engines. The 1979 production level represented a 26.75 percent increase (or 10,700 more units) over the 1978 production level. According to Mr. Xu, "This is a very rapid increase."

The quality of engines manufactured by the factory has also improved because of the application of "scientific principles of management." It should be noted that in China, enterprises constantly use the term *scientific management*, which has a very specific connotation in the West. In the West, *scientific management* refers to Taylorism and time-motion studies. When asked whether the term *scientific management* was a mistranslation, the Chinese answered that it is partially a mistranslation in that the term *scientific* is invariably equated with "most advanced and modern." On the other hand, it is not entirely inaccurate because most Chinese enterprises are trying to resume the time-motion studies that were introduced in the factories in the mid-1960s but were suspended from 1966 to 1976.

In China all products manufactured by the factories are ranked and designated as being of "inferior quality," "average quality," "good quality," "top quality," or "superior quality." In 1979 the 4115 diesel engines produced by the factory were rated as top quality. In the first six months of 1980 the 4115 diesel engines were rated as superior quality. The gasoline engines were rated as good quality for three consecutive seasons, beginning in 1979.

The assessment of the quality of the products in their industry is done by the Corporation of Automotive Industry, an agency higher than the factory. Twice a year the Corporation of Automotive Industry sends inspection teams to the respective factories under its jurisdiction. The inspection team comprises representatives of the corporation, a research institute, and other factories. The inspection team compares the quality of the products manufactured by the various factories. In addition, the Ministry of Agriculture also inspects the various factories once or twice a year. The products are compared and rated on the three criteria of technical specification, size and dimensions of parts, and cleanliness of the product.

Mr. Xu was asked to identify the factors he sees as responsible for the success of the enterprise. He attributed the success primarily to improvements made in the area of management. Prior to 1978 there was confusion and chaos in the management of the factory. In 1978 the party committee and enterprise management decided to improve management in the factory. The factory implemented new policies that call on cadres and workers to fulfill quotas set by the state. In 1978 the target was to manufacture good-quality products. In 1979 the policy was to improve quality so as to surpass the past level attained. In the 1980s the target is to manufacture products of superior quality. The factory has adopted the following measures to assist in the attainment of this goal:

1. To train and educate the cadres and 10,000 workers: Currently, each department, workshop, work group, and team is discussing how to fulfill or overfulfill the production targets. In 1980 the gasoline and diesel engines manufactured by the factory were rated as top quality.

2. To learn advanced management techniques from abroad, particularly in the areas of administration and quality control: The factory seeks to popularize the TQC system. Reorganization and restructuring of the enterprise will be based on the Yugoslav model. The deputy directors are given the authority to make decisions and do not have to refer everything to the director.

3. To launch socialist labor emulation drives twice a year: Mass discussions are carried out among workers on how to fulfill production quotas. During these sessions, the workers are indoctrinated about the importance of making suggestions for improving performance.

4. To encourage participation of workers in management through the Congress of Workers and Staff. The congress makes major decisions affecting the operations of the enterprise, listens to criticisms, and offers suggestions for improving performance.

Wages and Bonuses

In China there are two categories of wages, one set applying to government organizations and the other to industrial enterprise. Under the government category there are thirty grades of wages, ranging from 30 to 300 yuan. In the industrial-enterprise category there are twenty grades, ranging from 34 to 220 yuan. Both categories of wages are used simultaneously in the Beijing Internal Combustion Factory because some of the workers and cadres were previously associated with government organizations. The latter retain their government scale. Workers and cadres who were transferred from other factories retained the enterprise scale.

The wage scales for cadres fall into three general categories:

1. Directors and deputy directors earn between 140 and 160 yuan per month but may go as high as 220 yuan. The chief engineer, who is also the factory director, is the highest paid person in the factory, earning 220 yuan per month.

2. The chiefs of the subsections earn 100–120 yuan per month.

3. Cadres in the workshops earn 70–80 yuan per month.

Technicians receive a monthly salary of 80 yuan or more, and engineers earn 100 to 120 yuan. Workers' wages are governed by the eight-grade scale, and range from 34 to 107 yuan per month.

Bonuses generally average 3–3.5 months' wages. For example, if a worker earns 50 yuan per month, his or her bonuses for the year will average 150–165 yuan. (Note: The government has now stipulated that bonuses may not exceed 2 months' salary.) The amount of bonus paid varies from workshop to workshop. In the machine and foundry workshops, bonuses generally average 2.5

months' wages. In the maintenance, tooling, and power workshops, bonuses generally average 2.8–3 months' wages. For cadres and technicians in the sections and workshops, bonuses generally average 2 months' wages.

The average wage for a worker is 50 yuan per month. The average bonus is 11 yuan per month, so that a monthly take-home pay is 61 yuan. The average wage for the Beijing Internal Combustion Factory is below the national average because the factory has recruited many new workers in the past few years. Before 1966 the average wage of a worker in the factory was 66 yuan.

Bonuses are distributed on both an individual and a group basis. Individual bonuses are given according to the marks received by the individual worker at the monthly evaluation sessions. The higher the mark, the larger the bonus. At the end of every six months there is a socialist labor emulation drive. On the basis of their performances, several workshops are selected as advanced units and receive bonuses. The workshop then distributes the group bonus among the workers.

Export

Since the engines produced by the Beijing Internal Combustion Factory are fitted onto jeeps and tractors manufactured in China, exports of the factory's products are tied to exports of jeeps and tractors. In 1979 only 1–2 percent of the factory's total production was exported.

The Beijing Qing Hur Woolen Mill

Information in this case was provided by Mr. Wang, the deputy director, and other top management personnel at the Beijing Qing Hur Woolen Mill.

History and Overview

The factory is located in the northern suburbs of Beijing. It was established in 1908, during the last years of the Qing (Ching) dynasty, with equipment and technology imported from Britain. In the first half of the twentieth century the factory continued to use looms that were installed in the early 1900s. The factory developed slowly in the first four decades of its existence, and in 1949 operations were at a virtual standstill. There were only 300–400 employees.

The Qing Hur Woolen Mill is a state-owned enterprise. Shortly after 1949 the existing facilities at the factory were modified. The old buildings were demolished, and in 1951 the facilities were expanded and new equipment installed. Prior to 1951 the factory was only capable of manufacturing some rough materials. After 1951 it began production of precise spinning materials. The factory had 7,200 spindles and 120 looms. Of these 120 looms, 90 had shuttles. The remaining 30 looms were modified.

The factory continued to expand throughout the 1950s. In 1956 the factory had 10,000 spindles, with most of its equipment imported from abroad, primarily from Japan. In 1958 more machines were installed, and production capacity was further expanded. In the same year the factory began the manufacture of homespun bedspreads.

In 1960 the factory employed a total of 5,000 workers, a relatively large number compared with figures for other factories in the light-industrial sector. At that time the factory was reorganized in order to overcome difficulties in management and in the conduct of foreign trade. The factory was split into three plants, all located in the same vicinity. Qing Hur is one of these plants. Each plant has its own separate leadership and organization structure, and each is treated as an independent accounting unit and is responsible for its own profits and losses. The three plants engage in technical exchanges among themselves.

Qing Hur specializes in the manufacture of high-quality woolen fabrics. A meter of woolen fabric sells for approximately 20 yuan. In 1980 the factory manufactured over 1,000 varieties of woolen fabrics. The variety of products changes according to customers' needs. Products are manufactured both for domestic consumption and for export. Qing Hur now trades with several dozen different countries and regions. In 1980 the plant expected to export some 30 percent of its total production. Consistent with the government's decision to expand the light-industrial and textile sectors to increase exports, the plant seeks to expand its exports in the years ahead. It has established a new workshop that will export up to 90 percent of its production.

Qing Hur now employs 2,900 workers, 2,500 of them fairly advanced in years. Approximately 59 percent of the workers are female, but only one-third of the cadres are female. The mill has 73 technical cadres, 40 of whom are engineers.

Organizational Structure

The administrative organization in the mill is headed by the factory director, who is also the chief engineer, and five deputy directors who assist the director in running the factory. The administrative organization is under the leadership of the party committee. As noted previously, in the second half of 1980 five enterprises in Beijing experimented with the trial policy of placing the factory director under the leadership of the Congress of Workers and Staff. Again, it is not known whether the Beijing Qing Hur plant is among the five experimental units. The Qing Hur Woolen Mill is divided into six workshops, each of which performs a particular process. For example, there is a spinning workshop, a weaving workshop, a dyeing workshop, and a finishing workshop. Most of the woolen fabrics produced are dyed, not printed.

In addition to the six production workshops, there are two auxiliary workshops. One, the energy workshop, is in charge of water, electricity, and air conditioning. The other, the spare-parts workshop, is responsible for repairs and assembly. The spare-parts workshop also manufactures some of the machines used in the plant.

Besides the workshops, there are several functional sections: the technical-research section, the inspection section, the design section, the accounting section, the safety section, the planning section, the labor and personnel section, the technical-production section, the supply and marketing section, the administrative-office section, and a clinic that provides preventive medical care and medical treatment for minor injuries. For more serious medical problems, the mill contracts the services of a nearby hospital.

The titles of the heads of these functional sections are nonuniform. For instance, the administrative-office section is headed by the factory director, whereas the technical-research institute is headed by a deputy director. The functional sections are of two kinds: those with both cadres and workers, and those with cadres only. For example, the inspection section comprises both cadres and workers, whereas the accounting section is staffed by cadres only.

Each workshop is headed by a workshop director. The size of the workshop varies; the production workshops have up to 400 workers, whereas the auxiliary workshops have approximately 100 workers. Each workshop comprises several work groups. The work group is the smallest unit within the plant. The size of the work group varies depending on the production function. The size of the work group ranges from three to twenty individuals. Each work group holds discussion sessions twice a week to discuss problems encountered in the production process and ways of improving performance. Each session lasts twenty to thirty minutes.

In each workshop there are several eight-hour shifts. Most workshops have three shifts, but one workshop now has four shifts, although only three can operate on any given day. The fourth shift is on a standby basis. The practice of having four shifts was introduced in 1979. Its advantages are primarily twofold. First, the existence of the fourth shift will ensure that each shift is fully staffed. Since most of the workers are fairly advanced in years, they often fall sick. The fourth shift ensures that each shift will operate at its maximum capacity. Second, most of the workers in this plant are women, and their work is very labor intensive. The fourth shift can be used to reduce the number of hours worked per week. With four shifts, each worker works only five days a week, rather than six. Under this system each worker would work two day shifts, two mid-shifts, and two night shifts, and would then take two days off. The five-day work week gives female workers more time to do housework and take care of their families. In the words of Mr. Wang, this policy "shows our government's concern for women." Male workers also enjoy the same benefits. This new practice is warmly received by the workers, and enterprise management believes it enhances productivity. Most factories in the textile and light-industrial sectors will adopt this practice in the future.

Some workshops do not have shifts. The maintenance workshop, for instance, operates only from 8:00 a.m. to 5:00 p.m.

Reforms Introduced under the Three-Year Plan

Mr. Wang identified the following reforms that have been implemented under the Three-Year Plan for Readjustment:

1. Consistent with the national policy on readjustment, restructuring, consolidation, and improvement of China's economy, the plant has built a new workshop and modified existing facilities in others. Updating existing facilities requires less capital investment and yields more economical results.

The new workshop, which will export up to 90 percent of its products, performs only spinning and weaving but does no dyeing. In this plant the dyeing workshop has the greatest potential for expansion. In the past year or two the mill has expanded its dyeing capacities, resulting in a subsequent expansion of spinning and weaving capacities. By increasing dyeing capacities, the plant has increased overall production capacity by 50 percent.

The mill has also purchased a computer worth 200,000 yuan to assist in production planning and scheduling. Qing Hur is the only textile mill in China that has a computer. The computer, manufactured in Beijing, has a 3K capacity. The memory capacity of the computer was expanded in 1981. Although the cost of the computer is phenomenally high, management explained that because the computer was manufactured by a neighboring factory in Beijing, it was possible to obtain the computer relatively quickly. Importing one from abroad would take a very long time.

2. Since 1978 China has experimented with reforms in the administration and running of enterprises. The Qing Hur plant is one of eight experimental units throughout the country. Three of the experimental units are in Shanghai, two in Tianjin, and three in Beijing. These eight enterprises are engaged in all types of industries, ranging from heavy to light. The experimental reforms introduced in these eight factories are basically the same as those introduced in the 6,600 enterprises in the provinces of Sichuan, Anhui, and Zhejiang. These 6,600 enterprises are managed by the provincial authorities. The eight experimental units, on the other hand, are under the direct leadership of the State Economic Commission. China wants to introduce management reforms at both the central and the provincial levels.

In response to the question of whether the principles embodied in the Anshan Charter; "In Industry, Learn from Daqing"; and the Thirty-Point Decision on Industry are still adhered to in the operations of the enterprise, Mr. Wang replied that the mill only adopts those principles that are correct and relevant. Irrelevant principles are abandoned (in chapter 2, only the relevant principles were cited). The mill upholds the principle that "practice is the sole criterion for truth."

In response to the question of whether the mill adheres to the principles of the "two participations" (management participation in labor and labor participation in management) and the "three-in-one combinations" (management, technicians, and workers taking part in decision making), Mr. Wang's personal opinion is that these are correct principles. However, in his words, "I cannot say that they are absolutely correct." It depends on the conditions in the factory. During the Cultural Revolution, cadres had to spend an inordinate amount of time in physical labor, leaving little time for management. Mr. Wang noted: "The purpose of the cadre is not to engage in physical labor. Through labor, the cadre could become more aware of the problems confronting the workers. If the cadre engages in too much physical labor, then he is not a cadre. Cadres should engage in mental labor, not physical labor."

Under the present system, workers participate in decision making through the Congress of Workers and Staff. It is important to receive input from the workers on decisions which affect them. The mill plans to expand the powers of the congress so that it can decide which cadres should be promoted. It should also be allowed to make major decisions. In the second half of 1980 the powers of the Congress of Workers and Staff at the experimental units were greatly expanded.

3. The mill has adopted the system of electing workshop directors through secret balloting and plans to expand this process gradually to higher levels.

4. Besides implementing the party's economic policies, the mill has also adopted the party's policy of training technical cadres. The mill seeks to promote technically competent people where possible. Most workshop directors are technical cadres or skilled workers.

5. Since 1978 the mill has adhered to the policy of establishing rules and regulations to be followed in operating machinery and equipment and in the production process. Each worker is given a worker's manual and is expected to abide strictly by the rules and regulations set forth therein.

Wages, Bonuses, and Other Welfare Benefits

Wages in this enterprise are basically the same as those in other woolen mills. The monthly wage for workers ranges from 38 yuan to more than 90 yuan.

Engineers who graduated from universities between 1958 and 1960 earn an average of more than 60 yuan. Those that graduated in the earlier 1950s earn more than 100 yuan. The mill seeks to upgrade the wages of the technicians; however, since the base is low, it is difficult to make very rapid improvements. The factory director earns 170 yuan per month.

In response to the question of whether he believes that wage rates should be commensurate with the factory's economic performance, Mr. Wang said that he "definitely hopes it will be implemented in the future."

Bonuses generally average 15 percent of the workers' wage. As a lingering effect of the Gang of Four's stress on egalitarianism, there is little difference in the percentage of bonuses awarded workers and cadres. Reforms in this regard have been made. In this plant the bonus index assigned to first-line workers who take part in production is 1, whereas that assigned to cadres is 1.2. For example, if a worker receives 7 yuan in bonus, the cadre will receive 8.4 yuan. Mr. Wang believes that this policy will be continued in the future.

With the implementation of the four-shift system, those workers who want to work overtime cannot do so because there are already four shifts. Hence, there is no extra work for them. Workers in some workshops do work overtime, however. The rate for overtime work is the same as the regular wage. Overtime work depends on production needs, subject to a general plan that must be approved by the factory administration. Workers on the night shifts receive an extra subsidy for food. On national holidays (seven per year) workers receive double pay. There is no double pay for working on weekends.

Besides the seven national holidays, workers and cadres have no annual vacations. Only teachers at technical night schools are entitled to annual vacations.

The mill provides child-care facilities for its workers. Parents pay only 8 yuan per month per child for such facilities. Since this is hardly sufficient to cover the operating costs of the center, the government subsidizes the operations of the day-care facilities. Such subsidies amount to approximately 20 yuan per child per month.

The factory provides low-cost housing for its workers. Approximately 50 percent of the workers live in the factory. Monthly rent for a two-bedroom apartment is 2.40 yuan, or 10 fen (cents) per square meter. For those workers who do not live in the factory, the government subsidizes 70 percent of the workers' transportation costs to and from work.

The mill also provides cafeteria facilities. Lunch costs 20–30 fen. For 60 fen one could purchase a very sumptuous meal. Workers are allowed half-hour lunch breaks.

Productivity

Each worker produces approximately 20,000 yuan worth of products per year. As a result of the current expansion of building facilities, the productivity rate has temporarily declined.

Qing Hur is an advanced factory and has been designated as a model in the industry. It is advanced in some production functions but not in all areas. In general, the factories in Beijing, Shanghai, and Tianjin have better conditions and management than enterprises located in China's hinterlands.

Recently, two kinds of products manufactured by the Qing Hur plant were cited as the best in the country. In addition, ten other fabrics manufactured by the mill are ranked as good-quality products.

The absenteeism rate for the mill as a whole ranges from 2 to 3.5 percent. This is low compared with figures for other factories.

When asked to identify the reasons for the success of the mill, Mr. Wang cited, first, the leadership provided by the party. Since the fall of the Gang of Four, the workers have become more enthusiastic about their work because they see a brighter future ahead of them. The cadres and workers in the mill are united in their commitment to the goals of the Four Modernizations, and "factionalism is not strong." Second, the mill has correctly implemented the party's policies on economic management and the training of technical cadres. Cadres receive training through the Tube University. Each cadre attends the lectures sponsored by the Central Broadcasting University twice a week. Each session lasts one-and-a-half hours. The mill also runs a technical night school for its cadres, technicians, and workers. The factory has its own teaching staff. In addition, the mill invites outside speakers.

During the Cultural Revolution, moral encouragement was emphasized. Now, the principle of "more work, more pay" is followed. Bonuses are given at the end of every month and every year.

Reprimand

The mill uses several methods for dealing with delinquent workers: education, warning, serious warning, and dismissal. The last of these is used only where the individual has committed a criminal offense.

The Beijing No. 3 Textile Mill

The information provided in this case is based on an interview with the chief of the planning section and other management personnel at the Beijing No. 3 Textile Mill.

History and Overview

The Beijing No. 3 Textile Mill is a state-owned enterprise under the administration of the Textile Bureau at the municipal-government level. Construction on the mill was begun in 1954, and the factory went into operation in 1957. The mill has 100,000 spindles and 3,000 textile machines. In 1980 it employed 8,000 workers. The factory occupies a total floor space of 90,000 square meters. Living quarters for employees occupy another 90,000 square meters. Fewer than half the workers live in the factory's living quarters.

Approximately 60–70 percent of the mill's workers are female. One-third of the administrative and technical cadres are female. The reason for the relatively low percentage of women at the cadre level is the lower educational levels attained among women. Most technical cadres are university graduates, and prior to 1949 very few women attended universities.

All goals are handed down by the state. The state sets four targets with respect to quantity, quality and variety, profit, and contract. The enterprise must fulfill these four quotas. In determining the four targets, the state coordinates and consults with the enterprise. Thus the enterprise can have an input at the planning stage. However, once the targets have been approved by the state, the enterprise has no discretion to change any of them.

When the state sets the quotas, it also formulates a plan to supply raw materials to the mill under a unified system. The mill obtains all its supplies through one source, a supplying corporation, which also provides raw cotton to other mills.

The state also specifies the marketing plans for distribution of the mill's output. A fixed percentage is allocated for export, and the balance is for domestic consumption. The enterprise management notes that the biggest problem confronting the mill is that demand exceeds supply—that is, the mill cannot meet the needs of the market. There is also a problem with respect to the variety of products needed to supply domestic and overseas markets. The mill does not perform any market analysis to determine market needs. It receives all its information from the Ministry of Foreign Trade and the Ministry of Commerce. The latter tells the factory what to produce for the domestic market, whereas the former specifies the demands for the overseas market. The mill has little flexibility with respect to the variety of products it can produce. To overcome the problem of variety, the mill has increased the variety of spindles.

Recently, the mill has been granted greater autonomy in terms of variety of production. After fulfilling the quotas set by the state, the mill may exercise some discretion in terms of the variety of products to be produced.

Although there are no work manuals, the job is clearly understood by all. Safety standards are not very high—some, but not all, workers wear face masks. Workers do not wear earmuffs to cut down on the noise level.

Organizational Structure

The mill has adopted a system of division of responsibility whereby the factory director and deputy directors operate under the leadership of the party committee. The party committee is the leading organ in the factory. After important decisions are made by the party committee, the factory director and deputy directors are responsible for implementing them. In the past there was no division of labor between the party committee and the factory administration. The party committee performed all administrative functions. The implementation of the system of division of labor means that after the party committee makes all the major production and administration decisions, the work is carried out by the factory administration. The party committee thus has time to engage in political and ideological work—that is, to heighten the workers' enthusiasm toward work and to increase productivity.

Under the leadership of the party committee, there is a manager's office, which is the administrative organization. The manager's office includes nine people: one factory director, who is also a member of the party committee; five deputy directors, who are all members of the party committee (the deputy director responsible for production is also the chief engineer); and three deputy chief engineers. These last three are not members of the party committee. Besides the factory director and the five deputy directors who are members of the party committee, there are four other members of the party committee who are not responsible for administrative work. These four party-committee members are in charge of political affairs. They are the secretary of the party committee, two vice-secretaries, and one director of political affairs.

In most instances the five deputy directors report to the factory director on important matters. The chief engineer and deputy chief engineers are responsible for technical work. They are not required to report to the party committee on most of their activities. They report directly to the party committee only where the workers' livelihood and welfare are concerned.

There are three levels of administrative organization. First, there is the line organization. Under the manager's office, there are seven workshops, each headed by a director and deputy directors. Workshop directors are responsible for production plans, for solving technical problems that arise in the course of production, and for all personnel matters in their respective workshops. They are assisted by the deputy directors in the dispensation of these functions. The seven workshops are: (1) cleaning, (2) raw cotton yarn, (3) spinning, (4) second level of spinning (where two threads are spun into one), (5) beaming (where spun threads are prepared for weaving), (6) weaving, and (7) cloth inspection. Below the level of the workshops are work groups, which in turn are divided into teams and shifts. Each work group is headed by a supervisor. The supervisor of each team and shift is under the leadership of the director of the workshop.

Besides the line organization, there is the staff organization, which includes six sections: (1) planning, (2) finance, (3) technical, (4) personnel (which deals with workers' welfare and wages), (5) product inspection, and (6) office of the secretary of the factory director. The head of each section is designated the chief. The sections are parallel to the workshop level and are under the direct leadership of the factory director. The chiefs of the various sections direct and supervise the activities of the factory. The position of section chief is on a par with that of workshop director.

In each workshop there are several individuals responsible for functional activities such as planning and personnel matters. These people report directly to the workshop director but receive guidance from the chiefs of the sections. At the shift level there are also people responsible for performing these various functional activities. There are five workers in each shift who are responsible for safety, technical problems, product examination, and so on. These workers are under the leadership of the production group or shift to which they belong, but they also receive guidance from the staff organization.

The size of the workshop varies depending on the type of work performed. The small workshops have more than 100 people, whereas the large workshops have 2,000 workers. The size of the work group varies depending on the nature of the work performed. At the work-group level each supervisor is in charge of between eight and thirty workers.

Structure of the Party Committee

Every workshop has both an administrative organization and a political organization. The party committee is the political organization. As mentioned previously, each workshop is headed by a director and several deputy directors. The relationship between the director, the deputy directors, and the workers is one of leadership. However, in the political organization the relationship is not one of leadership. All members of the party committee vote on issues, and the majority rules. In each workshop there is a party general branch. In the party general branch there are also functional organizations known as sections, which are at the same level as the workshops. These are the organizational section, the propaganda section, the trade-union section, and the league-members section. The relationship of the party general branch to the workshop is not one of leadership, but one of supervision to ensure that state quotas are met.

Every production group has a party branch. Again, the relationship is not one of leadership, but one of supervision to ensure that state plans are fulfilled. The party groups are the lowest level in the line organization.

All workers must attend political study sessions at least once a week. Each session lasts between sixty and ninety minutes. All workers also must attend a weekly technical study session that also lasts sixty to ninety minutes.

In response to the question of whether this type of structure is typical of organizations throughout the country, the chief of the planning section responded that this structure is typical of textile mills in the country as a whole, but was not sure whether the structure was typical for factories in other industries. There are exceptions, however, particularly among factories established before 1949. The organization structure in such enterprises are "usually very scattered." Some of the older factories have an additional level known as the branch factory level. As far as the chief of the planning section is aware, some factories in Shanghai have this additional level, whereas in Beijing none do.

In response to the question of whether management feels that changes ought to be made in the existing organizational structure and, if so, when such changes will be implemented, the chief of the planning section responded that the existing administrative structure is borrowed from the USSR. The factory is contemplating changes because the existing structure is too cumbersome. The mill plans to reduce the number of staff organizations (sections) and the number of administrative staff members. These changes were under discussion during my June 1980 visit. Enterprise management did not know when these changes would be implemented.

Reforms

Since 1978 the following reforms have been adopted:

1. Since March 1980 the mill has implemented the four-shift system. Only three shifts are in operation at a time, with the fourth on a standby basis. The mill operates on Sundays but is closed on the seven national holidays. All workers work seven-and-a-half hours per day, with a half-hour lunch break.
2. The factory has implemented the system of electing workshop directors through a secret ballot.
3. The factory has implemented the Total Quality Control system.

Wages, Bonuses, and Other Welfare Benefits

The monthly salary for the factory director is 130 yuan. The monthly wage for workers ranges from 50 to 102 yuan, with an average of 55 yuan. Apprentices are paid less than 50 yuan. Administrative and technical cadres earn between 40 and 130 yuan, with an average of 60–80 yuan.

Bonuses cannot exceed 10 percent of the total wage. Bonuses are of two kinds: group and individual. The factory distributes bonuses to the various workshops according to their respective performances. The workshop in turn distributes the group bonus to every work group and shift based on its respective performance. In each group the bonus is then divided among the workers. The chief of the planning section believes that a combination of material and moral incentives is most effective in motivating workers to heighten performance.

Consistent with national policy, the retirement age for female workers is fifty, that for male workers sixty. The retirement age for female cadres is fifty-five. If a worker falls ill, he or she still is paid. Upon retirement, the worker receives at least 70 percent of his or her last month's wages. The percentage received depends on the number of years the worker has been with the factory. If the worker has worked for more than thirty years, he or she receives 100 percent of the final month's wage. If he has been with the factory for twenty years, he receives 75–80 percent of his last month's wage. Since most workers join the factory at eighteen, the mill does not have workers who have been employed for only a short period of time before retirement. A worker who sustains injury or is permanently disabled while working on the job receives 100 percent of pay. A permanently disabled worker receives additional benefits. The mill sends someone to his or her house to help with the housework and with other problems.

Productivity

In 1979 cotton-yarn production totaled 160 million tons. In the same year, cotton-cloth production reached 110 million meters. Twenty million meters of cotton cloth were exported. Cotton-yarn production reached 20,000 tons. Cotton yarns are not exported. Every year the amount of profit and tax turned over to the state by the mill is equal to one-and-a-half times the total capital investment.

In 1979 the value of products produced per worker was 19,000 yuan. Besides using this as a measure of productivity, the mill compares its own performance with that of other textile mills. It also compares the number of workers other mills need to manufacture every 100 square meters of cotton cloth.

In 1979 the Beijing No. 3 Textile Mill overfulfilled the state quota by 5 percent. Management attributes this success to: (1) the introduction of technical innovations and reforms in 1979, as discussed previously; and (2) improvements made through the installation of a new spinning machine and through widening of the looms.

In terms of productivity, the Beijing No. 3 Textile Mill is ranked at an upper-middle level among all textile mills in the country. It is not the most productive mill in China. From 1978 onward, productivity increased at the rate of 10 percent per year. The projected increase for the future is also 10 percent per year.

Since 1978 the situation in the factory has improved. One of its products was nominated as the best in the country in 1979, and another product was cited as the best in the country in 1980. Enterprise management attributed this success to the strengthening of management work. During the Cultural Revolution, management work was seriously disrupted. The mill emphasizes discipline on the part of the workers and has also adopted the Total Quality Control system.

According to the chief of the planning section, the mill's products enjoy a high reputation in both the domestic and the overseas markets. Its products are exported to Southeast Asia, Europe, Africa, the United States, and Canada. Exports fall into three categories: (1) those exported after printing and dyeing, (2) those exported before printing and dyeing, and (3) those exported as apparel. The factory does not undertake printing and dyeing, which are done by a neighboring factory. The products exported to Canada have undergone printing and dyeing.

The absenteeism rate is approximately 4 percent. This does not affect production at all because the fourth shift is always on standby. During the Cultural Revolution, the absenteeism rate was as high as 15 percent, which certainly had a negative effect on productivity. There is no turnover rate except for retirement and illness. Workers may request leaves of absence in order to attend to important affairs.

Reprimands

Workers cannot be dismissed, nor can economic sanctions be imposed for noncompliance. Hence the mill resorts to reforming delinquent workers through education.

With respect to the resolution of conflicts, there are basically two methods: where the situation is clear-cut, the supervisor points out who is right and who is wrong. Where the situation is not clear-cut, the factory tries to resolve differences through small groups that decide among themselves who is right and who is wrong.

The Beijing Jewelry Factory

The information provided in this case was obtained in an interview with top mangement personnel at the Beijing Jewelry Factory.

History and Overview

The Beijing Jewelry Factory is a collectively owned enterprise under the administration of the Second Light Industrial Bureau. After 1949 artisans were scattered all over the city of Beijing. The state then implemented the policy of industrialization and the "three transformations." The latter refers to the organization of individual agricultural producers and individual artisans into collectives, and the transformation of privately owned industries into state- or collectively owned enterprises. By 1956 the three transformations were largely completed.

The Beijing Jewelry Factory was formally organized in 1952. At that time the collective comprised some 200 artisans from different parts of the city. They pooled their capital together (totaling 120 yuan) to establish this factory. The collective was deficient in funds, but the government was not then in a position to lend a large amount of money to a small handicrafts factory. Since Beijing is the former capital of the Ming and Qing dynasties, there were many artisans in the city who used to serve the emperors and the ruling elite. After 1949 these artisans retained their skills. At that time the factory was engaged primarily in the embroidery of opera clothes.

During the Cultural Revolution, the policy of "abandoning the four olds" was implemented. Only eight operas with revolutionary themes were allowed to be performed. As a result, the production of feudal clothes was prohibited. Consequently, the factory had to change its product line. The artisans were in a quandary as to what to produce. For a time they made embroideries of the quotations of Chairman Mao and Mao buttons. They also learned papercut techniques from Shanghai and began the production of papercuts. The working conditions in the factory at that time were not good, and some workers undertook production in their own homes.

In 1970 the factory constructed two buildings to expand its production capacity. It then employed 700 workers. Besides embroidery, the factory began to manufacture jewelry, such as rings, bracelets, necklaces, and other ornamental displays. Characters representing such concepts as "love," "longevity," or "prosperity" were prohibited during the Cultural Revolution. Most of the factory's ornamental products are made of silver, and some of gold-plated silver. Some of the ornamental products are inlaid with precious stones, such as jade and agate. The factory also manufactures cloisonné.

The present work force still stands at 700. Cadres make up 8–9 percent of the work force. Approximately 75 percent of the work force is female.

Most of the factory's products are exported through the Jewelry Corporation and the Arts and Handicrafts Corporation under the Ministry of Foreign Trade. The factory has no direct contact with foreign buyers. Foreign customers place their orders through the two corporations under the Ministry of Foreign Trade. The latter then issues production quotas to the factory.

Theoretically, the factory is allowed to have direct contact with foreign buyers. In practice, however, the factory has no chance to establish direct contacts with foreign firms because it has no overseas representatives or offices. Consequently, foreign firms do not know of its existence. The foreign firms only know about the foreign trade corporations. During their buying trips to China, representatives of foreign firms are accompanied by members of the foreign trade corporations. In response to the question of whether the factory anticipates more direct contact with foreign buyers with the decentralization of foreign-trade activities, enterprise management responded: "After reading the papers on the subject, we wanted to change this practice [of no direct contacts with the foreign buyer] because of the problems inherent in it. But we think there is little opportunity for change."

The raw materials used in production, such as silver and gold, are supplied from local sources. These supplies are guaranteed by the state.

Since 1979 heavier emphasis has been placed on the use of contracts. In response to the question of who assumes responsibility if the factory fails to meet a contract, the answer was that the corporations under the Ministry of Foreign Trade will bear the loss because the enterprise sells its goods to the corporations at a wholesale price. The corporations reap a certain margin of the profit on the goods exported. Enterprise managers were quick to point out, however, that it is rare that they would not fulfill a contract. A dispute over the contract would normally be resolved through mutual consultation. Even with the establishment of economic courts in August 1979, most problems continue to be solved through mutual discussions. The greatest problem confronting the factory at the moment is that demand exceeds supply.

In response to the question of whether industrialization will result in a lessening of importance of the handicrafts industry, enterprise management replied in the negative. China will modernize in the Chinese way. China cannot abandon the handicrafts industry because of its long tradition and, more important, because of the country's large population. China intends to expand labor-intensive industries in order to employ more workers. The government prefers the policy of full employment at lower wages to that of unemployment of a certain percentage of the population at higher wages. Industrialization permits the factory to use machines to make certain component parts.

Organizational Structure

The administrative organization is headed by a general manager under the leadership of the party committee. The general manager is assisted by three deputy managers who are responsible for production and planning.

The factory is made up of six workshops and one office. The six workshops are (1) production, (2) technical design, (3) administrative, (4) supply and marketing, (5) finance and accounting, and (6) equipment. The supply and marketing workshop is responsible for purchasing some raw materials and for establishing contacts with the Arts and Handicrafts Corporation and the Jewelry Corporation. There are about 100 people in each workshop, and each is headed by a workshop director and deputy directors. The factory director and deputy directors do not engage in production. Under each workshop there are groups and shifts. There are ten people to a work group, and the work-group leader engages in production.

The system of Congress of Workers and Staff has been implemented in most state-owned enterprises, but not in this factory, which is collectively owned.

Productivity

In 1979 the output value per worker was 15,000 yuan. This is about the same as that for other factories in the same industry. In 1979 the factory overfulfilled the quota by 40–50 percent, attributing its success to the use of the bonus system.

The productivity rate of this factory is about the same as that for other state-owned enterprises. The only difference between collectively owned and state-owned enterprises is in the treatment of profits. The collectively owned enterprise turns its profits to the local authorities (in this case the Beijing Municipal Government), whereas state-owned enterprises hand their profits to the central government. Otherwise, state-owned and collectively owned enterprises are similar in terms of structure and management.

In 1979 the absenteeism rate was approximately 5 percent.

Wages and Bonuses

The wage structure is fairly complex. The eight-grade wage structure for workers in collectively owned enterprises is different from that for state-owned enterprises. Even in state-owned enterprises there are variations because some of these were privately owned prior to 1956. Only enterprises in the mining, railway, and telecommunications sectors have unified standards.

In 1977 the eight-grade wage structure in this factory underwent modification. After 1977 the wage for the first-grade worker was increased from 30 to 33 yuan, the wage for the second-grade worker was raised from 36 to 38.6 yuan, and that for the third-grade worker was increased from 42 to 45.2 yuan. The wage for the fourth-grade worker is 48 yuan. In 1980 further wage adjustments were made. This made the wage structure even more complex. There is no uniform wage structure for the Beijing Council of Workers. In 1980 it was decided that no worker can receive an increase of more than 7 yuan per month.

Bonuses may not exceed more than 7 percent of a worker's total wage. Bonuses are given on the basis of the worker's performance. Workers are evaluated on the three criteria of quality, quantity, and attitude toward work. The latter is defined as attendance at political study sessions after work hours.

Sanctions

If the worker does not fulfill the production target, his or her bonus will be reduced. The factory cannot reduce the wage or dismiss the worker. The factory tries to reform delinquent workers by encouraging them to emulate the behavior of the advanced workers.

The Beijing No. 4 Cosmetics Factory

The information presented in this case was obtained in an interview with management personnel at the Beijing No. 4 Cosmetics Factory.

History and Overview

The Beijing No. 4 Cosmetics Factory is a collectively owned enterprise, established in July 1961. At that time it was a small factory, employing fewer than 100 workers and producing only three or four products. Now it produces more than seventy varieties of cosmetics and other toiletries, primarily for domestic consumption. Some creams are exported to Southeast Asian countries and a small proportion to European countries.

The factory currently has a work force totaling 347 people, 41 of whom work as administrative cadres. This includes the cadres in the party committee.

Organizational Structure

The administrative organization is headed by the general manager under the leadership of the party committee. The general manager, who is assisted by several deputy managers, is concurrently a member of the party committee. The general manager is responsible for administrative work. In the administrative organization there are several levels and several functional sections, similar to those in the state-owned enterprises described earlier. Some of the deputy managers also assume responsibility for technology and production.

The factory is made up of seven workshops: (1) production and planning, (2) technical inspection, (3) accounting and finance, (4) labor and wages, (5) supply and marketing, (6) administrative office, and (7) logistics.

The structure of the party committee is similar to that of the state-owned enterprise. The number of personnel in the administrative committee is roughly the same as the figure for the party committee.

In response to a question about the types of changes enterprise management plans to implement in the future, the following were identified. First, the factory seeks to strengthen the role of management and to improve the system of workers' bonuses, the production command system, and the labor system. This last item refers to labor discipline. The absenteeism rate in 1979 was 10 percent. In 1980 it was 5 percent. During the Cultural Revolution, it was as high as 20 percent. Enterprise management sees a definite relationship between the use of bonuses and lowered absenteeism. Another reason that absenteeism was lower in 1980 was that older workers had retired. The factory has implemented stricter regulations for taking leaves of absence. In the past the worker had only to inform the group leader orally that he would be absent from work. Now the worker must submit a written statement to the team leader. If the worker wants to take three days off, he must submit the written application to the department responsible for production. If the worker wants to take more than three days off, he must get the official approval of the general manager. All workers are given work manuals pertaining to the operation of machinery and equipment and other organizational processes.

A second goal of management is to improve the equipment used in production in order to upgrade the quality and variety of products manufactured. A third goal is to learn the experiences of other advanced factories in the country.

Productivity

The productivity of the enterprise is measured along two dimensions: (1) the total value of output per worker per year; and (2) the total output (including only personnel engaged in production). The total output value per worker per year is approximately 25,000 yuan, about average for the industry. In 1979 the factory overfulfilled the state quota by 17 percent. In 1980 it expects to overfulfill the quota by 20 percent.

The factory is trying to improve the system for evaluating the performance of cadres. Workers do not evaluate the performance of the cadres. The evaluation is performed by the cadres themselves through mutual discussion. Absenteeism is used as a criterion in the evaluation process. The factory realizes the problems inherent in this system of evaluation and seeks to improve it. However, this goal has not yet been accomplished. Some of the schemes currently under consideration include the use of a scoring system with a possible total of 100 points. The administration would draw up a list of criteria, and each cadre would be evaluated on each criterion. For example, if a cadre is absent, he or she might receive a -1.

Another possible method would be to keep a record of cadres' performance and behavior, which would be signed by the section chief every week. The record would keep track of the types of activities the cadres engaged in and how they behaved.

Wages and Bonuses

Wages are fairly similar to those in other enterprises. The average wage of a worker is 45 yuan. The average wage for cadres is 50-55 yuan. Because some cadres were promoted from the level of workers, they continue to receive workers' wages. Cadres are promoted more frequently than are workers.

Until mid-1980 the factory had received two wage increases. The first was in 1972, when some workers got an increase. The other wage increase was in 1977 and was part of a national wage increase.

Bonuses average 10–15 percent of the worker's wage. There is a certain degree of flexibility in this regard. Cadres generally receive a slightly lower percentage as bonus, but the difference is minimal. In this factory workers receive varying rates of bonuses, whereas cadres receive a uniform amount. The factory is trying to learn from the steel mills, where the cadres get a higher percentage of bonuses.

Sanctions

With respect to the resolution of conflicts, trivial cases are resolved within the team through mutual discussion. The team leader criticizes and educates the wrongdoers. Major conflicts are resolved with the assistance of the party committee. In cases of serious offenses, the worker is disciplined.

Sanctions include education, having the wrongdoer engage in written self-criticism, warning, serious warning, and keeping a record of how the wrongdoer is making amends for his misdeeds. The factory has implemented the new system of dismissing workers. For example, one worker was absent from his job for a week without good reason, and he deceived enterprise management about the reason for his absence. Now the factory retains him on a trial basis for one year. If his performance during this trial period is poor, he will be dismissed.

Economic sanctions are also imposed. If a worker is absent for one day in a month, he will not receive a bonus. The principal form of misdemeanor in this factory is absenteeism.

In cases of theft or sabotage of machinery, there will be more severe economic penalties. The wrongdoers must also make compensation.

The Beijing No. 1 Carpet Factory

The information provided in this case was obtained through an interview with management personnel at the Beijing No. 1 Carpet Factory.

History and Overview

The Beijing No. 1 Carpet Factory is a collectively owned enterprise, one of nine carpet factories belonging to the Carpet Corporation. The Carpet Corporation is under the administration of the Second Light Industrial Bureau of the municipal government of Beijing.

The enterprise, established in 1958 through the collective efforts of individual artisans and small producers, has 1,400 workers. Approximately 60 percent of the workers and administrative cadres are female. The factory specializes in handmade carpets; and manufactures four varieties of handmade carpets: (1) Beijing style (this has a very long tradition; it is made of pure wool and cotton threads supplied from Xinjiang and Xijang [Tibet] provinces); (2) artistic style; (3) colored-weaving style; and (4) monotone sculptured carpets.

The factory is similar to state-owned enterprises in terms of management and organizational structure. The only difference is that it is treated as an independent accounting unit that is responsible for its own profits and losses. If it runs into financial difficulties, it can ask for loans.

Organizational Structure

The structure of the factory is similar to that for the Beijing No. 3 Textile Mill. The organizational setup is similar to that for most other enterprises in the country. There is a party committee, a party general branch, a manager's office, workshops, work groups, functional sections, and political sections. The staff organization, under the leadership of the general manager and the deputy managers, is responsible for the overall coordination of activities carried out by the various workshops.

The factory is made up of several workshops: design, weaving, dyeing, clipping, and washing. The designs are provided by a design institute that is separate from the enterprise but operates under the Second Light Industrial Bureau. Like all other factories, the enterprise has a medical clinic in the factory.

Production per year is approximately 56,000 square meters, and the products are primarily exported overseas. Most of the exports go to Europe, North America, and certain parts of Asia. All the exports are sold through the Ministry of Foreign Trade. The production plans are handed down by the state, and the products are sold according to state plans. Hence there is no difference between this collectively owned enterprise and a state-owned enterprise in this respect. The Second Light Industrial Bureau of Beijing sets the production quota according to market demands under a unified planning system. The enterprise does not carry out any planning activity on its own.

With the expansion of foreign trade, the factory has tried to recruit more workers, construct new buildings or renovate existing ones (the dyeing workshop was under renovation at the time of my visit), and carry out technical training. Compared with machine-made carpets, the quantity of handmade carpets exported is small. Consequently, the managers are debating whether or not to expand their production capacities.

The factory cannot dismiss its workers. The work manuals are written on blackboards. There is no written procedure for production. The absenteeism rate in the factory is low, although management would not specify the exact figure.

Wages and Bonuses

The average wage for a worker is 50 yuan. Wages for cadres and the bonus system are similar to those for state-owned enterprises. The wages for apprentices are much lower. In their two years of apprenticeship, apprentices earn only 20 yuan per month and are not entitled to bonuses.

There are four shifts of workers. The shift that is on rest does not receive a bonus. The factory employs many young people.

The Beijing Jade Factory

The information presented in this case was obtained through an interview with management personnel at the Beijing Jade Factory.

History and Overview

This is a collectively owned enterprise that was formed in 1958 through the merging of four cooperatives. The factory has a work force of 1,500 employees, 100 of whom are employed as cadres. Eight hundred of the employees are female.

Most of the products are exported, primarily to North America. These exports are handled by the Ministry of Foreign Trade. The factory has no direct contact with foreign customers. Items for export are manufactured according to specifications given by the Ministry of Foreign Trade. The factory uses its own designs to a large extent. The carving is done by hand, and it sometimes takes three years to complete a single article.

With the expansion of foreign trade, the managers are not sure what changes will be made. They may engage in some compensation trade and some processing work for foreign firms.

Under the Three-Year Plan for Readjustment, the factory has adopted the following measures to improve its operations:

1. The factory seeks to improve the quality and variety of its products. The variety differs across enterprises. On the one hand, the factory is trying to revive traditional Chinese art. On the other hand, it must cope with overseas demands and incorporate the ideas of its foreign customers.

2. The factory places heavy emphasis on production value, quantity, capital consumption, profit, quality, labor productivity, and variety.
3. The factory seeks to increase productivity through modification and improvement of existing machinery, and the use of modern equipment and tools.
4. The factory seeks to reduce consumption of raw materials.

Organizational Structure

The administrative organization is headed by a general manager under the leadership of the party committee. Three deputy managers assist the general manager. There are eight workshops in the factory, which are divided according to the variety of products manufactured. In addition, there are functional sections, such as the personnel section, which is responsible for the workers' livelihood and wages. The functional sections, which are on the same level as the workshops, provide guidance and assistance to the workshops. There is only one shift of workers.

There is no written manual for the workers. Workers in the factory have to attend political study sessions. The frequency of such study sessions is not fixed. The current theme for discussion at the political study sessions is how to attain the goals of the Four Modernizations and how to carry out party policies and directives and improve productivity.

The factory encourages worker participation in management through the Congress of Workers and Staff and through suggestion boxes.

Productivity

In 1979 the factory just fulfilled the state quota by producing commodities worth 15 million yuan. Enterprise management attributed the success to the following factors: (1) political stability and unity among the workers, (2) workers' enthusiasm, and (3) good management.

Every month the factory inspects the performance of the various work units. The factory then reports its performance to the higher authorities, the Second Bureau of Light Industry, and the Special Arts and Handicrafts Corporation.

The average absenteeism rate is 7 percent. Sometimes this drops to 4 percent. The reason for the relatively high absenteeism rate is that most of the skilled craftsmen are fairly advanced in age, and there is a relatively high proportion of women workers, who are more susceptible to illnesses.

Statistics on the performance of the work groups are compiled and posted throughout the workshops.

Wages and Bonuses

The average wage of a worker is 50 yuan, and bonuses average more than 10 percent of wages. Individual bonuses are given on the basis of the worker's performance. The workers are evaluated on the following criteria: attitude toward work (whether they obey rules and regulations, work hard, try to reduce energy consumption, help each other, and offer good suggestions); quality; and quantity.

Differences between State- and Collectively Owned Enterprises

Enterprise management then went on to discuss the two major differences between state- and collectively owned enterprises. First, collectively owned enterprises do not have state investment. Such enterprises are formed through the process of merging several cooperatives and individual producers. Second, collectively owned enterprises assume responsibility for part of their own profits and losses. Their profits are handed over to the bureau and are shared by more than 200 factories within the bureau. Of course, the losses are also shared. If the factory suffers a loss, this loss is borne by the others in the bureau. The bureau tries to analyze the reasons for the failure of a particular enterprise. The bureau encourages all enterprises to make profits, but there is a certain degree of flexibility for each factory. If the government decides that the product manufactured by a factory is essential, then the factory will be compensated for any loss incurred in the process of production. However, most of the factories within the bureau are profitable. For state-owned enterprises, the enterprise does not assume responsibility for its profits and losses. As pointed out previously, changes are being made in this respect in the 6,600 experimental units.

These are the two major differences between state-owned and collectively owned enterprises. State- and collectively owned enterprises are similar in terms of management and organization structure.

10 Organizational Processes

This chapter seeks to examine several aspects of organizational functioning, such as team spirit among workers, relations between labor and management, recruitment of workers, promotion to managerial and technical positions, decision making, reprimands, participative management, and the role of the trade unions and the Labor Bureau.

Cooperative or Team Spirit

North American culture emphasizes individualism. However, there is a growing awareness among industrial psychologists, organizational behaviorists, management, and workers that the formation of groups, whether formal or informal, can increase the likelihood of meeting organizational goals. Many books and articles have been published on the beneficial aspects of group formation in organizations. Some of these advantages include:

1. "Internal and external demands in modern organizations require much more interdependence and coordination of effort" (Nord 1972, p. 416).
2. Groups help to satisfy or fulfill a number of individual needs, including the need for affiliation, and can help reduce stress among group members.
3. Groups may provide a means of self-definition.
4. Groups can facilitate and/or improve the quality of decision making. (This is subject to debate; however, it is not the purpose here to go into the disadvantages of group problem solving).

Socialist Emulation Drives

The leaders of the PRC, perhaps more than their Western counterparts, are aware of the need for cooperative effort. They realize that without an underlying spirit of cooperation, the billion people who make up China's population would be nothing but a "heap of loose sand"—a term used by Dr. Sun Yat-sen, founder of the Chinese Republic in 1911, to describe the Chinese at the turn of the twentieth century. In present-day China, although competition is used in the factories to stimulate workers to heighten their performance, it is always balanced by an emphasis on the need to help one another to do better. This combination of competition and cooperation is best demonstrated in what are commonly referred to as socialist labor emulation drives. From time to time certain factories, work units, and individuals are designated as advanced factories, units, or workers. These serve as models that other factories, work units, and workers can emulate, learn from, and attempt to equal.

The first socialist labor emulation drive was launched in Harbin in northeastern China shortly after that city's liberation in 1947. These drives are designed to serve two major purposes: (1) to develop friendly competition between factories, workshops, and individuals so that they will surpass their past performance records; and (2) to help the less advanced units and workers catch up with the more advanced ones. The latter notion is foreign to U.S. enterprises. In China the most productive unit or person is not supposed to develop a complacent attitude or to remain aloof from the less productive units and workers. Rather, the aim of such emulation campaigns is to develop a spirit of cooperation and support in which the more advanced units and individuals help the less productive ones improve their performance.

Most factories have emulation committees that meet periodically to appraise and compare the performance of the different work units or individuals. In the Shenyang Heavy Machinery Factory, the emulation committee meets once a month to appraise and compare the various workshops and work groups on the six norms of output, quality, consumption of raw and semifinished materials, safety, record of attendance, and cleaning up. The workshops or work groups that have fulfilled the six norms well are commended and may be cited as "redbanner" or advanced units. This status is publicized throughout the factory. The names of advanced work teams, with little red flags pinned beside them, are displayed on emulation charts throughout the workshop. At the end of each quarter, the performance of the work units is summarized. Work units that have performed consistently well over the quarter are commended. Photographs and names of these pacesetters and advanced work units are displayed in the show windows strategically situated at the entrance to the factory.

In enterprises throughout China one sees colorful charts drawn on blackboards and huge posters complete with statistics indicating the targets set for the various workshops and groups and the results attained in the emulation campaigns. Little red paper flags are pinned next to the winner's name.

Need for Affiliation

In organizational psychology literature, an index known as the *need for affiliation* score (nAff) was developed for measuring the need to belong to a group. McClelland (1963) found that the nAff score for Taiwan in the 1950s was little different from that for China in the 1920s, whereas the score for the PRC in the 1950s was substantially higher, although it was still below the international average. Despite methodological problems inherent in McClelland's measures of the nAff score (which will not be discussed here), most observers of post-1949 Chinese society are impressed with the spirit of cooperation that prevails among the majority of the people.

In ancient China and in modern Taiwan the family is the nucleus of social organization. Thus interpersonal obligations are defined solely in terms of the family system. Chinese Communist party leaders realized that this attitude was obsolete and inadequate for guiding the Chinese in the modern industrial world. China's leaders have tried to revive the ancient concept that emphasized that "all men living under heaven are my brothers." This principle, though propounded by an ancient Chinese philosopher, was never put into practice. China's leaders believe that if every Chinese could broaden his view to look on the state as his own family and extend the interpersonal obligations that were once rendered only to family members, then there would be cooperation among all inhabitants of the country. An individual who acquires this new spirit and outlook will be more receptive to criticism and suggestions from peers and even from subordinates, more willing to cooperate and share responsibility, and more willing to work toward the broad objectives of the state, even if this involves temporary inconvenience and sacrifice on one's part. The belief that people in a truly cohesive group, sharing the same ideology and committed to the same goals, can work better than can isolated individuals, each with his own self-interest and concern, is similar to what U.S. psychologists call *group dynamics*.

Even though the Chinese government has been unable to eradicate totally the roots of self-interest, of giving one's family priority over the state and all others, visitors to China and Chinese who have lived in post-1949 China are greatly impressed with the altruistic spirit characteristic of most Chinese they encounter. Dr. Paul Lin, a professor at McGill University, recalled his own experience in China in 1960–1961, when there was a national food shortage in the country. "To see people sharing even then was a touching spiritual experience" (*Vancouver Sun*, February 12, 1974). Richman's statement (1969, p. 280) that "individual employees within Chinese enterprises tend to have a greater sense of cooperation, altruism and team spirit in the collective and national interest than in the Soviet industry" still holds in 1980.

This spirit of altruism and cooperation is basic to constructive group interaction, to the accommodation necessary in participative management, and to the need for management to become better aware of the problems confronting the workers.

Participative Management

In the West, from the turn of the century to the mid-1930s, Taylor's notion of scientific management held sway in the field of industrial management. However, with the publication of the Hawthorne Studies in the 1930s and later work in the evolution of organizational-behavior theories, the assumptions made under the classical theory were found to be inaccurate.

It is debatable whether the leaders of the CCP had ever read or been made aware of the works of Western participatory management theorists, for as far back as the mid-1930s Mao had expounded the principle of "democratic centralism" in the three main fields—the army, the party, and among the masses.

As applied to industrial enterprises, this theory calls for a "system which combines a high degree of centralization with a high degree of democracy." Although all enterprises must be subject to the leadership of the party and the state, workers must be allowed to become "masters" in the factory by participating in the management of the enterprise (*Selected Works*, volume 4, 1975, p. 420). Mao may have arrived at a theory of participatory management not through the route of experimental observations, as was done in the West, but primarily through direct observation of the masses and through logical necessity. Prior to 1949 the ordinary people suffered tremendously under the ruling class, who completely ignored their needs and wishes. Even though a de-Maoification campaign is presently underway in China, as pointed out in a previous chapter, the major purpose of the campaign is not to destroy all of Mao Zedong's contributions to the establishment of the PRC. Rather, the objective of the present campaign is to show that Mao is not a deity and hence could make mistakes, and that China should assess critically whether the policies and guidelines laid down by Mao are appropriate to China's present conditions. In order to enlist the continued support of the masses, it is imperative to involve them in decisions that affect them. Hence participatory democracy is still emphasized and practiced in most industrial enterprises today.

The official party line on the principle of participatory management took shape in the Charter of the Anshan Iron and Steel Company. The Anshan Charter set forth several principles to reform the system of administration and workers' participation, including the dual principles of the "two participations" and the "three-in-one combinations." The two participations refer to management participation in productive labor and worker participation in management. The three-in-one combinations refer to the inclusion of managers, technicians, and workers in the formulation and implementation of decisions affecting the enterprise's operations.

The degree of worker participation in management and management participation in labor has oscillated with periods of ideological reform. During the Cultural Revolution, these principles were interpreted in such a way that management spent an inordinate amount of time in physical labor, while ignoring administrative functions; meanwhile, persons who might have lacked technical competence were involved in running the factories. In periods of political tranquillity the workers generally respect the expertise of management. Under

China's current drive toward the goals of socialist modernization, there is an emphasis on technical competence, expertise, and leadership abilities. However, workers' opinions are solicited and taken into consideration in formulating plans, solving problems, and implementing policies. In 1980 management personnel did not engage in production per se but were required to go among the masses in order to become aware of the problems confronting the workers in the workplace. On the whole, the workers do not feel alienated either from management or from the enterprise itself. They have a strong sense of belonging, a sense of being masters in their own factories. They know that they have a say in the running of the organization and that their needs and welfare will not be unduly ignored.

In the post-Mao era, the principal vehicle through which workers participate in management is the Congress of Workers and Staff. China's leaders advocate the establishment of such workers' congresses in all enterprises. By the second half of 1980 over 80 percent of the enterprises in the cities of Beijing, Shanghai, and Tianjin had reinstituted Congresses of Workers and Staff. By the first quarter of 1981 congresses had been set up in all the large and medium-sized enterprises.

In the Tianjin Clock and Watch Factory, for instance, the Congress of Workers and Staff was established in 1957 under the leadership of the factory's party committee. The congress has been convened every year except for the eight years between 1966 and 1974. At each congress the factory's leadership report on their work over the past year, listen to criticisms and suggestions by the representatives, and make resolutions on various matters. An inspection group is elected to check on the implementation of the resolutions adopted once every three months. Representatives to the congress were elected directly by the workers and staff. All workers and staff have the right to vote and stand for election, provided they meet the following qualifications: (1) be politically and ideologically sound; (2) be productive, fulfill assignments, and abide by rules and regulations; (3) have close ties with the workers; and (4) be good at soliciting the workers' opinions and transmitting the spirit of the resolutions adopted. A total of 246 representatives attended the 1978 congress held at the Tianjin Clock and Watch Factory. Of these, 66 percent were workers, 26 percent were cadres, and 8 percent were technicians. When the congress is not in session, the representatives are divided into several groups on the basis of workshops, sections, or offices. Each group elects one member to the inspection group of the congress. This group checks on the implementation of the resolutions adopted by the congress every quarter; reports to the party committee, the cadres, or the workers and staff, respectively, on problems it has discovered; commends those who have implemented the resolutions well and criticizes those who have performed badly; and recommends ways and means of solving outstanding problems. The trade union attached to each enterprise is a working body of the congress and directs the work of the inspection group (*Beijing Review,* June 8, 1979).

In October 1980 the powers of the Congress of Workers and Staff were broadened. In some factories the congress is given the following authorities:

1. It has the authority to prepare and implement the annual budget and pro-
    duction plan for the enterprise. The congress is also empowered to prepare
    plans for plant expansion and increasing efficiency of operations.
2. It has the right to supervise research and development activities within the
    enterprise.
3. It has the authority to make decisions governing wages, workers' welfare
    benefits, working conditions, and such other actions as may benefit the
    workers.
4. It has the right to establish, revise, or abolish work rules, and to publish
    a manual of administrative procedures.
5. It has the authority to change the administrative system.
7. It has the right to administer the disciplinary system.
8. It has the right to supervise the election of workshop directors, section
    chiefs, and shift leaders through the process of secret balloting. It is also
    empowered to supervise the work of the cadres (*Beijing Review,* October
    20, 1980; pp. 3–4; *China Reconstructs;* May 1981, p. 18).

In five enterprises in Beijing the factory director has been placed under the leadership of the Congress of Workers and Staff instead of that of the party committee.

In addition to the Congress of Workers and Staff, the party requires that the party committee members, the factory director, and deputy directors go among the workers as frequently as possible to keep themselves abreast of actual situations on the shop floor. Meetings between cadres and workers are scheduled regularly so that any problem encountered in production can be brought up for discussion before the party committee and the working committee. In decisions on important matters, the workers' opinions are solicited so that their views can be heard and their concerns taken into consideration. In all workshops, work shifts, and work groups, there are workers in charge of equipment, safety devices, sanitation, materials, attendance records, the checking and testing of products, and the study of socialist principles. These workers are engaged in production and are elected by their fellow workers to help the leadership in management. In addition, workers take part in other administrative and technical meetings of the enterprise. In the Kailuan Coal Mines, for instance, workers participate in the committees for long-range planning, industrial design, and technical innovation, and in most administrative groups in grass-roots production units (*Kailuan Story* 1977).

Although participatory management is time consuming and may occasionally result in confusion because the formal authority structure is deemphasized, nevertheless the benefits that accrue from such a system seem to far outweigh the advantages. Some of the advantages are as follows:

1. Participatory management serves as a good motivating device. As mentioned previously, the sense of belonging to the enterprise makes the workers committed to the goals and activities of the organization. As is true in the West, workers' commitment to organizational goals is usually reflected in increased productivity or heightened performance, and in a reduction in turnover and absenteeism rates. In China the problem of turnover is irrelevant because of the system of job assignment by the state labor bureaus. However, we can get a rough idea of the effectiveness of such a system from the standpoint of absenteeism. Before 1949 the average absenteeism rate for the nation ranged from 10 to 20 percent annually. In 1966 the Chinese enterprises visited by Richman had an annual average absenteeism rate of about 1-2 percent (Richman 1969, pp. 260–261). Richman noted that most workers were "less frustrated, . . . identify more closely with organizational objectives, have a greater sense of purpose, commitment, and are better motivated and more productive than they were in old China" (1969, p. 260). The same held true during my visit to factories in 1979 and 1980. The absenteeism rate in most enterprises did not exceed 5 percent.

2. "Two heads are better than one." When the opinions of the workers are tapped, in many instances they have something valid to offer to the organization. Richman (1969, p. 258) noted that perhaps this "makes more sense than meets the eye" because China does not have a large contingent of highly skilled workers.

3. The system of participatory management brings workers and management closer together. Hence misunderstandings, communication breakdowns, and conflicts of group interests can be reduced. Moreover, by staying in close touch with the workers, management personnel can become more aware of the needs and problems encountered by workers on the job and thus can improve their own style of leadership.

4. Participatory management combats the attitude of "bureaucratism at the top, irresponsibility at the bottom" (Meisner 1972, p. 724). The system of participatory democracy keeps the people occupying top management positions from becoming too complacent and authoritarian. At the same time, workers are sensitized to management's problems, particularly with respect to cost reduction. Meisner related an anecdote of workers in a factory he visited who were not aware of the costs of knitted gloves used on the job. As a result, they "kept changing for new ones as soon as small holes or rips appeared." Having been introduced to such problems by taking part in budget-planning sessions, they "tend to repair damaged gloves themselves, thus saving dozens of gloves a month" (Meisner 1972, pp. 723–724).

5. The ideal factory director is one who has worked his way up through the ranks. This emphasizes the proletarian background of the people in senior positions. The system of participatory management provides a training ground for the development of such personnel.

6. Participatory management improves the quality of the organizational climate prevailing within the work unit. Research has shown that workers' perceptions of the organizational climate are strongly related to the outcome variables in the organization and can affect organizational performance (Taguiri and Litwin 1969; Pritchard and Karasick 1973). In China's efforts to attain the goals of the Four Modernizations, it is important that members have positive perceptions of the organizational climate because these are conducive to greater commitment to organizational goals and to heightened job performance.

Recruitment of Workers

Article 10 of the 1978 Constitution stipulates that "he who does not work, neither shall he eat" and that "work is an honorable duty for every citizen able to work." All able-bodied persons in China must work in order to earn their means of livelihood. In 1956 China adopted a system whereby the state labor bureaus in the various towns and cities were responsible for the recruitment and placement of all workers and staff members in state-owned enterprises.

Under this system workers have had the right to refuse a job assignment. However, this means that their names are again placed into the common pool of people applying for jobs. It may be some time before another suitable opening comes along. This, coupled with the fact that most people have been indoctrinated since birth to serve the people and the state wholeheartedly, has meant that in practice most people have accepted the jobs assigned to them by the state. The enterprises, on the other hand, have had no choice of personnel whatsoever.

In 1979 the state introduced, on a trial basis, the method of recruiting workers in the various trades and professions through examination. Applicants were examined in general and specialized subjects to determine their suitability for a particular position for which they were applying. This ensured a better fit between the requirements of industry, on the one hand, and the interests and aspirations of the applicants, on the other. This policy is conducive to industrial growth because it ensures that workers employed in a particular enterprise will possess the minimal qualifications for performing their jobs satisfactorily. The government noted that this new method has been warmly received by both job applicants and enterprises, and the practice may become more widespread in the future. As mentioned previously, collectively owned enterprises are free to recruit their workers from neighboring communities and elsewhere.

Since 1980 workers have been permitted to seek employment through the traditional labor bureaus or through their own efforts under an overall state plan (*Beijing Review,* October 27, 1980, p. 18).

Employment

In China today there are still many people waiting for jobs. China does not use the term *unemployment,* preferring the term *waiting for employment.* In the Chinese view "waiting for employment" and "employment" are not identical. However, after a fairly lengthy discussion with Sun Jen, chief of the Division of Policy Research at the Labor Bureau, it was not clear how the two differ in practice. According to Mr. Sun, people waiting for employment generally come from three categories. First, there are graduates of senior middle schools who have failed the university entrance exams. They do not demand work but want to spend more time studying for the subsequent year's entrance examination. The category includes workers who are sick and need to rest at home, as well as those who must help their families with housework. As pointed out in a previous chapter, all university graduates are employed upon graduation.

Another category of workers classified as waiting for employment are those who have completed several years of military service and are waiting for job assignments by the local governments. They do not receive wages while waiting for employment, but they receive a lump sum when they retire from the army.

A third category of workers waiting for employment includes the young intellectuals (that is, middle-school graduates) who were sent to work in the countryside during the Cultural Revolution. Now they want to be transferred back to the cities. In the waiting period, if they continue to work in the countryside, they receive salaries. However, if they return home to the cities before a job becomes available, they do not receive salaries.

Besides these three categories of people, there are instances in which individuals demand employment very urgently but cannot get work.

According to Mr. Sun, the problem of unemployment was solved during the 1950s when the government provided jobs for 4 million people. The present problem of waiting for employment arose for two reasons. First, after the 1950s the population grew very rapidly. In 1949 the population stood at 540 million. Since 1949 the population has increased at a rate of approximately 19 per 1,000 annually. At the end of 1978 the population stood at 975.23 million. In 1979 China's population was 78 percent higher than in 1949 (*Beijing Review,* November 16, 1979, pp. 17-24).

Second, between 1966 and 1976 the productivity rate increased very slowly. In fact, between 1974 and 1976 the Chinese economy was brought to the verge of collapse. These two factors have given rise to the present situation wherein a considerable number of workers are waiting for jobs. The government tries to solve this problem through two principal means.

The first method is population control The government hopes to attain the target of zero population growth by the year 2000. Several measures have been adopted to attain this goal:

1. Education and dissemination of birth control methods are provided.
2. Free contraceptives are available and offices for family planning have been established throughout the country.
3. Free male and female sterilization and induced abortions are available.
4. Couples are encouraged to subscribe to the one-child policy through the use of material incentives, which, in urban areas, include monthly health subsidies of 5 yuan a month until the child is 14 years old; priority in admission to kindergartens, primary and middle schools, and university, and in the allocation of jobs; free medical care; and exemption from tuition fees. In addition, a family that subscribes to the one-child policy is allocated the same amount of living space as a family of four. In rural areas a family that agrees to have only one child will receive a monthly sum equal to 3 work points (in the countryside, work points provide the basis for calculation of monthly wages and bonuses) until the child is fourteen. The child will be allotted the same amount of grain as an adult. and in the distribution of plots for private use, the child will receive a 1.5 share (*Beijing Review,* April 13, 1979, pp. 4–5).
5. Economic sanctions are imposed on those who insist on having more than two children. In Tianjin, for instance, parents who have had more than two children after the introduction of the one-child policy must pay the state or the collective a sum equal to 10 percent of their wages every month. The authorities justify this measure by arguing that given the generous welfare benefits provided by the state in terms of day-care facilities and health benefits, the state in fact subsidizes every child a family has. For example, the parents pay only two-thirds of the costs of operating a nursery or day-care center, and the state subsidizes the remaining one-third. Consequently, it is only fair that those families with more than two children repay the state in some way (*Beijing Review,* November 16, 1979, p. 25).
6. People are encouraged to marry late. In the 1981 Marriage Law, the legal age for men to contract marriage has been raised from twenty to twenty-two, and that for women from eighteen to twenty. In addition, it is prescribed in the law that "both husband and wife have the obligation to practice family planning."

China has established a State Family Planning Commission to regulate and implement family-planning policies throughout the country. These measures have yielded results. In 1980 China's natural population-growth rate was 11.0

per 1,000, compared with 20.99 per 1,000 in 1973 and 11.7 per 1,000 in 1979 (*China Reconstructs,* May 1981, p. 4). Despite the decline in population-growth rate, because of the rapid population increase in the preceding two-and-a-half decades, there are still new laborers waiting for jobs every year. From 1977 to 1980 the government provided jobs for 26.6 million youths (*Beijing Review,* February 23, 1981, p. 8). However, given that 63.4 percent of the country's population is under thirty years of age (the average age nationwide in 1978 was twenty-six), the problem of creating new jobs is likely to remain. The government estimates that each year for the next ten years, it must provide an additional 5 million jobs to accommodate those who are ready to enter the work force. Therefore, according to Mr. Sun, the problem of waiting for employment will persist for at least the next ten years.

The second method of decreasing unemployment is to develop the national economy. Since 80 percent of China's people still depend on agriculture as their principal means of livelihood, the government has undertaken measures to stimulate the growth of the rural economy. These include the diversification of the rural economy to include such fields as animal husbandry and forestry, and the development of secondary industries such as the processing of agricultural products.

In the cities the economic structure has been readjusted in order to increase employment. This readjustment includes the establishment of collectively owned enterprises and individual operators, and the development of light and textile industries and of the commercial and service-trade sectors. The advantages of establishing collectively owned enterprises were discussed in a previous chapter. In the future the government will pay greater attention to the development of commercial and service trades and to the light-industrial and textile sectors, which were neglected in the first twenty-five years of the PRC's history. In 1957, for instance, 14.5 percent of the urban work force was employed in the commercial and service trades, whereas in 1977 only 9.5 percent of the workers were employed in these sectors (*Beijing Review,* August 3, 1979, p. 2). In 1965, 23 percent of the urban work force was employed in collectively owned enterprises. In 1976 this figure was down to 20.9 percent. For every 1 million yuan invested in fixed assets in the heavy industrial sector, 90 jobs are provided. This compares with 250 jobs for the same amount of fixed assets in the light-industrial sector (*Beijing Review,* October 27, 1980, p. 18).

China will also expand and develop labor-intensive industries such as various light industries, tourism, and service trades. In realizing the goals of the Four Modernizations, although it is important to achieve automation in certain areas, given China's objective conditions (a large labor force and a lack of capital), the leadership see the need to develop medium-sized and small enterprises and labor-intensive industries.

In addition to the aforementioned two methods of resolving the problem of waiting for employment, the government will also consider exporting workers.

There are some arguments in China about whether this policy should be pursued. Up to now there has been no pure export of laborers. There are cases in which the China Construction Engineering Corporation (CCEC), which was established in 1957, has undertaken contract projects overseas by sending technicians, management personnel, and workers. By 1978 the corporation had completed 500 engineering projects in more than fifty countries throughout the world. In February 1979 the CCEC began to undertake complete projects, including surveying, design, and construction. By September 1979 the CCEC had signed seventy-two contracts with foreign countries (*Beijing Review*, October 27, 1980, pp. 21–23). As China expands its economic relationships with foreign countries, it plans to engage in more contract projects overseas. According to Mr. Sun, China does not anticipate the export of a great number of laborers overseas for two reasons. First, China has a policy of self-reliance. It has always tried to resolve its own problems. He cited as examples the construction of "new" China and the resolution of the food situation, both accomplished primarily through the country's own efforts. Second, China cannot imagine that any other country could absorb its 400-million-person labor force. The CCEC sends only a few thousand people abroad each year to engage in construction projects. Furthermore, the corporation sends only qualified individuals abroad. Many of the youth who are waiting for employment do not have the necessary skills to be sent overseas.

The government insists that the practice of sending laborers to work in foreign countries will not result in a repetition of the situation that occurred in the late nineteenth and early twentieth centuries. As the deputy managing director of the CCEC, Zhang Enshu, explains it, the workers who were exported in the nineteenth century toiled as coolies and "had to sell themselves to traders in human flesh." Under the present system, the workers belong to state enterprises. While abroad, they receive four to five times the wage they normally earn in China. All their accommodations and medical expenses are paid for, and they work only forty-eight hours a week (*Beijing Review*, October 27, 1980, pp. 22–23). They work for less than two years in a foreign country and enjoy holidays. In addition, they are entitled to one month's paid vacation every year and free trips back to China. The purposes of these projects are primarily three-fold: (1) to exchange knowledge and learn from the advanced countries; (2) to promote friendly relations between China and other countries; and (3) to earn foreign exchange.

Promotion to Managerial Level

In the past managerial personnel were appointed or selected from among those workers who were considered both red and expert. This was done through recommendation and discussion by fellow workers, party committee members, and management personnel in the enterprises concerned.

With the current emphasis on technical competence and leadership abilities as two important qualifications for managerial positions, reforms in the cadre system have been implemented on an experimental basis. Some of these reforms include the recruitment of managerial personnel through examinations and the election of cadres through a secret ballot. In the first half of 1981 factory directors were elected in 900 enterprises, workshop directors were elected in 10,000 enterprises, and section chiefs and work-group leaders were elected in some 30,000 enterprises throughout the country (*Beijing Review,* May 11, 1981, p. 6).

Several factories have adopted the method of recruiting managerial personnel through examinations. The Shanghai No. 17 Cotton Mill was one of the first factories to adopt this method. In 1979, 151 management personnel retired from the mill. Instead of relying on the traditional recommendation and discussion sessions, the leading cadres in the cotton mill used the examination system to determine which workers were eligible for promotion to managerial positions in the functional areas of planning, statistics, and accounting. All applicants had to meet the following criteria in order to be eligible for promotion: (1) must have at least two years of work experience; (2) must be under 35 years of age; (3) must have an education equivalent to that of a senior-middle-school graduate; and (4) must be in good health and hard working. Of the 235 candidates who sat for the exams, the 67 who obtained the highest scores were promoted to managerial positions.

The system of electing cadres at various levels through secret balloting, except at the level of factory director, was introduced at a united company of agriculture, industry, and commerce in Jiangxi Province's Yiyang County at the beginning of 1979. The principal characteristics of the new system included the following:

1. Cadres are elected once a year through a secret ballot. Each worker is entitled to one vote. Those cadres who receive more than 50 percent of the votes are reelected, whereas those who received less than 30 percent are forced to resign. In borderline cases (in instances where the cadre receives 30–50 percent of the votes), he or she may remain in the position provided he or she demonstrates a willingness to correct past deficiencies and make amends in the future.
2. Opinion polls are held once every six months to appraise the work of elected cadres.
3. Workers' opinions are solicited through the use of opinion boxes. These opinions are reviewed regularly, and the cadres concerned must seriously consider all suggestions put forward. For example, the cadre must explain why a particular suggestion cannot be adopted, or why and how he will go about implementing a particular suggestion.
4. Cadres will receive different types of subsidy according to their positions and contributions to the enterprise.

Since the implementation of the system, incompetent cadres have been demoted and replaced by competent ones who have the support of the majority of workers (*Beijing Review,* February 11, 1980, p. 6). This system has attracted attention throughout the country. The practice of electing workshop directors through secret balloting has been adopted at most factories, as discussed in chapter 9.

Changes in the methods of appointment to managerial positions place heavy emphasis on competence and leadership abilities, which are crucial to the effective and efficient functioning of organizations. All of this is conducive to the goal of socialist modernization.

Recruitment of Engineers

In the past, experienced workers could be promoted to the ranks of engineers in their respective factories through recommendations and discussions by fellow workers, party committee members, and management personnel. Graduates of colleges and institutes of science and technology were also recruited as engineers. Since 1979 some state-owned enterprises have used examinations to determine workers' eligibility for promotion to the rank of engineer.

In the first half of 1979 some 1,500 workers, cadres, and technicians at the Anshan Iron and Steel Company sat for the college basic-theory and specialty-theory examinations sponsored by the company. Upon successful completion of the written exam, the candidates answered questions before 300 groups of examiners organized by the different factories and mines attached to the company. In the oral exams the candidates demonstrated their abilities to solve concrete technical problems. Eight hundred seventy-seven people, half of them workers, obtained passing grades and were awarded certificates and appointed engineers for the company. This practice ensured that only qualified individuals could be recruited to the ranks of engineers and senior technicians.

To attain the goals of the Four Modernizations, it is necessary to develop a large contingent of technicians and scientists. In 1979 China had only 1.5 million engineers and technicians. To foster the rapid growth of a large pool of competent engineers and technicians, in early 1980 the State Council promulgated the provisional regulations concerning titles for engineers and technicians. Henceforth, titles would fall into five categories:

1. *Senior engineer:* This is equivalent to the level of professor and associate professor.
2. *Engineer:* This is equivalent to the level of lecturer.
3. *Assistant engineer:* This is equivalent to the level of assistant lecturer.
4. *Master technician.*
5. *Technician.*

Specific requirements and methods of appraisal are clearly delineated for each category. The principal criterion is technical competence. The number of years of schooling and service in an organization will also be considered (*Beijing Review,* January 28, 1980, p. 8). Examinations for the purpose of recruitment and promotion will be held once every year, or once every two to three years. However, those with outstanding achievements may take the exams at any time and may be double-promoted (that is, skip a category).

Redness versus Expertness

Since the establishment of the PRC in 1949, the government has pursued the policy that only those judged to be both "red" and "expert" can be nominated as advanced workers or promoted to top management. *Redness* refers to political soundness, and *expertness* to technical competence. Controversy has centered on how these principles should be applied in practice. Specifically, questions about the criteria for redness and expertness have arisen. In times of political upheaval, redness was often used as the only criterion for judging a worker's eligibility for nomination as an advanced worker and for promotion to top management. In those years many who indulged in political demagoguery were selected even if they lacked the necessary technical skills. This led to widespread inefficiency and chaos in the operations and management of enterprises; it explains in part why China's economy was brought to the brink of collapse between 1974 and 1976. Since 1976 most factories and enterprises have adopted a more pragmatic approach to the application of the principles of redness and expertness.

The use of examinations to determine a candidate's level of technical competence, as described in the previous two sections, and the specific practices followed in other enterprises, such as the one to be described here, indicate that the Chinese authorities are now placing an increasing emphasis on expertness in determining a person's suitability for advancement and promotion in an organization. A case in point is the photoelectrical institute under the Chinese Academy of Sciences. In the course of nominating advanced workers for the institute, a heated debate arose about the eligibility of one of the candidates, a researcher named Liu Tiehsheng. Liu had completed his university training in precision machinery in 1965 and had worked for the institute since then. When Liu learned that there were only a few people in the institute who could translate foreign scientific literature, he volunteered to do the work. Through assiduous study, he acquired a good command of several foreign languages, including English, Russian, French, German, and Japanese. His contributions over a four-year period included the translation of over seventy articles on science and technology and the compilation of a French-Chinese dictionary of photographic optics. Those who opposed his nomination argued that Liu was not qualified because he spent most of his time studying technical literature and therefore did not meet the criterion of redness. The majority of the organization's members argued, however, that redness implies "having a correct political orientation and being dedicated to serving the socialist cause and the people," whereas expertness required that the person be proficient in his own field of work in order to make contributions to building socialism. They argued that Liu fitted the bill because the relationship between politics and vocational work, or between redness and expertness, was a dialectical one. Politics is the commander and vocational work the commanded. "Politics must be put in command of vocational work and . . . politics must help promote vocational work." A person who does a good job must be committed to the goals of the country and hence must be ideologically sound (*Beijing Review,* October 27, 1978, p. 15). Most enterprises in China now realize that redness is a necessary but insufficient criterion for nomination as advanced worker or promotion to management and have espoused a more pragmatic approach. The authoritative *Beijing Review* (March 3, 1980, p. 26) published the following criteria for redness and expertness: "Loving one's socialist motherland, working consciously for socialism and serving the people, is red. While holding to socialism politically, one who earnestly learns his vocational skills, works hard to do a good job and makes contributions to society is considered red and expert."

Role of Factory Director

The role of the factory director has undergone several changes since the founding of the PRC in 1949. Soon after 1949 China's industrial development came under Soviet influence. Kao Kang, the chairman of the first State Planning Commission, was pro-Soviet. By 1950 entire industrial plants were imported from the USSR, along with Soviet advisors and management techniques. The Soviet model of one-man leadership was adopted. Under this system, the factory director had exclusive power in major decisions pertaining to finance, production plans, personnel, and technical problems. The factory director also had the power to overrule decisions of the party committee. Opposition to one-man management grew, however; in 1955 Kao Kang was dismissed from office. In 1958, following Mao Zedong's directive on strengthening party leadership and following the mass line, the principle of one-man leadership was replaced by the system of division of responsibility.

This shift in the role and authority of the leader has its parallels in management-theory development in the West. In the early 1900s, under the assumptions of scientific management, the leader of a group or organization had to guide the functioning of all aspects of the organization because the employees were seen as passive and unwilling to take responsibility.

In the late 1930s Lewin and his colleagues investigated the effects of authoritarian, democratic, and laissez-faire leadership on children's performance in a group. The studies showed that under an authoritarian leader, group members "tended to be more submissive and dependent on the leader." Moreover, there was less unity among group members, and member relationships could be characterized as "more aggressive and domineering." When the leader is altogether absent, however, the quality of work deteriorates. On the other hand, under more democratic leadership, the group was found to be more cohesive, and the members were usually happier and more satisfied and tended to be more productive in most of their activities (Nord 1972, p. 506).

Although the relationships between leadership style, employee performance, and satisfaction are still unclear, the current trend in most Western organizations is toward a more democratic leadership style. Management realizes that when good human relations prevail in work situations, workers tend to be more productive.

Mao came to power with the support of the workers and the peasants—the people who had been oppressed in the past. One of the principal aims of the new regime was to abolish class distinction. Mao recognized, however, that classes could not be eliminated all at once. Consequently, in the interim period the principle of democratic centralism must be put into practice, under which the party leads and directs, but only to the extent needed to bring about or nurture the "correct attitude" among the masses.

Despite the fact that it is not yet feasible to eliminate leadership altogether, an effort must be made to give the people real power. Those in leadership positions are expected to act according to the following guiding principle offered by Mao in 1948: "Guard against arrogance. For anyone in a leading position, this is a matter of principle and an important condition for maintaining unity. Even those who have made no serious mistakes and have achieved very great success in their work should not be arrogant" (Selected Works, vol. 3, 1975, p. 411).

In many respects Chinese workers appear to be more powerful vis-à-vis their superiors than their Western counterparts. They are encouraged to be outspokenly critical of any situation in which they feel they have been unfairly treated or where they feel improvement could be made. The ideal management-labor relationship in China is one of peaceful cooperation. The aim is not for one party or group to dominate over the other, but for both parties to learn from each other and to carry out the responsibilities and duties assigned to each.

This system of division of responsibility was abolished between 1966 and 1976, when the factories established revolutionary committees. After 1976 the revolutionary committees at most enterprises were dissolved, except where government administration was integrated with management. The system of division of responsibility was once again instituted, with the party committee making all major decisions through collective decision before implementation by the factory director. In 1981 the government called for a separation of party administration from factory administration. The party committee will no longer be responsible for administrative duties but will concentrate on party work. The factory administration is to be headed by the factory director under the leadership of the Congress of Workers and Staff.

In order to understand the operations of Chinese industrial enterprises, it is important to consider the role and functions of the Labor Bureau and the trade unions.

Labor Bureau

The information provided in this section was obtained in an interview with Sun Jen, chief of the Division of Policy Research at the Labor Bureau.

The Labor Bureau was established in 1975. Its forerunner was the Ministry of Labor, established in 1949. Only the name has been changed; the functions of the bureau are the same as those of the former ministry, with one exception. Shortly after 1949 private and semiprivate enterprises still existed in China. The Ministry of Labor, among its various activities, was then in charge of relationships between the capitalists and the workers. By 1956 all industries were nationalized. Hence the Ministry of Labor no longer had to perform this function. However, even the personnel in the bureau are the same as those in the ministry. For example, Sun Jan has been with the bureau since 1949. The reason for the name change is that in the West, ministry may mean cabinet ministry. In 1975 the name was changed to Labor Bureau to indicate that it is an agency under the State Council.

Functions of the Labor Bureau

The Labor Bureau has jurisdiction over three related areas: (1) the employment and training of workers; (2) wages and welfare benefits for workers; and (3) safety and health standards for workers. The Labor Bureau is an administrative organization that oversees the aforementioned activities. It does not perform specific activities or directly manage the activities outlined here. The enterprises are responsible for carrying out the specific activities in the foregoing three categories. The objectives of the Labor Bureau are primarily twofold: (1) to fulfill or overfulfill the national economic-development plan; and (2) to improve the welfare, living and health conditions, and technical level of the workers. To accomplish these two broad objectives, the Labor Bureau carries out the following activities:

1. The bureau drafts laws and regulations pertaining to employment, training, wages, welfare benefits, and safety and health standards. These rules and

regulations, which require the approval of the State Council, provide the general guidelines and principles to which all enterprises must adhere. Enterprises do enjoy some flexibility in the enforcement of these guidelines to fit the factory's objective conditions.

2. The bureau formulates an overall plan that governs various aspects of the labor force. This includes the allocation of the labor force according to the national economic-development plan, wages and wage increases, training of workers, and labor security. The bureau does not assign workers directly to the factory. Each factory drafts a plan of employment needs, and the local labor bureaus assign workers to factories.

3. The bureau tries to resolve all problems relating to labor, wages, and workers' welfare that cannot be solved by the enterprises and the local labor bureaus.

4. The bureau supervises and evaluates the work of the various enterprises with respect to the implementation of labor laws and regulations.

Relationship with Trade Unions

Trade unions are nongovernmental agencies, whereas the Labor Bureau is a government organization. The aims of the trade unions and the Labor Bureau are the same, but the two differ in their operations. There is a division of responsibility between the bureau and the trade unions. The role of the bureau is primarily administrative—making rules and regulations. The trade unions are nongovernmental representatives of the workers. Since the objectives of the two are the same, the relationships between the Labor Bureau and the trade unions are very close. The bureau relies on the trade unions for the accomplishment of its objectives, and the trade unions reflect and relay the demands of the workers to the bureau.

Trade Unions

The All-China Federation of Trade Unions, which is the leading national body of trade unions, was established in May 1925. Except for the period 1967–1978, when they were forced to suspend their activities, trade unions have played an important role in Chinese society.

Chinese trade unions are mass organizations of the working class, formed on a voluntary basis under the leadership of the CCP. Membership is open to workers and staff members in factories, shops, schools, hospitals, and scientific-research institutes, whether they are engaged in physical or mental labor and regardless of nationality, sex, and religion. In 1980 there were 376,000 trade-union organizations at the grass-roots level. These are staffed by 243,000 full-time cadres. In addition, there are 7.7 million trade-union activists. Total membership in the various trade unions amounted to 61 million, of whom 30 million are women (*Beijing Review,* May 11, 1981, p. 6). Anyone who wants to join a trade union must submit an application and is admitted only after a group discussion and approval by the trade union at the grass-roots level.

Trade unions are organized according to trade and geographical location. Each factory, school, and hospital has a union. There is a regional and a national industrial union for each particular branch. For instance, under the National Federation of Railway Trade Unions, there is a regional railway union in every railway bureau. Local federations of trade unions are also established in provinces, municipalities, and autonomous regions. The All-China Federation of Trade Unions is the leading body of all trade unions across the country.

Although the Constitution provides for the right to strike, strikes and walkouts are very rare because enterprises are either state owned or collectively owned. The trade unions emphasize the spirit of cooperation between workers and management, as discussed in the previous section. This notion is foreign to the Western world, in which the trade union is viewed by the workers as a citadel from which they can bargain with management from a position of strength. In the West management and labor are viewed as having basically conflicting interests.

The activities performed by the trade unions in China are primarily fourfold:

1. They serve as a link between the party and the masses. On the one hand, the trade unions transmit the workers' opinions and needs to the party in order to provide a basis for the latter to formulate or readjust its principles and policies. On the other hand, the trade unions educate the workers to understand and properly implement the party's policies.

2. They serve as a communist school. The trade unions conduct ideological, cultural, and technical-education programs among the workers. They run spare-time schools, cultural palaces, and recreational halls; launch socialist labor emulation campaigns; and prepare workers for enterprise-management functions. In 1980 trade unions throughout the country ran 3,669 educational institutes at various levels, which were attended by 1.13 million workers and staff members (*Beijing Review,* April 27, 1981, p. 5).

3. They serve as a pillar of state power. Trade unions organize workers to fulfill state production plans; educate them to observe the Constitution, laws, and policies of the state; and recommend outstanding workers to leading posts at various levels of the party. Under the Four Modernizations program, they mobilize the workers and staff members to support and implement reforms in the economic structure and the system of industrial management.

4. They promote the welfare of the workers. In addition to organizing schools and recreational halls, trade unions also run workers' sanatoria and assist workers to solve problems—for example, by building houses with funds

provided by factories, and by rehabilitating workers who have committed mistakes in the past. In 1980 trade unions ran 130 sanatoria throughout the country. In 1981 trade unions allocated 50 million yuan to provide rest and recuperation facilities for 200,000 workers in these sanatoria (*Beijing Review,* May 11, 1981, p. 6).

In summary, the function of the trade union is primarily to promote cooperation, stimulate workers' enthusiasm toward work, and boost morale among the workers. The reason that trade unions in China have developed along such lines is comprehensible only in light of the cooperative spirit that prevails in the country. From an analysis of the functions performed by the trade unions, it can be seen that they will continue to play a major role in educating and training workers, organizing them to fulfill state production plans, and promoting welfare and improving the standards of living of the masses of people—all of which are important prerequisites to the success of the Four Modernizations program.

Disputes between Workers and Enterprises

In the past disputes between workers and enterprises were resolved through the process of mutual consultation by trade unions and workers, on the one side, and the administrative organization of the enterprise on the other. Since the objectives of the administrative organization and those of the trade unions are identical in China, there is little or no contradiction between the workers and the enterprise. Therefore, most disputes can be resolved easily through consultation.

However, Sun Jen, chief of the Division of Policy Research at the Labor Bureau, admits that largely because of differences in perceptions, conflicts do arise. Disputes that cannot be resolved through the process of mutual consultation are submitted to a higher organization for settlement. For enterprise administration, there are several administrative levels. The enterprise can turn the case over to the administrative bureau at the provincial or municipal level. If it cannot be resolved at this level, it will be submitted to the ministry at the national level. The trade unions can turn a matter over to the city or provincial levels of the union. If the dispute cannot be resolved at these levels, the matter will be forwarded to the trade union at the national level.

The Labor Bureau functions on behalf of the government and is responsible for the implementation, supervision, and monitoring of labor rules and regulations. If a dispute arises with respect to labor rules and regulations, the Labor Bureau intervenes to help resolve it. Formerly, China's legal system was incomplete. The Labor Bureau is discussing how changes pertaining to labor-management conflicts can be made. The Labor Bureau is considering the establishment of an arbitration organization within the bureau. This will be an administrative organ of government. If arbitration does not work, then the dispute can be handed over to the economic courts, whose aim is to resolve economic disputes. Some workers and enterprises can sue and be sued in court.

Criminal offenses are settled in a court of law. For example, a coal-mine gas explosion in Jilin Province resulted in the death of several dozen workers. Upon investigation, it was found that the explosion occurred because administrative personnel did not follow regulations. Hence the matter was submitted to the law courts. The court handed down a sentence of three years' imprisonment (with delayed sentence) for the administrative personnel responsible for the explosion. Most workers thought the sentence was too light and voiced their discontent in the newspapers. Mr. Sun noted that the trade unions represent the workers' interests and speak on their behalf. They guarantee the rights of the workers according to laws and regulations. In this case the trade unions conducted some investigations on their own and asked the court to reopen the case.

Demands of Workers

Sun Jen, chief of the Division of Policy Research at the Labor Bureau, indicated that this is a complex issue because of individual differences in demands and differences according to the various professions. However, workers' demands can be categorized into three general areas:

1. Workers hope that there will be political stability and unity. This concern is especially dominant among older and middle-aged workers because of their personal experiences. They hope the government will be able to strengthen the legal system and provide for democratic life. They also hope the government will provide education and help people develop good social habits and customs.

Within the enterprise, they hope that management will be strengthened. Between 1966 and 1976 chaos prevailed. Although order has now been restored in most areas, some unhealthy tendencies remain. Compared with the advanced countries, China's system of management is fairly undeveloped.

2. In general, workers want to improve their knowledge and skills. This demand is especially prevalent among young and middle-aged workers because many of them did not receive a good education during the Cultural Revolution. Where possible, they hope to engage in full-time study or, otherwise, in spare-time education.

Middle-aged workers want to improve their technical and management skills. Workers who are fairly advanced in years also try their best to make some progress.

3. During the past two decades, wage increases were minimal and the standard of living of the workers did not improve rapidly. Workers hope their standards of living will improve more quickly in the future. However, according to Mr. Sun, most workers understand that China must first develop its production. They appreciate and support the government's efforts in these directions.

Comparatively speaking, middle-aged workers make greater demands because they have families to support. Middle-aged workers want higher wages and larger living quarters for their families. Cultural and educational demands are more important to the young workers. Because they do not have families to support, they prefer material goods such as tape recorders, transistors, and cameras.

Reprimands

Chinese enterprises use two primary means for dealing with individuals who have deviated from the work and performance standards prescribed by the state and the enterprise. The first is patient talks, criticism, and political indoctrination. The other involves more drastic measures such as economic sanctions, demotion, or dismissal from the job.

Patient Talks, Criticism, and Political Indoctrination

At the quarterly meetings of the Congress of Workers and Staff, the representatives report on the implementation of resolutions passed at the congress and on the work performed by cadres and workers. Those who have performed well are commended, but those who have erred are criticized. The purpose of such criticism is not to tarnish a person's reputation or to breed ill feelings among fellow workers, but to help those who have erred see what is wrong, what needs to be done, and how to change for the better.

This technique of criticism reminds one of T-group sessions in the West, although the extent of the measures taken varies significantly from one culture to the other. The aims of the two are basically similar—to make the individual in the group realize his or her own shortcomings. Once he has adopted the correct attitude or value as his own, the individual emerges from such sessions as a changed and, it is hoped, improved person.

At these mass criticism meetings an individual who has erred is criticized by everyone present. He may try to defend himself at first, but at some point he must be made to realize the error of his attitudes and behavior. He openly confesses to all present that he has erred in the past. At this point the group members change their attitude toward the individual from one of bitter criticism to one of forgiveness and acceptance; like the lost sheep who has strayed from the fold, he is warmly received back into the group.

Criticism is often combined with patient talks and political indoctrination. At the Anshan Iron and Steel Company, some workers came under the influence of the Gang of Four. They deliberately created disturbances in the factory. After 1976 the leadership of the enterprise decided to take corrective action. Some units in the Anshan Iron and Steel Company tried to reform these troublemakers through labor, but the results were unsatisfactory. The party members found that a more effective way of handling these offenders was to treat them as class brothers and help them see why they were wrong and how they could make amends. For example, Wang Yiling, a veteran worker, volunteered to take on the education of one of these offenders, Shan Shaoshun. Every morning Wang had heart-to-heart talks with Shan on the way to work. On holidays Wang invited Shan to dine at his house and play with his children. When an opportunity arose, Wang told Shan about the differences between pre-1949 and post-1949 China, how things had changed for the better, and how he should be grateful to the party for these changes. Whenever Shan showed the slightest progress, Wang immediately encouraged him. Through patient talks and warm gestures toward Shan, Wang was able to help him correct his ways.

The party committee of the Anshan Iron and Steel Company educated some other offenders through ideological work and criticism of the Gang of Four. Party members patiently explained to the offenders why they erred and how they had fallen victim to the Gang. These patient talks and analyses are conducted until the individual realizes his mistakes and agrees to make amends. Because some individuals might relapse into bad ways, the party considers it necessary to continue educating them whenever they show signs of reverting to their past habits.

Demotion, Dismissal, and Economic Sanctions

In accordance with the practice of giving rewards and bonuses to those who fulfill or overfulfill their production quotas, it has been proposed that those who do not meet production quotas should be punished. Punishment would include economic sanctions such as reduction of wages or the imposition of fines. The government also called on enterprises to establish the practice of removing or dismissing leading cadres who consistently fail to show progress in their performance, as well as individuals who through negligence have caused the enterprise to incur severe losses.

A case in point is the Bohai incident (*Beijing Review,* August 4, 1980, p. 7; September 8, 1980). On November 25, 1979, the oil rig Bohai No. 2 capsized, resulting in a loss of seventy-two lives and over 37 million yuan. This was the most serious accident in the history of the petroleum industry. Upon investigation, it was found that the accident occurred because the administration ignored both the instructions laid down by the shipyard that built the oil rig and the operational rules of the bureau. In the investigation it was discovered that the head of the oil rig radioed headquarters three times and made three separate requests for three tugboats to be sent to tow the platform. Headquarters ignored the requests by sending only one 8,000-horsepower tugboat. Furthermore, on the morning of the fateful day, headquarters received gale warnings from weather observatories in Tianjin, Hebei, and Shandong. However, headquarters ignored these warnings and ordered the towing operation to proceed according to schedule. Upon further investigation it was found that from 1975 to 1979 there were 1,043 offshore accidents, which took 105 lives and caused serious injury to 114 people. Many such disasters could be attributed to the negligence of cadres at the ministry. The investigation further showed that the Ministry of Petroleum Industry did not try to unravel the causes of the Bohai accident and did not report all the facts to the State Council. Because of this, Song Zheming, the minister of the petroleum industry, was dismissed from his position; and Vice-Premier Kang Shien, who is in charge of the petroleum industry, was given a demerit of the first grade. Other cadres who were directly responsible for the accident received prison sentences ranging from one to four years.

In late 1978, for instance, the secretary of the Guangzhou Tractor Plant's party committee was removed because the tractors produced by the plant since its establishment in 1966 were substandard in quality. In early 1978 the plant was ordered to stop production and make the necessary readjustments. Several months elapsed with no improvement. After investigation by members of the state and provincial authorities, it was found that the secretary of the factory's party committee was irresponsible and did not have the technical skills necessary to run the plant. He was removed from his position.

At present most enterprises still adhere to the "iron rice bowl" practice, or system of lifetime employment. In vernacular Chinese, *rice bowl* is the synonym for "job" and "wages," and *iron* stands for "guarantee" and "unbreakable." Hence the term *iron rice bowl* means a secure job and guaranteed income for life after one is employed by an enterprise.

All workers in China are either permanent or temporary. *Permanent workers* in China are those who, once employed by a factory, will work until retirement as long as they do not become criminals or commit any serious offenses. An enterprise that has a special task can request *temporary workers* to help out for a few days, weeks or months—up to a year. Such workers will be informed beforehand that the assignment is only temporary. Temporary workers generally make up less than 10 percent of the workers employed in an enterprise. Temporary workers are drawn from the pool of people waiting for employment, and from the peasantry. During the winter months, for instance, the offices must be heated, and some peasants are hired temporarily for this purpose.

The practice of lifetime employment was adopted for permanent workers after 1949. To date, permanent workers cannot be dismissed because their livelihood is guaranteed. The worker's job is guaranteed as long as he reports to work. The enterprise is responsible for the worker's welfare, his health, and even his death. His whole life is guaranteed by the factory—hence the concept of the iron rice bowl.

This policy may be changed in the future. In July 1979 Xue Muqiao, a noted Chinese economist, wrote an article entitled "Some Ideas on the Employment Question in Urban Areas," wherein he argued that the policy of the iron rice bowl is not conducive to increased labor productivity and the goals of the Four Modernizations. This arises primarily because the worker becomes complacent and feels secure that no matter how badly he performs on the job, he will not be dismissed from the enterprise altogether. This article stimulated lively debate among the people. Among the principal opponents of the abandonment of this system was Liu Zizhen, an office worker. In September 1979 he wrote an article in the *Beijing Ribao,* entitled "The Iron Rice Bowl Should Not Be Smashed." Liu argued that this system was a manifestation of the superiority of socialism and therefore must be upheld. Middle-ground policies recommended by others include the implementation of an examination system to be administered by the labor departments; only those employed through an examination would be given the "iron rice bowl." Another proposal is for the testing of employees every year to determine whether they deserve promotion and wage increases (*Beijing Review,* November 30, 1979, p. 4). The issue of whether the "iron rice bowl should be smashed" is still under discussion. The benefit that accrues from the system lies in the security it provides for the workers. However, there are obvious problems associated with the system, especially where management is poor and political education inadequate. The workers may become complacent and not try to improve their performance.

Mr. Sun indicated that "when we say we want to make changes, we mean we will change the defects and retain the benefits." The Labor Bureau has not yet worked out any specific method for the change. In the past every enterprise had to guarantee employment and could not increase or decrease the number of workers. In the future society will have to help solve the employment problem. According to Mr. Sun, a likely future course of action is as follows: the enterprise will be able to lay off some workers according to production needs. In some provinces and cities, the labor bureaus have set up labor-service corporations that can undertake this job. Enterprises that need extra workers temporarily can apply to the labor-service corporations. These corporations can organize the surplus workers to study and carry on some production functions. In this way the workers' livelihood can be guaranteed. At present some of the workers displaced through mergers and consolidation of enterprises engage in study in order to improve their technical skills. Some large enterprises also form labor-service corporations within the enterprise.

In the future an enterprise will be able to reduce its work force. Society will assume the responsibility of guaranteeing the workers' livelihood. However, the enterprise must also share some responsibility. The government will enact laws to protect the workers in this regard; the state is opposed to any policy whereby an enterprise could lay off workers at will. The principle behind such changes is to allow the enterprise some autonomy and discretion to increase or reduce the number of workers according to production needs. At the same time the enterprise must guarantee the workers' livelihood and their jobs.

In light of the imposition of economic sanctions against some workers, demotion and dismissal of workers in some enterprises, and the reforms made in other aspects of organizational functioning to promote greater efficiency, it appears that some kind of change in the system of lifetime employment will be made in the future to make employees more accountable for their performance on the job.

11 Foreign Trade

In light of the important role assigned to foreign trade in China's pursuit of the goals of the Four Modernizations, no discussion of Chinese industrial society would be complete without a brief examination of the country's foreign-trade policies and a discussion of its prospects for the future.

In 1977, when China embarked on the Four Modernizations program, its leaders were confronted with the harsh reality that the country had lagged seriously behind other advanced nations in terms of technological developments, efficiency, and productivity in various sectors of the national economy. In its efforts to modernize and catch up with the advanced economies, China hopes to compress several decades of progress and development into a mere twenty-two years.

The Chinese view technological transfer through trade and other forms of economic exchange and technical cooperation as expedient and efficient means of bringing about this goal. By learning from other countries' experiences, China hopes to avoid duplicating mistakes made by others in the development process. This will greatly reduce the time and effort needed to attain modernization. Though difficult, this is not impossible. A good case in point is the Japanese automobile industry. In 1951 automobile production in Japan stood at 38,490 units. By 1970 this figure had risen to 5,289,157 units. In twenty years Japan has grown from an insignificant manufacturer of motor vehicles to become the second-largest producer of motor vehicles in the world in 1967 (*Automobile Facts* 1977). In 1980 Japan overtook the United States as the world's largest manufacturer of cars and trucks. The reasons for the phenomenal success of the Japanese automobile industry and its ability to make a quantum leap within a relatively short period of time are manifold. One factor was that Japan was the last of the leading automotive manufacturers in the world to enter the field of automobile production. Because of this late entry, Japan benefited from the experiences accumulated by the other leading automotive manufacturers, and thus avoided repeating many of the mistakes that had temporarily hampered or retarded the growth of its North American and European counterparts in the past (Tung 1981b). From the beginning (that is, after 1945), Japan had access to modern technology and production techniques. This saved the Japanese from investing in equipment, machinery and know-how that would soon be rendered obsolete, as happened from the 1890s to the 1920s on the North American and European continents. Advanced techniques were largely imported to Japan in the form of licensing arrangements, primarily from the United States. Between

1950 and 1966 Japan had access to some 805 patent rights or technical-assistance programs (Hunsberger 1964, pp. 81–83).

This brief illustration is not designed to indicate that China could definitely compress the time needed to modernize through importation of foreign technology and learning from other countries' experiences. Rather, the case of the Japanese automobile industry highlights two points: (1) it is possible to condense many decades of experimentation and development into a much shorter time span; and (2) technological transfer through importation and other forms of economic cooperation appear to be efficient and expedient means of bringing about rapid growth and development. This explains why the Chinese government views foreign trade as a "vital cog in the modernization wheel" (*China Trader,* March 1980, p. 8). Through imports China can gain access to advanced technology and equipment. This same end can also be achieved through other forms of economic cooperation, including joint ventures, compensation trade, licensing, and processing arrangements. In order to pay for these imports, China needs hard currency. This is where China's exports come into the picture. Chinese exports provide the means of earning foreign exchange.

Numerous issues are raised in connection with China's foreign-trade practices and management. In the past few years several books have been published on China's foreign-trade practices and policies (Hsiao 1977; *China's Foreign Trade,* 1978; Liu and Wang 1980). Instead of presenting a lengthy discourse on all aspects of China's foreign-trade practices and policies, this chapter highlights a few key elements. These include a brief overview of

1. the principles governing China's foreign-trade policies, particularly with respect to import and export
2. recent reforms made in the structure and management of foreign trade, including alternative methods of economic cooperation and financing arrangements, and the establishment of special economic zones
3. the organizations that regulate foreign-trade activities, including the Foreign Investment Commission, the Import-Export Commission, the China International Trust and Investment Corporation, the China Council for the Promotion of International Trade, the Ministry of Foreign Trade, and the various foreign-trade corporations
4. the role of the Bank of China and the People's Insurance Company of China in China's foreign trade

This chapter is designed to draw the reader's attention to those areas, organizations, and issues that affect the management and conduct of China's foreign trade. It should be noted at the outset that rapid changes in all aspects of China's economy, including the foreign-trade sector, have already rendered obsolete some of the policies and practices reported in the publications cited previously. The same note of caution should be applied to the policies and practices discussed in this chapter. Although every attempt has been made to incorporate the latest reforms and changes made in the structure and management of foreign trade up to the first quarter of 1981, it would be safe to assume that additions or modifications to the list of reforms will be forthcoming in the next few years.

Principles Governing China's Foreign-Trade Policies

China's political and economic relations with foreign countries are based on five principles:

1. mutual respect for sovereignty and territorial integrity
2. mutual nonaggression
3. noninterference in each other's internal affairs
4. equality and mutual benefit
5. peaceful coexistence (*First Session of the Fifth National People's Congress,* 1978)

China's foreign-trade policies are also governed by the same principles. Specifically, the emphasis is on equality, mutual benefit, independence, and self-reliance.

Equality and Mutual Benefit

In his "Report on the Work of the Government" delivered at the First Session of the Fifth National People's Congress, Hua Guofeng identified the dual purposes of foreign trade as: (1) supplying each other's needs, and (2) promoting production and economic prosperity among the nations of the world (*First Session,* 1978). The Chinese attach great importance to this principle and "maintain that foreign trade should always benefit both trading parties and not one party alone, still less should it be harmful to the other party" (*China's Foreign Trade,* 1978, p. 8). This serves to explain the Chinese preference for resolving issues between parties through negotiations and mutual discussions and for arriving at decisions through consensus rather than voting.

This principle also governs China's import and export policies. In practice this means that "trade must be based on the capabilities and needs of both trading partners" (Liu and Wang 1980, p. 5). Consequently, China would not purchase commodities that do not meet the country's needs or fit its objective conditions. The principles with respect to imports can be summarized as follows:

1. Products that could be manufactured at home must not be imported. This is designed to stimulate the growth of other sectors of the country's economy.

There are several exceptions to this policy, however, including importation for diplomatic reasons, under special arrangements with other countries, and to increase the variety of goods available in the domestic market (*China Trader*, March 1980; Liu and Wang 1980).

2. Raw materials that are not produced domestically or are in short supply, but that are required in the process of production should be imported (*China Trader*, March 1980).

3. Since a major reason for importing is to facilitate technological transfer, advanced but *appropriate* technology that fits in with China's national priorities and objective conditions must be imported.

The emphasis on appropriateness stems from China's awareness that its prevailing conditions are very different from those in the advanced nations. China has abundant manpower, but the educational levels and technical skills of most workers are not high. Consequently, the high level of automation suited to the needs of advanced economies may be inappropriate for China's present conditions. At present the development of labor-intensive industries and the purchase of equipment requiring smaller capital investments are more in line with China's objective conditions. According to Liu Lixin, a vice-president of the People's Construction Bank of China, it is not necessary to introduce the "most advanced technology" in all instances. Rather, the country should seek to "introduce more practical technology" that takes in more labor and requires less capital investment (*Beijing Review*, August 25, 1980, p. 25). In importing technical equipment, the Chinese adhere to the principle of "making foreign things serve China" in order to compress the time needed for China to attain modernization (*China's Foreign Trade*, 1978).

The policies governing the export of Chinese commodities are, first, that those materials that are needed at home should be exported in restricted amounts, since the goal of the Four Modernizations is to improve the people's livelihood (*China Trader*, March 1980); and, second, that in order to earn foreign exchange to fuel China's modernization efforts, priority should be given to the development of textile and light-industrial products. These products typically require low capital investments, generate fairly quick returns on investment, and have a market overseas. Over the past several years, textile products alone have accounted for over 20 percent of the total value of China's exports.

Independence and Self-Reliance

During the Cultural Revolution, the principle of self-reliance was almost synonymous with economic isolationism. This principle is now interpreted to mean that foreign assistance should be accepted as long as it does not impinge on China's national sovereignty, and that the country should rely primarily on its own efforts. In China's opinion, this principle does not conflict with foreign trade, but complements it. Through trade and other forms of economic cooperation, the time China needs to advance its level of technological development can be compressed. This would enable the Chinese to be technologically independent sooner than would otherwise be the case (*China's Foreign Trade*, 1978, p. 6).

Reforms in the Structure and Management of Foreign Trade

To promote foreign trade, China has undertaken a series of reforms since 1978 that is designed to improve the conduct of foreign trade. Further changes are contemplated. The following is a cursory review of the most salient reforms made since then and others that are contemplated.

Establishment of Domestic Corporations

In 1978 China established a number of domestic corporations under the respective ministries. These corporations determine what equipment should be purchased. The names of some of these corporations and the respective ministries to which they belong are as follows:

1. China Agriculture Machinery Corporation, under the First Ministry of Machine Building
2. China Cereals and Oils Corporation, under the Ministry of Agriculture and Forestry
3. China Seed Corporation, under the Ministry of Agriculture and Forestry
4. China Chemical Construction Corporation, under the Ministry of Chemical Industry
5. China National Chemical Fibers Corporation, under the Ministry of Textiles
6. China Coal Industrial Technique and Equipment Corporation, under the Ministry of the Coal Industry
7. China National Feedstuffs Corporation, under the Ministry of Commerce
8. China National Geological Exploration Corporation, under the State Geology Bureau
9. China National Oil and Natural Gas Exploration and Development Corporation, under the China Petroleum Corporation and the Ministry of Petroleum
10. China Petroleum Corporation, under the Ministry of Petroleum
11. China National Radio Equipment Corporation, under the Fourth Ministry of Machine Building
12. China National Underwater Cable and Construction Corporation, under the Ministry of Posts and Telegraphs

13. China Railway Technical and Equipment Corporation, under the Ministry of Posts and Telegraphs
14. China Waste Materials Reclamation Corporation, under the Ministry of Public Health (*Doing Business with China,* 1979, p. 7).

According to Richard Chen, the director of China development at Occidental Petroleum Corporation (Tung 1981a), by dealing directly with the domestic corporations and their respective ministries, which are the end users, one is dealing with the core of the business.

Decentralization of Foreign-Trade Activities

In 1979 the two provinces of Guangdong and Fujian and the three cities of Beijing, Shanghai, and Tianjin were granted greater autonomy in the conduct of foreign trade. The foreign-trade corporations at these provincial and municipal levels are empowered to conduct foreign trade directly with foreign firms and to conclude contracts and agreements valued under U.S. $3 million without Foreign Investment Commission approval. After the conclusion of such contracts, copies of the agreements must be sent to the Foreign Investment Commission for filing so that the latter can coordinate activities related to foreign trade. Investments over U.S. $3 million require the approval of the Foreign Investment Commission. As of January 1, 1980, twenty-one provinces, three municipalities, and five autonomous regions began to transact business directly with foreign firms through their newly established foreign-trade corporations (*China Business Review,* September–October 1980).

In addition to the authority granted to certain provinces and municipalities, Vice-Premier Yao Yilin, the minister in charge of the State Planning Commission, indicated that certain large enterprises and associations will be allowed to conduct trade directly with foreigners on an experimental basis. These enterprises will be allowed to retain a share of the foreign exchange thus earned for expansion of the enterprise's production capacities or for improving workers' welfare (*Beijing Review,* September 22, 1980, p. 42). The results of these experiments will then be evaluated before the government decides whether such changes should be extended to more enterprises throughout the country.

Recently, the concern has been raised that the continued policy of readjustment of China's economy may lead to a recentralization of foreign-trade activities. *Beijing Review* noted that because of inexperience on the part of many enterprises and local authorities, problems arose in the implementation of some of the aforementioned changes. However, the solution to these problems lies not in recentralization but in "improved management [which involves] . . . among other things, government intervention in certain important matters." The government is now studying the foreign-trade structure and management of the advanced nations to learn from their positive experiences (*Beijing Review,* March 9, 1981, p. 3).

Special Economic Zones

In October 1977 Foreign Trade Minister Li Qiang announced China's decision to establish "special economic zones" in certain designated regions to expand China's trade with foreign countries. This concept is similar to the foreign-trade zones or free-trade zones in the United States. In China, in the designated special economic zones, priority will be given to the manufacture of products for sales overseas (*Business PRC,* 1980). Some of the regions that have been designated as special economic zones are Shenzhen, which is situated along the Chinese–Hong Kong border; Zhuhai, which is located along the Chinese-Macao border; Shantou (Swatow); and Fujian.

In early 1980 the China Merchants Steam Navigation Company (CMSN) began development of Shekou, an industrial zone in Shenzen. CMSN invested U.S. $20 million in land reclamation and leveling of sites in Shekou. In March 1980 CMSN made available 10 million square feet of land in this region for long-term lease (twenty-five or more years) at U.S. $0.40 to U.S. $0.80 per square foot. Wages for workers in Shekou will be the average between the Guangdong and Hong Kong wage scales. For details of regulations governing the operation of enterprises in the special economic zones see appendix J.

Overall Control by the State

With the decentralization of foreign-trade activities, the state must undertake policies and legislation to ensure uniformity in foreign-trade practices throughout China. After all, China is a centrally planned economy, and the role of the five-year and ten-year plans cannot be downplayed. Hence foreign trade must be subject to a centrally unified plan.

To ensure some degree of homogeneity in trade practices, import and export licenses will be used. In addition, exchange controls will be tightened (*Beijing Review,* September 22, 1980, p. 42). For the full text of the provisional regulations for exchange control of the PRC, see appendix I. In January 1981 China devalued its currency. The new exchange rate is fixed at 2.8 yuan to U.S. $1. This is almost double the former rate of 1.56 yuan to U.S. $1 (*China Business Review,* January–February 1981, p. 18). Laws pertaining to the conduct of foreign trade and forms of economic cooperation have already been promulgated or are being drafted. Examples of the legislation that has been drafted are the Joint Venture Law (see appendix A); the Income Tax Law pertaining to joint ventures (see appendix C); the regulations governing the operations of the special economic zones (see appendix J); interim regulations governing the establishment of resident offices of foreign enterprises (see appendix G); and the Individual Income Tax Law, which affects wage earners making more than 800 yuan per month. Given the low wage rate in China, this law will affect only foreigners residing in China and workers employed in joint-venture enterprises (see appendix E). Other laws, such as company laws, patent laws, mercantile laws, and enterprise management laws, were still in the drafting stage as of late 1980.

In early 1980 the State Council reestablished the General Administration of Customs to coordinate the work of the various customs units and to give "full play to the powers and functions of the customs" (*Beijing Review,* March 3, 1980, p. 7). The General Administration of Customs was first established in 1949 but was renamed the Administration Bureau of Customs in 1960. At all points of entry and exit, the General Administration of Customs will supervise and manage all imports and exports to and from China to ensure that they comply with existing regulations governing the import and export of goods to and from China. Existing policies and regulations are now being reviewed by the General Administration, and new legislations will be enacted. Besides the policies and regulations affecting all imports and exports, local customs regulations may also be applied. However, these must be submitted to the State Council for approval.

Development of Infrastructure

In order to expand foreign trade, China's infrastructure must be developed. This includes the construction of railroads, the development of networks of communication, the modernization of harbors and wharves, and the expansion of the merchant-marine fleet. The development of China's infrastructure has been given priority in the Three-Year Plan for Readjustment (1979–1981) and the new Ten-Year Plan (1981–1990).

Fairs and Trade Exhibitions

Most foreign traders are familiar with the semiannual Guangzhou Commodities Trade Fairs (Canton Trade Fair). Beginning with the 1979 autumn fair, representatives of the Chinese factories manufacturing the products were present at the negotiations to listen to customers' demands and opinions. This unprecedented procedure should improve the quality of future trade negotiations between China and foreign partners as the Chinese manufacture of the products can receive input and give immediate feedback on production-related problems. Another change was to open the fairgrounds year round. Previously the Guangzhou Fair was held twice a year, once in spring and once in autumn, each time for about a month. The authorities have now decided to open the exhibition halls year round so that the Chinese foreign-trade corporations and foreign firms can display their products (*Beijing Review,* November 2, 1979, pp. 6–7).

Even though transactions and negotiations for business contracts are now conducted at different levels in the major cities of China, the Guangzhou Trade Fair continues to play an important role in the sale of Chinese products. Some 24,000 businessmen from ninety-seven countries attended the autumn 1979 Guangzhou Trade Fair, for instance. The volume and value of transactions at the autumn 1979 fair surpassed all previous levels. For example, the amount of chemical products sold more than doubled that of the previous autumn's fair. The sale of metals and mining products was up by 50 percent (*Beijing Review,* November 23, 1979).

In addition to the semiannual Guangzhou Trade Fairs, fairs and trade exhibitions designed to acquaint foreign buyers with Chinese products are held in major cities in China and throughout the world. For example, in the fall of 1980 both the United States and China held national exhibitions in each other's countries.

Use of Foreign Credit

China has abandoned its former policy of rejecting foreign aid and has entered into long-, medium-, and short-term loans with governments and private financial institutions. It has also gained admission to international financial institutions such as the International Monetary Fund and the World Bank. Policies governing the use of foreign credit are discussed in a subsequent section.

New Forms of Economic Cooperation

Besides importing and exporting, China has engaged in new forms of economic cooperation and exchange with other countries. The principal forms are as follows.

Joint Venture. In July 1979 the Joint Venture Law was promulgated. It allows for a minimum of 25-percent investment and a maximum of 99 percent. As Rong Yiren, chairman of the board of directors of China International Trust and Investment Corporation, noted, investments of less than 25 percent will be permitted under special circumstances—for example, where advanced technology is involved. One-hundred-percent equity investment will be allowed where high technology is involved. However, the latter will not be considered joint ventures, and the foreign investor will have 100-percent control over the management of such operations (speech by Rong Yiren, 1979). The details of the Joint Venture

Law are contained in appendix A. The major features of the law are as follows:

1. The government guarantees to protect the property invested by the foreign partner. Profits and earnings derived from such ventures could be remitted home after the payment of taxes.
2. Corporate income tax for the majority of joint ventures (for exceptions, see appendix C) will be lower than that in the United States in general.
3. There will be incentives for reinvestment of profits and earnings of such ventures in China.
4. Decisions will be arrived at through consensus and mutual discussions rather than by voting.

Compensatory Trade. This refers to an economic arrangement whereby in return for contributions of capital, technological know-how, or equipment, the foreign investor would be paid in the form of goods, not foreign exchange. This payment of goods could be in the form either of direct products (products manufactured through the project established under the compensation trade arrangement) or of indirect products (products not manufactured through the project established under the compensation trade arrangement, but mutually agreed on by both parties) (*China Trader,* March 1980).

One of the early projects using this form of arrangement is the Beijing Xuanwu Radio Components Factory for the manufacture of carbon-film resistors. Capital and equipment were provided by the foreign partner, and China provided the factory building and fuel. The capital cost of the equipment and interest will be paid off within three years of the date of operation with money earned from processing (*China's Foreign Trade,* 1980, p. 9). Development of energy resources such as oil and coal would lend itself to this type of economic arrangement.

Cooperative or Joint Production. This could take the form of a technology transfer. Under this type of arrangement, the foreign partner supplies the equipment, technological know-how, and personnel to train Chinese workers so that the latter can manufacture complete sets of equipment or parts thereof.

An example of this type of arrangement is the one entered into between Bell Helicopter and China to product twin-engine helicopters. There is no equity investment on the part of Bell Helicopter. A substantial portion of the technological transfer involves the training of Chinese management personnel and engineers in Bell Helicopter's Fort Worth, Texas, branch. Some managers and engineers from Bell Helicopter were sent to Harbin, China, to train Chinese personnel there (*China Business Review,* November–December 1979).

Other forms of economic cooperation that could be subsumed under the general category of cooperative and joint production include assembly and processing of materials. For instance, the foreign investor may provide all raw material and equipment, and China might supply the labor force for assembly. In some instances it may be necessary for the foreign investor to provide personnel to train the Chinese workers. The products would then be assembled by the Chinese workers, for which a fee is paid by the investor (*China Trader*, March 1980).

The arrangement for processing of materials is used when China has the production capability but lacks the raw materials required for processing. This arrangement can take one of four forms. First, the foreign investor may supply all the raw materials. The Chinese enterprise then processes the raw materials for a fee. Second, the foreign investor may supply a portion of the raw materials. On delivery of the finished products, payment for the raw materials is deducted from the price of the finished items. A third form occurs in cases where China lacks the machinery or equipment necessary to produce goods up to a certain quality or standard. Under such circumstances, this machinery and equipment is imported duty free. Payment for such machinery is deducted from the processing fee. A fourth form arises in cases where China cannot supply certain components of an export item that are necessary to meet the foreign investors' specifications. Under this arrangement, the investor supplies those components and deducts their cost from the price of the finished items (*China Trader*, March 1980).

Licensing. In order to gain access to foreign technology, China has indicated an interest in licensing arrangements for the production of locomotive parts and of microelectronic, telecommunications, food-processing, and construction equipment. Under this type of arrangement, the licenser receives a lump-sum royalty payment (around 10–20 percent) upon signing the contract. The balance is paid before or after start-up of the plant, depending on the situation. Besides pure licensing arrangements, the Chinese are interested in combining licensing with joint-production arrangements. A possible objection that foreign investors may have to licensing arrangements is that currently China is not a member of the Convention for the Protection of Industrial Property. However, China has indicated a willingness to join the convention. China is also currently drafting its patent laws (*China Business Review*, March–April 1980).

Sales and Purchase Contracts. In addition to the aforementioned types of economic arrangements that have been adopted since 1978, sales and purchase contracts are still widely used in China's foreign-trade practices. These are generally one of two types: First, there is the formal contract wherein all relevant details are clearly spelled out. This form is generally used for new customers or in the purchase of bulk commodities and important equipment. Second, the sales-confirmation format is generally used with long-time customers and in small contracts.

Prices are generally determined through consultation and are based on pre-vailaing international market prices. Sales and purchase contracts could be quoted on a CIF, FOB, or C&F basis. The Chinese prefer FOB for imports of bulk commodities or full-boat cargo because their own ships can be used. Terms of payment can take the form of letter of credit, collection, installment, or deferred payment. The last of these is most often used in the sale or purchase of heavy machinery, complete plants, and other commodities that generally require a long production period. Interest is charged at prevailing international rates. Payment can be made in Chinese currency, the currency of the country of the contracting party, or the currency of a third country.

The packaging clause is generally arrived at through discussion. The follow-ing stipulations may be included in the contract: (1) trademarks as specified by the customer; (2) use of customer's containers and packing materials; and (3) packaging and presentation specified by the customer (*China's Foreign Trade*, 1979, pp. 8–9).

Organizations that Govern the Conduct of Foreign Trade

In the past all foreign-trade activity was conducted through the national foreign-trade corporations, which report directly to the Ministry of Foreign Trade. With China's decision to expand the role of foreign trade, changes have been made in the structure and management of such trade. Figure 11–1 presents a simplified chart of the different hierarchical levels in China's present foreign-trade struc-ture. Only the hierarchical levels (who reports to whom) and the names of the principal organizations involved in China's foreign trade are presented. The in-formation in this section was based on interviews with officials of the respective organizations, unless otherwise stated.

Under the State Council, there are nine commissions: the State Planning Commission, the State Economic Commission, the State Construction Commis-sion, the Finance and Commerce Commission, the State Science Commission, the Commission of Energy (established in 1980), the State Machine Building Commission (established in 1980), the Foreign Investment Commission, and the Import-Export Commission. The last two were established in 1979. The other commissions for which no dates of establishment were given were established shortly after 1949.

The Foreign Investment Commission and the Import-Export Commission

Of the nine commissions under the State Council, the two that are directly con-cerned with the conduct of foreign trade are the Foreign Investment Commission

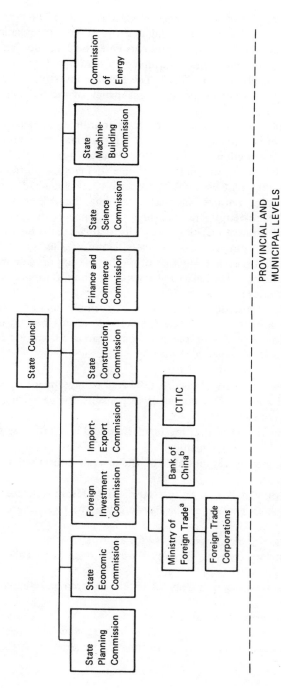

Foreign Trade Corporations/Import-Export Commissions

[a] A vice-minister of the Ministry of Foreign Trade is also a vice-chairman of the Foreign Investment Commission.
[b] A director of the Bank of China is also a vice-chairman of the Foreign Investment Commission.

Figure 11-1. China's Foreign-Trade Structure

and the Import-Export Commission. Both were established in July 1979 and are headed by Vice-Premier Gu Mu. These two commissions are in fact one organization; that is, they share the same departments and personnel. Both are housed in the same building. This building was formerly occupied by the China Council for the Promotion of International Trade (CCPIT). The Foreign Investment Commission and Import-Export Commission took up occupancy of the building at the end of 1980.

The overall mission of the two commissions is to coordinate all activities relating to foreign trade, international finance, and international cooperation. They perform two separate functions, however. The Foreign Investment Commission directs and controls investment and is responsible for investment projects at home and abroad, including joint ventures. As of July 1980 China had established several small-scale joint ventures overseas, including the Peking Duck Restaurant in Tokyo and joint-venture relationships with some of its overseas sales agents for the sale of Chinese machine tools. Up to July 1980 China had not established joint manufacturing facilities overseas. However, the country is actively pursuing such possibilities. The function of the Import-Export Commission, as its name suggests, is to draft legislation regulating China's imports and exports and to oversee activities in these areas.

Both commissions draft legislation and assist in the formulation of foreign-trade plans. Both report directly to the State Council. However, they do not implement trade plans. The activities of the two commissions are carried out by the following bureaus, each of which is headed by a director.

1. The Foreign Investment Control Bureau is in charge of investment opportunities at home and abroad. This bureau is responsible for approving or disapproving all joint ventures.
2. The Legal Bureau is in charge of drafting regulations and laws affecting the conduct of foreign trade and investment.
3. The Coordination Bureau is responsible for the overall coordination of foreign trade.
4. The General Office Bureau is an administrative office responsible for internal affairs and the coordination of the day-to-day activities of the commissions.
5. The Export Bureau has primary responsibility for exports.
6. The Technology Transfer/Licensing/Turnkey Bureau is responsible for compensatory trade arrangements.
7. The Research and Investigation Bureau conducts research pertaining to foreign trade.
8. The Consulting Bureau provides consulting and advice.
9. The Manufacturing or Processing of Materials Bureau is a new bureau established to deal with arrangements for processing of materials that China

enters into with foreign investors. Most of the products manufactured under such arrangements are exported.

10. The Government Loans Bureau deals with loans from other governments.

Besides these bureaus, the commissions run the Institute of International Economics and Management. The institute offers postgraduate courses in international business and economics. The institute began enrolling students in September 1980, and its campus is currently under construction in the outskirts of Beijing. For the time being, the Bureau of Research and Investigation is responsible for establishing the institute. When completed, the institute will be on the same level as the other bureaus.

Joint-Venture Approvals. According to officials at the Foreign Investment Commission, foreign firms interested in pursuing joint-venture relationships with China should first contact the Ministry of Foreign Trade or the China International Trust and Investment Corporation (CITIC). After the contracts have been negotiated between CITIC and a foreign partner, they must be submitted to the Foreign Investment Commission for approval. For the two provinces of Guangdong and Fujian and the "three big cities" of Shanghai, Tianjin, and Beijing, which have been granted greater autonomy in the conduct of foreign trade, approvals are handled differently. For contracts and projects valued at under U.S. $3 million, the foreign-trade organizations at these provincial and municipal levels may sign agreements directly with the foreign investors. However, copies of all such contracts and agreements must be sent to the Foreign Investment Commission for filing. This allows the latter to coordinate foreign-trade activities in the country. Projects exceeding U.S. $3 million would require the approval of the Foreign Investment Commission.

Relationship with the China Council for the Promotion of International Trade (CCPIT). CCPIT is not a business entity—that is, it does not handle business transactions on its own. Rather, CCPIT is a nongovernment service organization whose purpose is to promote trade. Its role is to introduce foreign corporations and investors to the respective ministries. It provides information to foreign investors about trading and investing in China but cannot make decisions about foreign investment. It sponsors exhibitions overseas. The overseas representatives of CCPIT are attached to the commercial sections of the Chinese embassies abroad. A foreign firm may contact one of these embassy representatives, who in turn may introduce the foreign firm to the Foreign Investment Commission.

At present, because of the lack of personnel, the Foreign Investment Commission does not have overseas offices to handle inquiries from foreign investors. In the future it may set up overseas offices. If and when this occurs, inquiries should be answered more promptly. Inquiries are currently made through the embassies and are generally handled by CCPIT representatives who have no decision-making authority. Consequently, they must direct everything to Beijing for approval, which may account for the inordinate delays in responding to inquiries.

The Ministry of Foreign Trade

Prior to the establishment of the Foreign Investment Commission, the Ministry of Foreign Trade reported directly to the State Council. Now it reports directly to the Foreign Investment Commission, which in turn reports to the State Council. The Ministry of Foreign Trade is under the direction and control of the Foreign Investment Commission. The ministry formulates its own plans and submits them to the Foreign Investment Commission for approval. The national foreign-trade corporations, which are under the Ministry of Foreign Trade, are responsible for implementing these plans.

The Ministry of Foreign Trade was established in 1952. Until then it was a department of the Ministry of Trade. In 1952 the latter ministry was split into two: the Ministry of Commerce, which deals with domestic trade; and the Ministry of Foreign Trade, which handles overseas trade. In the past all foreign-trade activities were concentrated in the Ministry of Foreign Trade. All activities were centralized because China's system of foreign trade was patterned after that of the USSR and other East European countries.

There are a dozen national import/export trade corporations under the Ministry of Foreign Trade. Each of these foreign-trade corporations has representatives in Hong Kong and nearly all the developed nations. However, these representatives have no authority to make decisions and must refer everything to Beijing.

The Ministry of Foreign Trade, which is set up for administrative purposes, has several departments:

1. The import department supervises all imports to China.
2. The export department supervises all exports from China.
3. Four territorial departments handle trade matters with countries in each of the following territories:
   a. Soviet-bloc countries
   b. Africa and the Middle East
   c. developed countries such as the United States, Canada, and Western Europe
   d. East and Southeast Asia, including Japan

Each of the four territorial departments prepares and drafts trade agreements and conducts negotiations with the countries concerned. The draft agreements are then submitted to the State Council for approval. After this approval is received, these territorial departments are responsible for executing the agreements.

4. The financial and accounting department is in charge of financial matters.
5. The trade-planning department drafts plans for the conduct of foreign trade.
6. The statistical department compiles trade figures on different countries of the world.
7. The personnel department is responsible for the employment of personnel for the national foreign-trade corporations and the ministry.
8. The Research Institute of International Trade conducts research on international-trade matters and performs market analysis. Each foreign-trade corporation has its own research division.

How will decentralization of foreign trade affect the functionings of the Ministry of Foreign Trade? According to Wang Lieh-wang, division chief, Research Institute of International Trade, even though the two provinces and the three cities have more authority to conduct trade directly with foreign firms, these provincial and municipal authorities will continue to have close connections with the ministry, other ministries, and the central government. Each of these two provinces and three cities now has its own general foreign-trade corporation. Each controls a number of import/export trade corporations, whose functions are divided according to different categories of commodities, similar to those at the national level. They are quite independent of the Ministry of Foreign Trade. The foreign-trade corporations in the two provinces and the three cities have the authority to negotiate both sales and purchase contracts by themselves. The ministry will not intervene in their activities and negotiations because of the sheer volume of contracts being negotiated. The ministry will, however, control their pricing policies. Both the central and local governments have the power to supervise pricing of commodities. Theoretically, there should be uniform pricing; that is, there should be no undercutting of prices to promote sales. However, it is almost impossible to regulate every single commodity. With the government's decision to float prices of certain nonessential commodities in the domestic market to stimulate competition among enterprises, this policy of uniform pricing on export items may be modified in the future.

With decentralization, the Ministry of Foreign Trade would have to change its method of administration. Before decentralization, import and export activities were concentrated in the hands of the central government. Consequently, there was no need to issue import and export licenses. Decentralization necessitates the use of import/export licenses to ensure some degree of uniformity in practices and to coordinate foreign-trade activities. With decentralization, the Ministry of Foreign Trade will relegate a substantial portion of the import/export activities it formerly performed. These will be transferred to the provincial authorities and to a select number of large state-owned enterprises. Since it takes time to train personnel at the provincial, municipal, and enterprise levels to deal directly with foreign firms on trade matters, the ministry will provide technical assistance in the interim period. In the future the ministry will not conduct business transactions as it now does but will act as an agent and derive a commission from the foreign-trade corporations.

To train personnel for these new foreign-trade corporations in the provinces and the three cities, the Ministry of Foreign Trade has established an Institute of Foreign Trade, which offers a four- to five-year program. The subjects taught in the institute are similar to those offered by equivalent colleges in other countries. The primary focus is on foreign language, which is a major problem for China at the moment.

The China International Trust and Investment Corporation

In July 1979 the State Council authorized the establishment of the China International Trust and Investment Corporation (CITIC). The corporation formally went into operation in October 1979. It is a state-owned enterprise operating under the leadership of the State Council. Unlike the CCPIT, which is not empowered to conduct business transactions, CITIC is a business organization that is authorized to carry out business transactions and make investments. The corporation is responsible for its own profits and losses. The Foreign Investment Commission is its superior organization and formulates investment policies and guidelines. In addition, all agreements negotiated between CITIC and a foreign investor require the approval of the Foreign Investment Commission.

CITIC was set up for the primary purpose of implementing the mission stipulated at the Third Session of the National People's Congress—that of economic construction and socialist modernization of China. In order to attain this goal, China must actively seek foreign investment. CITIC is set up for facilitating investment in China. If a foreign investor wants to establish a joint venture or some other form of economic cooperation within China, CITIC will try to find an appropriate Chinese partner, and vice versa. At the moment the emphasis is on investing in China, since the main purpose of foreign investment is to accelerate the Four Modernizations. However, CITIC does not rule out the possibility of making investments outside China in the future.

As discussed previously, economic cooperation between China and foreign investors may take many forms, including joint venture, compensation trade, coproduction, technology transfer, and processing of materials from abroad. With the exception of processing of materials, which is handled by the Ministry of Foreign Trade, CITIC is actively involved in promoting and facilitating all these forms of economic cooperation. CITIC will entertain almost any type of foreign investment as long as it is profitable to China. CITIC raises funds abroad for investment projects in China, accepts funds from foreign investors by issuing debentures of the corporation, and may also serve as an agent in the issue of shares pertaining to investments in China. CITIC performs all activities related to investment—introducing appropriate partners, participating in negotiations, and signing the agreement. Once the project has gone into operation, CITIC supervises it to the end. It will also act as consultant, witness, or agent under contract for foreign investors with respect to advanced technology and equipment. CITIC may also undertake investments on its own account if it is interested in a project. The corporation has start-up capital of 200 million yuan. CITIC is primarily concerned with investment projects, whereas the Ministry of Foreign Trade is primarily concerned with commodity purchasing and selling.

In order to promote investment in China, Rong Yiren, together with high-ranking officials from the different ministries, visited the United States in the last quarter of 1979. During this tour they publicized the functions of CITIC and met with U.S. corporate executives to discuss different ways of promoting economic exchanges between China and the United States. To better acquaint foreign investors with the corporation, the managers and deputies of CITIC will visit foreign countries on a regular basis. CITIC also invites foreign investors to China to discuss the prospects for investment there.

Even though the corporation was officially established in October 1979, it has been in business unofficially since July 1979. Initially, its work was confined to public relations. On October 4, 1979, the first board of directors' meeting was held. On that date the establishment of the corporation was officially announced, and the statutes of the corporation were approved by the State Council (see appendix H for a copy of CITIC's statutes). There are a total of forty-four directors, five of them from Hong Kong and Macau. The other thirty-nine directors are from different parts of China. They were selected because of their expertise and past experience in the field of investment. Some of them were eminent industrialists in pre-1949 China. The chairman of the board of directors, Rong Yiren, was one of the most successful industrialists in China prior to 1949. He is also the vice-chairman of the National Committee of the Chinese People's Political Consultative Conference (*Beijing Review,* April 28, 1980). The board of directors meets annually but, when necessary, may meet more frequently. The main functions of the board of directors are to inspect the annual report and to formulate work plans for the next stage. Decisions are reached through negotiations and mutual agreement, not by majority vote.

The vice-chairman of the board of directors is Lei Renmin, former vice-minister of foreign trade. Under him, there are three executive directors: Mr. Wu, who is executive director and vice-president of CITIC's Hong Kong branch; Mr. Chen, who is vice-president of CITIC in China and was formerly associated with the Bank of China's London branch; and Mr. Wang, who received the Ph.D. in economics in West Germany in the 1930s and was a Shanghai financier in pre-1949 China.

There are two levels of management, the first of which is the vice-president level. Below the vice-presidents there are four departments: administration, business, financing, and real estate.

By early July 1980, within nine months of its establishment, CITIC has met with some 3,000 foreign investors. Most of the overseas investors are from the United States, Japan, and West Germany. As of early July 1980 they had signed fifty agreements, letters of intent, or minutes with foreign investors. These agreements include joint ventures, coproduction, technology transfer, leasing, and compensation trade. However, most of them are for joint ventures and co-production. CITIC has also concluded three contracts that require Foreign Investment Commission approval. Some of the projects concluded include the formation of the China Orient Leasing Company, a project involving the Japanese Orient Leasing Company, one of the companies in Beijing, and CITIC. In its initial phase of operation, the China Orient Leasing Company will only lease machinery. Later on, it may lease other things as well. Mr. Rong also signed a letter or intent with the Chase Manhattan Bank, providing for the establishment of working offices in Beijing and New York. At the time of the interview in July 1980, the CITIC official indicated that CITIC has several dozen projects under discussion and more than a hundred projects that require proper partners. It has a staff of fifty members who must review more than two hundred projects. As of July 1980 CITIC had no overseas representatives other than those in Hong Kong. If necessary, it may set up branch offices overseas.

Foreign Trade Corporations at the Provincial
and Municipal Levels

In addition to the aforementioned organizations that are concerned with the conduct of foreign trade at the national level, foreign-trade corporations and import/export commissions have been set up at the provincial and municipal levels to trade directly with foreign investors. This is in keeping with the goal of decentralizing foreign-trade activities. According to the September–October 1980 issue of *China Business Review* (p. 3), as of January 1, 1981, twenty-one provinces, three municipalities, and five autonomous regions will begin to conduct foreign trade directly through their own foreign-trade corporations. The foreign-trade corporations at the provincial and municipal levels will be under the control of the provinces and municipalities.

The Bank of China's Role in Foreign Trade and Investments

The Bank of China (BOC) was established in 1912. Prior to 1949 it was both an official and a commercial bank. In 1953 the Political Council (forerunner of the present-day State Council) designated the Bank of China as the bank licensed to engage in foreign exchange. To date it is the only bank in China that specializes in foreign exchange. The Bank of China handles overseas business, whereas the People's Bank of China (PBOC) engages in domestic business. In order to meet the needs of the Four Modernizations, reforms were made to the BOC in 1979. Prior to 1979 the BOC was under the leadership of the PBOC. In 1979 the BOC was designated by the State Council as the specialized foreign-exchange bank under the direct leadership of the State Council. The BOC is an independent foreign-exchange institution. Usually, it transacts foreign business by itself. However, in cases involving important policies, the BOC reports them to the State Council through the PBOC.

The main task of the BOC is to organize, utilize, accumulate, and manage foreign exchange. It also handles various kinds of foreign-exchange transactions, as well as international financial activities. The activities undertaken by the Bank of China include the following:

1. Settle international trade and nontrade business.
2. Make loans and deposits with international banks. The BOC makes deposits and takes out loans with foreign banks and deals with remittances by overseas Chinese. It also engages in international financial negotiations.
3. Make foreign-exchange loans and desposits. The BOC lends to domestic institutions that require foreign exchange. For example, if a Chinese enterprise wants to import a certain piece of equipment from abroad, the loan will be made to the ministry. It also handles renminbi (Chinese currency) deposits and loans for the foreign-trade corporations.
4. Handle gold and silver transactions.
5. Organize and take part in syndicated loans with foreign banks.
6. Enter into joint ventures with overseas banks and overseas companies. In early 1980 the Bank of China formed a financial company with the First National Bank of Chicago and the Industrial Bank of Japan. Each of the three aforementioned partners contributed 30 percent. The remaining 10 percent is held by a Chinese foreign-trade institution in Hong Kong, the Hwa-yun Company. The Bank of China also organized another financial company with the Hong Kong Golden Wall Bank and the Bank of Tokyo. The Hong Kong bank holds 35 percent of the equity share, the Bank of Tokyo holds 50 percent, and the Bank of China holds the remaining 15 percent.
7. Issue bonds and other certificates bearing monetary values.
8. Undertake international trust. The BOC also gives advice to business concerns. The overseas branches of the BOC can deal with various kinds of foreign exchange with the permission of the authorities of the country in which they operate.

Use of Foreign Funds

Prior to 1978 the use of foreign loans was virtually prohibited. In those days the Bank of China did not borrow any money from foreign countries, although the

BOC did engage in foreign business then because it made deposits in foreign banks, and vice versa. Other financial arrangements, such as deferred trade, were utilized. In 1978 the government stated that in order to facilitate the socialist modernization of China, the country would have to adopt international financial methods to absorb foreign capital. Even in the current Three-Year Plan for Readjustment, China will continue to utilize foreign funds, primarily from governmental and international agencies, although it will also avail itself of commercial bank loans, provided the terms are "fair and reasonable" (*Beijing Review,* April 6, 1981). After 1978 the Bank of China borrowed some money from foreign countries, generally in the form of buyers' credit. It has also entered into agreements with foreign banks and governments. In late 1979 the Japanese government extended a long-term low-interest 50-billion-yuan loan to China at an annual interest rate of 3 percent. Principal and interest are to be repaid over thirty years, after a ten-year grace period. The agreement also provides for the negotiation of additional loans each year between 1980 and 1986, up to a total value of $1.5 billion. These loans will be administered by the Bank of China and are not tied to Japanese exports; that is, they could be used to purchase commodities not manufactured in Japan (*China Business Review,* January–February 1980). The line of credit available to China is estimated at $26 billion. However, China stresses its ability to pay. According to the BOC official, during the Three-Year Plan for Readjustment, foreign capital will be utilized in accordance with the principle of economic readjustment. After the period of readjustment, China may use more the foreign credit currently available to it. In the interim period of readjustment, foreign capital will be used primarily for equipping and modernizing existing enterprises in China. In the future China will not utilize foreign capital for large-scale projects or those that extend over a long period of time. In February 1981 China decided to suspend the second phase of the Baoshan Iron and Steel Works in Shanghai (*Time,* March 16, 1981, p. 68). There had been a feeling in China for quite some time that projects should not be undertaken that would require importation of whole plants, as was the case for the Baoshan Iron and Steel Works.

Stability of Chinese Currency

In the view of Mr. Tang, deputy general manager of the Bank of China, international trade will not affect the stability of the renminbi (Chinese) currency because world prices and domestic prices are separate. When the price of materials in the international market fluctuates, this does not influence domestic prices because the latter are set by the government.

Impact of Entry of IMF and World Bank

In the first quarter of 1980 China gained admission to the International Monetary Fund (IMF) and the World Bank. As a member country, China will actively participate in the activities of the two institutions and act according to its rights and obligations. China will also strengthen its financial relationships and expand economic ties with all member countries. In June 1980 a delegation from the IMF visited the BOC to gather information in order to solve procedural problems. China's entry into the IMF and the World Bank will give it access to cheap credit and to new issues of the special drawing rights (SDRs).

Problems Confronting the Bank of China

According to Mr. Tang, the Bank of China is confronted with problems in three areas. Each of these is discussed in this section, along with the measures taken by the BOC to rectify these problems.

First, with the socialist modernization of the country, the role of the BOC will increase. The bank's facilities will be used more often, and the bank will be required to undertake more and more varied functions. Mr. Tang felt that the bank is not yet fully equipped to meet all these demands. The structure and methods of transactions adopted by the BOC are backward compared with those of the largest banks in the developed countries.

Second, many cadres and staff members of the BOC lack the management and technical skills needed to carry out the greatly expanded activities of the bank. Finally, the communication networks and equipment now used by the BOC are old-fashioned.

To rectify this situation, the Bank of China has adopted the following measures:

1. The BOC has sent delegations overseas to study the operations of foreign banks with advanced management techniques.
2. Cadres with basic business knowledge and foreign-language skills are sent abroad as trainees for a period of one or two years. Most of the trainees are now being sent to London. In the future some will be sent to the United States and Japan. Many foreign banks have offered to help in this respect, but because the BOC lacks personnel with sufficient language skills, it could not take advantage of many of these offers at the moment.
3. Several local universities and institutions have established international financial departments to train graduates in foreign-exchange management.

4. In various branches of the BOC, training classes have been established for the cadres.
5. The BOC seeks to improve the communication network and equipments. The bank has some computers and will expand the capacities of existing computers. In addition, it will try to improve communications with the International Clearing House.

Role of Insurance in China's Foreign Trade and Investment

With the expansion of foreign trade and other forms of economic cooperation, cargo shipments and properties invested must be protected against loss by means of insurance. According to Article 8 of the China Joint Venture Law, all joint ventures operating in China must take out insurance through the People's Insurance Company of China (PICC).

The PICC is a state-owned enterprise established in 1949. It differs from the Insurance Commission, whose purpose is to supervise all insurance companies in China. The Insurance Commission is housed within the People's Bank of China. The PICC is supervised by the People's Bank of China.

The PICC transacts different kinds of insurance business. It underwrites all marine insurance and reinsurance business that is international. With the expansion of foreign trade, it will underwrite new classes of coverage, such as offshore drilling rigs, contractors' risk, surety bonds, performance bonds, credit insurance, and so on—in short, all the coverages that are required to meet the needs of joint ventures and foreign trade.

In late 1979 two new categories of insurances were added. One is for contract failure and the other for political risk. Under the former the PICC will compensate losses caused by failure to fulfill contracts. Political-risk insurance covers losses suffered as a result of wars, riots, government confiscation, requisition, or restrictions. However, it does not cover government measures taken in response to actions by the insured that violate the law (*Beijing Review,* February 11, 1980).

The PICC underwrites domestic insurance, including insurance for property and transportation of goods (*Beijing Review,* February 11, 1980), Further, it handles liability insurance for foreigners in China, such as foreign travelers, diplomatic legation and cars, and so on.

Besides the PICC, there are two insurance companies in China, the China Insurance Company and the Taiping Insurance Company, both of which have headquarters in Beijing. These two insurance companies operate overseas and have branch offices in Hong Kong, Macau, and Singapore. They deal with overseas business and underwrite maritime insurance abroad. For example, when China exports to Singapore, the Singapore importers can insure with the Taiping Insurance Company. With respect to both imports and exports, the consignees have full discretion to choose their insurance agents.

The PICC has connections with more than 900 insurance companies in over 100 countries. These foreign insurance companies act as surveying and settling agencies. The PICC has entered into a fifty-fifty joint venture with the American International Group, Inc., to set up the China-American Insurance Company, which began operations on October 1, 1980 (Tung 1981a).

According to a PICC official, the premiums it charges are comparable to, if not lower than, those in the United States. If there is no claim, it issues a no-claim bonus. The company's premiums will be adjusted periodically according to international standards and other relevant information.

With respect to settlement of claims, the PICC indicated that if a claim has been established, it will pay. If there is a dispute, it will try to negotiate with the client first. It prefers to settle disputes through mutual discussion and negotiation. However, if both parties cannot resolve their differences through mutual discussion, the matter will go to court. The claimant chooses the place of arbitration. Even after the case has been submitted to court, the PICC will continue to try to resolve the matter through negotiations. Mr. Li, deputy manager of the PICC, indicated that 90 percent of cases in which a lawsuit has commenced have ultimately been settled out of court.

With the expansion of foreign trade and investments within China, the PICC has had to assume greatly expanded activities. To meet these needs, the PICC has established training programs. In 1980 it set up an international insurance faculty in one of the colleges in China. This is a four-year program. PICC's branch offices throughout China also organize insurance courses to train their own cadres and staff members. In addition, they send some of the trainees overseas. By July 1980 they had sent eight trainees to the United Kingdom to work with insurance companies such as Lloyd's of London. Other insurance companies have also offered to help, but again there is the problem of the shortage of personnel possessing sufficient language skills.

Foreign-Trade Prospects for the Future

Under the current Three-Year Plan for Readjustment, a number of contracts with foreign firms have been canceled or suspended temporarily (*Time,* March 16, 1981, p. 68). The Chinese government points out that the purpose of readjustment is not to curtail or decrease foreign trade and economic cooperation (*Beijing Review,* March 9, 1981), as evidenced by the fact that China's overall foreign trade grew by 20 percent in 1980 and is expected to increase by 10 percent more in 1981 (*Time,* March 16, 1981, p. 68). Rather, the purpose is to bring about orderly development of China's economy based on a more pragmatic appraisal of the country's needs and limitations for the time being. The Three-Year Plan for Readjustment, if successfully implemented, will provide a more solid base for the growth of China's economy, including the foreign-trade sector. As indicated previously, if China had harbored unrealistic goals, its efforts to modernize might have collapsed. Such an occurrence would be more detrimental to the growth and development of foreign trade.

In the interim period of readjustment, even though business negotiations have slowed down and a number of projects have been canceled or temporarily suspended, the former U.S. ambassador to China, Leonard Woodcock, advised foreign firms not to abandon their efforts because "the Chinese do, in fact, stick with old friends who have stood by them when the going gets easier" (*Pacific Basin Quarterly,* December 1979, p. 3). Ambassador Woodcock's point is well taken. The Chinese are very appreciative of those people and firms that stand by them through hard times, and will duly reward them when the opportunity arises. In fact, one of the criteria the Chinese use in their selection of suitable partners for offshore oil-development projects—indeed, in a variety of projects—is "previous working relationships between China and the foreign firm" (Tung 1981a). This attitude stems in part from the Chinese preference for building long-term relationships with its business partners and associates. Consequently, as China modernizes and the standard of living of its people rises, firms that have a history of good working relationships with the Chinese stand to gain by having access to a market that constitutes a quarter of humanity.

12 Performance in Chinese Industrial Enterprises

In the West organizations are primarily concerned with efficiency and effectiveness in meeting organizational goals. Organizations constantly strive to be effective and to achieve greater efficiency in their operations. In China the government's concern is the same, especially in the new era of socialist modernization. The Chinese government has declared that the mission of the new era is to make an all-out effort to transform the country's relatively backward economy to equal "the first ranks of the world" by the year 2000.

This chapter examines performance in Chinese industrial enterprises. In assessing performance, it may be inappropriate to compare the productivity rates of a Chinese enterprise with those of a U.S. firm manufacturing the same or a similar product, or the output value per Chinese worker with that of his U.S. counterpart. Such comparisons would not be meaningful for several reasons. First, the efficiency of an enterprise is largely determined by the firm's method of acquisition of raw materials and resources as inputs for production; by the transformation processes that convert inputs into outputs; and by the quantity and quality of outputs. The United States is a capitalist economy in which market forces have complete freedom to determine the firm's method of acquisition of resources and means of distribution of output. China, by contrast, is a planned socialist economy that until very recently completely ignored market forces in the allocation and acquisition of raw materials and in the distribution of outputs. Until very recently Chinese enterprises were run solely by administrative means. They were not treated as independent accounting units and hence were not held responsible for their own profits and losses. Their function was simply to meet production targets set by the state. These production targets are part of a large, centrally derived and administered plan. Hence efficiency appeared to be the concern not of the individual enterprise, but of the state.

Second, the two countries' levels of technological development differ greatly. During my 1979 visit to the Anshan Iron and Steel Company, a leader in the industry, I noted that the computers used in the factory were at least fifteen or twenty years behind those used in the United States today. In the Qinghur No. 3 Textile Mill, the sole textile factory in China with a computer installation, the computer has a capacity of only 3K. In general, the equipment and machinery in use in most industrial enterprises throughout China, including the advanced units, are obsolete by U.S. standards. Most knowledgeable observers indicate that there is at least a ten- to fifteen-year lag in Chinese technology behind those of the advanced capitalist economies. As Vice-Premier Fang Yi candidly admitted: "Taking the overall situation into consideration, China is backward as compared with the West and Japan. It is no loss of face to admit backwardness. On the other hand, we want to catch up and eliminate this gain" (*China Business Review*, November–December 1979, p. 28). In finance and management techniques, officials concede that they are still using techniques borrowed from the USSR in the early 1950's.

A third factor is that the educational level in China is low. As pointed out previously, only 3 percent of the industrial work force has technical skills equivalent to those of an engineer or technician. An overwhelming majority of Chinese workers have no education beyond junior middle school. This factor, coupled with the dependence on obsolete machinery and equipment, means that the methods of operation in many enterprises are primitive by U.S. standards.

Finally, most U.S. industries are capital intensive, whereas most industries in China are labor intensive. Visitors to Chinese oil fields were struck by the fact that huge pipes were hauled manually by literally hundreds of men, whereas in the United States such pipes could be handled by a single piece of heavy machinery. Although the Chinese government has encouraged the importation of advanced technology, machinery, and equipment, it has also emphasized the need to consider China's objective conditions—an abundant work force and scarce foreign exchange. Consequently, where appropriate, more labor-intensive machinery should be used in order to provide employment and to conserve foreign exchange. Since there appears to be no immediate solution to the problems of a huge labor force and scarce foreign exchange, it is likely that the policy of encouraging the use of labor-intensive technology will continue to be enforced.

Given the tremendous differences between the United States and China in terms of systems of economic management and levels of educational and technological development, it would be meaningless to compare the productivity rates and output value per worker of the two countries. The Chinese do not try to hide their backwardness. Hua Guofeng revealed some disturbing figures about the sad state of China's industries in his "Report on the Work of the Government," delivered at the Second Session of the Fifth National People's Congress, on June 18, 1979. He noted that in mid-1979 the productivity rate in the large industrial enterprises in China was one-fifth to one-tenth of those in the developed capitalist economies (*Beijing Review*, August 17, 1979, p. 13). He indicated that 24 percent of the state-owned enterprises were operating at a loss and that 43 percent of the industrial products manufactured by the key enterprises were below the highest quality levels attained in the past. Moreover, some 55 percent of the enterprises must conserve both raw and semifinshed materials in order to match the lowest levels previously attained (*Beijing Review*, July 6, 1979, p. 13). Hence there was a need for immediate change, beginning with the reforms embodied in the Three-Year Plan (1979–1981) for readjustment, restructuring, consolidation, and improvement of China's economy.

Until very recently, concrete statistics on various aspects of organizational functioning were not readily available. On June 27, 1979, for the first time in twenty-three years, the State Statistical Bureau released detailed statistics on

a variety of matters. In light of these factors, it appears that a more me
analysis would be an assessment of the positive and negative factors th
effectiveness, productivity, and performance in Chinese industrial en
Such an assessement would help us determine whether Chinese industrial enterprises have the necessary ingredients for improving their performance in the
future.

Factors Affecting Performance

As pointed out in chapter 1, besides the general consensus that organizational
effectiveness is desirable and that it should be assessed and measured, there is
little agreement among researchers about how organizational effectiveness
should be operationalized and measured. Figure 1-1 presented a simplified
framework listing variables generally hypothesized to affect organizational outcomes. The model hypothesizes that societal-environment variables, organizational-environment variables, and personal variables all influence organizational
effectiveness.

Most of the variables included in the societal-environment, organizational-
environment, and personal categories have been examined in the preceding chapters. The purpose here is to assess each of these briefly as it affects performance
in Chinese industrial enterprises.

The level of technological development and the educational skills of Chinese
workers are low. The government acknowledges these negative factors and recognizes the need to import advanced technology and equipment and to develop the
technical skills of the industrial workers at all levels as rapidly as possible. Unless
China can develop a large contingent of skilled workers, import advanced technology, and successfully absorb such technology to narrow the technological gap
that now exists between China and the advanced nations—to build up a strong
base for developing technical innovations domestically at a later date—the country's dream of becoming a modern nation will be shattered, and the productivity
levels of China's industrial enterprises will lag behind those of the advanced
capitalist economies.

The economic system of management, with its heavy reliance on administrative means, is cumbersome, often leads to bottleneck situations, tends to stifle
creativity, and delays the flow of information to and from the central authorities. All these factors could retard growth among Chinese enterprises. In addition, overcentralization of authority in the hands of the State Planning Commission—which sets production targets, allocates resources, distributes outputs,
and takes on the enterprises' profits and losses—is not conducive to increasing
productivity among workers at all levels. Enterprise management and workers
blindly pursue state production plans and have little concern with efficient use
of raw materials and the quality of outputs because they know that they will
only be held accountable for meeting the production targets set by the state.
They have little initiative to contribute beyond these production targets. Thus
the minimal standards and targets set by the state become the maximum toward

which enterprise employees will work. At the same time, ignoring market forces means that commodities that are not in high demand are produced, whereas other needed products are manufactured in insufficient quantities. This leads to waste and prevents the people's standard of living from rising commensurately with increased industrial output.

The positive aspect of state planning is that the state acts as a regulatory agency, allocating scarce resources, ensuring minimal standards of living among the people, curbing inflation, coordinating activities among various sectors of the economy, and providing guidelines for the systematic development of various sectors of the country. This was especially necessary in the early years of the PRC, when sociopolitical and economic conditions were in disrepair. At that time only a strong central authority could bring about swift and orderly mobilization of resources, undertake large-scale construction projects, set the country on a path of growth after decades of stagnation, and bring about relatively stable economic growth.

Capitalist economies, including the United States, now recognize the need for the government to exercise some form of control over various sectors of the economy to ensure orderly development, as witnessed by the increasing number of governmental rules and regulations imposed upon the operations of private industrial enterprises. However, there should be a limit to the extent and amount of control exercised by the government. The Chinese government, recognizing the limitations inherent in overcentralization of authority in the hands of the State Planning Commission, is experimenting with the policy of granting greater autonomy to the respective enterprises in planning, decision making, and handling of financial matters. Initial results of the experimental reforms among a select group of 6,600 enterprises have been encouraging so far. If such reforms continue to stimulate greater initiative among enterprise managers to take on greater responsibilities and aim for higher efficiency then productivity will increase in the future.

When political indoctrination or ideology is used as a unifying spirit to guide people to engage in constructive activities, to spur people to shake off the shackles of poverty and of economic and technological stagnation, and to motivate them to strive for the early attainment of socialist modernization, then ideology can have a positive influence on performance in industrial organizations. However, in its extreme form, when ideology becomes an end in itself rather than a means to an end (as happened during the Great Leap Forward and the Cultural Revolution), then ideology can prove dysfunctional to economic growth and development by leading to an abandonment of economic goals and to a situation in which only those who excel in political pedagogy, regardless of their technical competence, are put in charge of running enterprises. The government has taken measures to prevent the recurrence of such disruptive political upheavals by offering guidelines on the correct approach to the study of Marxism-Leninism-Mao Zedong Thought, by implementing the policy that "practice is the sole criterion for truth," by preventing the development of a personality cult around any single individual, and by emphasizing the need for collective leadership. If China can enjoy fairly stable political conditions at home and abroad for a relatively long period of time, wherein ideology serves to reinforce the need for progress and development, then improvements may be made in the operations and management of industrial enterprises.

Since the founding of the PRC, the government has tried to develop correct attitudes among the people toward work, productive labor, the need for achievement, and the need for technical innovation and revolution. In the new era of socialist modernization, these attributes are emphasized more than ever before, as evidenced by the reinstitution of exams for college entrance, for recruitment of workers into organizations, and for promotion of personnel to managerial positions and positions as engineers, so that only the best and the brightest will take on the responsibility of running enterprises in the future. This is a positive development in terms of improving productivity in the future, because research has shown a high correlation between the achievement drive of a country's people and the country's level of economic development. When high achievers are put in charge of running the enterprises, they will undoubtedly set tougher standards and goad others to aim higher, be more efficient and produce more and better-quality products and services.

The motivational devices now in vogue in industrial enterprises are designed to reinforce the goal of increasing productivity. In the first place, rewards are directly tied to individual performance, so that those who produce more and perform better will receive higher wages. In the second place, the government has made efforts to make consumer goods more widely available, so that people can appreciate the value of money and see the link between increased productivity, higher wages, and a higher standard of living. At this time, although economic sanctions (such as reduction in wages, fines, and demotion) are beginning to be used in certain enterprises, these are still not practiced on a wide scale. Furthermore, the system of lifetime employment, though having its merits, tends to breed complacency and irresponsibility because some workers know that no matter how badly they perform, they will not be dismissed from the organization. The government is contemplating changes in the area. Unless unproductive and delinquent workers see that poor performance leads to penalties, they will have little incentive to change their ways.

The establishment of the Congress of Workers and Staff, the principle of participative management, and the role of the trade unions all tend to foster better relations between enterprise management and workers and to have a positive impact on organizational members' perception of the organizational climate. This translates into smoother operations and implementation of production plans. With the reinstitution of the examination system and the restoration of titles such as engineer, some concern has been raised that this may lead to the development of a managerial elite class who will become increasingly removed from the workers. These practices do pose a threat in terms of widening the gap between management and personnel, but they should not become a negative factor with respect to improving performance in the factories as long as the gap does not become too wide and relations between the two parties do not become so strained that both sides cannot get together and work toward common goals. Moreover, the government contends that this phenomenon is unlikely to occur because of the measures the party has taken to emphasize the need for cadres to set good examples, to go among the masses, and not to seek special privileges. It remains to be seen whether these measures are sufficient to offset the development of unhealthy tendencies. As pointed out previously, as long as these changes are kept within limits, they should not have an adverse affect on productivity.

On the whole, it appears that the government is cognizant of the factors that could affect performance of industrial enterprises and is trying to enhance the positive factors, to correct the negative ones, and to check the development of unhealthy tendencies that may hinder industrial growth. Between 1949 and 1979 the government showed that even in the face of great adversity, China could time and again follow reason and foster the growth of positive factors. Despite the fact that productivity levels in many industrial enterprises are still very low compared with those of the advanced nations, it must be recognized that China has come a long way in a relatively short period of time from the incredible disorganization and disorientation that prevailed before 1949. China would have been unable to make such rapid strides in its industrial growth and development had it not been for the existence of the positive factors mentioned previously. With the government's current emphasis on the need for socialist modernization, and its call for changes to overcome limitations in China's systems of industrial and economic management, it is likely that Chinese industrial enterprises will be able to accomplish far greater and better things in the coming decades, provided the government continues to adhere to its present policies.

A variety of management reforms implemented on a trial basis in a number of enterprises have produced encouraging results so far. A case in point is the Sichuan experiment discussed in chapter 9. By 1980 Sichuan-style experiments had been introduced in some 6,600 enterprises throughout the country. Although these account for only 16 percent of all the state-owned enterprises in China, in 1980 these 6,600 enterprises accounted for 60 and 70 percent, respectively, of China's total industrial output values and profits from state-owned enterprises. Initial findings of the results obtained in the 6,600 enterprises showed that, through management reforms, the majority of enterprises were able to increase their production substantially, thereby earning higher profits, which in turn translated into more revenue for the state and higher incomes for the workers. Of the profits earned by these enterprises, in 1980 a full 87 percent went to the state, and 10 percent was retained by the respective enterprises for their own use (*Beijing Review*, April 6, 1981).

Problem Areas

Despite these encouraging results, several problems (both real and potential) remain that could adversely affect the outlook for increased productivity. These problem areas were discussed throughout the various chapters and can be summarized as follows.

First, whether there is grass-roots support for these types of management reform. The advanced or key factories tend to support management reforms that grant greater autonomy to the individual enterprises in handling financial matters, and that directly tie the availability of capital and other resources to the performance of the enterprise. The less advanced units, which by far constitute the majority of enterprises in the country, may view these reforms in a different light. They may be apprehensive that the new system will lead to wider disparity between advanced and less advanced units. In the past the enterprise was not treated as an independent accounting unit and hence was not responsible for its own losses. With the new management reforms, however, enterprises will be held responsible for any losses. In addition, the availability of capital, funds for bonus distribution, and other resources will be tied to the performance of the enterprise. Hence the less advanced units may perceive their material interests to be adversely affected by these reforms. Enterprises that consistently suffer losses will be consolidated and merged with more successful ones. In 1980, 19,300 enterprises were consolidated or merged to form 1,900 specialized companies or general plants (*Beijing Review*, April 27, 1981). Even though the workers who are temporarily displaced through consolidation process continue to receive their wages and are trained in a new technical skill at the labor-service organizations to prepare them for their next job assignment, these reforms may still be negatively perceived by the less productive units.

Second, the use of bonuses to reward increased output must be balanced by the imposition of sanctions on those who fail to perform up to standard. Even though the policy of imposing economic sanctions on those who failed to perform well has been introduced and practiced in some enterprises over the past two years, the policy of dismissing incompetent individuals from the organization has not been implemented. As pointed out previously, the system of lifetime employment, though having its merits, tends to breed complacency and irresponsibility because workers know that they will not be dismissed from the organization, regardless of their performance. In order to spur production and improve the quality of services and products, workers must see the relationship between noncompliance or substandard performance and economic sanctions and dismissal.

Third, for the first twenty-nine years of the PRC's existence, the prices of commodities remained fairly stable. In November 1979 price controls on nonessential commodities were lifted. The prices of many of these nonessential commodities rose substantially. The inflation rate for nonessential commodities reached 6 percent for 1980. To rectify the situation, the government has adopted several measures to check inflation. However, if these measures are insufficient, inflation could quickly eat up any increase in the workers' wages.

Fourth, although many of the reforms are based on sound economic logic, the country should be alert to the possibility of the occurrence of what in the West is known as the *Hawthorne effect*. The term *Hawthorne effect* refers to the famous time-motion studies conducted at the Hawthorne Works of the Western Electric Company in Chicago in the 1930s to determine the effects that changes in the work environment would have on the performance and productivity rates of workers. In these studies it was found that increased productivity could be attributed in part to the fact that the people included in the experiment felt they were the center of attention. Hence the government and the enterprises should determine whether any of the increased productivity in the experimental units can be attributed to the Hawthorne effect. If such a phenonmenon is in operation, once the novelty of the experiment, of being in the limelight, wears off, productivity may drop.

Finally, despite arguments to the effect that socialist planning is compatible with the market mechanism and that the antithesis of planned economic development is not the market but spontaneity and anarchy in production (Jiang 1980), China still must wrestle with some of the inherent contradictions between the use of socialist planning and the market mechanism.

China should be alert to these problems and potential problems in order to raise the productivity levels of the nation as a whole. Unless the country takes sufficient measures to correct these problems, they could adversely affect the prospects for increased productivity and hence could retard China's economic growth and development.

13 Conclusion

The foregoing chapters have provided some insights into post-Mao industrial society. Specifically, the book focused on industrial growth and development since the establishment of the PRC in 1949, and on the political, socioeconomic, and legal forces that shape Chinese industrial society. This included an analysis of the motivations behind the Four Modernizations program, the factors that could affect the success or failure of socialist modernization; the role of ideology in post-Mao industrial society; the political and legal systems in China; sociocultural factors that influence and shape the Chinese mentality and outlook toward work and society at large; various aspects of the functioning and operation of Chinese industrial enterprises, and whether these practices are conducive to increased productivity and heightened performance in the future; and the role of foreign trade in China's economic development. In the main, the changes and reforms that have been introduced in the political, socioeconomic, and legal arenas appear to facilitate economic growth and development. To many people, the crucial question is not whether China will actually be able to catch up with the advanced world by the year 2000, but whether the country will remain committed to the goals of the Four Modernizations. If the country could remain committed to these goals and could sustain steady economic growth, uninterrupted by political and ideological upheavals, over the next two decades, this in itself would represent a colossal feat.

As mentioned previously, the Chinese are anxious to learn new management techniques from abroad in order to improve the overall efficiency of their enterprises. Consequently, the coming years will see the adoption of new practices and procedures in China. However, it would be erroneous to assume that China will transplant Western management techniques in their entirety and apply them indiscriminately to Chinese factories. Even in their espousal of the socialist principles of Marxism-Leninism, the Chinese have done some preliminary screening and have sinicized Marxism-Leninism somewhat before implementing its principles. China's leaders are aware of the tremendous differences, both cultural and economic, between socialist China and the Western capitalist nations. Time and again they have emphasized that China should only adopt those practices and procedures that would be suited to the peculiar conditions of the country.

Throughout history the Chinese have proved to be a pragmatic people with a willingness to change along with the times. This attribute, above all, may account for the fact that China has survived for thousands of years despite the civil wars that occurred between the various imperial dynasties, despite foreign domination of the country during the Yuan dynasty by the Monguls and during the Qing (Ching) dynasty by the Manchus; and despite a semicolonial status for almost 150 years under the Western imperialist powers. Time and again the Chinese have proved that they could rebuild their country. Since the latest debacle of the Gang of Four, which brought the country to the verge of political, economic, and social collapse—a plight that ended only five years ago—China has recovered sufficiently to show rising productivity in various sectors of the economy. It is the Chinese ability to survive in face of tremendous adversity, and, even more remarkable, to recover from havoc and disaster, that has intrigued Western observers for so long. Many of these fine qualities and attributes are kept alive today in the organization and running of Chinese industrial enterprises. These are of interest to researchers studying the principles of organizational theory and behavior. When the Chinese indicate an eagerness to learn advanced management techniques from the West, they are most interested in areas such as cost accounting, quality control, techniques of cost-benefit analysis, forecasting, how to accommodate market factors in drafting the state production and purchasing plans, and how to raise worker productivity. This does not mean an abandonment of the principles and practices that have served the country well over the past three decades.

For the academician, although Chinese management theories and techniques are fairly underdeveloped compared with those of the advanced nations, China does provide an interesting case for study and comparison. For some, the country's experiences represent a large-scale social experiment. Under the Communist party the Chinese have become fairly effectively organized and mobilized to develop the productive forces of the country. Although many of the principles and techniques currently in vogue in China may not be applicable to the United States, given the tremendous cultural, political, and economic differences that exist, nevertheless, it would benefit researchers and academicians to be aware of such differences and similarities. Knowledge of the similarities and differences in various aspects of organizational functioning and processes, such as leader-member relations and motivational practices in the two countries, could assist theorists and researchers of comparative management, organizational theory, and organizational behavior to better understand how broad environmental variables, such as ideology and socioeconomic variables, can influence the functioning and effectiveness of organizations. Comparisons of similarities and differences would enable researchers to have a better comprehension of the antecedents and outcomes of certain organizational practices or variables, and the dynamics of the relationships between such variables. Such knowledge would prove invaluable in the development of principles of organizational theory and organizational behavior, and would contribute to the development of better models of comparative management, which could be very important to the advancement of theory and knowledge in international business.

From the practitioner's perspective, the role assigned to foreign trade in China's Four Modernizations program signals a new era of expanded trade and economic cooperation between China and the advanced capitalist economies. For example, the trade figures between the United States and China for the year ending 1979, the first year of normalization, were more than double those for the preceding year. Within a year of normalization, China has become the United States' largest communist trading partner, and the United States is China's third-largest trading partner, behind Hong Kong and Japan *(London Times,* September 17, 1980). Many firms in the developed West are eager to get into the Chinese market because of the vast potential a country of that size holds for the firm's future profitability. China's commitment to the goals of the Four Modernizations poses opportunities for foreign businesses to become involved in the development, and subsequently to reap the fruits of modernization of a hitherto largely untapped market of a billion people. A further stimulus to trade and economic cooperation between China and other countries was provided by the enactment of the Joint Venture Laws on July 1, 1979. This law gives foreign firms the opportunity to set up factories and manufacturing facilities within China. In 1980, the first year after the enactment of the Joint Venture Laws, some 20 joint ventures and 300 cooperative arrangements were approved by the Foreign Investment Commission *(Beijing Review,* April 20, 1981). Although some Chinese and foreign observers express concern that economic intercourse with capitalist economies may lead to an abandonment of the socialist road and result in exploitation of China by foreign capitalists, the Chinese authorities are fond of quoting Lenin's 1921 remarks in this regard: "We shall not grudge him (foreign capitalists) even 150 percent in profits, provided the conditions of our workers are improved." Consequently, it is written into the Joint Venture Laws that the investments and assets of foreign partners in China will be protected by the Chinese government.

Several joint-venture projects are currently being implemented and many other forms of economic cooperation and exchange are under negotiation. In order to benefit fully from such joint-venture relationships, it is imperative that the non-Chinese partner have a basic understanding of the various forces that influence Chinese industrial society, its foreign-trade practices, the running of enterprises, and the motivation of Chinese workers. Such knowledge would enhance the chances of gaining access to the China market, would facilitate the operations of joint-venture arrangements, and would increase the probability of success of economic cooperation with the Chinese.

Bibliography

Automobile Facts and Figures. 1977. Automobile Manufacturers Association, Inc.

Atkinson, J.W., and Feather, N.T., eds. 1966. *A theory of achievement motivation*. New York: Wiley.

Barnett, R.B. 1968. *China after Mao*. Cambridge, Mass.: Harvard University Press.

Beijing Review, various issues, 1978-1981.

Burns, E. 1935. *A handbook of Marxism*. New York: International Publishers.

Business PRC, vol. 3, no. 2 (1980).

Business Week, May 20, 1978.

Central Intelligence Agency. 1978. *China: In pursuit of economic modernization*. Washington, D.C.: National Foreign Assessment Center.

Chen, N.R. 1979. *China's economy and foreign trade, 1978-1979*. Washington, D.C.: U.S. Department of Commerce, Office of East-West Country Affairs.

Cheng, S. 1974. *A glance at China's economy*. Beijing: Foreign Languages Press.

China Business Review, various issues, 1979-1981.

China's Foreign Trade, various issues, 1979-1980.

China's foreign trade and its management. 1978. Hong Kong: Chung Hwa Book, Ltd.

China International Trust and Investment Corporation. 1979. Beijing.

China Reconstructs, various issues, 1979-1981.

China Trader. March 1980. Hong Kong: Sino Communication Company.

Clarke, D.E. 1973. Measures of Achievement and Affiliation Motivation. *Review of Educational Research* 43:41-52.

Cockerell, M. 1980. The incredible Chinese news machine. *The Listener*, September 18, pp. 354-356.

Cofer, C.N., and Appley, M.H. 1965. *Motivation: Theory and research*. New York: Wiley.

Constitution of the People's Republic of China. 1978. Beijing: Foreign Languages Press.

Creel, H.G. 1953. *Chinese thought*. New York: Mentor.

Current Background. 1951. Hong Kong: American Consulate General, no. 89.

Doing Business with China. 1979. Washington, D.C. U.S. Department of Commerce.

Duncan, R.B. 1972. Characteristics of organizational environments and perceived environmental uncertainty. *Administrative Science Quarterly* 17:313-327.

Eleventh National Congress of the Communist Party of China (Documents). 1977. Beijing: Foreign Languages Press.

Excerpts from *The selected works of Zhou Enlai*, vol. 1. In *Beijing Review*, March 2, 1981, pp. 8-11.

Farmer, R.N., and Richman, B.M. 1965. *Comparative management and economic progress*. Homewood, Ill.: Richard D. Irwin.

First Session of the Fifth National People's Congress of the People's Republic of China (Documents). 1978. Beijing: Foreign Languages Press.

Fortune, October 23, 1978.

Guangming Ribao, September 18, 1979.

Herdan, I. 1976. *Introduction to China*. London: Anglo-Chinese Educational Institute.

Hsiao, G.T. 1977. *The foreign trade of china*. Berkeley: University of California Press.

Hsu, R.B. 1977. The political economy of rural health care in China. *Review of Radical Political Economics* 9:134–140.

Huang, K. 1981. How to assess Chairman Mao and Mao Zedong Thought. *Beijing Review*, April 27, 1981, pp. 15–23.

Hunsberger, W.S. 1964. *Japan and the U.S. in world trade*. New York: Harper and Row.

Jiang, Y. 1980. The theory of an enterprise-based economy. *Social Sciences in China* 1:48–66.

The Kailuan story. 1977. Beijing: Foreign Languages Press.

Katz, D., and Kahn, R.L. 1978. *The social psychology of organizations*, 2nd ed. New York: Wiley.

Kraar, L. 1975. A high-level sales pitch for shoppers from Peking. *Fortune* (November):108–113, 187–190.

Laaksonen, O. 1975. The structure and management of Chinese enterprises. *Finnish Journal of Business Economics*, pp. 1–22.

Lawler, E.E.; Hall, D.T.; and Oldham, G.R. 1974. Organizational climate: Relationship to organization structure, process and performance. *Organizational Behavior and Human Performance* 11:139–155.

Lawrence, P.R., and Lorsch, J.W. 1967. *Organization and environment: Managing differentiation and integration*. Homewood, Ill.: Richard D. Irwin.

Li, V.H. 1980. A perspective on the new legalization drive. In N.T. Wang, ed., *Business with China: An international reassessment*. New York: Pergamon Press.

Lin, Z. 1980. Initial reform in China's economic structure. *Social Sciences in China* 3:172–194.

Liu, C., and Wang, L. 1980. *China's foreign trade*. Hong Kong: China Translation and Printing Services.

Liu, G., and Zhao, R. 1979. Relationship between the plan and the market in a socialist economy. *Jingji Yanjiu (Economic Studies)* 5.

London Times, September 14, 1980.

London Times, September 17, 1980.

McClelland, D.C. 1961. *The achieving society*. Princeton, N.J.: Van Nostrand.

———. 1963. Motivational patterns in South-East Asia with special reference to the Chinese case. *Journal of Social Issues* 19:6–19.

Meisner, M. 1972. The Shenyang Transformer Factory: A profile. *China Quarterly*, pp. 717–737.

Miller, W.H. 1979. China flirts with capitalism. *Industry Week*, August 6, 1979, pp. 38–44.

National conference on *learning from Daqing in industry (Selected documents)*. 1977. Beijing: Foreign Languages Press.

Negandhi, A.R., and Prasad, S.B. 1975. *The frightening angels: A study of U.S. multinationals in developing countries*. Kent, Ohio: Kent State University Press.

New China, U.S.-China People's Friendship Association, New York (Winter 1979).

Nord, W., ed. 1972. *Concepts and controversies in organizational behavior*. Santa Monica, Calif.: Goodyear Publishing Company.

Oh, T.K. 1976. Theory Y in the People's Republic of China. *California Management Review* 19:77–84.

Pacific Basin Quarterly, Special issue (December 1979).

Pervin, L.A. 1968. Performance and satisfaction as a function of individual-environment fit. *Psychological Bulletin* 69:56–68.

Pincus, F.L. 1979. Higher education and socialist transformation in the People's Republic of China since 1970. *Review of Radical Political Economics* 11:24–48.

Pritchard, R., and Karasick, B. 1973. The effects of organizational climate on managerial job performance and job satisfaction. *Organizational Behavior and Human Performance* 9:110–119.

Ren, T.; Sun, H.; and Liu, J. 1980. Investigation report: Enterprises in Sichuan acquire greater independence. *Social Sciences in China* 1:201–215.

Renmin Ribao, various issues, 1979–1981.

Richman, B.M. 1969. *Industrial society in Communist China*. New York: Random House.

Riskin, C. 1975. Workers' incentives in Chinese industry. In *China: A reassessment of the economy*, Compendium of papers submitted to the Joint Economic Committee, Congress of the United States. Washington, D.C.: U.S. Government Printing Office, pp. 199–244.

Rong Yiren, chairman of the board of directors of the China International Trust and Investment Corporation, Speech at the American Chamber of Commerce, Hong Kong, November 9, 1979.

Rumyantsei, A. 1969. Maoism and the anti-Marxist essence of its philosophy. *Communist Viewpoint* 1:31–34.

Schurmann, H.F. 1968. *Ideology and organization in Communist China*, 2nd ed. Berkeley: University of California Press.

Schwartz, B.I. 1951. *Chinese communism and the rise of Mao*. Cambridge, Mass.: Harvard University Press.

Seattle Post-Intelligence, December 17, 1979.

Selected works of Mao Zedong, vol. 1. 1975. Beijing: Foreign Languages Press.

———, vol. 3. 1975. Beijing: Foreign Languages Press.

———, vol. 4. 1975. Beijing: Foreign Languages Press.

_____, vol. 5. 1977. Beijing: Foreign Languages Press.

Stein, H., and Stein, M. 1978. America reflected in a Chinese mirror. *Fortune,* March 13, pp. 53–60.

A study in socialist productivity since the establishment of the People's Republic of China, vol. 2. 1978. Shanghai: People's Press.

Sun, Y. 1980. What is the origin of the law of value? *Social Sciences in China* 3:155–171.

Taguiri, R., and Litwin, G., eds. 1969. *Organizational climate: Explorations of a concept.* Cambridge, Mass.: Harvard University Press.

Time, various issues, 1978–1981.

Thompson, J.D. 1967. *Organizations in action.* New York: McGraw-Hill.

Thorndike, R.L. 1949. *Personnel selection: Test and measurement techniques.* New York: Wiley.

Tomlinson, A.C. 1980. Some perspectives on financing China's projects. In N.T. Wang, ed., *Business with China: An International reassessment.* New York: Pergamon Press.

Tung, R.L. 1979. Dimensions of organizational environments: An exploratory study of their impact on organization structure. *Academy of Management Journal* 22:672–693.

_____. 1980. *Management practices in China.* In China: International Business Series. New York: Pergamon Press.

_____. 1981a. *U.S.–China trade negotiations.* New York: Pergamon Press.

_____. 1981b. International trade in automobiles: The product life cycle approach. Paper presented at the National Meetings of the Academy of International Business, Montreal, October 15–17, 1981.

_____. 1981c. Patterns of motivation in Chinese industrial enterprises. *Academy of Management Review* 6:487–494.

Vancouver Sun, February 12, 1974.

The Washington Post, March 30, 1981.

Weinbaum, B. 1976. Women in transition to socialism: Perspectives on the Chinese. *Review of Radical Political Economics* 8:34–57.

Xue, M. 1979. *A study in the problems of the socialist economy.* Beijing: People's Press.

_____, 1980. *Several problems concerning China's present economy.* Beijing: People's Press.

Yao, L., ed. 1979. *Readjustment, restructuring, consolidation and improvement of the national economy.* Beijing: People's Press.

Yuchtman, E., and Seashore, S.E. 1967. A systems resource approach to organizational effectiveness. *American Sociological Review* 32:891–903.

Zhou, Z. 1981. Newspapers in China. *Beijing Review,* May 18, 1981, pp. 23–29.

Appendix A:
The Law of the People's Republic of China on Joint Ventures Using Chinese and Foreign Investment

(Adopted by the Second Session of the Fifth National People's Congress on July 1, 1979)

Article 1

With a view to expanding international economic cooperation and technological exchange, the People's Republic of China permits foreign companies, enterprises, other economic entities, or individuals (hereinafter referred to as foreign participants) to incorporate themselves, within the territory of the People's Republic of China, into joint ventures with Chinese companies, enterprises, or other economic entities (hereinafter referred to as Chinese participants) on the principle of equality and mutual benefit and subject to authorization by the Chinese government.

Article 2

The Chinese government protects, by the legislation in force, the resources invested by a foreign participant in a joint venture and the profits due him pursuant to the agreements, contracts, and articles of association authorized by the Chinese government as well as his other lawful rights and interests. All the activities of a joint venture shall be governed by the laws, decrees, and pertinent rules and regulations of the People's Republic of China.

Article 3

A joint venture shall apply to the Foreign Investment Commission of the People's Republic of China for authorization of the agreements and contracts concluded between the parties to the venture and the articles of association of the venture formulated by them, and the commission shall authorize or

From *Beijing Review*, July 20, 1979, pp. 24–26.

reject these documents within three months. When authorized, the joint venture shall register with the General Administration for Industry and Commerce of the People's Republic of China and start operations under license.

Article 4

A joint venture shall take the form of a limited-liability company.

In the registered capital of a joint venture, the proportion of the investment contributed by the foreign participant(s) shall in general not be less than 25 percent.

The profits, risks, and losses of a joint venture shall be shared by the parties to the venture in proportion to their contributions to the registered capital.

The transfer of one party's share in the registered capital shall be effected only with the consent of the other parties to the venture.

Article 5

Each party to a joint venture may contribute cash, capital goods, industrial property rights, and so on, as its investment in the venture.

The technology or equipment contributed by any foreign participant as investment shall be truly advanced and appropriate to China's needs. In cases of losses caused by deception through the intentional provision of outdated equipment or technology, compensation shall be paid for the losses.

The investment contributed by a Chinese participant may include the right to the use of a site provided for the joint venture during the period of its operation. In case such a contribution does not constitute a part of the investment from the Chinese participant, the joint venture shall pay the Chinese government for its use.

The various contributions referred to in the present article shall be specified in the contracts concerning the joint venture or in its articles of association, and the value of each contribution (excluding that of the site) shall be ascertained by the parties to the venture through joint assessment.

Article 6

A joint venture shall have a board of directors with a composition stipulated in the contracts and the articles of association after consultation between the parties to the venture, and each director shall be appointed or removed by his own side. The board of directors shall have a chairman appointed by the Chinese participant and one or two vice-chairmen appointed by the foreign participant(s). In handling an important problem, the board of directors shall reach decision through consultation by the participants on the principle of equality and mutual benefit.

The board of directors is empowered to discuss and take action on, pursuant to the provisions of the articles of association of the joint venture, all fundamental issues concerning the venture, namely, expansion projects; production and business programs; the budget; distribution of profits; plans concerning manpower and pay scales; the termination of business; the appointment or hiring of the president, the vice-president(s), the chief engineer, the treasurer, and the auditors, as well as their functions and powers and their remuneration; and so forth.

The president and vice-president(s) (or the general manager and assistant general manager(s) in a factory) shall be chosen from the various parties to the joint venture.

Procedures covering employment and discharge of the workers and staff members of a joint venture shall be stipulated according to law in the agreement or contract concluded between the parties to the venture.

Article 7

The net profit of a joint venture shall be distributed between the parties to the venture in proportion to their respective shares in the registered capital after the payment of a joint-venture income tax on its gross profit pursuant to the tax laws of the People's Republic of China and after the deductions therefrom as stipulated in the articles of association of the venture for the reserve funds, the bonus and welfare funds for the workers and staff members, and the expansion funds of the venture.

A joint venture equipped with up-to-date technology by world standards may apply for a reduction of or exemption from income tax for the first two to three profit-making years.

A foreign participant who reinvests any part of his share of the net profit within Chinese territory may apply for the restitution of a part of the income tax paid.

Article 8

A joint venture shall open an account with the Bank of China or a bank approved by the Bank of China.

A joint venture shall conduct its foreign-exchange transactions in accordance with the Foreign Exchange Regulations of the People's Republic of China.

A joint venture may, in its business operations, obtain funds from foreign banks directly.

The insurances appropriate to a joint venture shall be furnished by Chinese insurance companies.

Article 9

The production and business programs of a joint venture shall be filed with the authorities concerned and shall be implemented through business contracts.

In its purchase of required raw and semiprocessed materials, fuels, auxiliary equipment, and so forth, a joint venture should give first priority to Chinese sources, but may also acquire them directly from the world market with its own foreign-exchange funds.

A joint venture is encouraged to market its products outside China. It may distribute its export products on foreign markets through direct channels or its associated agencies or China's foreign-trade establishments. Its products may also be distributed on the Chinese market.

Wherever necessary, a joint venture may set up affiliated agencies outside China.

Article 10

The net profit that a foreign participant receives as his share after executing his obligations under the pertinent laws and agreements and contracts, the funds he receives at the time when the joint venture terminates or winds up its operations, and his other funds may be remitted abroad through the Bank of China in accordance with the foreign-exchange regulations and in the currency or currencies specified in the contracts concerning the joint venture.

A foreign participant shall receive encouragements for depositing in the Bank of China any part of the foreign exchange that he is entitled to remit abroad.

Article 11

The wages, salaries, or other legitimate income earned by a foreign worker or staff member of a joint venture, after payment of the personal income tax under the tax laws of the People's Republic of China, may be remitted abroad through the Bank of China in accordance with the foreign-exchange regulations.

Article 12

The contract period of a joint venture may be agreed on between the parties to the venture according to its particular line of business and circumstances. The period may be extended upon expiration through agreement between the parties, subject to authorization by the Foreign Investment Commission of the

People's Republic of China. Any application for such extension shall be made six months before the expiration of the contract.

Article 13

In cases of heavy losses, the failure of any party to a joint venture to execute its obligations under the contracts or the articles of association of the venture, force majeure, and so forth, prior to the expiration of the contract period of a joint venture, the contract may be terminated before the date of expiration by consultation and agreement between the parties and through authorization by the Foreign Investment Commission of the People's Republic of China and registration with the General Administration for Industry and Commerce. In cases of losses caused by breach of the contract(s) by a party to the venture, the financial responsibility shall be borne by the said party.

Article 14

Disputes arising between the parties to a joint venture that the board of directors fails to settle through consultation may be settled through conciliation or arbitration by an arbitral body of China or through arbitration by an arbitral body agreed on by the parties.

Article 15

The present law comes into force on the date of its promulgation. The power of amendment is vested in the National People's Congress.

Appendix B: Regulations on the Registration of Joint Ventures Using Chinese and Foreign Investment

(Approved by the State Council of the People's Republic of China on July 26, 1980)

Article 1

The present regulations are worked out in accordance with stipulations laid down in the "Law of the People's Republic of China on Joint Ventures using Chinese and Foreign Investment" and for the purpose of registering such ventures to protect their legitimate operations.

Article 2

A joint venture using Chinese and foreign investment should, within one month after being approved by the Foreign Investment Commission of the People's Republic of China, register with the General Administration for Industry and Commerce of the People's Republic of China.

The General Administration for Industry and Commerce authorizes the administrative bureaus for industry and commerce in the provinces, municipalities, and autonomous regions to register joint ventures using Chinese and foreign investment in their localities. Licenses for operations shall be issued to the said joint ventures after examination by the General Administration for Industry and Commerce of the People's Republic of China.

Article 3

In applying for registration, a joint venture using Chinese and foreign investment should produce the following documents:

1. the document of approval issued by the Foreign Investment Commission of the People's Republic of China;

From *China's Foreign Trade*, Supplement to no. 6 (1980), pp. 12–13.

2.   the agreement on the joint venture reached by the various parties involved, the contract and the articles of association of the venture, in both Chinese and foreign language and each in triplicate; and

3.   a duplicate of the license and other documents issued by the departments concerned under the government of the country (or region) from which the foreign participants in the joint venture come.

Article 4

In applying for registration of a joint venture using Chinese and foreign investment, a registration form shall be completed in Chinese and foreign language, in triplicate. Items to be registered include the name of the venture, its address, scope of production and business, forms of production and business, registered capital of the parties concerned, chairman and vice-chairmen of the board of directors, general manager and deputy general managers or general director or deputy directors of the plant, the number and date of approval on the document, the size of the entire staff, and the number of foreign workers and staff members.

Article 5

A joint venture using Chinese and foreign investment is regarded as having officially been established the day when a license for its operation is issued to it, and the legitimate production and business shall be protected by the law of the People's Republic of China.

An unregistered enterprise shall not be permitted to go into operation.

Article 6

A joint venture using Chinese and foreign investment shall, by producing the license for its operation, open an account with the Bank of China or another bank approved by the Bank of China, and register with the local tax bureau for payment of taxes.

Article 7

In cases where a joint venture using Chinese and foreign investment desires to move to a new site, shift its production, increase or cut or transfer the registered capital, or extend the contract period, the said venture shall, within one month after approval by the Foreign Investment Commission of the People's Republic of China, register the changes with the Administrative Bureau for Industry and Commerce in the province, municipality, or autonomous region where it is located.

In cases where changes to other items are effected, the said venture shall have to forward at the end of the year a written report about these changes to the Administrative Bureau for Industry and Commerce in the province, municipality, or autonomous region where it is located.

Article 8

In registering or getting its changes registered, a joint venture using Chinese and foreign investment shall pay the registration fee or the fee for getting its changes registered, the sum of which is to be fixed by the General Administration for Industry and Commerce of the People's Republic of China.

Article 9

A joint venture using Chinese and foreign investment upon the expiration of the contract period of the venture or desirous of terminating the contract before its expiration date, shall upon production of the document of approval issued by the Foreign Investment Commission of the People's Republic of China register for the nullification of the contract with the Administrative Bureau for Industry and Commerce in the province, municipality, or autonomous region where it is located. The license of the said venture shall be handed in for cancellation after examination by the General Administration for Industry and Commerce of the People's Republic of China.

Article 10

The General Administration for Industry and Commerce of the People's Republic of China and the Administrative Bureaus for Industry and Commerce in the provinces, municipalities, and autonomous regions are authorized to supervise and inspect the joint ventures using Chinese and foreign investment in the areas they govern. In cases of violations of the present regulations, the violator shall be given a warning or be fined in accordance with the varying degrees of seriousness in each specific case.

Article 11

The present regulations come into force on the date of its promulgation.

Appendix C:
The Income-Tax Law of the People's Republic of China Concerning Joint Ventures with Chinese and Foreign Investment

(Adopted and Entered into Force at the Third Session of the Fifth National People's Congress on September 10, 1980)

Article 1

Income tax shall be levied in accordance with this law on the income derived from production, business, and other sources by any joint venture with Chinese and foreign investment (hereinafter called *joint venture* for short) in the People's Republic of China.

Income tax on the income derived from production, business, and other sources by branches within or outside the territory of China of such joint ventures shall be paid by their head office.

Article 2

The taxable income of a joint venture shall be the net income in a tax year after deduction of costs, expenses, and losses in that year.

Article 3

The income-tax rate on joint ventures shall be 30 percent. In addition, a local surtax of 10 percent of the assessed income tax shall be levied.

The income-tax rates on joint ventures exploiting petroleum, natural gas, and other resources shall be stipulated separately.

Article 4

In the case of a foreign participant in a joint venture remitting its share of the profit from China, an income tax of 10 percent shall be levied on the remitted amount.

From *Beijing Review*, October 6, 1980, pp. 18–20.

Article 5

A newly established joint venture scheduled to operate for a period of ten years or more may, upon approval of the tax authorities of an application filed by the enterprise, be exempted from income tax in the first profit-making year and allowed a 50-percent reduction in the second and third years.

With the approval of the Ministry of Finance of the People's Republic of China, joint ventures engaged in such low-profit operations as farming and forestry or located in remote, economically underdeveloped outlying areas may be allowed a 15–20 percent reduction in income tax for a period of ten years following the expiration of the term for exemptions and reductions mentioned in the preceding paragraph.

Article 6

A participant in a joint venture that invests its share of profit in China for a period of not less than five years may, upon approval by the tax authorities of an application filed by the said participant, obtain a refund of 40 percent of the income tax paid on the reinvested amount. A participant that withdraws its reinvested funds within five years shall pay back the tax amount refunded.

Article 7

Losses incurred by a joint venture in a tax year may be carried over to the next tax year and made up with a matching amount drawn from that year's income. Should the income in the subsequent tax year be insufficient to make up for the said losses, the balance may be made up with further deductions against income year by year over a period not exceeding five years.

Article 8

Income tax on joint ventures shall be levied on an annual basis and paid in quarterly installments. Such provisional payment shall be made within fifteen days after the end of each quarter. The final settlement shall be made within three months of the end of a tax year. Excess payments shall be refunded by the tax authorities or deficiencies made good by the taxpayer.

Article 9

Joint ventures shall file their provisional income-tax returns with the local tax authority within the period prescribed for provisional payments. The taxpayer shall file its final annual income-tax return together with its final accounts within three months of the end of the tax year.

Article 10

Income tax levied on joint ventures shall be computed in terms of Renminbi (RMB). Income in foreign currency shall be assessed according to the exchange rate quoted by the State General Administration of Exchange Control of the People's Republic of China and shall be taxed in Renminbi.

Article 11

When joint ventures go into operation or when they change the nature of their business, change their address, close down, or make changes in or transfer registered capital, such joint ventures shall register with the General Administrative Bureau for Industry and Commerce of the People's Republic of China and, within thirty days of such registration, present the relevant certificates to the local tax authority for tax registration.

Article 12

The tax authorities have the right to investigate the financial affairs, account books, and tax situation of any joint venture. The joint venture must make all reports according to the facts and provide all relevant information and shall not conceal the facts or refuse to cooperate.

Article 13

A joint venture must pay its tax within the prescribed time limit. In cases of failure to pay within the prescribed time limit, the appropriate tax authority, in addition to setting a new time limit for tax payment, shall surcharge overdue payments at 0.5 percent of the overdue tax for every day in arrears, starting from the first day of default.

Article 14

The tax authorities may, acting at their discretion, impose a penalty on any joint venture that has violated the provisions of articles 9, 11, and 12 of this law.

In dealing with any joint venture that has evaded or refused to pay tax, the tax authorities may, in addition to pursuing the tax, impose a penalty of not more than five times the amount of tax underpaid or not paid, according to the seriousness of the offense. Cases of gross violation may be handled by the local people's courts according to law.

Article 15

In cases of disputes with tax authorities about tax payment, joint ventures must pay tax according to the relevant regulations first before applying to higher tax authorities for reconsideration. If they do not accept the decisions made after such reconsideration, they can bring the matter before the local people's courts.

Article 16

Income tax paid by a joint venture or its branch in other countries may be credited against the assessed income tax of the head office as foreign tax credit.

Where agreements on avoidance of double taxation have been concluded between the People's Republic of China and the government of another country, income-tax credits shall be handled in accordance with the provisions of the related agreements.

Article 17

Detailed rules and regulations for the implementation of this law shall be formulated by the Ministry of Finance of the People's Republic of China.

Article 18

This law shall come into force from the date of promulgation.

Appendix D: Detailed Rules and Regulations for the Implementation of the Income-Tax Law of the People's Republic of China Concerning Joint Ventures with Chinese and Foreign Investment

Article 1

These detailed rules and regulations are formulated in accordance with the provisions of Article 17 of the Income Tax Law of the People's Republic of China Concerning Joint Ventures with Chinese and Foreign Investment (hereinafter called *tax law* for short).

Article 2

"Income derived from production and business" mentioned in Article 1 of the tax law means income from the production and business operations in industry, mining, communications, transportation, agriculture, forestry, animal husbandry, fisheries, poultry farming, commerce, tourism, food and drink, service, and other trades.

"Incomes from other sources" mentioned in Article 1 of the tax law covers dividends; bonuses; interests; and income from lease or transfer of property, patent right, proprietary technology, ownership of trademarks, copyright, and other sources.

Article 3

"A local surtax of 10 percent of the assessed income tax" in Article 3 of the tax law means a surtax to be computed and levied according to the actual amount of income tax paid by the joint ventures.

From *Beijing Review*, March 30, 1981, pp. 23–25.

Reduction or exemption of local surtax on account of special circumstances shall be decided by the people's government of the province, municipality, or autonomous region in which the joint venture is located.

Article 4

A foreign participant in a joint venture, which wants to remit its share of profits from China, shall report to the local tax authorities. The remitting agency shall withhold an income tax of 10 percent from the remittance. No tax shall be levied on that part of its share of profits which is not remitted from China.

Article 5

"The first profit-making year" mentioned in Article 5 of the tax law means the year in which a joint venture has begun making profit after its losses in the initial stage of operation have been made up in accordance with the provisions of Article 7 of the tax law.

Article 6

A participant in a joint venture, which invests its share of profit in this enterprise or in other joint ventures with Chinese and foreign investment for a period of not less than five years in succession, may receive a refund of 40 percent of the income tax already paid on the reinvested amount upon the examination and approval of the certificate of the invested enterprise by the tax authorities to which the tax was paid.

Article 7

The tax year for joint ventures starts from January 1 and ends on December 31 in the Gregorian calendar.

Article 8

The amount of taxable income shall be computed by the following formulas:

1. Industry:
   a. Cost of production of the year is equal to direct material used in production of the year plus direct wages plus manufacturing expenses.

    b.   Cost of product of the year is equal to inventory of semifinished product at the beginning of the year and in-production product plus cost of production of the year minus inventory of semifinished product at the end of the year and in-production product.

    c.   Cost of sale of product is equal to cost of product of the year plus inventory of product at the beginning of the year minus inventory of product at the end of the year.

    d.   Net volume of sale of product is equal to total volume of sale of product minus (sales returns plus sales allowance).

    e.   Profit from sale of product is equal to net volume of sale of product minus taxes on sales minus cost of sale of product minus (selling expenses plus administrative expenses).

    f.   Amount of taxable income is equal to profit from sale of product plus profit from other operations plus nonoperating income minus nonoperating expenditure.

2. Commerce:

    a.   Net volume of sale is equal to total volume of sale minus (sales returns plus sales allowance).

    b.   Cost of sales is equal to inventory of merchandise at the beginning of the year plus [purchase of the year minus (purchase returned plus purchase discount) plus purchase expenses] minus inventory of merchandise at the end of the year.

    c.   Sale profit is equal to net volume of sale minus sales tax minus cost of sales minus (selling expenses plus overhead expenses).

    d.   Amount of taxable income is equal to sale profit plus profit from other operations plus nonoperating income minus nonoperating expenditure.

3. Service trades:

    a.   Net business income is equal to gross business income minus (business tax plus operating expenses plus overhead expenses).

    b.   Amount of taxable income is equal to net business income plus nonoperating income minus nonoperating expenditure.

4. Other lines of operation:

For other lines of operation, refer to the aforementioned formulas for calculation.

Article 9

The following items shall not be counted as cost, expense, or loss in computing the amount of taxable income:

1. expenditure on the purchase or construction of machinery, equipment, buildings, facilities, and other fixed assets;

2. expenditure on the purchase of intangible assets;
3. interest on capital;
4. income-tax payment and local surtax payment;
5. penalty for illegal operations and losses in the form of confiscated property;
6. overdue tax payment and tax penalty;
7. losses from windstorms, floods, and fire risks covered by insurance indemnity;
8. donations and contributions other than those for public-welfare and relief purposes;
9. that part of the entertainment expenses for operating purposes above the quota of 3 per 1,000 of the total sale income in the tax year or above the quota of 10 per 1,000 of the total operational income and those entertainment expenses that are not relevant to production and operation.

Article 10

Depreciation of fixed assets in use shall be calculated on an annual basis. Fixed assets of joint ventures cover houses, buildings, machinery and other mechanical apparatus, means of transport, and other equipment for the purpose of production with useful life of more than one year. But items with a per-unit value of less than 500 yuan and a short useful life can be itemized as expenses according to the actual number in use.

Article 11

Fixed assets shall be assessed according to the original price.

For fixed assets used as investment, the original price shall be the purchase price plus transport fees, installation expenses, and other related expenses incurred before they are put to use.

For self-made and self-built fixed assets, the original price shall be the actual expenditures incurred in the course of manufacture or construction.

Article 12

In depreciating fixed assets, the residual value shall be assessed first and deducted from the original price, the principle being making the residual value at 10 percent of the original price; those requiring to retain a little or no residual value shall be submitted for approval to the local tax authorities.

The depreciation of fixed assets shall generally be computed in average by the straight-line method.

Article 13

The useful life for computing depreciation of fixed assets is as follows:

1. The minimum useful life for houses and buildings is twenty years.
2. The minimum useful life for trains, ships, machines and equipment, and other facilities for the purpose of production is ten years.
3. The minimum useful life for electronic equipment and means of transport other than trains and ships is five years.

For cases where the fixed assets of joint ventures, owing to special reasons, need to accelerate depreciation or where methods of depreciation need to be modified, applications shall be submitted by the said ventures to the local tax authorities for examination and then relayed level by level to the Ministry of Finance of the People's Republic of China for approval.

Article 14

Expenditures arising from the increase of value of fixed assets in use as a result of technical reform shall not be listed as expense.

The fixed assets continuing in use after full depreciation shall no longer be depreciated.

Article 15

The balance of the gain of joint ventures derived from sale of fixed assets at the current price after the net sum of nondepreciated assets or the residual value is deducted shall enter the year's loss and gain account.

Article 16

Intangible assets such as technical know-how, patent right, ownership of trademarks, copyright, ownership of sites and other royalties used as investment shall be assessed by amortization according to the sums provided in the agreements or contracts from the year they begin in use; for the intangible assets that are bought in at a fixed price, the actual payment shall be assessed from the year they are put in use.

The aforementioned intangible assets, with provision of time limit for use, shall be assessed by amortization according to the provision of time limit for use; those without the provision shall be assessed by amortization in ten years.

Article 17

Expenses arising during the period of preparation for a joint venture shall be amortized after it goes into production or business, with the amount of amortization not exceeding 20 percent each year.

Article 18

Inventory of merchandise, raw materials, in-production products, semifinished products, finished products, and by-products shall be computed according to the cost price. For the method of computation, the joint ventures may choose one of the following: first-in first-out, shifting average, and weighted average. In those cases where a change in the method of computation is necessary, it shall be submitted for approval to the local tax authorities.

Article 19

Income tax to be paid in quarterly installments as prescribed in Article 8 of the tax law may be computed as one-fourth of the planned annual profit or the actual income in the preceding year.

Article 20

Joint ventures shall file their income-tax returns and their final accounting statements with the local tax authorities within the prescribed period irrespective of profit or loss in the tax year and send the reports on auditing by the chartered public accountants registered in the People's Republic of China.

The accounting statements submitted by branches of joint ventures within China to their head offices shall be submitted to the local tax authorities at the same time for reference.

Article 21

Joint ventures shall file tax returns within the time limit set by the tax law. In case of failure to submit the tax returns within the prescribed time limit owing to special circumstances, application should be submitted in the said time limit, and the time limit may be appropriately extended upon the approval of the local tax authorities.

The final day of the time limit for tax payment and filing tax returns may be extended if it falls on an official holiday.

Article 22

Income of joint ventures in foreign currency shall be assessed according to the exchange rate quoted by the State General Administration of Foreign Exchange Control on the day when the tax-payment certificates are made out and shall be taxed in Renminbi.

Article 23

The accounting on the accrual basis shall be practiced for revenue and expenditure of joint ventures. All accounting records shall be accurate and perfect and shall have lawful vouchers as the basis for entry account.

Article 24

The method of finance and accounting of joint ventures shall be submitted to local tax authorities for reference.

When the method of finance and accounting of joint ventures contradicts the provisions of the tax law, tax payments shall be computed according to the provisions of the tax law.

Article 25

Vouchers for accounting, accounting books, and reports used by joint ventures shall be recorded in the Chinese language or in both Chinese and foreign language.

Accounting vouchers, accounting books, and reports shall be kept for at least fifteen years.

Article 26

Sales invoices and business receipts shall be submitted for approval to the local tax authorities before they are used.

Article 27

Officials sent by tax authorities shall produce identification cards when investigating the financial affairs, accounting books, and tax situation of a joint venture and undertake to keep them secret.

Article 28

Tax authorities may impose a penalty of not more than 5,000 yuan on a joint venture that has violated the provisions of Articles 9, 11, and 12 of the tax law according to the seriousness of the case.

Article 29

Tax authorities may impose a penalty of not more than 5,000 yuan on a joint venture that has violated the provisions of paragraph 2 of Article 25, and Article 26 of these detailed rules and regulations.

Article 30

Tax authorities shall serve notices on cases involving penalties in accordance with the relevant provisions of the tax law and these detailed rules and regulations.

Article 31

When a joint venture applies for reconsideration in accordance with the provisions of Article 15 of the tax law, the tax authorities concerned are required to make decisions within three months after receiving the application.

Article 32

Income tax paid abroad by joint ventures or its branches on their income earned outside China may be credited against the amount of income tax to be paid by their head offices upon presenting the foreign tax-payment certificate. But the credit amount shall not exceed the payable tax on the income abroad computed according to the tax rate prescribed by China's tax law.

Article 33

Income-tax returns and tax-payment certificates used by joint ventures are to be printed by the General Taxation Bureau of the Ministry of Finance of the People's Republic of China.

Article 34

The right of interpreting the provisions of these detailed rules and regulations resides with the Ministry of Finance of the People's Republic of China.

Article 35

These detailed rules and regulations come into force on the same date as the publication and enforcement of the Income Tax Law of the People's Republic of China Concerning Joint Ventures with Chinese and Foreign Investment.

Appendix E: Individual Income-Tax Law of the People's Republic of China

(Adopted by the Third Session of the Fifth National People's Congress on September 10, 1980)

Article 1

An individual income tax shall be levied in accordance with the provisions of this law on the incomes gained within or outside China by any individual residing for one year or more in the People's Republic of China.

For individuals not residing in the People's Republic of China or individuals residing in China less than one year, individual income tax shall be levied only on that income gained within China.

Article 2

Individual income tax shall be levied on the following categories of income:

1. wages and salaries;
2. compensation for personal services;
3. royalties;
4. interest, dividends, and bonuses;
5. income from lease of property; and
6. other kinds of income specified as taxable by the Ministry of Finance of the People's Republic of China.

Article 3

Individual income tax rates:

1. Income from wages and salaries in excess of specific amounts shall be taxed at progressive rates ranging from 5 percent to 45 percent (see appended tax-rate table).

From *China's Foreign Trade*, Supplement to no. 6 (1980), pp. 10–12.

2. Income from compensation for personal services, royalties, interest, dividends, bonuses, lease of property, and other kinds of income shall be taxed at a flat rate of 20 percent.

Article 4

The following categories of income shall be exempted from individual income tax:

1. prizes and awards for scientific, technological, or cultural achievements;
2. interest on savings deposits in the state banks and credit cooperatives of the People's Republic of China;
3. welfare benefits, survivors' pensions, and relief payments;
4. insurance indemnities;
5. military severance pay, decommission or demobilization pay for cadres and fighters of the armed forces;
6. severance pay or retirement pay for cadres, staff members, and workers;
7. salaries of diplomatic officials of foreign embassies and consulates in China;
8. tax-free incomes as stipulated in international conventions to which China is a party or as stipulated in agreements China has signed;
9. incomes approved as tax free by the Ministry of Finance of the People's Republic of China.

Article 5

The amount of taxable income shall be computed as follows:

1. For income from wages or salaries, a monthly deduction of 800 yuan shall be allowed; that part in excess of 800 yuan shall be taxed.
2. For income from compensation for personal services, royalties, or lease of property, a deduction of 800 yuan shall be allowed for expenses if the amount in a single payment is less than 4,000 yuan; for single payments in excess of 4,000 yuan, a deduction of 20 percent shall be allowed. The balance remaining after deduction shall be taxed.
3. Interest, dividends, bonuses, or other kinds of income shall be taxed on the full amount received in each payment.

Article 6

For individual income tax, the income earner shall be the party responsible for paying the tax and the paying unit shall be the withholding agent. Taxpayers not covered by withholding are required personally to file declarations of their income and pay tax themselves.

Article 7

Taxes withheld each month by a witholding agent and those to be paid each month by taxpayers filing personal returns shall be turned in to the state treasury and the tax return submitted to the tax authority within the first seven days of the following month.

Any taxpayer who earns income outside China shall pay the tax due to the state treasury and submit a tax return to the tax authority within thrity days of the end of each year.

Article 8

All incomes shall be computed in terms of Renminbi. Income in foreign currency shall be assessed according to the exchange rate quoted by the State General Administration of Foreign Exchange Control of the People's Republic of China, and shall be taxed in Renminbi.

Article 9

The tax authorities have the right to conduct investigations concerning the payment of tax. Withholding agents and taxpayers filing personal returns must report according to the facts and provide all relevant information and shall not refuse or conceal the facts.

Article 10

A commission of 1 percent of the tax amount withheld shall be paid to the withholding agents.

Article 11

A withholding agent or a taxpayer filing personal returns must pay the tax due within the prescribed time limits. In cases of failure to pay within the prescribed time limits, the appropriate tax authority, in addition to setting a new time limit for tax payment, shall surcharge overdue payments at 0.5 percent of the overdue tax for every day in arrears, starting from the first day of default.

Article 12

The tax authorities may, acting at their discretion, impose a penalty on a withholding agent or on a taxpayer filing personal returns who has violated the provisions of Article 9 of this law.

In dealing with those who have concealed income or evaded or refused to pay tax, the tax authorities may, in addition to pursuing the tax, impose a penalty not more than five times the amount of tax underpaid or not paid, according to the seriousness of the offense. Cases of gross violation shall be handled by the local people's courts according to the law.

Article 13

In cases of disputes with the tax authorities over the payment of taxes, the withholding agent or taxpayer filing personal returns must pay taxes according to the relevant regulations first before applying to higher tax authorities for reconsideration. If they do not accept the decisions made after such reconsideration, they can bring the matter before the local people's courts.

Article 14

Detailed rules and regulations for the implementation of this law shall be formulated by the Ministry of Finance of the People's Republic of China.

Article 15

This law shall come into force from the date of promulgation.

Individual Income-Tax Rates
(Applicable to wages and salaries)

Grade	Range of Income	Tax Rate (%)
1	Monthly income of 800 yuan and less	Exempt
2	Monthly income from 801 to 1,500 yuan	5
3	Monthly income from 1,501 to 3,000 yuan	10
4	Monthly income from 3,001 to 6,000 yuan	20
5	Monthly income from 6,001 to 9,000 yuan	30
6	Monthly income from 9,001 to 12,000 yuan	40
7	Monthly income above 12,000 yuan	45

Appendix F: Regulations on Labor Management in Joint Ventures Using Chinese and Foreign Investment

(Approved by the State Council of the People's Republic of China on July 26, 1980)

Article 1

Labor-management problems concerning joint ventures using Chinese and foreign investment (hereinafter referred to as *joint ventures*) should be handled in accordance with the regulations, in addition to the pertinent stipulations in Article 6 of the "Law of the People's Republic of China on Joint Ventures using Chinese and Foreign Investment."

Article 2

Matters pertaining to employment, dismissal, and resignation of the workers and staff members; tasks of production and other work; wage and awards and punishment; working time and vacation; labor insurance and welfare; labor protection and labor discipline in joint ventures should be stipulated in the labor contracts signed.

A labor contract is to be signed collectively by a joint venture and the trade-union organization formed in the joint venture. A relatively small joint venture may sign contracts with the workers and staff members individually.

A signed labor contract must be submitted to the labor-management department of the provincial, autonomous regional, or municipal people's government for approval.

Article 3

The workers and staff members of a joint venture either recommended by the authorities in the locality in charge of the joint venture or the labor-management

From *China's Foreign Trade*, Supplement to no. 6 (1980), pp. 13–14.

department, or recruited by the joint venture itself with the consent of the labor-management department, should all be selected by the joint venture through examination for their qualifications.

Joint ventures may run workers' schools and training courses for the training of managerial personnel and skilled workers.

Article 4

With regard to the surplus workers and staff members as a result of changes in production and technical conditions of the joint venture, those who fail to meet the requirements after training and are not suitable for other work can be discharged. However, this must be done in line with the stipulations in the labor contract, and the enterprise must give compensation to these workers.

The dismissed workers and staff members will receive assignment for other work from the authorities in charge of the joint venture or the labor-management department.

Article 5

The joint venture may, according to the seriousness of the case, take action against those workers or staff members who have violated rules and regulations of the enterprise that result in certain bad consequences. Punishment by discharges must be reported to the authorities in charge of the joint venture and the labor-management department for approval.

Article 6

With regard to the dismissal and punishment of workers and staff members by the joint venture, the trade union has the right to raise an objection if it considers them unreasonable, and send representatives to seek a solution through consultation with the board of directors. Should the consultation fail to arrive at a solution, the matter will be handled in accordance with the procedures set forth in Article 14 of the present regulations.

Article 7

When workers and staff members of a joint venture, on account of special conditions, submit resignation to the enterprise through the trade union in accordance with the labor contract, the enterprise should give its consent.

Article 8

The wage level of the workers and staff members in a joint venture will be determined at 120 to 150 percent of the real wages of the workers and staff members of state-owned enterprises of the same trade in the locality.

Article 9

The wage standards, the forms of wages paid, and bonus and subsidy systems are to be discussed and decided on by the board of directors.

Article 10

The bonuses and welfare funds drawn by the joint venture from the profits must be used as bonuses, awards, and collective welfare and should not be misappropriated.

Article 11

A joint venture must pay for the Chinese workers' and staff members' labor insurance, cover their medical expenses and various kinds of government subsidies in line with the standards prevailing in state-owned enterprises.

Article 12

The employment of foreign workers and staff members and their dismissal, resignation, pay, welfare and social insurances, and other matters concerned should all be stipulated in the employment contracts.

Article 13

Joint ventures must implement the relevant rules and regulations of the Chinese government on labor protection and ensure safety in production. The labor-management department of the Chinese government is authorized to supervise and inspect their implementation.

Article 14

Labor disputes occurring in a joint venture should first of all be solved through consultation by both parties. If consultation fails to arrive at a solution, either party or both parties may request arbitration by the labor-management department of the people's government of the province, autonomous region, or municipality where the joint venture is located. Either party that disagrees to the arbitration may file a suit at the people's court.

Article 15

The right of interpretation of the present regulations belongs to the State Bureau of Labor of the People's Republic of China.

Article 16

The regulations come into force on the date of its promulgation.

Appendix G:
Interim Regulations Governing the Control of Resident Offices of Foreign Enterprises
(Promulgated by the State Council of the People's Republic of China on October 30, 1980)

Article 1

The regulations hereunder are formulated with a view to facilitating the development of international economic and trade contacts and the control of resident offices in China of foreign companies, enterprises, and other economic organizations (referred to hereafter as *foreign enterprises*).

Article 2

Any foreign enterprise desiring to establish resident office in China should first of all apply for permission and after securing approval go through the registration procedure.

No foreign enterprise is allowed to start business activities in the nature of those of a resident office before approval is granted and the registration procedure completed.

Article 3

A foreign enterprise, when applying for permission to establish a resident office in China, should produce the following documents and reference materials:

1. an application form signed by the chairman of the board of directors or the general manager of that enterprise, including such details as the name of the resident office to be set up, the name(s) of the responsible member(s), the scope and duration of activity, and the site of the office;
2. the legal document sanctioning the operation of that enterprise issued by the authorities of the country or the region in which that enterprise operates;

From *Beijing Review*, December 15, 1980, pp. 25–26.

3. the capital creditability document issued by the banking institution(s) that has business contacts with that enterprise;
4. the credentials and brief biographies of the members of the resident office appointed by that enterprise.

A banking or insurance institution that desires to open a resident office should, apart from producing the documents and reference materials as specified in items 1, 2, and 4 of the foregoing section, produce at the same time an annual report on the assets and liabilities and losses and profits of the head office of that enterprise, its constitution, and the composition of its board of directors.

Article 4

Applications of foreign enterprises for permission to establish resident offices are to be approved by one of the following organizations:

1. A trader, manufacturer, or shipping agent should apply to the Ministry of Foreign Trade of the People's Republic of China for approval.
2. A banking or insurance institution should apply to the People's Bank of China for approval.
3. A maritime shipping operator or a maritime shipping agent should apply to the Ministry of Communications of the People's Republic of China for approval.
4. An air-transport enterprise should apply to the General Administration of Civil Aviation of China for approval.
5. Enterprises outside these lines of activity should, according to the nature of their operations, apply to the proper commissions, ministries, or bureaus under the government of the People's Republic of China for approval.

Article 5

When granted approval to establish a resident office, a foreign enterprise should, within thirty days of the date of approval, go to the General Administration for Industry and Commerce of the People's Republic of China on the strength of the approval document and go through the registration procedure of filling in a registration form and paying the registration fees before it is issued a registration certificate. The original approval document should be recalled in case of failure to register within the deadline.

Article 6

After approval for the establishment of a resident office is granted in accordance with the stipulations in Article 4, the members of that office and their families should, on the strength of the approval document, apply to the local public-security organ for residence permission before they are issued residence permits.

Article 7

A resident office, when desiring to change its name, its responsible member(s), scope of operation, duration, or site, should apply to the original approval-issuing organization and, after securing approval, go to the General Administration for Industry and Commerce of the People's Republic of China on the strength of the approval document and go through the procedure for effecting a change in registration and pay the fees. It should also go through the procedure with the local public-security organ for changing the residence permits.

Article 8

A resident office should, on the strength of the registration certificate and in accordance with the relevant stipulations of the Bank of China, open an account in the Bank of China or in any bank which the Bank of China may designate.

Article 9

A resident office and its members should, in accordance with the stipulations of Chinese tax laws, go through the tax laws, go through the tax registration procedure with the local tax office, and pay taxes in accordance with the regulations.

Article 10

A resident office and its members should declare to China's House of Customs the imported office articles, articles for daily use, and means of transport, and pay customs duties and industrial and commercial unified tax as stipulated.

Imported vehicles and ships should be registered with the local public-security organ before the license plates and permits are issued. Fees should be paid to the local tax office for the use of the license plates for such vehicles and ships.

Unauthorized transfer or sale of the aforementioned imported goods is not permitted. In the event of a necessary transfer or sale, an application should be submitted to the House of Customs and approval obtained before such a transfer or sale can be effected. Imported goods can be sold only to designated shops.

Article 11

A resident office should entrust local service units for foreigners or such other units as may be designated by the Chinese government on such matters as renting a house or engaging the service of Chinese personnel.

Article 12

The government of the People's Republic of China undertakes to protect, in accordance with law, the legitimate rights and interests of resident offices and their members and facilitate their normal business activities.

Article 13

The resident offices are not allowed to set up radio stations on Chinese territory. They should apply to the local telecommunications bureaus for the renting of such commercial communications lines or communications equipments as may be necessary for their business operations.

Article 14

The members of a resident office and their families should abide by Chinese laws, decrees, and relevant regulations in all their activities in China and in entering and leaving China.

Article 15

In case a resident office and its members violate the "Interim Regulations" or they are engaged in other law-breaking activities, the proper Chinese authorities have the power to look into the cases and deal with them in accordance with law.

Article 16

A resident office should submit written notification of its termination of its operations to the original approval-granting organization thirty days before the duration of its operation expires or if it decides to end its business activities before the due date and, after clearing up its debts, paying its taxes, and winding up other related matters, go through the formalities with the original registration-certificate-issuing organization for canceling the registration and turn in the certificate.

The foreign enterprise that the said resident office represented should continue to be held responsible for any matter that the said resident office may leave unfinished at the time of its termination.

Article 17

Those resident offices that have already been established with approval should, within thirty days of the promulgation of the "Interim Regulations," go through the procedure of registration with the General Administration for Industry and Commerce of the People's Republic of China on the strength of the documents of approval.

Article 18

Any other matters that are not covered in the "Interim Regulations" should be handled in accordance with the relevant Chinese laws, decrees, and regulations.

Article 19

The "Interim Regulations" should apply to any foreign enterprise that desires to appoint a resident representative(s) as to those desiring to establish resident offices.

Article 20

The "Interim Regulations" go into effect on the day of promulgation.

Appendix H:
Statutes of Association of the China International Trust and Investment Corporation

1. General Principles

Article 1

The China International Trust and Investment Corporation (CITIC) (hereafter called *the Corporation*) is a state-owned socialist enterprise operating under the direct leadership of the State Council of the People's Republic of China.

Article 2

The function of the Corporation is to introduce, absorb, and apply foreign investment and advanced technology, and to import advanced equipment and bring in advanced technology for purposes of China's national construction and promotion of socialist modernization of our country pursuant to the provisions of the Law of the People's Republic of China on Joint Ventures Using Chinese and Foreign Investment and other relevant laws and regulations.

Article 3

The capital of the Corporation shall be 200,000,000 yuan (Renminbi).

Article 4

The Corporation shall resolutely abide by socialist principles, observe economic laws in its operations, and employ modern and scientific methods of management.

Article 5

The head office of the Corporation shall be in Beijing, with a branch office in Xianggang (Hong Kong). Other branch offices, subsidiaries, subbranch offices, or agencies shall be set up inside and outside of China when the need arises.

From China International Trust and Investment Corporation, Beijing (1979).

2. Scope of Operation

Article 6

The Corporation shall undertake under commission of foreign corporations, enterprises, other economic entities, or individuals to negotiate and enter into short-term or long-term joint-venture agreements and related contracts with the various local administrations and departments in China, and the corporations, enterprises, and other economic entities thereunder; and shall render them services by way of making introductions, giving consultation, and providing information for the purposes of setting up joint ventures and short-term or long-term technological cooperation.

Article 7

The Corporation shall undertake under commission of the different ministries and local administrations and departments in China, and the corporations, enterprises, and other economic entities thereunder, to negotiate and enter into short-term or long-term joint-venture agreements and related contracts with foreign corporations, enterprises, other economic entities, or individuals; and shall render them services by way of making introductions, giving consultation, and providing information for the purposes of setting up joint ventures and short-term or long-term technological cooperation.

Article 8

The Corporation shall accept funds from foreign corporations, enterprises, other economic entities, or individuals, or shall raise funds abroad for investment in China by using debentures of the Corporation or by serving as agents in the issue of the shares related to investment in China, and shall handle trustee business of short-term or long-term investments in China.

Article 9

The Corporation shall render services to foreign corporations, foreign enterprises, other foreign economic entities, or individuals; and to the different ministries, administrations, and departments in China; and the corporations, enterprises, and other economic entities thereunder by way of providing introduction to and information on the relevant laws and regulations, taxation provisions, foreign-exchange control, wages for labor, accounting, and auditing on joint-venture enterprises.

Article 10

The Corporation may act as agents under contract with foreign manufacturers and merchants in business activities relating to advanced technology and equipment.

Article 11

The Corporation may out of business necessity engage in joint ventures inside and outside of China, or make investment single-handed by itself.

3. Organization

Article 12

The highest organ of authority of the Corporation is the board of directors. The board of directors consists of a chairman, vice-chairmen, executive directors, and directors nominated by the State Council. The functions of the board are:

1. to lay down the short-term and long-term business policies and operational programs of the Corporation pursuant to the spirit of directives from the State Council;
2. to appoint the president and vice-presidents, subject to the State Council's approval of such appointments;
3. to examine and approve the infrastructure of the Corporation and the setting up and closing down of its branches and subsidiaries inside and outside of China as proposed by the president;
4. to examine and approve the above-norm investment projects as submitted by the president;
5. to examine and approve the Corporation's annual financial reports and proposals for distribution of profits as submitted by the president;
6. to receive and examine the reports of the president on the work of the Corporation;
7. to make reports to the State Council on the major business activities of the Corporation.

Article 13

The president shall be responsible for the overall operation and administration of the Corporation. The vice-presidents shall assist him in his work. The functions of the president shall be:

1. to carry out effectively the business policies and operational programs of the Corporation as laid down by the board of directors;
2. to be responsible for organizing the infrastructure of the Corporation and its branches and subsidiaries inside and outside of China, to appoint and dismiss the key officers and foreign specialists of the Corporation, and to make reports to the board of directors for record on file;
3. to examine and make decisions on investment projects, to submit reports to the board of directors on the above-norm investment projects for approval;

4. to submit to the board of directors the annual financial reports and pro-
    posals for distribution of profits;
5. to make periodic reports to the board of directors regularly on the work
    of the Corporation.

4. Management

Article 14

The Corporation shall establish its own independent business operation with
an independent financial and accounting system.

Article 15

The Corporation shall devise and adopt appropriate operational plans and
measures to suit its short-term and long-term business policies and operational
programs in order to carry on the business of the Corporation in a planned
and effective manner.

Article 16

The joint-venture projects undertaken by the Corporation in trust must posses the
ability to redeem in foreign exchange. The Corporation shall be under an obligation to examine, supervise, and promote the work of such joint-venture projects.

Article 17

The Corporation shall conduct individual audits of accounts of the entrusted
investment projects and review their economic performance.

Article 18

The Corporation shall employ its personnel according to their merits, and shall
try out a contract system in employing its staff members. The Corporation
shall effectively adopt a wage system on the principle of distribution of reward
in proportion to work done and shall promote and censure them according
to performance gradings.

5. Others

Article 19

These articles of statute shall become effective as of the date of approval by the
State Council. The same applies in the event of alterations.

Appendix I:
Provisional Regulations for Exchange Control of the People's Republic of China
(Promulgated by the State Council on December 18, 1980; Entered into Force on March 1, 1981)

Chapter I: General Provisions

Article 1

These provisional regulations are formulated for the purpose of strengthening exchange control, increasing national foreign-exchange income, and economizing on foreign-exchange expenditure so as to expedite the national economic growth and safeguard the rights and interests of the country.

All foreign-exchange income and expenditure; the issuance and circulation of all kinds of payment instruments in foreign currency; dispatch and carriage into and out of the People's Republic of China of foreign exchange, precious metals, and payment instruments in foreign currency shall be governed by these regulations.

Article 2

Foreign exchange herein mentioned refers to:

1. foreign currencies, including bank notes, coins, and so forth;
2. securities in foreign currency, including government bonds, treasury bills, corporate bonds and debentures, shares, interest and dividend coupons, and so forth;
3. instruments payable in foreign currency, including bills, drafts, checks, bank deposit certificates, postal savings certificates, and so forth;
4. other foreign-exchange funds.

From *Beijing Review*, January 26, 1981, pp. 25–28.

Article 3

The People's Republic of China pursues the policy of centralized control and unified management of foreign exchange by the state.

The administrative organ in charge of exchange control of the People's Republic of China is the State General Administration of Exchange Control (SGAEC) and its branch offices.

The specialized foreign-exchange bank of the People's Republic of China is the Bank of China. No other financial institution shall engage in foreign-exchange business, unless approved by the SGAEC.

Article 4

All Chinese and foreign organizations and individuals in the People's Republic of China must, unless otherwise stipulated by law or decree or in these regulations, sell their foreign-exchange proceeds to the Bank of China. Any foreign exchange required is to be sold to them by the Bank of China in accordance with the quota approved by the state or with relevant regulations.

The circulation, use, and mortgage of foreign currency in the People's Republic of China are prohibited. Unauthorized sales and purchases of foreign exchange and unlawfully seizing possession of foreign exchange in whatever ways and by whatever means are prohibited.

Chapter II: Exchange Control Relating to State Organizations and Collective Economic Units

Article 5

Foreign-exchange income and expenditure of state organs, armed-forces units, nongovernmental bodies, educational institutions, state enterprises, government establishments, and urban and rural collective economic units in China (hereinafter referred to as *domestic organizations*) are all subject to control according to plan.

Domestic organizations are permitted to retain a proportion of their foreign-exchange receipts in accordance with relevant regulations.

Article 6

Unless approved by the SGAEC or its branch offices, domestic organizations shall not: possess foreign exchange; deposit foreign exchange abroad; offset foreign-exchange expenditure against foreign-exchange income; or use the foreign exchange belonging to state organs stationed abroad or Chinese enterprises and establishments resident in foreign countries or in Hong Kong and Macao, by way of borrowing or acquisition.

Article 7

Unless approved by the State Council, domestic organizations shall not issue securities with foreign-exchange value inside or outside China.

Article 8

Departments under the State Council and people's governments of various provinces, municipalities, and autonomous regions shall compile annual overall plans for domestic organizations under their respective jurisdiction whereby loans may be accepted from banks or enterprises in foreign countries or in Hong Kong and Macao. These plans shall be submitted to the SGAEC and the Foreign Investment Commission for examination and forwarded to the State Council for approval.

The procedure for examining and approving individual borrowings shall be prescribed separately.

Article 9

The portion of foreign exchange retained by domestic organizations, nontrade foreign exchange and foreign exchange under compensatory trade received in advance for later payments, funds borrowed in convertible foreign currency, and other foreign exchange held with the approval of the SGAEC or its branch offices must be placed in foreign-currency deposit accounts or foreign-currency quota accounts to be opened with the Bank of China, and must be used within the prescribed scope and be subject to the supervision of the Bank of China.

Article 10

When domestic organizations import or export goods, the banks handling the transactions shall check their foreign-exchange receipts and payments either against the import or export licenses duly verified by the customs or against the customs declaration forms for imports or exports.

Article 11

State organs stationed abroad must use foreign exchange according to the plan approved by the state.

The operating profits of enterprises and establishments in foreign countries or in Hong Kong and Macao must, except for the portion kept locally as working funds according to the plan approved by the state, be transferred back on scheduled time and be sold to the Bank of China.

No Chinese organization stationed abroad is permitted to keep foreign exchange for domestic organizations without authorization.

Article 12

Delegations and work groups sent temporarily to foreign countries or to Hong Kong and Macao must use foreign exchange according to their respective specific plans and must, upon their return, promptly transfer back to China their surplus foreign exchange to be checked by and sold to the Bank of China.

Foreign exchange earned in their various business activities by the delegations and work groups referred to in the foregoing paragraph, and by members thereof, must be promptly transferred back to China and must not be kept abroad without the approval of the SGAEC or its branch offices.

Chapter III: Exchange Control Relating to Individuals

Article 13

Foreign exchange remitted from foreign countries or from Hong Kong and Macao to Chinese or foreign nationals or stateless persons residing in China must be sold to the Bank of China, except the portion retained as permitted by the state.

Article 14

Chinese and foreign nationals and stateless persons residing in China are permitted to keep in their own possession foreign exchange already in China.

The foreign exchange referred to in the preceding paragraph shall not, without authorization, be carried out or sent out of China either in person or by others or by post. If the owners wish to sell the foreign exchange, they must sell it to the Bank of China and are permitted to retain a portion thereof as convertible foreign currency according to the percentage prescribed by the state.

Article 15

When foreign exchange that has been kept in foreign countries or in Hong Kong and Macao by Chinese residents in China prior to the founding of the People's Republic of China, by overseas Chinese prior to their returning to and settling down in China, or by Hong Kong and Macao compatriots prior to their returning to and settling down in their home places is transferred to China, the owners are permitted to retain a portion thereof as convertible foreign currency according to the percentage prescribed by the state.

Article 16

When foreign exchange belonging personally to individuals sent to work or study in foreign countries or in Hong Kong and Macao is remitted or brought back to China, the owners returning after completion of their missions are permitted to retain the entire amount as convertible foreign currency.

Article 17

The percentages of foreign-exchange retention permitted under Articles 13, 14, and 15 of these regulations shall be prescribed separately.

Foreign exchange retained by individuals as permitted under Articles 13, 14, 15, and 16 of these regulations must be deposited with the Bank of China. These foreign-exchange deposits may be sold to the Bank of China or remitted out of China against certification by the Bank of China. It is, however, not permitted, without authorization, to carry or send deposit certificates out of China either in person or by others or by post.

Article 18

Foreign exchange remitted or brought into China from foreign countries or from Hong Kong and Macao by foreign nationals coming to China; by overseas Chinese and Hong Kong and Macao compatriots returning for a short stay; by foreign experts, technicians, staff members, and workers engaged to work in domestic organizations; and by foreign students and trainees may be kept in their own possession, sold to or deposited with the Bank of China, or remitted or taken out of China.

Article 19

Chinese and foreign nationals and stateless persons residing in China may apply to the local branch offices of the SGAEC for the purchase of foreign exchange to be remitted or taken out of China. When approved, the required foreign exchange will be sold to the applicants by the Bank of China.

When foreign experts, technicians, staff members, and workers engaged to work in domestic organizations require foreign exchange to be remitted or taken out of China, the Bank of China will deal with their applications in accordance with the stipulations in the contracts or agreements.

Chapter IV: Exchange Control Relating to Foreign Representatives in China and Their Personnel

Article 20

Foreign exchange remitted or brought into China from foreign countries or from Hong Kong and Macao by foreign diplomatic missions, consulates, official commercial offices, offices of international organizations and nongovernmental bodies resident in China, diplomatic officials and consuls, as well as members of the permanent staff of the aforementioned units, may be kept in their own possession, sold to or deposited with the Bank of China, or remitted or taken out of China.

Article 21

The conversion into foreign currency, if required, of visa and certification fees received in Renminbi from Chinese citizens by foreign diplomatic missions and consulates in China, is subject to approval by the SGAEC or its branch offices.

Chapter V: Exchange Control Relating to Enterprises with Overseas Chinese Capital, Enterprises with Foreign Capital, and Chinese and Foreign Joint Ventures and Their Personnel

Article 22

All foreign-exchange receipts of enterprises with overseas Chinese capital, enterprises with foreign capital, and Chinese and foreign joint ventures must be deposited with the Bank of China; and all their foreign-exchange disbursements must be paid from their foreign-exchange deposit accounts.

The enterprises referred to in the preceding paragraph must submit periodic reports and statements of their foreign-exchange business to the SGAEC or its branch offices, all of which are empowered to inspect their activities with respect to their foreign-exchange receipts and payments.

Article 23

Except where otherwise approved by the SGAEC or its branch offices, Renminbi should in all cases be used in the settlement of accounts between enterprises with overseas Chinese capital, enterprises with foreign capital, Chinese and foreign joint ventures, and other enterprises and individuals residing in the People's Republic of China.

Article 24

Enterprises with overseas Chinese capital, enterprises with foreign capital, and foreign partners in Chinese and foreign ventures may apply to the Bank of China for remitting abroad their net profits after tax as well as other legitimate earnings by debiting the foreign-exchange deposit accounts of the enterprises concerned.

The enterprises and foreign partners referred to in the preceding paragraph should apply to the SGAEC or its branch offices for transferring foreign-exchange deposit accounts of the enterprises concerned.

Article 25

An amount not exceeding 50 percent of their net wages and other legitimate earnings after tax may be remitted or taken out of China in foreign currency by staff members and workers of foreign nationality and those from Hong Kong and Macao employed by enterprises with overseas Chinese capital, enterprises with foreign capital, and Chinese and foreign joint ventures.

Article 26

Enterprises with overseas Chinese capital, enterprises with foreign capital, and Chinese and foreign joint ventures that wind up operations in accordance with legal procedure should be responsible for the liquidation within the scheduled period of their outstanding liabilities and taxes due in China, under the joint supervision of the relevant departments in charge and the SGAEC or its branch offices.

Chapter VI: Control Relating to Carrying Foreign Exchange, Precious Metals and Payment Instruments in Foreign Currency into and Out of China

Article 27

No restriction on the amount is imposed on the carrying into China of foreign exchange, precious metals, and objects made from them; but declaration to the customs is required at the place of entry.

To carry foreign exchange out of China or to carry out of China the foreign exchange previously brought in shall be permitted by the customs against certification by the Bank of China or against the original declaration form at the time of entry.

To carry out of China precious metals and objects made from them or to carry out of China the precious metals and objects made from them previously brought in shall be permitted by the customs according to the specific circumstances as prescribed by the government regulations or against the original declaration form at the time of entry.

Article 28

Renminbi travelers' checks, travelers' letters of credit, and other Renminbi payment instruments convertible into foreign currency may be brought into China against declaration to the customs, and taken out of China against certification by the Bank of China or against the original declaration form at the time of entry.

Article 29

Unless otherwise approved by the SGAEC or its branch offices, the carrying or sending out of China either in person or by others or by post of the following documents and securities held by Chinese residing in China is not permitted: bonds; debentures; share certificates issued abroad; title deeds for real estate abroad; documents or deeds necessary in dealing with creditor's right or owner's right to possession regarding inheritance, real estate, and other foreign-exchange assets.

Article 30

The carrying or sending out of China of Renminbi checks, drafts, passbooks, deposit certificates, and other Renminbi instruments held by Chinese or foreign nationals or stateless persons residing in China is not permitted, either in person or by others or by post.

Chapter VII: Supplementary Provisions

Article 31

All units and individuals have the right to report any violation of these regulations. Rewards shall be given to such units or individuals according to the merit of the report. Violators shall be penalized by the SGAEC or its branch offices, by the departments of public security, by the departments of administration of industry and commerce, or by the customs. According to the seriousness of the offense, the penalties may take the form of compulsory exchange of the foreign currency for Renminbi, or fine or confiscation of the properties or both, or punishment by judicial authorities according to law.

Article 32

The exchange-control regulations for special economic zones, for trade in border areas, and for personal dealings between inhabitants across the border shall be formulated by the people's governments of the provinces, municipalities, and autonomous regions concerned with the spirit of these regulations and in light of specific local conditions, and shall be enforced on the approval of the State Council.

Article 33

Detailed provisions for the enforcement of these regulations shall be formulated by the SGAEC.

Article 34

These regulations shall come into force on March 1, 1981.

Appendix J:
Regulations on Special Economic Zones in Guangdong Province

(Approved by the Fifteenth Session of the Standing Committee of the Fifth National People's Congress on August 26, 1980)

Chapter I: General Principles

Article 1

Certain areas are delineated from the three cities of Shenzhen, Zhuhai, and Shantou in Guangdong Province to form special economic zones (hereinafter referred to as *special zones*) in order to develop external economic cooperation and technical exchanges and promote the socialist modernization program. In the special zones, foreign citizens, overseas Chinese, compatriots in Hong Kong and Macao, and their companies and enterprises (hereinafter referred to as *investors*) are encouraged to open factories or set up enterprises and other establishments with their own investment or undertake joint ventures with Chinese investment, and their assets, due profits, and other legitimate rights and interests are legally protected.

Article 2

Enterprises and individuals in the special zones must abide by the laws, decrees, and related regulations of the People's Republic of China. Where there are specific provisions contained in the present regulations, they have to be observed as stipulated herewith.

Article 3

A Guangdong Provincial Administration of Special Economic Zones is set up to exercise unified management of the special zones on behalf of the Guangdong Provincial People's Government.

From *China's Foreign Trade*, Supplement to no. 6 (1980), pp. 14–15.

Article 4

In the special zones investors are offered a wide scope of operation, favorable conditions for such operation are created, and stable business sites are guaranteed. All items of industry, agriculture, livestock, breeding, fish breeding and poultry farming, tourism, housing and construction, research and manufacture involving high technologies and techniques that have positive significance in international economic cooperation and technical exchanges, as well as other trades of common interest to investors and the Chinese side, can be established with foreign investment or in joint venture with Chinese investment.

Article 5

Land-leveling projects and various public utilities in the special zones, such as water supply, drainage, power supply, roads, wharves, communications, and warehouses, are undertaken by the Guangdong Provincial Administration of Special Economic Zones. When necessary, foreign-capital participation in their development can be considered.

Article 6

Specialists at home and abroad and personages who are enthusiastic about China's modernization program will be invited by each of the special zones to form an advisory board as a consultative body for that special zone.

Chapter II: Registration and Operation

Article 7

Investors wishing to open factories or take up various economic undertakings with their investment should apply to the Guangdong Provincial Administration of the Special Economic Zones, and will be issued licenses of registry and use of land after examination and approval.

Article 8

Investors can open accounts and deal with matters related to foreign exchange in the Bank of China in the special zones or other banks set up in the special zones with China's approval.

Investors can apply for insurance policies at the People's Insurance Company of China in the special zones and other insurance companies set up in the special zones with China's approval.

Article 9

Products of the enterprises in the special zones are to be sold in the international market. If an enterprise wants to sell its products in the domestic market in China, it must have the approval of the Guangdong Provincial Administration of Special Economic Zones and pay customs duties.

Article 10

Investors can operate their enterprises independently in the special zones and employ foreign personnel for technical and administrative work.

Article 11

If investors want to terminate their business in the special zones, they should submit the reasons for their termination to the Guangdong Provincial Administration of Special Economic Zones, go through related procedures, and clear the debts. The assets of the closed enterprises can be transferred, and the funds can be remitted out of China.

Chapter III: Preferential Treatment

Article 12

The land in the special zones remain the property of the People's Republic of China. Land to be used by investors will be provided according to actual needs; and the length of tenure, rent, and method of payment will be given favorable consideration according to the different trades and uses. Concrete methods will be specified separately.

Article 13

Machinery, spare parts, raw materials, vehicles, and other means of production for the enterprises in the special zones are exempted from import duties. The necessary consumer goods shall be subject to full or lower import duties or exempted, depending on the merits of each case. Imports of the aforementioned goods and exports of products of the special zones must go through existing customs procedures.

Article 14

The rate of income tax levied on the enterprises in the special zones is to be 15 percent. Special preferential treatment will be given to enterprises established within two years of the promulgation of these regulations, enterprises with an investment of U.S. $5 million or more, and enterprises involving advanced technologies or having a longer cycle of capital turnover.

Article 15

Legitimate after-tax profits of the investors, salaries, and other proper earnings after paying personal income tax of the foreign, overseas Chinese, and Hong Kong and Macao workers and staff members of the enterprises in the special zones can be remitted out of China through the Bank of China or other banks in the special zones in line with the zone's foreign-exchange control measures.

Article 16

Investors who reinvest their profits in the special zones for five years or longer may apply for exemption of income tax on profits from such investment.

Article 17

Enterprises in the special zones are encouraged to use Chinese-made machinery, raw materials, and other goods. Preferential prices will be offered on the basis of the export prices of China's similar commodities and settled in foreign exchange. These products and materials can be shipped directly to the special zones with the vouchers of the selling units.

Article 18

Entry and exit procedures will be simplified and convenience offered to the foreigners, overseas Chinese, and compatriots in Hong Kong and Macao going in and out of the special zones.

Chapter IV: Labor Management

Article 19

Labor-service companies are to be set up in each of the special zones. Chinese staff members and workers to be employed by enterprises in the special zones are to be recommended by the local labor-service companies or recruited by the investors with the consent of the Guangdong Provincial Administration of Special Economic Zones. Enterprises can test them before employment and sign labor contracts with them.

Article 20

The employees of the enterprises in the special zones are to be managed by the enterprises according to their business requirements and, if necessary, can be dismissed in line with the provisions of the labor contracts.

Employees of the enterprises in the special zones can submit resignation to their enterprises according to the provisions of the labor contracts.

Article 21

Scales and forms of the wages, award methods, labor insurance, and various state subsidies of the Chinese staff members and workers in the enterprises are to be included in the contracts signed between the enterprises and the employees in accordance with the stipulations of the Guangdong Provincial Administration of Special Economic Zones.

Article 22

Enterprises in the special zones should have the necessary measures for labor protection to ensure that the staff members and workers work in safe and hygienic conditions.

Chapter V: Administration

Article 23

The Guangdong Provincial Administration of Special Economic Zones exercises the following functions:

1. draw up development plans for the special zones and organize for their implementation;
2. examine and approve investment projects of investors in the special zones;
3. deal with the registration of industrial and commercial enterprises in the special zones and with land allotment;
4. coordinate the working relations among the banking, insurance, taxation, customs, frontier inspection, postal and telecommunications, and other organizations in the special zones;
5. provide staff members and workers needed by the enterprises in the special zones and protect the legitimate rights and interests of these staff members and workers;
6. run education, cultural, health, and other public welfare facilities in the special zones;
7. maintain law and order in the special zones and protect according to law the persons and properties in the special zones from encroachment.

Article 24

The Shenzhen Special Zone is under the direct jurisdiction of the Guangdong Provincial Administration of Special Economic Zones. Necessary agencies are to be set up in the Zhuhai and Shantou Special zones.

Article 25

A Guandong Provincial Special Economic Zones Development Company is to be set up to cope with the economic activities in the special zones. Its scope of business includes fund raising and trust investment, operating enterprises or joint ventures with investors in the special zones, acting as agents for the investors in the special zones in matters related to sales and purchases with other parts of China outside the special zones, and providng services for business talks.

Chapter VI: Appendix

Article 26

These regulations shall be enforced after their adoption by the Guangdong Provincial People's Congress and after they have been submitted to and approved by the Standing Committee of the National People's Congress of the People's Republic of China.

Appendix K:
China's Marriage Law
(Adopted at the Third Session of the Fifth National People's Congress on September 10, 1980)

Chapter I: General Principles

Article 1

This law is the fundamental code governing marriage and family relations.

Article 2

The marriage system based on the free choice of partners, on monogamy, and on equal rights for the sexes, is put into effect.

The lawful rights and interests of women, children, and the aged are protected. Family planning is practiced.

Article 3

Marriage upon arbitrary decision by any third party, mercenary marriage, and any other acts of interference in the freedom of marriage are prohibited. The exaction of money or gifts in connection with marriage is prohibited.

Bigamy is prohibited. Within the family, maltreatment and desertion are prohibited.

Chapter II: Marriage Contract

Article 4

Marriage must be based on the complete willingness of the two parties. Neither party shall use compulsion, and no third party is allowed to interfere.

From *Beijing Review*, March 16, 1981, pp. 24–27.

Article 5

No marriage shall be contracted before the man has reached twenty-two years of age and the woman twenty years of age. Late marriage and late childbirth should be encouraged.

Article 6

Marriage is not permitted in any of the following circumstances: (1) where the man and woman are lineal relatives by blood or collateral relatives by blood (up to the third degree of relationship); (2) where one party is suffering from leprosy, a cure not having been effected, or from any other disease that is regarded by medical science as rendering a person unfit for marriage.

Article 7

Both the man and the woman desiring to contract a marriage shall register in person with the marriage-registration office. If the proposed marriage is found to be in conformity with the provisions of this law, registration shall be granted and a marriage certificate issued. The relationship of husband and wife is established when a marriage certificate is acquired.

Article 8

After a marriage has been registered, the woman may become a member of the man's family, or the man may become a member of the woman's family, according to the agreed wishes of the two parties.

Chapter III: Family Relations

Article 9

Husband and wife enjoy equal status in the home.

Article 10

Husband and wife each has the right to use his or her family name.

Article 11

Both husband and wife have the freedom to engage in production, to work, to study, and to participate in social activities; neither party is allowed to restrain or interfere with the other.

Article 12

Husband and wife are in duty bound to practice family planning.

Article 13

The property acquired during the period in which husband and wife are under contract of marriage is in the joint possession of the two parties unless they have agreed otherwise.

Husband and wife enjoy equal rights in the management of the property in their joint possession.

Article 14

Husband and wife have the duty to support and assist each other.

When one party fails to perform this duty, the party in need of support and assistance has the right to demand that the other party pay the cost of support and assistance.

Article 15

Parents have the duty to rear and educate their children; children have the duty to support and assist their parents.

When parents fail to perform this duty, their children who are minors or who are not capable of living on their own have the right to demand that their parents pay for their care.

When children fail to perform the duty of supporting their parents, parents who have lost the ability to work or have difficulties in providing for themselves have the right to demand that their children pay for their support.

Infanticide by drowning and any other acts causing serious harm to infants are prohibited.

Article 16

Children may adopt either their father's or their mother's family name.

Article 17

Parents have the right and duty to subject their children who are minors to discipline and to protect them. When children who are minors have done harm to the state, to the collective, or to any other person, their parents are in duty bound to compensate for any economic loss.

Article 18

Husband and wife have the right to inherit each other's property.

Parents and children have the right to inherit each other's property.

Article 19

Children born out of wedlock enjoy the same rights as children born in lawful wedlock. No person shall harm them or discriminate against them.

The father of a child born out of wedlock must bear part or the whole of the cost of maintenance and education of the child until he or she can live on his or her own.

Article 20

The state protects lawful adoption. The relevant provisions in this law governing the relations between parents and children are applicable to the rights and duties in the relations between foster parents and their foster children.

The rights and duties in the relations between foster children and their natural parents are terminated on the establishment of relationship of adoption.

Article 21

No maltreatment or discrimination is allowed between stepparents and their stepchildren.

The relevant provisions in this law governing the relations between parents and children are applicable to the rights and duties in the relations between stepfathers or stepmothers and their stepchildren who receive care and education from their stepparents.

Article 22

Grandparents or maternal grandparents who have the capacity to bear the relevant costs have the duty to rear their grandchildren or maternal grandchildren who are minors and whose parents are deceased. Grandchildren and maternal grandchildren who have the capacity to bear the relevant costs have the duty to support and assist their grandparents or maternal grandparents whose children are deceased.

Article 23

Elder brothers or elder sisters who have the capacity to bear the relevant costs have the duty to rear their minor younger brothers or sisters whose parents either are deceased or have no capacity to rear them.

Chapter IV: Divorce

Article 24

Divorce is granted when husband and wife both desire it. Both parties should apply for divorce to the marriage-registration office. The marriage-registration office, after clearly establishing that divorce is desired by both parties and that appropriate measures have been taken for the care of any children and property, should issue the divorce certificate without delay.

Article 25

When one party insists on divorce, the organizations concerned may try to effect a reconciliation, or the party may appeal directly to the people's court for divorce.

In dealing with a divorce case, the people's court should try to bring about a reconciliation between the parties. In cases of complete alienation of mutual affection, and when mediation has failed, divorce should be granted.

Article 26

If the spouse of a member of the armed forces on active service insists on divorce, consent must be obtained from the member concerned.

Article 27

The husband is not allowed to apply for a divorce when his wife is pregnant or within one year after the birth of a child. This restriction does not apply in the case of the wife applying for divorce, or when the people's court deems it absolutely necessary to agree to deal with a divorce application by the husband.

Article 28

After divorce, if both parties desire to resume husband-and-wife relations, they should apply to the marriage-registration office for a registration of remarriage. The marriage-registration office should accept such a registration.

Article 29

The blood ties between parents and children are not ended by the divorce of the parents. Whether the father or the mother has the custody of the children, they remain the children of both parties.

After divorce, both parents continue to have the right and duty to rear and educate their children.

The guiding principle after divorce is to allow the mother to have the custody of a breast-fed infant. If a dispute arises between the two parties over the guardianship of a child after weaning and agreement cannot be reached, the people's court should make a judgment in accordance with the rights and interests of the child and the circumstances of both parties.

Article 30

If, after divorce, one party is given custody of a child, the other party is responsible for part or all of the necessary cost of the maintenance and education of the child. The two parties should reach an agreement regarding the amount of the cost and the duration of its payment for such maintenance and education. If such an agreement is lacking, the people's court should make a judgment.

Article 31

In case of divorce, the disposal of the property in the joint possession of husband and wife is subject to agreement between the two parties. In cases where agreement cannot be reached, the people's court should make a judgment after taking into consideration the actual state of the family property and the rights and interests of the wife and the child or children.

Article 32

In cases of divorce, debts incurred jointly by husband and wife during the period of their married life should be paid off out of their joint property. In cases where such property is insufficient to pay off such debts, the two parties should work out an agreement with regard to the payment; if an agreement cannot be reached, the people's court should make a judgment. Debts incurred separately by the husband or wife should be paid off by the party responsible.

Article 33

In case of divorce, if one party has maintenance difficulties, the other party should render appropriate financial assistance. Both parties should work out an agreement with regard to the details; in case an agreement cannot be reached, the people's court should make a judgment.

Chapter V: By-Laws

Article 34

Persons violating this law should be subject to administrative disciplinary measures or legal sanctions according to law and the circumstances.

Article 35

In cases where the relevant party refuses to execute judgments or rulings regarding maintenance, costs of upbringing, or support, or regarding the division or inheritance of property, the people's court has the power to enforce their execution in accordance with the law. The organizations concerned have the duty to assist such execution.

Article 36

The people's congresses and their standing committees in national autonomous regions may enact certain modifications or supplementary articles in keeping with the principles of this law and in conformity with the actual conditions prevailing among the minority nationalities of the locality in regard to marriage and family relations. But such provisions enacted by autonomous prefectures and autonomous counties must be submitted to the standing committee of the provincial or regional people's congresses for ratification. Provisions enacted by autonomous regions must be submitted to the Standing Committee of the National People's Congress for the record.

Article 37

This law comes into force on January 1, 1981.

The Marriage Law of the People's Republic of China promulgated on May 1, 1950, shall be repealed as of the date of the coming into force of this law.

Appendix L:
Basic Principles of the
Law of Criminal
Procedure
(Effective January 1, 1980)

Principle 1

Exercise powers and functions according to law. Article 3 stipulates: "The public security organ conducts the investigation, provisional apprehension and pretrial of the criminal cases. The people's procuratorate is in charge of approving arrests, conducting procuratorial control (including investigation), and preferring public charges. The people's court administers justice. No government organs, people's organizations or individuals other than these shall have such powers." These are the three organs that implement laws and supervise law enforcement.

Principle 2

Relying on the masses. Article 4 stipulates: In criminal proceedings, the people's court, the people's procuratorate, and the public-security organ "shall rely on the masses."

As all criminals commit their offenses against the masses, they are bound to leave some traces of their actions among the people. Therefore, if we rely on the masses when making investigations, we can clear up cases more quickly and more accurately.

Judicial organs must canvass people's opinions widely and get their help—this is a special feature of the Chinese legal system. Professional judicial workers and professional legal knowledge are indispensable. But practice in past years proves that support and cooperation from the masses are important conditions in breaking cases and handling them correctly as well as in preventing the occurrence of crime.

Principle 3

Base oneself on facts, take law as the criterion. Article 4 stipulates: In criminal proceedings, the people's court, the people's procuratorate, and the public-security organ "shall base themselves on facts and take law as the criterion."

From *Beijing Review*, June 9, 1980, pp. 23–26.

Taking law as the criterion means the laws must be complied with, their enforcement must be strict, and lawbreakers must be dealt with.

The law of criminal procedure stipulates: In dealing with all cases, "stress should be laid on evidence and investigation, and one should not be too ready to believe the confession of an accused. An accused shall not be sentenced without evidence other than his confession; he shall be convicted and punished on the basis of sufficient evidence even without his confession" (Article 35). "It is strictly forbidden to extort confession by torture or to gather evidence by illegal means such as threats, enticement, or deception" (Article 32).

Articles 68 and 115 stipulate that a witness should produce true evidence and testimony. He will be dealt with according to law if he intentionally commits perjury or conceals evidence.

Principle 4

All citizens are equal before the law. Article 4 stipulates: In criminal proceedings, "in the application of the law, all citizens are deemed equal; no privilege whatsoever is permissible before the law." With respect to administration of the law, all citizens are equal irrespective of nationality, race, sex, profession, social origin, religious belief, education, property, or term of residence. Anyone who violates the law will be held criminally responsible regardless of his social position.

Principle 5

Division of work and responsibilities, coordination, and mutual restriction. Article 5 stipulates: "In criminal proceedings, the people's court, the people's procuratorate, and the public-security organ shall have a division of work and responsibilities, and coordinate and restrict one another, so as to guarantee accurate and effective enforcement of law." Accordingly, a number of specific regulations have been drawn up with respect to the law of criminal procedure:

"The arrest of an accused shall be carried out by the public-security organ upon approval by the people's procuratorate or decision by the people's court" (Article 39).

"Where the public-security organ considers a decision of nonapproval of arrest made by the people's procuratorate to be incorrect, it may request a reconsideration" (Article 49).

Where the people's procuratorate "finds out about an unlawful practice on the part of the public-security organ engaging in an investigation, the latter shall be instructed to put it right" (Article 52).

"Upon conclusion of an investigation conducted by the public-security organ, a written opinion for a public charge or exemption from a public charge shall be prepared, which shall be transmitted together with the files of the case and the evidence to the people's procuratorate at the same level for examination and decision" (Article 93).

Where the public-security organ holds that a decision of exemption from a public charge taken by a people's procuratorate on a case transferred from a public-security organ is incorrect, it may request a reconsideration; and where its request is rejected, it may submit the case to the people's procuratorate at the next higher level for reexamination (Article 102).

The people's court should examine a case for which a public charge has been preferred by the people's procuratorate. It may turn the case back to the people's procuratorate for additional investigation if "the main facts are unclear and the evidence is insufficient. It may request the people's procuratorate to withdraw the charge where the offence need not be punished" (Article 108).

Where the people's procuratorate "considers a judgment or a ruling of first instance handed down by the people's court at the same level to be definitely in error, it shall lodge a protest against the judgment or the ruling to the people's court at the next higher level" (Article 130).

"The procurator present is entitled to express his opinions to the bench for putting right any violation of law at the hearing when discovered" (Article 112).

Principle 6

The various nationalities use their own spoken and written languages in criminal proceedings. Article 6 stipulates: "Citizens of all nationalities have the right to use their own languages in criminal proceedings. The people's court, the people's procuratorate, and the public-security organ shall provide interpretation for a litigant participant unacquainted with the spoken and written language commonly used in the locality. In districts compactly inhabited by a minority nationality or by a number of nationalities, trials and inquiries shall be conducted in the commonly used spoken language in the locality; and written judgments, public notices, and other documents issued in the commonly used written language in the locality." This stipulation takes into account that China is a multinational country. (China has fifty-five minority nationalities besides the Han nationality).

Principle 7

A trial of second instance is a trial of final instance. Article 143 stipulates: "Either the judgment or ruling derived from a trial of second instance or that handed down by the Supreme People's Court shall be that of final instance."

In China the local people's courts are divided into three levels: basic people's courts, intermediate people's courts, and higher people's courts. At the national level there is the Supreme People's Court. A litigant contesting a judgment of first instance rendered by a local people's court at any level has the right to file an appeal to the people's court at the next higher level. The local people's procuratorate may lodge a protest against a judgment to the people's court at the next higher level. Judgment of an appellant case or protested case (a case of second instance) at the people's court at the next higher level is a judgment of final instance.

The reason that a litigant has the right to file an appeal and a people's procuratorate to lodge a protest against a judgment of first instance is to enable the people's court at the next higher level to examine whether the judgment of first instance made by the people's court is correct or not in the confirmation of facts and in the application of law. In this way the people's court at the next higher level can correct a possible mistake in time.

Principle 8

Open trial. Article 8 stipulates: "The people's court conducts all trials publicly, unless otherwise provided for by the present law." Cases not to be tried publicly are those where state secrets or individual privacy are involved or in which the offenders are minors.

Conducting public trials enables the masses to supervise the trials and to receive legal education, and puts the court in a better position to make a correct judgment or just ruling.

Principle 9

The accused has the right of defense. The principle of defense stipulated by the law of criminal procedure is: "The accused has the right of defense, and the people's court is obliged to guarantee that he has defense" (Article 8).

The chapter on defense stipulates: "Besides exercising the right to defend himself, an accused must entrust any of the following people with his defense: (1) lawyers; (2) citizens recommended by a people's organization or the institution in which the accused works, or those approved by the people's court; or (3) close relatives or guardians of the accused" (Article 26).

"The people's court shall assign an advocate for the accused if he has not called in any" (Article 27).

The law of criminal procedure stipulates: "A defense lawyer may inspect the files in question, acquaint himself with the details of the case, and interview and correspond with the accused. The other advocates may, upon permission of the people's court, be informed of the details of the case and interview and correspond with the accused" (Article 29).

Principle 10

Participation of people's assessors in trials. Article 9 stipulates: The people's court practices a system of participation by the people's assessors at a trial. The chapter on trial group stipulates: In cases of first instance in the basic people's court and the intermediate people's court, justice is administered by a collegiate bench made up of a judge and two people's assessors. In cases of first instance in the higher people's court and the Supreme People's Court, justice is administered by a collegiate bench made up of one to three judges and two to four people's assessors. Article 105 stipulates: "The people's assessors, during the exercise of their functions in the people's court, have equal rights with the judges."

According to the law, people's assessors are elected by citizens simultaneously with the election of deputies to primary people's congresses (the people's congress is an organ of state power). This electoral system, which was suspended during the Cultural Revolution, is now being resumed. At present the people's assessors are recommended by the organizations concerned (factories, schools, people's communes, and so on), and formally invited by the people's court after consultation between the people's court or judicial-administration department and these organizations.

Principle 11

Rights of litigant participants guaranteed. "A litigant participant has the right to bring an accusation against a judge, a procurator or an investigator who has encroached on the litigant rights of a citizen or committed an act of personal insult" (Article 10).

Litigant participants enjoy full rights in proceedings, such as: the accused has the right to defend himself or entrust an advocate to defend him; he has the right to ask a judge, a procurator, or an investigator who is in some way interested in the case to withdraw; he has the right to call in new witnesses and a special witness, and to gather new evidence; during court trial he has the right to examine evidence, to debate, and to make a final statement; and he has the right to file an appeal against a judgment of first instance.

Principle 12

Principles for not pursuing criminal liability. Article 11 stipulates: In any of the following circumstances, no criminal liability shall be pursued: where the offense is obviously a petty one, the harm done is insignificant, and the case is thus not deemed to be a criminal offense; where the prescription has expired (for instance, an offender unapprehended and unpunished for five years, in a case where the maximum term of sentence for his crime is less than five years); where the offender has been exempted from penalty by a special pardon; where no private charge has been made or where such a charge has been withdrawn in a case that, according to the criminal law, shall not be accepted unless a complaint is lodged.

Index

About the Author

Rosalie L. Tung received the Ph.D. from the University of British Columbia. She is an associate professor of management at The Wharton School of Finance and Commerce, University of Pennsylvania. She was formerly on the faculties of The University of California at Los Angeles, the University of Manchester Institute of Science and Technology (England), and the University of Oregon. She was invited as the first foreign expert to teach management at the Foreign Investment Commission, the highest agency under the Chinese State Council that approves all joint ventures and major forms of foreign investment. She has been included in the 1982 edition of *The International Who's Who of Intellectuals,* 1981 edition of *The World's Who's Who of Women,* the 1981–1982 edition of *Who's Who of American Women,* and *The Directory of Distinguished Americans,* for outstanding contributions in her field. She is the author of *Management Practices in China,* and *U.S.–China Trade Negotiations.* Dr. Tung has also published widely on the subjects of international management and organizational theory in leading journals, including the *Columbia Journal of World Business,* the *Academy of Management Journal,* the *Academy of Management Review,* the *Journal of Vocational Behavior,* the *Business Graduate* (United Kingdom), and the *Journal of International Business Studies.*

Dr. Tung is a reviewer of peer proposals for the National Science Foundation. She is a member of the Academy of International Business, the Academy of Management, the American Management Association, the American Economic Association, the American Institute of Decision Sciences, the American Psychological Association, and the International Association of Applied Psychology.